Energy, Climate and the Environment Series

Series Editor: **David Elliott**, Emeritus Professor of Technology, Open University, UK

Titles include:

Luca Anceschi and Jonathan Symons (*editors*)
ENERGY SECURITY IN THE ERA OF CLIMATE CHANGE
The Asia-Pacific Experience

Mehmet Efe Biresselioglu
EUROPEAN ENERGY SECURITY
Turkey's Future Role and Impact

David Elliott (*editor*)
NUCLEAR OR NOT?
Does Nuclear Power Have a Place in a Sustainable Future?

David Elliott (*editor*)
SUSTAINABLE ENERGY
Opportunities and Limitations

Horace Herring and Steve Sorrell (*editors*)
ENERGY EFFICIENCY AND SUSTAINABLE CONSUMPTION
The Rebound Effect

Matti Kojo and Tapio Litmanen (*editors*)
THE RENEWAL OF NUCLEAR POWER IN FINLAND

Antonio Marquina (*editor*)
GLOBAL WARMING AND CLIMATE CHANGE
Prospects and Policies in Asia and Europe

Catherine Mitchell
THE POLITICAL ECONOMY OF SUSTAINABLE ENERGY

Ivan Scrase and Gordon MacKerron (*editors*)
ENERGY FOR THE FUTURE
A New Agenda

Gill Seyfang
SUSTAINABLE CONSUMPTION, COMMUNITY ACTION AND THE NEW ECONOMICS
Seeds of Change

Joseph Szarka
WIND POWER IN EUROPE
Politics, Business and Society

David Toke
ECOLOGICAL MODERNISATION AND RENEWABLE ENERGY

Xu Yi-chong (*editor*)
NUCLEAR ENERGY DEVELOPMENT IN ASIA
Problems and Prospects

Xu Yi-chong
THE POLITICS OF NUCLEAR ENERGY IN CHINA
Energy, Climate and the Environment

Energy, Climate and the Environment
Series Standing Order ISBN 978-0-230-00800-7 (hb) 978-0-230-22150-5 (pb)
(*outside North America only*)

You can receive future titles in this series as they are published by placing a standing order. Please contact your bookseller or, in case of difficulty, write to us at the address below with your name and address, the title of the series and the ISBN quoted above.

Customer Services Department, Macmillan Distribution Ltd, Houndmills, Basingstoke, Hampshire RG21 6XS, England

Energy Security in the Era of Climate Change

The Asia-Pacific Experience

Edited by

Luca Anceschi

Lecturer in International Relations, LaTrobe University, Australia

Jonathan Symons

Assistant Professor, Department of Political Science, Lingnan University, Hong Kong

palgrave
macmillan

First published 2012 by
PALGRAVE MACMILLAN

Palgrave Macmillan in the UK is an imprint of Macmillan Publishers Limited, registered in England, company number 785998, of Houndmills, Basingstoke, Hampshire RG21 6XS.

Palgrave Macmillan in the US is a division of St Martin's Press LLC, 175 Fifth Avenue, New York, NY 10010.

Palgrave Macmillan is the global academic imprint of the above companies and has companies and representatives throughout the world.

Palgrave® and Macmillan® are registered trademarks in the United States, the United Kingdom, Europe and other countries.

ISBN 978-1-349-32711-9 ISBN 978-0-230-35536-1 (eBook)
DOI 10.1057/9780230355361

This book is printed on paper suitable for recycling and made from fully managed and sustained forest sources. Logging, pulping and manufacturing processes are expected to conform to the environmental regulations of the country of origin.

A catalogue record for this book is available from the British Library.

A catalog record for this book is available from the Library of Congress.

10 9 8 7 6 5 4 3 2 1
21 20 19 18 17 16 15 14 13 12

Contents

List of Tables

List of Figures

Series Preface

Concerns about the potential environmental, social and economic impacts of climate change have led to a major international debate over what could and should be done to reduce emissions of greenhouse gases, which are claimed to be the main cause. There is still a scientific debate over the likely scale of climate change, and the complex interactions between human activities and climate systems, but, in the words of no less than the former Governor of California, Arnold Schwarzenegger, *'I say the debate is over. We know the science, we see the threat, and the time for action is now.'*

Whatever we now do, there will have to be a lot of social and economic adaptation to climate change – preparing for increased flooding and other climate-related problems. However, the more fundamental response is to try to reduce or avoid the human activities that are seen as causing climate change. That means, primarily, trying to reduce or eliminate emission of greenhouse gasses from the combustion of fossil fuels in vehicles and power stations. Given that around 80% of the energy used in the world at present comes from these sources, this will be a major technological, economic and political undertaking. It will involve reducing demand for energy (via lifestyle choice changes), producing and using whatever energy we still need more efficiently (acquiring more from less), and supplying the reduced amount of energy from non-fossil sources (basically switching over to renewables and/or nuclear power).

Each of these options opens up a range of social, economic and environmental issues. Industrial society and modern consumer cultures have been based on the ever-expanding use of fossil fuels, so the changes required will inevitably be challenging. Perhaps equally inevitable are disagreements and conflicts over the merits and demerits of the various options and in relation to strategies and policies for pursuing them. These conflicts and associated debates sometimes concern technical issues, but there are usually also underlying political and ideological commitments and agendas which shape, or at least colour, the ostensibly technical debates. In particular, at times, technical assertions can be used to buttress specific policy frameworks in ways that subsequently prove to be flawed.

The aim of this series is to provide texts that lay out the technical, environmental and political issues relating to the various proposed policies for responding to climate change. The focus is not primarily on the science of climate change, or on the technological detail, although there will be accounts of the state of the art, to aid assessment of the viability of the various options. However, the main focus is the policy conflicts over which strategy to pursue. The series adopts a critical approach and attempts to identify flaws in emerging policies, propositions and assertions. In particular, it seeks to illuminate counter-intuitive assessments, conclusions and new perspectives. The aim is not simply to map the debates, but to explore their structure, their underlying assumptions and their limitations. Texts are incisive and authoritative sources of critical analysis and commentary, indicating clearly the divergent views that have emerged and also identifying the shortcomings of these views. However the books do not simply provide an overview; they also offer policy prescriptions.

The present volume looks at what has become a central energy and climate issue – energy security. While from an environmental perspective we should not rely on our fossil fuel inheritance, it is claimed that the viability of the global economy, and the economies of developing countries especially, require continued and perhaps even expanded use of coal, oil and gas. A major focus of geopolitics therefore concerns securing access to the remaining fossil resources. At the same time it seems certain that some of these resources (oil especially) will soon become depleted, the main debate being when, rather than if. Some hope that this will help resolve or reduce climate problems, but the reality is that when and if 'peak oil' is reached, there will be a shift to coal-derived oil, for use in vehicles, potentially making the emission problems even worse. More generally, a shift to gas is also likely, with shale gas seen as offering a respite from depletion. While that may reduce emissions temporarily, as may the adoption of carbon capture and storage, it is not a long-term solution, and access to gas reserves is variable geographically. That is particularly the case in the Asian Pacific area, the focus of this book, whereas there are still significant reserves of coal, and also (in Australia) uranium – with the issue of nuclear in Asia being the subject of earlier books in this series.

However, there are also enviable renewable energy resources, with China leading the way to their exploitation. In terms of energy security, quite apart from climate concerns, long term this must surely be the main way forward. Certainly some now argue that, although some renewable energy technology may be currently expensive in capital cost terms, longer term a renewably based energy system will be cheaper since, for most renewables, there are no fuel costs. Moreover, in the shorter term using renewable energy resources means less has to be spent on importing ever more expensive fossil fuels. Furthermore, the resource is more than adequate to sustain continued economic expansion – there are now several scenarios suggesting that renewables could supply nearly 100% of total global primary energy by 2050, if proper attention is also paid to energy efficiency.

This book explores the ways in which these various energy policy options are playing out in the Asia Pacific area. While fossil fuels clearly remain central, some look to nuclear, while others see renewables plus efficiency as the best option, and it is the latter perspective that informs much of the discussion in this text. But it goes well beyond that to look at the way in which international negotiations over development and climate strategies are being framed, and the limits and constraints imposed by national priorities and sectional interests. In its widest sense, as this book asserts, energy security must include security in relation to climate shocks, but there are real conflicts when attempts are made to discuss constraints on fossil fuel use. A key issue then is whether the vision of a sustainable future based on renewables and efficiency is sufficiently convincing to overcome resistance.

Acknowledgements

Previous versions of a number of papers included in this volume were originally presented at the workshop 'Energy Security in the Era of Climate Change: A Dialogue on Current Trends and Future Options' held at the Centre for Dialogue, La Trobe University.

The organisation of the workshop was supported by a generous grant from the Academy of Social Sciences in Australia.

The editors thank Professor Joseph A. Camilleri (Centre for Dialogue/School of Social Sciences, La Trobe University), for initiating the workshop and for his invaluable support and constant encouragement during the completion of this project.

Notes on Contributors

Ariana Alisjahbana is a master's student in Economics and Environmental Analysis and Policy in the Department of Geography and Environment at Boston University, USA.

Luca Anceschi is Lecturer in International Relations in the School of Social Sciences, La Trobe University, Melbourne, Australia.

Tulsi C. Bisht is Research Fellow at the Centre for Tourism and Services Research at Victoria University, Melbourne, Australia.

Joseph A. Camilleri is Professor of International Relations and founding Director of the Centre for Dialogue, La Trobe University, Melbourne, Australia.

Peter Christoff is Associate Professor in Environmental Studies in the Melbourne School of Land and Environment at the University of Melbourne, Australia.

Mark Diesendorf is Associate Professor and Deputy Director of the Institute of Environmental Studies at the University of New South Wales, Sydney, Australia.

Jim Falk is Director of the Australian Centre for Science, Innovation and Society at the University of Melbourne, Australia.

Leigh Glover is Associate Director and Senior Research Fellow at the Australasian Centre for the Governance and Management of Urban Transport at the University of Melbourne, Australia.

Anna Korppoo is a Senior Research Fellow at Fridtjof Nansen Institute, Oslo.

Mark Lister is Vice President of the Alternative Technology Association of Australia.

Maximilian Mayer is Lecturer and Managing Assistant at the Centre for Global Studies at the University of Bonn, Germany.

Ditya Agung Nurdianto is Head of Section at the Department of Foreign Affairs of the Republic of Indonesia.

Budy P. Resosudarmo is Associate Professor at the Arndt-Corden Department of Economics of the Crawford School of Economics and Government, Australian National University.

Hugh Saddler is Adjunct Professor jointly in the Crawford School of Economics and Government and the Fenner School of Environment and Society, Australian National University, and Principal Consultant in the Climate Change Business Unit of Pitt & Sherry.

Akihiro Sawa is Executive Senior Fellow at the 21st Century Public Policy Institute, Tokyo, Japan.

Peer Schouten is a PhD candidate at the School of Global Studies, University of Gothenburg, Germany, and editor-in-chief of *Theory Talks*.

Thomas Spencer is Research Fellow on Energy and Climate Policy at the Institut du Développement Durable et des Relations Internationales (IDDRI), Paris.

Jonathan Symons is Assistant Professor at the Political Science Department at Lingnan University, Hong Kong.

Xu Yi-chong is Research Professor of Politics and Public Policy at Griffith University, Brisbane, Australia.

List of Abbreviations

AAUs	assigned amount units
AEMC	Australian Energy Markets Commission
ANT	Actor Network Theory
AOSIS	Association of Small Island States
ASEAN	Association of Southeast Asian Nations
AWG-KP	Annex 1 Parties under the Kyoto Protocol
AWG-LCA	Ad Hoc Working Group on Long-Term Cooperative Action under the UNFCCC
BAU	Business as Usual
bcm	billion cubic meter
CCS	carbon capture and storage
CDM	Clean Development Mechanism
CEP	Caspian Environment Programme
CERs	Certified Emissions Reductions
CIS	Commonwealth of Independent States
CO_2	carbon dioxide
CO_2e	carbon dioxide equivalent
COP	Conference of the Parties
CPRS	Carbon Pollution Reduction Scheme (Aus)
CSE	Centre for Science and Environment (India)
DPJ	Democratic Party of Japan
EPA	Environmental Protection Agency (United States)
ESCOs	Energy Saving Companies
FDI	Foreign Direct Investment
FYP	Five Year Plan
GDP	gross domestic product
GEF	Global Environment Facility
GHG	greenhouse gas
GIS	Green Investment Scheme
GJ	gigajoule
g/kWh	grams per kilowatt-hour
GNP	gross national product
GRP	gross regional domestic product
Gt CO_2e	giga ton CO_2 emissions
GW	gigawatt
GWe	gigawatt electrical
GWh	gigawatt-hours
HDI	Human Development Index
IAEA	International Atomic Energy Agency

IEA	International Energy Agency
IEP	Integrated Energy Policy (India)
INC	Intergovernmental Negotiating Committee
IPCC	Intergovernmental Panel on Climate Change
JI	Joint Implementation
JUSCANNZ	Japan, the USA, Switzerland, Canada, Australia, Norway and New Zealand
kgoe	kg of oil equivalent
Ktoe	kilo tonnes of equivalent oil
kV	kilovolts
kWh	kilowatt-hour
LDP	Liberal Democratic Party (Japan)
LNG	liquefied natural gas
LPG	liquefied petroleum gas
LULUCF	Land Use, Land-Use Change and Forestry
m^3	cubic meter
MEF	Major Economies Forum on Energy and Climate
MEP	Ministry of Environmental Protection (China)
METI	Ministry of Economy, Trade and Industry (Japan)
MJ	megajoule
MOP	Meeting of the Parties to the Kyoto Protocol
MOX	mixed oxide
MRV	Measurable, Reportable and Verifiable
Mt	megatonne
Mt CO_2e	mega ton CO_2 emission
mtoe	million tons of oil equivalent
MW	megawatt
NAPCC	National Action Plan on Climate Change (India)
NDRC	National Development and Reform Commission (China)
NEA	National Energy Administration (China)
NEM	National Electricity Market (Australia)
NESA	National Energy Security Assessment (Australia)
NGO	non-governmental organisation
NOCs	National Oil Corporations
NO_x	nitrogen dioxide
OECD	Organization for Economic Development and Cooperation
Ofgem	Office of Gas and Electricity Markets (United Kingdom)
OPEC	Organization of the Petroleum Exporting Countries
PJ	petajoule
PLN	power line networking
ppm	parts-per-million
PV	photovoltaic

REDD+	Reducing Emissions from Deforestation and Degradation plus other measures
RET	Renewable Energy Target (Australia)
SASAC	State-owned Assets Supervision and Administration Commission (China)
SO_2	sulphur dioxide
tcm	trillion cubic meters
tmb	thousand million barrels
toe	tons of oil equivalent
TPES	Total Primary Energy Supply
TWh	terawatt-hour
UNCED	United Nations Conference on Environment and Development
UNDP	United Nations Developments Programme
UNFCCC	United Nations Framework Convention on Climate Change
WRI	World Resources Institute
WTO	World Trade Organization

Introduction: Challenges to Energy Security in the Era of Climate Change

Jonathan Symons

Coming decades will witness major transformations in global energy systems. Depletion of easily accessible reserves of oil and natural gas, dangerous climatic changes resulting from combustion of fossil fuels and the rise of new energy consumers – notably China and India – will make transformative change inevitable. In the West, discussion of energy security is often dominated by security concerns associated with both dependence on Middle Eastern oil and fears of a zero-sum competitive scramble for energy resources (Goldthau and Witte 2010, pp. 1–3). There is also alarm over the climate impacts of rapid growth in the developing world's greenhouse gas (GHG) emissions. However, recognition of these serious challenges should not be allowed to obscure the unambiguously positive aspects of changes in energy use. Across many developing countries, increases in energy use and GHG emissions are a consequence of expanding access to economic opportunity and modern energy. Viewed on a global scale, the primary challenge facing energy security policy is the task of managing the energy demands of 6.9 billion people within the context of ecological limits.

Although energy challenges have global dimensions, global institutions governing energy are relatively underdeveloped. Instead, energy security, understood in terms of achieving low-cost, diverse, stable energy supplies (Yergin, 2006, p. 70), is usually a goal of national policy making. States typically pursue 'energy security' policies in order to safeguard national economic competitiveness and security. However, in the twentieth century this traditional conception of energy security has increasingly been critiqued for ignoring the wider social and economic consequences of energy production. The threat posed by climate change is the most significant of these concerns. Since the energy sector is responsible for approximately 57 per cent of global GHG emissions – and estimates indicate that, if warming in excess of 2°C is to be avoided, global emissions need to be reduced by 60–80 per cent before 2050 – the linkage between these two issue areas is tight (IPCC, 2007). On 11 March 2011, just as this book was going to press, Japan was struck by a severe earthquake and ensuing tsunami that took the lives of thousands and caused critical damage to the Fukushima I Nuclear Power Plant. At the time of writing, the full extent of the nuclear disaster is not yet clear. However, this tragic incident has already deepened public concerns about nuclear energy globally and highlighted the difficult choices confronting climate and energy policy.

The most significant challenge that climate concerns pose to traditional energy security relates to price. Renewable energy sources are typically more expensive than conventional energy – and the most economically competitive low-emission options, such as nuclear and hydropower, are often politically controversial due to broader social and environmental concerns. The price pressure arising from climate mitigation policies cuts against the emphasis on affordable energy supply, which is central to the concept of energy security.

The *Stern Review of the Economics of Climate Change* calculated that the present-day economic value of future climate impacts resulting from each tonne of CO_2 emissions is approximately US$85 (the 'social cost of carbon') (Stern, 2006, p. 322). Were this externality to be internalised in the price of energy, it would radically reshape the economic competitiveness of different energy sources. First, gas, nuclear and renewable sectors would be bolstered at the expense of increases in the price of oil and especially coal. Second, this re-prioritisation of energy sources would reshape the value of national energy reserves and exports – states with significant coal deposits would be disadvantaged. If anxiety about rising fuel prices, which has already become a central political issue in many parts of the world, provides any guide it seems likely that there would be fierce political opposition to such changes.

In summary, a contradiction between climate and energy policy arises, as climate change mitigation requires use of comparatively expensive low-emissions energy sources. Moreover, at the same time as the threat of climate change is prompting reappraisal of traditional concepts of energy security, continued prioritisation of low-cost energy sources is preventing effective mitigation. These global challenges have attracted various international responses, the most significant of which are the United Nations Framework Agreement on Climate Change (UNFCCC) (1992), and subsequent agreements within the UNFCCC framework. However, global governance of energy remains limited. Cooperation among producer and consumer countries, such as in the Organisation of the Petroleum Exporting Countries (OPEC) and the International Energy Agency (IEA), has increased international coordination, but failed to raise the locus of energy governance from the national to the global level (Karlsson-Vinkhuyzen, 2010). While the IEA has been a key voice articulating the need for investment in low-emissions energy infrastructure, its own analysis highlights that almost two-thirds of growth in oil consumption before 2030 will occur in China (43 per cent) and India (19 per cent) – both of which are excluded from IEA membership (IEA, 2008, p. 77).

Reconceptualising energy security

In the light of these developments, this book addresses questions that arise from the apparent contradiction between climate and energy policies. It examines how energy security polices are, will and ideally should be transformed in the light of scientific evidence that many widely used sources of energy contribute to dangerous climatic change. Further, it addresses the conundrum of how to best reconceptualise energy security to take account of the unintended environmental consequences of energy production.

If a re-conceptualisation of 'energy security' is to assist in reconciling climate and energy policies, it must be shaped by an awareness of technological capacity, ecological limits and political possibilities. Consequently, this book's objectives include (1) exploration of the dynamics through which energy security concerns conflict with climate policy; (2) analysis of the potential for climate and energy policies to be made compatible; (3) investigation of the ways in which energy security is currently being reconceptualised within national political discourses; (4) assessment of the extent to which states' domestic and international climate policies (and consequently the global climate regime) have been shaped by energy security concerns and vice versa; and (5) identification of the potential for global initiatives to reshape the incentive structures facing states, so as to generate greater synergies between climate and energy security goals.

This book works towards a conception of energy security that factors in externalities of various kinds – how this should be achieved is debated among the various contributors. A first cut at the problem might seek to reform existing conceptions of energy security by taking account of the environmental and social externalities of energy generation. Energy security might then be understood as *the attainment of energy supply and use patterns that are consistent with achieving a good life for all*. Energy security, thus defined, could only be realised through global cooperation to achieve (1) secure, reliable and affordable supplies of energy that are (2) derived from ecologically and socially sustainable sources, while (3) bringing energy use patterns to a level where available supplies are sufficient.

This conception involves three significant departures from traditional concepts of energy security: it addresses social and economic externalities; it considers demand management as well as energy supply; and it makes global (rather than national) welfare the acknowledged goal of energy policy. Nevertheless, some contributors to this volume, such as Maximilian Mayer and Peer Schouten, see this response as inadequate – they argue that the anthropocentric view that humanity and the natural world are separable is the root cause of negative environmental externalities. As a result the concept of 'energy security' cannot be reformed so simply.

A number of chapters assess energy security at a conceptual level, while others consider the relationship between climate and energy concerns from the vantage of national policy makers in the Asia-Pacific region – understood here as the ensemble of major producers and consumers in a region approximately extending from the Caspian Sea to the Pacific Ocean. While traditional definitions of the Asia-Pacific region usually do not extend to the post-Soviet republics of Central Asia, we include this sub-region into our analysis, as Central Asia's energy exports are crucial components of the energy security strategies of key Asia-Pacific states, including the Russian Federation and the People's Republic of China. The states considered in Part II comprise almost half the global population (approximately 46 per cent) and account for well over half the projected global growth in energy demand over the coming two decades (IEA, 2008, p. 27). As the energy and climate policies pursued by these states will be crucial factors in shaping the global response to climate change, detailed examination of the factors shaping policy formation in the Asia-Pacific region is vital to an understanding of the global politics of climate and energy.

Outline of the book

The book is divided into three parts that consider the relationship between energy security and climate change conceptually (Part I), through national case studies concerning China, India, Japan, Russia, Indonesia, Australia and the five Central Asian states (Part II), and from the vantage of global governance (Part III). Movement between conceptual, local and global levels of analysis exposes recurring themes in climate and energy policy. These themes include the unintended consequences of anthropocentric attitudes, state capacity and popular resistance to the higher cost of low-emission energy sources, market failures that limit investment in new energy technologies and energy efficiency, the close association between energy choices and conceptions of the good life, the influence of energy exports over climate policy and conflicting conceptions of justice in global climate agreement-making.

Anthropocentricism

The opening chapter, by Maximilian Mayer and Peer Schouten, outlines the volume's most radical critique of energy security. Where other authors (e.g. Camilleri, Falk and Symons) argue that cooperative global energy governance will be needed to enable the environmental impacts of fossil fuel use to be addressed, Mayer and Schouten go further: they propose that it is necessary to reassess the relationship between humanity and nature and move beyond an anthropocentric worldview in order to address the shortcomings of existing energy security policy. In their view, any conception of energy security that holds nature as a 'matter of fact' which human agency acts upon in pursuit of shifting 'social' concerns, is likely to confront unexpected repercussions and so produce further insecurity. Instead, those factors that have previously been silenced as 'facts' to be operated on, must be considered primary subjects of concern when formulating conceptions of security.

State capacity and domestic resistance to pricing greenhouse gas emissions

Theoretically, the most economically efficient way to respond to climate change would be to impose a price on GHG emissions that builds the economic cost of environmental externalities into the cost of energy. Ideally, market mechanisms would then deliver environmental and energy outcomes in the most economically efficient manner. Any residual areas of market failure (such as underinvestment in energy research) could be addressed through targeted policy measures. While most chapters explore environmental externalities and examine various mechanisms through which these might be minimised (e.g. Diesendorf, Saddler), many also explore the key areas of political resistance to such changes.

Since most costs from climate change will arise in the distant future, winning acceptance for investment in climate change mitigation poses an extreme political challenge. Internalising the cost of future climate impacts within today's energy prices would impose significant costs on present-day populations, and the only reward for such sacrifice is a promise of future benefits. Moreover, appeals to national interest are blunted because while energy policy is shaped at a national level, the future costs of climate change will confront the globe as a whole. Most chapters in Part II explore these dynamics through discussion of local responses to climate policy. While much analysis focuses on popular resistance to energy-price rises, in Chapter 11 Leigh Glover presents another face of this dynamic. Glover analyses the way in which Australian energy security policy has advanced the interests of 'large corporate entities linked to the energy sector by directing public investment for private corporate gain', by 'influencing international negotiations to align with the interests of these parties' and 'locking-in' long-term reliance on fossil fuel energy systems.

In Chapter 9, Budy Resosudarmo, Ariana Alisjahbana and Ditya Nurdianto review Indonesia's energy-policy challenges. Given Indonesia's low levels of access to electricity, rapid economic growth and desire to reduce reliance on imported oil, officials plan to increase coal's share of electricity generation. While this development will increase energy-sector emissions, Indonesia has some room to move in climate policy because of low-cost abatement opportunities in forestry and peatland management – sectors that currently contribute the majority of national emissions. Their chapter identifies winding back energy price subsidies as the main challenge facing energy sector climate policy. At present, subsidies hold domestic fuel and electricity prices well below world prices. These generous subsidies, which have accounted for as much as 23 per cent of total government expenditure, overwhelmingly benefit more affluent urban residents, promote economically inefficient energy use and blunt the effectiveness of market-based policies that seek to reduce GHG emissions. Nevertheless, the riots and unrest that have occurred in response to previous price reforms suggest the government must tread carefully as it proceeds towards its goal of eliminating subsidies by 2025.

Xu Yi-chong takes analysis of domestic resistance to emissions reduction policy in a different direction by focusing on China's lack of state capacity to implement stated policies (Chapter 5). Xu paints a complex picture of China's energy challenges, which, given simultaneous expansion of demand for oil and access to modern energy, seems to reflect both first world and third world patterns. It is the complex interaction between fragmented governance, inconsistent policy making and inadequate legal and regulatory systems that, in Xu's view, has prevented the Chinese central government from achieving more stringent emissions restraint.

Akihiro Sawa's discussion of Japanese energy policy (Chapter 7) outlines some of the local specificity of resistance to low-emission energy sources. Given its limited land area and existing high energy efficiency standards, Japan's emissions mitigation options are extremely constrained – Sawa cites research suggesting that the marginal mitigation costs of domestic emissions reduction could be as much as US$500 per tonne. As a result, acquiring emissions credits from off-shore abatement projects might be expected to play a significant role in future climate policy. However, while Japan is well placed to achieve low-cost overseas emissions abatement through technology transfer, environmental activists are determined to prioritise more costly domestic emissions abatement over an international strategy. Here, the Fukushima incident will cast a long shadow over any future plans for nuclear expansion.

Market failures

Energy policy that seeks to address climate concerns needs to do more than create price signals. Various market failures mean that price signals alone are unlikely to shift consumption and investment patterns sufficiently. For example, inadequate investment in energy research can be attributed to the difficulty that private companies face in capturing the full benefits of research. Further, investment in energy infrastructure may be depressed by concerns about policy uncertainty and political instability.

In Chapter 2, Mark Lister explores the way in which non-price-sensitive market characteristics have resulted in the underutilisation of energy efficiency measures. Where estimates suggest that cost-neutral measures could reduce energy use and associated emissions by 30 per cent in some sectors, these opportunities have rarely been fully exploited (IPCC, 2007). Lister argues that private actors face multiple, non-financial barriers to improving energy efficiency that blunt responses to price signals. Among other factors, he considers irrational 'temporal discounting' of future gains; non-prioritisation of non-core business activities (since electricity normally comprises less than 3 per cent of business expenditure); split incentives (e.g. between landlords and tenants) which prevent full capture of savings from investment in energy efficiency; and transaction costs associated with achieving a large number of small energy savings.

Lister concludes that political leadership and construction of powerful narratives promoting the importance of energy efficiency will be required to drive sustained consideration of this important topic. Other contributors appear to confirm this observation. While most of the national case studies outline government plans for energy efficiency, few (besides China and Japan) report historical success in this area. In these cases efficiency measures were driven by government intervention and supply shortages rather than managed price signals. Hugh Saddler's analysis of international responses to the oil crises of the 1970s and establishment of the IEA in 1974 outlines how states (such as Japan) adopted end use energy efficiency in order to make national economies and energy systems less vulnerable to disruption (Chapter 3).

Energy and conceptions of the good life

As Joseph Camilleri elaborates in Chapter 14, human societies can be distinguished historically by the forms of energy that they have harnessed. The taming of fire, animal labour, water and wind marked significant transformation in ways of living. Since the Industrial Revolution, successive utilisation of coal, petroleum and gas has enabled a massive expansion of economic activity and human interconnectedness, which are hallmarks of the contemporary era of globalisation. Relationships between climate, energy source and forms of society are not only apparent historically; they also mark major divisions among contemporary human communities. For example, life opportunity and social structure are closely linked with access to energy. Many authors in this volume point to the ways in which contemporary energy choices relate not only to the technical challenge of mitigating climate change but also to broader social questions about the nature of the good life.

In Chapter 4, Mark Diesendorf assesses the respective strengths and risks associated with four different future energy scenarios that might potentially provide both climate and energy security: conventional nuclear, new generation nuclear, 'clean coal' and 'sustainable energy' involving efficient use of renewable energy. While largely rejecting the potential of 'clean coal', Diesendorf acknowledges that nuclear scenarios are likely to involve lower costs over the short term than the sustainable energy scenario. However, he argues that the latter is more attractive due to its association with a different societal vision. In Diesendorf's account a renewable energy system composed of a mix of centralised and local energy sources is likely to have lower risks than the nuclear scenario and be more consistent with a socially just society, as it will deliver more widely dispersed employment opportunities and allow households to achieve at least partial energy independence.

Energy exports, regime stability and resistance to climate mitigation

In Chapter 12, Peter Christoff surveys the policy positions of the largest 20 GHG emitters since 1992. He concludes that there is considerable diversity in the approaches taken by states that are dependent on energy imports. However, he finds that countries whose economies are heavily reliant on fossil fuel exports (e.g. Australia, Russia or Canada) have – with the notable exception of Norway – played a negative role within climate negotiations and have acted to weaken and delay agreement.

Christoff's analysis of the tendency for energy exporters to be climate mitigation laggards is borne out in the chapters concerning Russia (Chapter 8 by Anna Korppoo and Thomas Spencer) and the Central Asian states (Chapter 10 by Luca Anceschi). Korppoo and Spencer argue that few emissions mitigation policies have been introduced in Russia to date because Russia's commitment under the Kyoto Protocol (limiting emissions to the 1990 level) can be achieved without specific climate-focused measures, and public attitudes do not support voluntary action. Since Russia is the world's largest producer and exporter of natural gas, second largest exporter of oil, and obtains around half of tax revenues from the energy sector its major focus in climate negotiations has been on protecting the security of its energy exports.

Regime dependence on energy export revenue is even greater in Central Asia. After outlining the centrality of this region to the energy security strategies of China, Russia and the European Union, Anceschi argues that Central Asia's energy exporters have adopted an unusual conception of energy security. Since the stability of these regimes depends on energy revenue, Central Asian elites view energy security as the ability to guarantee a regular flow of energy exports. These dynamics have meant that the regional leaderships have shown limited interest in climate change mitigation, and have minimised their engagement in global climate initiatives. As a consequence, GHG emissions in Kazakhstan, Turkmenistan and Uzbekistan have risen significantly throughout the post-Soviet era.

Statism, justice and global governance

In Chapter 13, Jim Falk describes the challenge of achieving energy security in an era of climate change as requiring reconciliation of 'the needs and aspirations of humans as they live at small scales, with the needs and aspirations of the human race, who in the end must live and shape their future adaptively on a finite and stressed planet'. This argument, that if energy security and climate policy are to be reconciled then energy security must be pursued through cooperative global governance, is another of the volume's recurring themes. However, the call for cooperative, human-centred governance runs up against deep international division over how a global climate agreement should justly distribute the burdens of emissions abatement.

This divide is most sharply illustrated by the bitter dispute in climate negotiations over the application of the norm of 'common but differentiated responsibility'. Where major developing countries assert that the West has a moral duty to lead by making deep emissions cuts and providing financial and technological assistance, the United States (among others) replies that any agreement which does not impose binding and verifiable limits on leading developing economies is doomed to be ineffective. Tulsi Bisht's (Chapter 6) analysis of India's justifications for resisting a global agreement that imposes binding emissions limits on the developing world provides further insight into this dispute. Bisht first outlines India's arguments that Western states have historical responsibility for the accumulated 'stock' of GHGs, have comparatively high contemporary per capita emissions and, through their reluctance to unconditionally transfer green technologies, are proposing an agreement that would undermine the sovereignty of developing countries. However, he also points to growing concern about climate change threats within India and awareness that a relatively small Indian upper class lead lifestyles that create very high emissions levels.

The dispute over a just global response to climate change is further explored in Part III. It is clear that the vital public good of a safe climate can only be protected through some kind of international agreement. However, the final two chapters paint opposing pictures of the likelihood of an effective agreement being brokered. Where Joseph Camilleri (Chapter 14) outlines the ways in which existing responses to climate change achieve an unprecedented level of global cooperation, Jonathan Symons (Chapter 15) argues that although an ambitious global response to climate change would bring side benefits for aggregate energy security, such a cooperative outcome is unlikely. Nevertheless both agree that the success of negotiations over global climate governance will have profound consequences, not just for energy security, but also for the organisation of human societies the world over.

References

Goldthau, A. and J.M. Witte (2010), 'The role of rules and institutions in global energy: An introduction', in A. Goldthau and J.M. Witte (eds): *Global Energy Governance: The New Rules of the Game* (Washington, DC: Brookings Institution).

Intergovernmental Panel on Climate Change (IPCC) (2007), 'Summary for policymakers', in B. Metz, O.R. Davidson, P.R. Bosch, R. Dave and L.A. Meyer (eds): *Climate Change 2007: Mitigation. Contribution of Working Group III to the Fourth Assessment*

Report of the Intergovernmental Panel on Climate Change (Cambridge and New York: Cambridge University Press).
International Energy Agency (IEA) (2008), *World Energy Outlook 2008: Executive Summary* (Paris: International Energy Agency).
Karlsson-Vinkhuyzen, S. (2010), 'The United Nations and global energy governance: Past challenges, future choices', *Global Change, Peace & Security*, 22(2): 175–195.
Stern, N. (2006), *Stern Review on the Economics of Climate Change* (London: HM Treasury).
Yergin, D. (2006), 'Ensuring energy security', *Foreign Affairs*, 85(2): 69–82.

Part I

Conceptualising Energy Security in the Era of Climate Change

1
Energy Security and Climate Security under Conditions of the Anthropocene

Maximilian Mayer and Peer Schouten

> All members of the international community face a shared dilemma. To ensure well being for a growing population with unfulfilled needs and rising expectation we must grow our economies. Should we fail, we increase the risk of conflict and insecurity. To grow our economies we must continue to use more energy. Much of that energy will be in the form of fossil fuels. But if we use more fossil fuels we will accelerate climate change, which itself presents risks to the very security we are trying to build.
>
> (United Kingdom Mission to the United Nations, 2007)

Introduction

This chapter sets out to revisit energy security and climate security in light of the Anthropocene. We draw on the notion of the Anthropocene in order to ask what it means for conceptions of security that the environment has become an effect of human agency. The passage quoted above, which is a statement of the British Government in the 2007 United Nation Security Council debate on climate change and security, provides an ideal starting point for our considerations. The dilemma that stems from the costly downsides of the prolonged pursuit of energy security could not be expressed more plainly: the term 'security' appears inappropriate in 'energy security' as pursuing it threatens its very aim.

The Intergovernmental Panel on Climate Change (IPCC) has called attention to aspects of the same endemic danger, such as the challenge greenhouse gas emissions from consumption of natural resources present to the environment. But the challenge looms larger. Jane Lubchenco (1998, p. 491), for one, lucidly points out that:

> As the magnitude of human impacts on the ecological systems of the planet becomes apparent, there is increased realization of the intimate

connections between these systems and human health, the economy, social justice, and national security.

Another manifestation of the same dilemma is that the 2010 Gulf Coast oil spill, which President Barack Obama called 'the worst environmental disaster America has ever faced' (The White House, 2010), resulted directly from that nation's hunger for affordable mineral resources. We therefore ask: how is it possible that the security of nations depends on oil consumption on the one hand (Litfin, 2003), while the US President speaks of 'waging a battle' against an 'oil spill that is assaulting our shores and our citizens' on the other? Or, in more general terms, why has energy security policy caused widespread *in*securities?

Tackling this dilemma in an insightful way, Simon Dalby (2009) has hailed the notion of the Anthropocene as a new paradigm for global politics. The Anthropocene, a term imported from earth sciences, refers to a new geological period in which human actions have such an impact that we need to fundamentally rethink our relationship to the environment (Crutzen and Stroemer, 2000). Taking the work surrounding this notion as a starting point, this chapter offers a contribution to the unfolding debate on energy security in an era of climate change, in which the meaning and importance of the notion of the environment for contemporary security analysis has been of central concern (Krause, 2003).

Accepting that the Anthropocene is not only a geological era, but is also a concept that carries an urgent normative connotation, we here explore two of its implications for our understanding of energy security. Firstly, rethinking energy security in light of the Anthropocene means we cannot leave the externalities of its pursuit out of the picture. Attempts to rethink energy security for the twenty-first century that do not live up to this criterion are inadequate. Daniel Yergin (2006, p. 69), for instance, proposed a broadening of energy security so that it 'does not stand by itself but is lodged in the larger relations amongst nations and how they interact with one another'. This widening does not reach far enough. Nor can the inclusion of externalities be accomplished by simply adding the goal of 'limiting greenhouse gas emissions' to the traditional agenda of 'adequate, reliable, and affordable energy resources' (Verrastro and Sarah Ladislaw, 2007, p 103; Bradshaw, 2009).

If these were viable solutions, we might ask why so 'little progress' has been achieved in tackling the double challenge of energy security and climate change (Deutch, Lauvergeon, and Prawiraatmadja, 2007, p. 2). An array of econometric studies point to the intricate linkages, trade-offs and possible synergies between the pursuit of energy security and climate mitigation policies (cf. Turton and Barreto, 2006; Lefèvre, 2007; Brown and Huntington, 2008). Realising that fundamental insecurity persists despite successful attainment of energy security leads us to reconsider the premises upon which thinking about security is based. The first implication then is that under the Anthropocene, the factuality of the 'modern' separation between mankind and nature is breaking down to uncover a contested web of relations, not reflected in the confident ontology underpinning energy security.

Second and related, we need to take one step beyond discursive understandings of (energy) security. To conceptualise security as discourse and, subsequently, energy security as a discursive political agenda, is to adopt the language of 'radical constructivism' and to treat energy and climate security as 'merely' socially constructed. This comfortably removes from sight the many externalities of their pursuit. Instead, an adequate conception of energy security needs to incorporate the material processes by which we attain that security, and to conceptualise climate concerns 'as a reality at the intersection of its physical and social history' (Byrne and Glover, 2005, p. 6). The second implication of taking the Anthropocene seriously is that we must methodically treat security not as merely socially constructed but rather as also built up from – and threatened by – the very material elements that are mobilised and assembled in its pursuit. Taken together, these two implications mark a shift in the way in which the relationship between nature and human society conditions our understanding of security.

Outline of the chapter

In the following section, we first show how different scholars in debates surrounding security and the environment agree that our notion of 'security' needs to be rethought, as existing conceptualisations, based on a traditional meaning of 'national security', have proven of limited use in responding to environmental concerns,[1] to subsequently lay out what it would mean to rethink security in light of the Anthropocene.

The third section explores ways to incorporate energy security's externalities into the analysis. It does so by building on insights from the above theoretical debate while adding a conceptual twist. From an actor-network theory inspired perspective, we argue that rethinking energy security in light of the Anthropocene requires first rethinking the relationship between 'political' discourses on security and 'nature'. We propose that taking the Anthropocene condition seriously requires us to move beyond the discursive turn to consider energy security as an *assemblage*, constituted by and dependent on both 'social' and 'material' elements, and which in turn directly 'impacts' upon both – rather than being a social construct divorced from 'nature'. The section continues to analyse energy security and those agendas concerned with its externalities – environmental and climate security – as different ways of assembling the same elements from the biosphere. Showing how these agendas constitute 'agencies' by pushing and pulling the same elements reveals the interwovenness of, and feedback loops between, 'social' and 'natural' elements that are hidden by discursive representations of these agendas. Through examples, it shows how alternate renderings of climate security have tended to assemble the climate as a security issue in ways very similar to energy security agendas.

In the conclusion to this chapter, we argue that by considering these alternate agendas as political agencies working on the same elements in different ways, it becomes possible to pin down the shortcomings of energy security. We identify a series of focal points that must be addressed if the debate is to move further, and argue that the principles of inclusiveness and symmetry would enable us to unsettle our narrow understanding of security and create space for a broader range of concerns.

Conceptualising Security in the Anthropocene Era

Within critical security studies, security is understood as an 'essentially contested concept'. This entails recognition that invoking security involves specific actors uttering 'speech acts' that reveal conflicting interests, and subsequently, that security cannot be feasibly reduced to any single perspective. Security has thus come to be understood as a way of speaking about political issues; 'securitisation' refers to the discursive process by which an issue is elevated from normal politics and constituted as a priority issue that warrants extraordinary policies (Wæver, 1995; Huysmans, 2006). In this understanding, security is 'more socially constructed than objectively determined' (Barnett, 2001b, p. 2). Whereas this approach accounts for the contested and shifting nature of security, it also delinks 'discursive' security from an 'objectively determined' realm to which nature belongs. Recognising security as contested and partial reveals that any such agenda involves a contentious articulation of the relation between nature and security; an articulation developed by someone, for someone and for some purpose (Buzan, Wæver, and Wilde, 1998; Stern, 2005). Asking who this agenda serves, instead of accepting energy security as a universally shared goal, denaturalises the link between energy consumption and security.

Energy security: Securitising national consumption

Energy security is commonly understood as a political agenda concerned with governance of energy production and consumption in service of national economies. Securitising an issue like energy provision takes it out of the domain of normal politics and constitutes it as an exceptional concern. Importantly, the elevation of one particular kind of concern as a security issue reduces the broader environment to a slim object of political disagreement and silences it as a concern. Consequently, the imposed relationship between nature and security is quintessentially biased towards concerns stemming from a national interest, conflicting not only with other national interests but also with security conceptions foregrounding subnational or global interests (cf. Lubeck, Watts and Lipschutz, 2007). Firmly rooted in the realist framework that perceives the world beyond one's national borders as anarchic and relations with other states as antagonistic, energy security has been concerned with national referent objects with pre-given interests. These interests have been taken as preservation of a fixed supply of natural resources to feed a national economy in a manner that leaves ecology unproblematised. With energy security successfully securitised, only a very limited aspect of the relation between human agency and the natural environment receives political (and analytical) attention.

Environmental and climate security: Broadening the scope

This narrow understanding of energy security – while still in broad use – has come under heavy scrutiny, as is reflected in the broad debate about environmental security. Ironically, energy security's continued and effective purchase has given rise to even bigger threats to national security such as abrupt climate shifts (Barnett, 2001a; Dalby, 2002; Liotta, 2005).

Subsequently, these externalities also became securitised (Floyd, 2008; Trombetta, 2008). Since the mid-1990s, climate concerns have increasingly appeared in national security strategies, framed as threats to national well-being (Dalby, 2009). Recent efforts by various international institutions to separate out climate change into different measurable security issues (Brauch and Zundel, 2008; Brauch, 2009) can also be seen as applications of the same principle, in which the relationship between mankind and the environment is fixed again by securitisation. Environmental security becomes constructed 'in terms of technological and modernist managerial assertions of control within a geopolitical imaginary of states and territorial entities' (Dalby, 2002, p. 146). Again, successful securitisations of particular aspects of the relationship between human agency and the natural environment constitute the latter as a limited, stable and apprehensible object in service of or threatening the former. In this process, the reverse dynamic – by which human agency affects the natural environment – is by and large discarded.

Alternate securitisations such as environmental or climate security, despite some differences (Brzoska, 2009), are based on, and ultimately lead to, the same kind of reductionism as the energy security agenda. This reductionism is made evident by the lack of clear evidence for a straightforward pathway between environmental change and conflict, for linkage between fossil resources and interstate wars, or between climate change and societal collapse, despite almost 30 years of research (Mcab and Bailey, 2007; Dalby, 2009). We thus witness the same principle at work both in energy security and in alternate securitisations that challenge it by incorporating more matters of concern. Both energy security and climate security are thus contested securitisations, each with a limited and conflicting scope of matters of concern. To explore why Anthropogenic insecurity persists despite the efforts mobilised and concerns addressed by these agendas, we need to uncover what these dominant securitisations of energy and climate change share.

Nature black-boxed

The different agendas – energy security, environmental security and climate security – all present us with a reductionist account of the natural environment and how it is related to human agency. All three agendas are premised upon a modern, anthropocentric, ontological separation of nature and society, in which nature is a 'black box', a mechanical, factual entity that requires mastery.[2] Society, instead, is more fluid and determines what counts as a matter of concern that requires us to act upon nature in a certain way. Indeed, it is the concern of a social subject that drives the shifting securitisations of natural objects. Energy security reduces nature to a factual amount of barrels of oil per day, which is of importance to the demands set by a human referent object. While climate security broadens the concern to the social repercussions of this process, it is premised upon the same understanding and foregrounds the same social concerns. The content of both securitisations is social and disembedded from nature, which merely forms a passive context to be acted upon.

The Anthropocene: Unleashing mankind as a natural force

The anthropocentric understanding underpinning the aforementioned securitisations is challenged by insights from climate scientists; foregrounding the notion of the Anthropocene, they emphasise not human control over, but human influence on the environment (Hulme, 2010). Recognising the central role of humankind in geology and ecology since the Industrial Revolution, Nobel laureate Paul J. Crutzen proposed to call the period characterised by that influence the 'Anthropocene'. Crutzen and others have subsequently advocated a re-embedding of mankind in the environment as the point of departure for feasible social science (Clark and Munn, 1986; Crutzen and Stoermer, 2000; cf. Marsh 1874). They advocate a shift in focus from concerns such as building pipelines, ever-deeper offshore drilling, the calculation of arable land for food production and incentivising other nations to reduce emissions, to shifting climate patterns, rapidly decreasing water resources and the use of the atmosphere as a gigantic emissions dump. In other words, when global economic and consumption dynamics are considered an agency working upon nature, security becomes linked to different matters of concern.

But ultimately, the challenge goes further: it requires the reinterpretation of what security means in light of a different interpretation of modernity (cf. Litfin, 2003). Starting with the Industrial Revolution, mankind has gained unprecedented control over nature. Nature became, in the understanding of the Enlightenment, a force that can be understood, controlled and domesticated in a mechanistic way, to serve shifting social interests over time (Bauman, 1995).[3] Nature was made to behave like a classical economic commodity and reduced to a passive factor of production – 'land'.

Because nature appeared to react in a predictable way to our interventions, economics, politics and social theory became divorced from environmental considerations (Barry, 1999; Steffen, 2004).

Yet with increased control came unprecedented influence – 'we', indeed, 'now live on a human-dominated planet' (Lubchenco, 1998, p. 491). Ironically, due to human agency, nature has come to constitute a severe threat to livelihoods and whole nations, as illustrated by the small island states that are already beginning to move their citizens to secure lands. Furthermore, it is recognised that global and local feedback loops between nature and human interventions therein, as well as non-linear irreversible dynamics, could lead to unforeseen disasters eventually destabilising the global ecosystem (Hansen, 2005; Solomon and Intergovernmental Panel on Climate Change, 2007). As humans are rapidly changing global ecological systems – often with unpredictable and threatening results – the modernist understanding that a clear and easily defined difference exists between objective factors and dynamics of nature and the contingent processes of society is giving way to numerous continuing 'border conflicts' (Beck, 2002; Tsing, 2005). Adopting these premises, a different picture arises, consisting of intricate interwovenness, perpetual feedback loops and the essential embeddedness of the human enterprise in nature. Social scientists have gone as far as proclaiming the 'death of nature' in a naturalistic sense, that is, as an adversary to the social, and replacing it with an ontology of nature as a social phenomenon (Jokinen, 1997). In the following section, we explore what it means for our conception of 'security' in the cases of securitisations of energy, the environment and the climate, to merge the ontology of the social and the natural into one.

Energy Security, Environmental Security and Climate Security as Assemblages

This section draws upon insights from science and technology studies in general and actor-network theory in particular to provide an analysis of how energy, environmental and climate security can be understood as distinct 'assemblages' that enrol essentially the same elements but to different effects.[4] Securitisations of nature are understood not as 'social' constructions, but rather as associations both of 'social' and 'material' elements, involving political and economic practices, material flows, infrastructure and ecological environments as well as human resistance and narratives of national security.[5]

Security assemblages that perform and shape the world are here defined conceptually as networks of elements linked by actors or programmatic agencies.[6] This stance entails methodically moving beyond the discursive focus of securitisation. Rather than solely constituting security discourses *about* some aspect of nature, actors *involve* these aspects of nature by actively transforming them to fit a particular agenda (Rose and Miller, 1992; Latour, 1993). As such, the contested discourses of energy, environmental and climate security are hybrid agencies consisting of a 'complex blending of social and biophysical factors' (Forsyth, 2001, p. 150) working upon nature in definite – and finite – ways (Latour, 2004, 2005). In order to act upon such vast assemblages, all elements have to be translated into a language that permits intervention, by separating out what matters into economically or politically apprehensible concerns. The notion of 'translation' is pivotal for actor-network theory. It refers to 'all the negotiations, intrigues, calculations, acts of persuasion and violence thanks to which an actor or force takes, or causes to be conferred on itself, authority to speak or act on behalf of another actor or force' (Callon and Latour, 1992, p. 279). The notion thus literally captures the transformation of elements through the associations made by actors in a securitisation.

In line with the rich body of work surrounding such thinkers as Arne Naess and more recently Bruno Latour, who have each in their own way argued for a notion of the 'social' that incorporates both nature and mankind as matters of concern (Callon, 1986; Mol, 1998; Barry, 2001; Barad, 2003; Jasanoff, 2005; Asdal, 2008; Bingham and Hinchliffe, 2008; Morin, 2009; Gammon, 2010), we here summarise our analytical lens as based on the two criteria of inclusiveness and symmetry. *Inclusiveness* refers to the scope and breadth of a notion of security in terms of the elements assembled as endogenous matters of concern rather than as exogenous matters of fact.[7] Secondly, *symmetry* is a criterion that implies equal inclusion of both 'social' and 'natural' agencies and concerns. Thus, neither a notion of security focusing primarily on human concerns (as does energy security), nor privileging environmental concerns (as do radical variants of 'deep ecology') will suffice. Directing our attention instead to the hybrid agencies that assemble heterogeneous elements, hopefully avoids the bias that inevitably results in one-sided research endeavours and destructive or infeasible policy agendas, which have helped to bring about the Anthropocene era in the first place.

Assembling energy security

Energy security is commonly understood as 'simply the availability of sufficient supplies at affordable prices', that is, a variable of national economic growth to be secured through markets, political and, if necessary, military action. By extension, political and scholarly concern with energy security is premised on threats to the smooth functioning of national economies arising from sharp increases in prices, instability in oil-producing countries or geopolitical tensions. As such, hydrocarbon resources in general, and oil and gas reserves in particular,[8] are deemed the 'lifeblood of civilization'; for this reason, they are a central preoccupation of national security agendas (Zweig and Bi, 2005; Amineh and Houweling, 2007; Marquina Barrio, 2008; Moran and Russell, 2009).

While specific national energy security strategies may diverge as export and import countries follow diverging interests and strategic policies appear to compete with market-based approaches, their similarities by far outweigh their differences. The basic assumptions have remained constant over time. The standard contemporary understanding of energy security has not deviated from the canonical definition offered by the US Department of Energy in 1985 (as cited in Hirsch, 1987, p. 1472):

> Energy security means that adequate supplies of energy at reasonable cost are physically available to US consumers from both domestic and foreign sources. It means that the nation is less vulnerable to disruptions in energy supply and that it is better prepared to handle them if they should occur.

Ever since Winston Churchill made oil dependence a core concern of British strategy, energy policies have shared an emphasis on securing sustained national energy consumption patterns and a supply-side focus. The core matter of concern is thus the question 'whether there will be sufficient resources to meet the world's energy requirements in the decades ahead' (Yergin, 2006, p. 70). Politicians commonly invoke the 'national' rationale for the inevitable primacy of exploring new oil reserves, as President Obama's (2010) assertion illustrates:

> But the bottom line is this: given our energy needs, in order to sustain economic growth, produce jobs, and keep our businesses competitive, we're going to need to harness traditional sources of fuel even as we ramp up production of new sources of renewable, homegrown energy.

The security community as well as energy companies present energy security to their audience neatly cleaned up and seemingly consisting of only market efficiency and strategic concerns – while in fact it is made up just as much of material and other multifarious elements. It incorporates natural elements like the resource endowments of national territories and technical infrastructure like pipelines or oil tankers as much as it does 'social' or 'discursive' ones: a successful securitisation of nature that foregrounds secure access to energy (rather than for instance environmental concerns), needs to assemble 'social' actors consisting of oil companies, US legislators, refineries and platforms, deep sea drilling technologies, but also geothermal tendencies, global consumption habits and the downsides of alternative technologies.

Numerous studies illustrate the multifaceted and continuous assembling efforts of different agencies that the pursuit of energy security requires to keep the globe-spanning 'energy security assemblage' in place. US and Chinese oil companies work hand in hand with their respective governments, and, in the case of the United States, with the armed forces, in order to explore and extract crude oil (Klare, 2004; Mitchell, 2007). Oil companies, however, also must persistently organise the coupled processes of financial accumulation and crude oil extraction to stabilise the world oil market. The specific materiality of crude oil shapes not only the territorialisation of global productions networks but also the internal political structures of rentier states (Bridge, 2008; Labban, 2008). At a local level, the same assemblage requires production, distribution and regulation regimes across the globe, which involve multiple disparate issues to be enrolled and kept in place. Moreover, the car assemblage has restructured entire landscapes, has significantly changed urban planning and architecture as well as common patterns of leisure and work life. Car and oil companies, which are integral parts of the energy security assemblage, are also among the economically most powerful global enterprises (Merriman (2009), see also Urry, 2007).

It is equally important for our purpose to note what energy security *does not* incorporate as a matter of concern, namely, corrupt regimes financed by fossil revenues and plutocratic dictatorships and corruption in the global petroleum sector at large (McPherson and MacSearraigh, 2007), the resource curse (Collier, 2007), biodiversity surrounding coal mines and drilling platforms, the military as a major environmental polluter (Deudney, 1999; McNeil, 2009) and the consequences of energy consumption on the environment – all elements impacted by the pursuit of energy security. Distribution conflicts over oil revenues sustain civil wars, and can even threaten the subsistence of states where resource revenues reignite conflict along ethnic fault lines, sustaining the fragmentation of already weak states (Kaldor, Karl and Said, 2007; Watts, 2009).

Another example of how such externalities are actively silenced out of the energy security assemblage by the conscious efforts of agencies is that in the United States, the Global Climate Coalition organised by the fossil industries successfully undermined a widening of public and scientific concerns on the greenhouse effect throughout the 1990s (Levy and Egan, 1998, p. 343; Antilla, 2005). Similarly, influential international relation scholars, by invoking a supposedly established hierarchy of security issues, actively silence environmental concerns (Lacey, 2005). Through these seemingly disparate assembling agencies, energy security, with its restricted scope of concern, has largely managed to hold these elements stable as 'passive' matters of fact that react as expected to interventions stemming from our energy desires and present no cause for concern. By translating all elements into the economic terms of 'supply' and 'demand', the energy security assemblage produces a parsimonious social matter of concern. At the same time, this translation process silences and hides many elements and concerns that respond differently to petro-politics (cf. Çalişkan and Callon, 2010). While these social and material 'effects' are very much linked into the network of elements constituting the energy security assemblage, they are not represented as matters of concern and as such remain largely invisible 'border conflicts'.

Assembling environmental security

Environmental security is qualitatively different from energy security in so far as it does not represent a single parsimonious global assemblage. Instead, it points to the competition between interest groups that are differently affected by energy production processes such as mining, drilling or energy-related development projects (Peluso and Watts, 2001). The many cases of environmental securitisations thus present us with a more diffuse and confused array of matters of concern, ranging from local and transnational competing interest groups to wildlife diversity and the preservation of the 'Gold Coast' of California. They dissolve the rational language of resource supply and demand into a wide array of affected contradicting interests of humans, animals and whole ecosystems. By giving these actors a voice, environmental securitisations are assemblages revolving around different matters of concern.

The US reactions to the huge underwater oil spill in the Gulf of Mexico in May 2010 perfectly illustrate how energy and environmental security are at once linked and at odds. First, a draft climate bill which was to encourage oil drilling in US territory was hastily revised to take the opposing position (Broder, 2010b). Second, Governor Arnold Schwarzenegger halted oil exploration projects along the Californian Coast stating his most pressing concerns on television:

> All of you have seen when you turn on the television the devastation in the Gulf. And I'm sure that they also were assured that it is safe to drill. I see on TV the birds drenched in oil, the fishermen out of work, the massive oil spill, oil slick destroying our precious ecosystem. It will not happen here in California. (Rothfeld, 2010)

The sort of environmental security Schwarzenegger evokes here concerns oil, but it assembles it differently and draws in more elements than energy security does – including for instance birds, fisherman and the ecosystem. Instead of aggregate national concerns, it brings to the fore many of the consequences of oil production that are otherwise silenced. As such, it exposes matters of fact that are silenced by the energy security agenda and makes them matters of concern. Whereas the environmental security agenda is often treated as a separate concern from the energy security agenda, this example shows how environmental security is literally attached to the same assemblage of drilling platforms and submarine ecologies as energy security – an assemblage that is differently enrolled by invoking environmental concerns. To put it differently, the oilrig off the Gulf Coast, which had previously been a smooth-functioning technical element in an energy security assemblage, was revealed to be an unstable network of elements that could not simply be transposed to the Californian coast without possibly unacceptable environmental costs.

Where environmental securitisations gain in inclusiveness and symmetry *vis-à-vis* energy securitisations of related assemblages of elements, they point to much less straightforward policy agendas. The notion of 'security' underpinning environmental security is much less wedded to the policy-ready state centrism underpinning energy security. For instance, an environmental securitisation of the Arctic region extends the perspective from that of a single state to that of a hybrid referent object (consisting of biodiversity, indigenous people and mankind through potentially rising sea levels) threatened by crude oil production, industrial pollution and rising local temperatures (Martello, 2008; Kristoffersen and Young, 2010).

Assembling climate security

Climate security involves new programmatic agencies and further extends the range of concerns assembled to include – beyond local and regional transformation and pollution of livelihoods – long-term increases in average temperatures, the global interconnectedness of feedback loops and all kinds of linkages between disparate components of the biosphere (e.g. Overpeck and Cole, 2006; Lenton et al., 2008). Since only climate and earth sciences can detect and visualise the complex and increasingly non-linear dynamics of fragile global ecosystems that eventually need to be acted upon (Demeritt, 2001; Hulme, 2009; see also Taylor and Buttel, 1992), the scientific community represents a central agency assembling climate security (Mayer, forthcoming). The assembled elements are translated into the alarming language of 'abruptness' and 'tipping points' in ecological regimes (Risbey, 2008; see also Cox, 2002; Pearce, 2006; Fagan, 2008), as for instance here by US presidential science adviser John Holdren: 'Climate scientists worry about "tipping points" thresholds beyond which a small additional increase in average temperature or some associated climate variable results in major changes to the affected system' (ScienceDaily, 2010).

Furthermore, competing climate security assemblages refer to different referent objects that have to be secured accordingly. For instance, whereas climate scientists warn against very rapid changes in regional and local ecological systems with huge global environmental repercussions, think-tanks and strategists assemble the 'climate flickers' as amplifying local conflicts over resources and societal instability and leading to interstate rivalries and, ultimately, 'anarchy' (Schwartz and Randall, 2003; Borgerson, 2008; cf. Maas and Tänzler, 2009). Climate security assembled in the latter way echoes the environmental determinism of the 1990s and directly circles back to the logic of 'energy security' (cf.: Judkins, Smith, and Keys, 2008; Dalby, 2009). For example, a group of former US generals recently concluded that since climate change amplifies the problem of unstable governments it demands military stabilisation operations worldwide. The generals invoke the US resource supply as threatened: 'Political instability also makes access to African trade and resources, on which the US is reliant for both military and civilian uses, a riskier proposition' (CNA, 2007, p. 20).

In the Arctic, where rapid temperature increase has surpassed even recent scientific predictions (Leichenko and O'Brien, 2008, pp. 91–103), state agencies have started to react to rapid physical changes and enrolled them as threats to sovereignty and economic interests. Studies show that the sea ice over the North Pole might vanish completely within the next 30 years (Holland, Bitz, and Tremblay, 2006; Wang and Overland, 2009), which in turn renders existing assemblages of state practices unstable. Climate change is thus 'forcing the state system to confront its accepted suppositions about the relationship amongst land, state, territory, and nation' (Gerhardt et al., 2010, p. 999).

The rapid sea ice melting is enabling gas and oil exploration and opening up the Northwest Passage as a major new shipping route for world trade. Reacting to the exposure of multiple undetermined border demarcations, the Canadian government is rapidly extending its military presence at the American continent's northern rim in order to control the Northwest Passage and to assert its sovereignty claims (Byers, 2009). When Canada's Foreign Affairs Minister Lawrence Cannon labels his country an 'Arctic superpower', he is mainly referring to the abundant fossil reserves in the Arctic that would make Canada another 'Energy Superpower' (Boswell, 2009).

On the opposite side of the Arctic ocean, Russia's government tries to secure territorial claims and the interests of its national oil companies stretching over the whole North Pole by re-establishing its strategic 'bear' bombers' patrol flights and large-scale military drills (Zysk, 2010). During one of Premier Vladimir V. Putin's nature adventures to Franz Josef Land that received considerable attention in the Russian mass media, the Premier enrolled the polar bear, also figuring as national personification, as an element of the climate security assemblage. Emphasising at once Russia's 'profound strategic interests' in the Region, the dire consequences of ice shield reduction and sea ice melting for the animal's living conditions, 'the bear', he declared, 'is the real master of the Arctic' (Harding, 2010). In August 2007, Russian scientists, claiming the North Pole belongs to Russia, placed a titanium Russian flag on the North Pole seafloor.

Although nationalist rhetoric abounds, Denmark, Russia and Canada committed in the 2008 Ilulissat Declaration to solve their territorial disputes within the framework of international law. These nations are now funding huge scientific research projects to map the Arctic's continental shelves in preparation for 2013, when the United Nations (UN) seabed commission will finally determine which country owns the Arctic according to International Law. As such, geologists and lawyers, who shall determine which nations own the exclusive rights of exploiting the large gas and oil reserves under the Arctic seabed (Byers, 2009; Gerhardt et al., 2010), are drawn into climate security assemblages too. Meanwhile, Chinese scholars, seeing huge potential in the opening up of new trade routes, proclaim their nation's 'rights' in the Arctic region. The Chinese state connects itself with the rapid ecological changes in the Far North not only through research teams that make inroads into the region, but also via a formidable flotilla of new icebreakers (Jakobson, 2010; McLeary, 2010).

Other assembling agencies are also active. In contrast to these competitive regional postures, the diplomatic context of the ongoing international climate negotiations does not primarily enrol climate change as a threat to national sovereignty, territory and petro-politics. The 2009 Copenhagen Accord that has been signed by all major world powers, has set a 2-degree benchmark for stabilisation of the global average temperature (Broder, 2010a). Here, the stability of the earth system is assembled as the main matter of concern, and ecological change in the Arctic is not enrolled as a sovereignty issue, but as chemical dynamic (methane emissions) that pushes the whole earth system over a threshold (Sample, 2005).

Importantly, as the above examples show, environmental security and climate concerns push and pull the same elements that make up energy security assemblages, albeit in different directions. As discussed above, an oilrig off the Louisiana coast, while constructed as an element in securing energy supplies, can also be mobilised as part of an environmental security assemblage; and climate concerns can be mobilised to fortify the militarisation of an energy security agenda. Whereas climate security foregrounds human and natural concerns more or less on an equal level and includes more elements than either energy or environmental security assemblages do, it has proven more difficult to assemble the political agencies necessary to implement the agenda of climate mitigation. By symmetrically including the technical and natural elements and the social concerns assembled under the headers of the various agendas in our discussion, it becomes evident how each agenda links them differently and to what effect. Beyond mere securitisations, these distinct renderings actively transform the assembled elements to different, and competing, effects. What is also revealed is that the competing assembling efforts of energy, environment and climate securitisations are often blurred; overlapping ambiguities are enrolled in varying ways, but the strategic agencies of those spearheading an energy security assemblage always appear dominant.

Conclusions

This chapter started with a central dilemma of current world politics: we urgently need to balance the pursuit of energy security with broader social and ecological concerns. While various studies made important inroads in investigating the conditions enabling such a multidimensional balancing act, this chapter has argued that a tenacious issue remains – that existing conceptions of security do not accommodate broader environmental concerns. By revisiting the underpinnings of energy security in light of the *problématique* of the Anthropocene, we argue that it is only by considering both the consumption of hydrocarbon resources and the consequences of their extraction and usage as endogenous matters of concern that redefinitions of energy security will enjoy any success in unsettling unsustainable and treacherous patterns.

The main theoretical contribution of this chapter lies in conceptualising agendas pursuing energy, environmental and climate security not as social constructs but rather as assemblages. Progressive variants of security studies, including those critical of the traditional energy security agenda, have tended to treat security as part of the discursive realm, either as a discourse or as a securitisation, divorced from both technical problems and physical reality, thus requiring a different conceptual toolbox. In doing so, they run counter to the central tenet of the Anthropocene that modern human agency is currently the biggest natural force.

Drawing on insights from actor-network theory, this chapter entails three main points. Firstly, in conceptualising security as assemblages embedded in and linked to the very natural 'objects' they concern, it becomes apparent how competing programmatic efforts working upon nature in fact constitute it as an object amenable to intervention. They are not mere discursive narratives by politically organised groups of humans *about* nature, but rather transformations of nature. As an effect, as Dalby (2002, p. 194) puts it, we have learnt to represent nature 'as an unproblematic object, knowable via classification and experiment, and above all infinitely manipulable in the service of human purpose'.

Secondly, actor-network theory allows us to narrate the effects of competing discourses in a distinct way. The concurrent existence of competing definitions of the relationship between nature and security (that assemble from the same heterogeneous variety of elements but differently) points to the jostling inherent in politics in an inherently unstable world (Callon and Latour, 1992). A move in one node of these vast and complex assemblages reverberates all over because of the different feedback loops and interdependencies between elements: one 'human' intervention mediated by technology impacts on the environment, which in turn 'responds', leading to constrained human acts that modify the assemblages as a whole. By bringing the effects of these assembling efforts into the picture as matters of concern, the condition of the Anthropocene becomes apparent. Rather than critically lamenting capitalist social constructs or abstract but dangerous dominant discourses, we have shown how assemblages of energy, environmental or climate security only persist because of the active assembling efforts of actors and programmatic agencies. Highlighting these efforts is an essential part of actor-network theory and has the advantage of revealing concretely the specific political agencies that, geared at sustaining energy security, impact on nature in complex and varied ways.

Finally, through the notions of inclusiveness and symmetry, our approach uncovers the paradoxes of energy security by bringing the material back into analysis of energy security. Inclusiveness brings to the fore the externalities silenced by energy security, and symmetry shows that material and natural elements are as much a part of securitisations of energy as are discursive elements. We were thus able to shed a different light on the question of how it is possible that we might successfully attain energy security (e.g. successfully securitise the environment in a particular way) and yet deepen global insecurities.

Energy security is the most powerful amongst the securitisations of nature we discussed. It forms an assemblage that holds stable uncountable associations between huge material and financial flows, and enrols a wide array of actors and agencies. Neither environmental nor climate security, which are mostly small and regional or locally based assemblages, reach the parsimony and global scale of energy security. Under its header, the use of fossil fuels, national political legitimacy and the structure of the international system have become deeply intertwined. By analysing how the agencies upholding energy security assemblages neatly separate out the relevant concerns concerns in a language consisting of market efficiency and strategic tools, as well as how material linkages to such externalities as pollution, climate change and other environmental concerns become silenced, it becomes possible to assess the success of energy security. Energy security, with its restricted scope of concern, is anchored in an anthropocentric myth of limited social concerns prevailing over an extensive natural 'context' that can be filled and drilled with the proper technology.

The downside of this immense power is, ironically, the paradox of the Anthropocene: whereas human impact on ecological systems is growing quickly, it is at the same time hard to see how 'society' has increased its control over nature, when in fact converging lines and fragile complex interdependencies are laid bare by climate change. If the multiple forms of interwovenness of environment (encompassing the climate) and humans were assembled as sharing the status of matter of concern against which to measure interventions, energy security agendas would be less parsimonious, but energy consumption would possibly be better attuned to its consequences for the biosphere.

One of the main difficulties remaining is formulating policy or creating processes and institutions for the pursuit of balanced energy and climate security under conditions of the Anthropocene, that is, when nature is no longer naturalistic, and security no longer a socio-political construct. Answering this question is beyond the scope of this chapter. Yet, it becomes clear that conceptually, nature cannot be held constant as a 'matter of fact' to be acted upon by humans according to their shifting 'social' concerns. Instead of this anthropocentric worldview, the reality of (often differently) assembled referent objects – including those actors that are habitually silenced as pure 'facts' or others that we usually isolate from their surrounding (ecological) systems – should form the starting point when formulating security matters of concern. It is only by acknowledging this condition, for instance through the methodology of inclusiveness and symmetry, that one could begin to conceive of a notion of security that will not ultimately render us more *in*secure.

Notes

1. Susan Strange (1999) already stressed the systematic failure of the international system to limit environmental pollution. Simon Dalby (2002, p. xxiii) asserts that '[the] limitations of international relations thinking are especially acute when matters of global environmental politics and environmental security are concerned'. Anthony Giddens (2009) links the political economy of energy security to climate politics, and calls for radical changes in human interaction with nature to avoid disastrous climate change. Still others point to the intersection of energy security, climate change, food and water scarcity that places huge pressure on the international security (WBGU, 2007; Lee, 2009).
2. This argument has often been voiced as a (postmodern) analysis or critique against modern social sciences, cf. Latour (1993, 2004, 2005) and Beck (1995).
3. Also see Çalişkan and Callon (2009); Hall and Klitgaard (2006); Latour (1993); Polanyi (2001), for criticisms of the disembedding of different aspects of society and the complicity of different social sciences herein.
4. This section draws heavily on the work of actor-network theory (ANT) (Callon and Law, 1982, 1997; Callon, 1986; Latour, 1987, 2005; Law and Callon, 1988; Callon and Latour, 1992; Law, 1991, 1992, 2008; DeLanda, 2006; Law and Mol, 2008). For a more in-depth discussion and empirical applications of ANT within international security studies, see Schouten (2010, 2011).
5. Securitisation theory explicitly bases itself on a linguistic approach called 'speech act theory' deriving from the work of Searle (1965) and Austin (1962).
6. While the term 'assemblage' is a core ANT term referring both to a network of heterogeneous actors (be they material, human, discursive or natural) and any discursive representation of such a network (Latour, 2005), the term has also been gaining purchase in security studies to refer to networks of security actors cross-cutting public/private, formal/informal and local/global divides. See Abrahamsen and Williams (2009, 2011) and Schouten (2010) for a discussion of 'assemblages' that links both approaches.
7. As with much of the discussion in this section, this distinction between matters of concern and matters of fact derives from Latour (2005); any 'actant' or element can be assembled as a 'black box', that is, a stable building block, or as a capricious concern.
8. Due to the relative abundance and equal distribution, its material characteristics, and the lack of a global market coal (and biomass) is rarely a concern of energy security.

References

Abrahamsen, R. and M.C. Williams (2009), 'Security beyond the state: Global security assemblages in international politics', *International Political Sociology*, 3(1): 1–17.
Abrahamsen, R. and M.C. Williams (2011), *Security Beyond the State: Private Security in International Politics* (Cambridge-New York: Cambridge University Press).
Amineh, M.P. and H. Houweling (2007), 'Global energy security and its geopolitical impediments – The case of the Caspian region', *Perspectives on Global Development and Technology*, 6(1): 365–88.
Antilla, L. (2005), 'Climate of scepticism: US newspaper coverage of the science of climate change', *Global Environmental Change Part A*, 15(4): 338–52.
Asdal, K. (2008), 'Enacting things through numbers: Taking nature into account/ing', *Geoforum*, 39(1): 123–32.
Austin, J.L. (1962), *How to Do Things with Words* (Oxford: Clarendon Press).
Barad, K. (2003), 'Posthumanist performativity: Toward an understanding of how matter comes to matter', *Signs: Journal of Women in Culture and Society*, 28(3): 801–31.
Barnett, J. (2001a), *The Meaning of Environmental Security: Environmental Politics and Policy in the New Security Era* (New York: Zed Books).
Barnett, J. (2001b), 'Security and climate change', *Tyndall Centre for Climate Change Research Working Paper*, 7.
Barry, A. (2001), *Political Machines: Governing a Technological Society* (London-New York: Athlone Press).
Barry, J. (1999), *Environment and Social Theory* (London-New York: Routledge).
Bauman, Z. (1995), *Life in Fragments: Essays in Postmodern Morality* (Oxford-Cambridge, Mass.: Blackwell).
Beck, U. (1995), *Ecological Enlightenment: Essays on the Politics of the Risk Society* (Atlantic Highlands: Humanities Press).
Beck, U. (2002), *Ecological politics in an age of risk* (Cambridge; Malden, MA: Polity Press).
Bingham, N. and S. Hinchliffe (2008), 'Reconstituting natures: Articulating other modes of living together', *Geoforum*, 39(1): 83–7.
Borgerson, S.G. (2008), 'Arctic meltdown: The economic and security implications of global warming', *Foreign Affairs*, 87: 63–77.
Boswell, R. (2009). 'Canada is "Arctic superpower": Cannon', *National Post*, 28 June [http://www.nationalpost.com/news/story.html?id=1741776; accessed: 03 December 2010].
Bradshaw, M.J. (2009), 'The geopolitics of global energy security', *Geography Compass*, 3(5): 1920–37.
Brauch, H.G. (2009), *Facing Global Environmental Change: Environmental, Human, Energy, Food, Health and Water Security Concepts* (Berlin: Springer).
Brauch, H.G. and G. Zundel (2008), *Globalization and Environmental Challenges: Reconceptualizing Security in the 21st Century* (Berlin-New York: Springer).
Bridge, G. (2008), 'Global production networks and the extractive sector: Governing resource-based development', *Journal of Economic Geography*, 8(3): 389–419.
Broder, J.M. (2010a), 'China and India join climate accord', *New York Times*, 10 March [http://www.nytimes.com/2010/03/10/world/10climate.html; accessed: 03 December 2010].
Broder, J.M. (2010b), 'Senate gets a climate and energy bill, modified by a gulf spill that still grows', *New York Times*, 12 May [http://www.nytimes.com/2010/05/13/science/earth/13climate.html?ref=us; accessed: 03 December 2010].

Brown, S.P.A. and H.G. Huntington (2008), 'Energy security and climate change protection: Complementarity or tradeoff?', *Energy Policy*, 36(9): 3510–3.

Brzoska, M. (2009), 'The securitization of climate change and the power of conceptions of security', *Security and Peace*, 27(3): 137–45.

Buzan, B., O. Wæver and J.D. Wilde (1998), *Security: A New Framework for Analysis* (Boulder: Lynne Rienner).

Byers, M. (2009), *Who Owns the Arctic? Understanding Sovereignty Disputes in the North* (Vancouver: Douglas & McIntyre).

Byrne, J. and L. Glover (2005), 'Ellul and the weather', *Bulletin of Science, Technology and Society*, 25(1): 4–16.

Çalişkan, K. and M. Callon (2009), 'Economization, part 1: Shifting attention from the economy towards processes of economization', *Economy and Society*, 38(3): 369–98.

Çalişkan, K. and M. Callon (2010), 'Economization, part 2: A research programme for the study of markets', *Economy and Society*, 39(1): 1–32.

Callon, M. (1986), 'Some elements of a sociology of translation: Domestication of the scallops and the fishermen of St Brieuc Bay', in J. Law (ed.): *Power, Action and Belief: A New Sociology of Knowledge?* (London: Routledge).

Callon, M. and B. Latour (1992), 'Unscrewing the big Leviathan: How actors macrostructure reality and how sociologists help them to do so', in K. Knorr-Cetina and A.V. Cicourel (eds): *Advances in Social Theory and Methodology – Towards an Integration of Micro- and Macro-Sociologies* (London-Henley: Routledge/Kegan Paul).

Callon, M. and J. Law (1982), 'On interests and their transformation: Enrolment and counter-enrolment', *Social Studies of Science*, 12(4): 615–25.

Callon, M. and J. Law (1997), 'After the individual in society: Lessons on collectivity from science, technology and society', *The Canadian Journal of Sociology*, 22(2): 165–82.

Center for Naval Analyses (CNA) (2007), *National Security and the Threat of Climate Change* (Alexandria: CNA Corporation).

Clark, W.C. and R.E. Munn (1986), *Sustainable Development of the Biosphere* (Cambridge: Cambridge University Press).

Collier, P. (2007), *The Bottom Billion: Why the Poorest Countries Are Failing and What Can Be Done About It* (Oxford-New York: Oxford University Press).

Cox, J.D. (2002), *Climate Crash: Abrupt Climate Change and What It Means for Our Future* (Washington, DC: Joseph Henry Press).

Crutzen, P.J. and E.F. Stoermer (2000), 'The Anthropocene', *Global Change Newsletter*, 41: 17–8.

Dalby, S. (2002), *Environmental Security* (Minneapolis: University of Minnesota Press).

Dalby, S. (2009), *Security and Environmental Change* (Cambridge: Polity).

DeLanda, M. (2006), *A New Philosophy of Society: Assemblage Theory and Social Complexity* (London-New York: Continuum).

Demeritt, D. (2001), 'The construction of global warming and the politics of science', *Annals of the Association of American Geographers*, 91(2): 307–37.

Deudney, D. (1999), 'Environmental security. A critique', in D. Deudney and R.A. Matthew (eds): *SUNY Series in International Environmental Policy and Theory* (Albany: State University of New York Press).

Deutch, J., A. Lauvergeon and W. Prawiraatmadja (2007), *Energy Security and Climate Change* (Washington, Paris, Tokyo: The Trilateral Commission).

Fagan, B.M. (2008), *The Great Warming: Climate Change and the Rise and Fall of Civilizations* (New York: Bloomsbury Press).

Floyd, R. (2008), 'The environmental security debate and its significance for climate change', *The International Spectator: Italian Journal of International Affairs*, 43(3): 51–65.

Forsyth, T. (2001), 'Critical realism and political ecology', in A. Stainer and G. Lopez (eds): *After Postmodernism: Critical Realism?* (London: Athlone Press).

Gammon, E. (2010), 'Nature as adversary: The rise of modern economic conceptions of nature', *Economy and Society*, 39(2): 218–46.

Gerhardt, H., P.E. Steinberg, J. Tasch, S.J. Fabiano, and R. Shields (2010), 'Contested sovereignty in a changing Arctic', *Annals of the Association of American Geographers*, 100(4): 992–1002.

German Advisory Council on Global Change (WBGU) (2007), *World in Transition – Climate Change as a Security Risk* (London: Earthscan).

Giddens, A. (2009), *The Politics of Climate Change* (Cambridge-Malden: Polity).

Hall, C.A.S. and K.A. Klitgaard (2006), 'The need for a new, biophysical-based paradigm in economics for the second half of the age of oil', *International Journal of Transdisciplinary Research*, 1(1): 4–22.

Hansen, J.E. (2005), 'A slippery slope: How much global warming constitutes "dangerous anthropogenic interference"?', *Climatic Change*, 68(3): 269–79.

Harding, L. (2010), 'Vladimir Putin hugs polar bear on Arctic trip', *The Guardian*, 29 April [http://www.guardian.co.uk/world/2010/apr/29/vladimir-putin-polar-bear-arctic; accessed: 03 December 2010].

Hirsch, R.L. (1987), 'Impending United States energy crisis', *Science*, 235(4795): 1467–73.

Holland, M.M., C.M. Bitz, and B. Tremblay (2006), 'Future abrupt reductions in the summer Arctic sea ice', *Geophysical Research Letters*, 33(23): L23503.

Hulme, M. (2009), *Why We Disagree about Climate Change: Understanding Controversy, Inaction and Opportunity* (Cambridge: Cambridge University Press).

Hulme, M. (2010), 'Cosmopolitan climates: Hybridity, foresight and meaning', *Theory, Culture & Society*, 27(2/3): 277–88.

Huysmans, J. (2006), *The Politics of Insecurity: Fear, Migration, and Asylum in the EU* (New York: Routledge).

Jakobson, L. (2010), 'China prepares for an ice-free Arctic', *SIPRI Insights on Peace and Security*, 2010(2).

Jasanoff, S. (2005), 'In the democracies of DNA: Ontological uncertainty and political order in three states', *New Genetics and Society*, 24(2): 139–56.

Jokinen, P. (1997), 'Ulrich Beck: Ecological politics in an age of risk' [review], *Acta Sociologica*, 40(1): 114–8.

Judkins, G., M. Smith and E. Keys (2008), 'Determinism within human-environment research and the rediscovery of environmental causation', *The Geographical Journal*, 174: 17–29.

Kaldor, M., T.L. Karl and Y. Said (2007), *Oil wars* (London: Pluto).

Klare, M.T. (2004), *Blood and Oil: The Dangers and Consequences of America's Growing Petroleum Dependency* (New York: Metropolitan Books/Henry Holt & Co.).

Krause, K. (2003), 'Environmental security' [book review], *Environmental Change & Security Project Report* (9): 111–3.

Kristoffersen, B. and S. Young (2010), 'Geographies of security and statehood in Norway's "Battle of the North" ', *Geoforum*, 41(4): 577–84.

Labban, M. (2008), *Space, Oil, and Capital* (Abingdon-New York: Routledge).

Lacey, M. (2005), *Security and Climate Change – International Relations and the Limits of Realism* (London: Routledge).

Latour, B. (1987), *Science in Action: How to Follow Scientists and Engineers Through Society* (Cambridge: Harvard University Press).

Latour, B. (1993), *We Have Never Been Modern* (Cambridge: Harvard University Press).

Latour, B. (2004), *Politics of Nature: How to Bring the Sciences into Democracy* (Cambridge: Harvard University Press).

Latour, B. (2005), *Reassembling the Social: An Introduction to Actor-Network-Theory* (Oxford-New York: Oxford University Press).

Law, J. (ed.) (1991), *A Sociology of Monsters: Essays on Power, Technology and Domination* (London-New York: Routledge).

Law, J. (1992), 'Notes on the theory of the actor-network: Ordering, strategy, and heterogeneity', *Systemic Practice and Action Research*, 5(4): 379–93.

Law, J. (2008), 'On sociology and STS', *Sociological Review*, 56(4): 623–49.

Law, J., and A. Mol (2008), 'Globalisation in practice: On the politics of boiling pigswill', *Geoforum*, 39(1): 133–43.

Law, J., and M. Callon (1988), 'Engineering and sociology in a military aircraft project: A network analysis of technological change', *Social Problems*, 35(3): 284–97.

Lee, B. (2009), 'Managing the interlocking climate and resource challenges', *International Affairs*, 85(6): 1101–16.

Lefèvre, N. (2007), *Energy Security and Climate Policy: Assessing Interactions* (Paris: OECD/IEA).

Leichenko, R.M. and K.L. O'Brien (2008), *Environmental Change and Globalization: Double Exposures* (Oxford-New York: Oxford University Press).

Lenton, T.M., H. Held, E. Kriegler, J.W. Hall, W. Lucht, S. Rahmstorf, et al. (2008), 'Tipping elements in the Earth's climate system', *Proceedings of the National Academy of Sciences*, 105(6): 1786–93.

Levy, D.L. and D. Egan (1998), 'Capital contests: National and transnational channels of corporate influence on the climate change negotiations', *Politics and Society*, 26(3): 337–61.

Liotta, P.H. (2005), 'Through the looking glass: Creeping vulnerabilities and the reordering of security', *Security Dialogue*, 36(1): 49–70.

Litfin, K. (2003), 'Towards an integral perspective on world politics: Secularism, sovereignty and the challenge of global ecology', *Millennium – Journal of International Studies*, 32(1): 29–56.

Lubchenco, J. (1998), 'Entering the century of the environment: A new social contract for science', *Science*, 279(5350): 491–7.

Lubeck, P.M., M.J. Watts and R. Lipschutz (2007), *International Policy Report – Convergent Interests: US Energy Security and the "Securing" of Nigerian Democracy* (Washington: Center for International Policy).

Maas, A. and D. Tänzler (2009), *Regional Security Implications of Climate Change – A Synopsis* (Berlin: Adelphi Report Conducted for DG External Relations of the European Commission under a contract for the German Ministry for the Environment, Nature Protection and Nuclear Safety).

Marquina Barrio, A. (2008), *Energy Security: Visions from Asia and Europe* (New York: Palgrave Macmillan).

Marsh, G.P. (1874), *The Earth as Modified by Human Action* (New York: Scribner, Armstrong & Co).

Martello, M.L. (2008), 'Arctic indigenous peoples as representations and representatives of climate change', *Social Studies of Science*, 38(3): 351–76.

Mayer, M. (forthcoming), 'Chaotic climate change and security', in International Political Sociology' (Paper presented at the SGIR Conference Stockholm).

Mcab, R.M., and K.S. Bailey (2007), 'Latin America and the debate over environmental protection and national security', *DISAM Journal*, 29(4): 18–34 (December).
McLeary, P. (2010), 'The Arctic: China opens a new strategic front', *World Politics Review*, 19 May.
McNeil, J.R. (2009), 'The international system, great powers, and environmental change since 1900', in H.G. Brauch and Berghof-Stiftung für Konfliktforschung (eds): *Facing Global Environmental Change: Environmental, Human, Energy, Food, Health and Water Security Concepts* (Berlin: Springer).
McPherson, C. and S. MacSearraigh (2007), 'Corruption in the petroleum sector', in J.E. Campos and S. Pradhan (eds): *The Many Faces of Corruption: Tracking Vulnerabilities at the Sector Level* (Washington, DC: World Bank).
Merriman, P. (2009), 'Automobility and the geographies of the car', *Geography Compass*, 3(2): 586–99.
Mitchell, L. (2007), 'The black box: Inside Iraq's oil machine', *Harper's Magazine*, 81–3.
Mol, A. (1998), 'Ontological politics. A word and some questions', *Sociological Review*, 46(S): 74–89.
Moran, D. and J.A. Russell (2009), *Energy Security and Global Politics: The Militarization of Resource Management* (London-New York: Routledge).
Morin, M.E. (2009), 'Cohabitating in the globalised world: Peter Sloterdijk's global foams and Bruno Latour's cosmopolitics', *Environment and Planning: Society and Space*, 27(1): 58–72.
Obama, B. (2010), 'Obama's speech on energy security and offshore drilling', March 2010 [http://www.cfr.org/publication/21787/obamas_speech_on_energy_security_and_offshore_drilling_march_2010.html; accessed: 09 May 2010].
Overpeck, J.T. and J.E. Cole (2006), 'Abrupt change in Earth's climate system', *Annual Review of Environment and Resources*, 31(1): 1–31.
Pearce, F. (2006), *The Last Generation. How Nature Will Take Her Revenge for Climate Change* (London: Random House).
Peluso, N.L. and M. Watts (2001), *Violent Environments* (Ithaca: Cornell University Press).
Polanyi, K. (2001), *The Great Transformation: The Political and Economic Origins of Our Time* (Boston: Beacon Press).
Risbey, J.S. (2008), 'The new climate discourse: Alarmist or alarming?', *Global Environmental Change*, 18(1): 26–37.
Rose, N. and P. Miller (1992), 'Political power beyond the state: Problematics of government', *The British Journal of Sociology*, 43(2): 173–205.
Rothfeld, M. (2010), 'Schwarzenegger reverses course on off-shore drilling', *Los Angeles Times*, 3 May [http://latimesblogs.latimes.com/california-politics/2010/05/schwarzenegger-reverses-course-on-off-shore-drilling.html; accessed: 03 December 2010].
Sample, I. (2005), 'Warming hits "tipping point"', *Guardian*, 11 August [http://www.guardian.co.uk/environment/2005/aug/11/science.climatechange1; accessed: 03 December 2010].
Schouten, P. (2010), 'Security as controversy: Privatizing security inside global security assemblages' (Paper presented at the International Studies Association Annual Conference).
Schouten, P. (2011), 'Political topographies of private security in Sub-Saharan Africa', in T. Dietz, K. Havnevik, M. Kaag and T. Oestigaard (eds): *African Engagements – Africa Negotiating an Emerging Multipolar World* (Leiden: Brill).

Schwartz, P. and D. Randall (2003), *An Abrupt Climate Change Scenario and Its Implications for United States National Security. A report Commissioned by the US Defense Department* (Washington: Global Business Network).

ScienceDaily (2010), 'Climate "tipping points" may arrive without warning, says top forecaster', *Science Daily*, 10 February [http://www.sciencedaily.com/releases/2010/02/100209191445.htm; accessed: 03 December 2010].

Searle, J.R. (1965), 'What is a speech act?', in M. Black (ed.): *Philosophy in America* (Ithaca: Cornell University Press).

Solomon, S. and Intergovernmental Panel on Climate Change (2007), *Climate Change 2007 – The Physical Science Basis: Contribution of Working Group I to the Fourth Assessment Report of the Intergovernmental Panel on Climate Change* (Cambridge-New York: Cambridge University Press).

Steffen, W.L. (2004), *Global Change and the Earth System: A Planet Under Pressure* (Berlin-New York: Springer).

Stern, M. (2005), *Naming Security – Constructing Identity: 'Mayan Women' in Guatemala on the Eve of 'Peace'* (Manchester: Manchester University Press).

Strange, S. (1999), 'The Westfailure system', *Review of International Studies*, 25(3): 345–54.

Taylor, P.J. and F.H. Buttel (1992), 'How do we know we have global environmental problems? Science and the globalization of environmental discourse', *Geoforum*, 23(3): 405–16.

The White House (2010), 'Remarks by the President to the Nation on the BP Oil Spill', 15 June [http://www.whitehouse.gov/the-press-office/remarks-president-nation-bp-oil-spill; accessed: 30 June 2010].

Trombetta, M.J. (2008), 'Environmental security and climate change: Analysing the discourse', *Cambridge Review of International Affairs*, 21(4): 585–602.

Tsing, A.L. (2005), *Friction: An Ethnography of Global Connection* (Princeton: Princeton University Press).

Turton, H. and L. Barreto (2006), 'Long-term security of energy supply and climate change', *Energy Policy*, 34(15): 2232–50.

United Kingdom Mission to the United Nations (2007), *Energy, Security and Climate – Security Council Open Debate: UK Concept Paper* [http://gc.nautilus.org/Nautilus/australia/reframing/cc-security/sec-council; accessed: 03 December 2010].

Urry, J. (2007), *Mobilities* (Cambridge: Polity).

Verrastro, F. and Sarah Ladislaw, S. (2007), 'Providing energy security in an interdependent world', *The Washington Quarterly*, 30(4): 95–104.

Wæver, O. (1995), 'Securitization and desecuritization', in R.D. Lipschutz (ed.): *On Security* (New York: Columbia University Press).

Wang, M. and J.E. Overland (2009), 'A sea ice free summer Arctic within 30 years?' *Geophysical Research Letters*, 36(7): L07502.

Watts, M. (2009), 'Crude politics: Life and death on the Nigerian oil fields' (University of Berkeley, Department of Geography Working Paper, 25).

Yergin, D. (2006), 'Ensuring energy security', *Foreign Affairs*, 85(2): 69–82.

Zweig, D. and J. Bi (2005), 'China's global hunt for energy', *Foreign Affairs*, 84(5): 25–38.

Zysk, K. (2010), 'Russia's Arctic strategy: Ambitions and constraints', *Joint Force Quarterly*, 57: 104–11.

2
Unmasking the Invisible Giant: Energy Efficiency in the Politics of Climate and Energy

Mark Lister

Introduction

Climate change constraints and ever-increasing global energy requirements can only be reconciled to create global energy security if we can attain energy supply and use patterns that are consistent with progress towards a good life for all. There are two fundamental activities to be undertaken in this endeavour: one relates to energy supply and its climate change impacts (see Chapter 1, pp. 21–22); the other, to energy demand. Every unit of energy supply that is produced cleanly contributes the same amount to the climate change solution as every equivalent unit of energy that, through reduced usage, does not need to be supplied in the first place. When it comes to addressing climate change and therefore securing our energy future, clean energy supply and reduced energy demand are two sides of the same coin.

Every balanced analysis of climate change mitigation points to energy efficiency as the most cost-effective means of reducing global carbon dioxide emissions. In addition to the direct reduction in costs per unit of actual energy consumed, reducing demand by eliminating non-productive waste means that the difficult social, cultural and geopolitical issues associated with securing energy supplies can be, if not avoided altogether, at least deferred in many instances. This 'buying of time' is a key recommendation for establishing a clear focus on energy efficiency in the immediate term, allowing more expensive solutions to become commercially ready for later rollout.

Somewhat paradoxically, while energy efficiency has long been recognised as the most cost-effective response to worldwide greenhouse emissions reductions, much public and political focus has been on the emissions intensity of electricity generation. In the Australian context, which is the principal experience applied in this chapter, there has been a disproportionate public emphasis on the exorbitant cost of re-configuring our electricity supply system, the concept of an emissions 'cap' and resultant emissions price that will be prescribed by emissions trading, and the importance of a supply-side target that ensures renewable energy contributes an increasing portion of electricity generation. Reduction of energy waste has not always featured as heavily in the discussion (see Chapter 11, p. 200).

This chapter examines why this might be the case, and points to some of the changes that are required to capitalise on the potential contribution that energy efficiency can make to improving global energy security. First, this potential is explored quantitatively, by examining what opportunities may exist to reduce energy demand and the economic and environmental contribution that this may make. The discussion is focussed to some extent on Australia as a case study; this relates to the author's direct experience in leading energy efficiency advocacy efforts in that country. However, the discussion of cultural bias also applies within other developed countries. Second, the chapter considers, in some detail, why energy efficiency's potential is not being realised at present. In addition to a set of well-understood barriers, I argue that there is social and historical bias against measures to reduce energy demand compared with other, more costly alternatives. The chapter concludes with some observations on alternative approaches that may be required to scale up the acceptability and implementation of energy efficiency measures.

The global potential for energy efficiency

According to reports by the Intergovernmental Panel on Climate Change (IPCC), particularly its 2007 report received from Working Group III (IPCC, 2007), there is global potential to cost-effectively reduce approximately 30 per cent of projected baseline emissions from the residential and commercial building sectors alone by 2020; this potential is the highest amongst all sectors studied. There are also measures that can cost-effectively save energy in other end-use sectors (see Figure 2.1).[1]

Another key factor in assessing energy efficiency's potential is the abundance of opportunities that are economically attractive. This sets energy efficiency apart from other measures to reduce emissions and improve energy security. For example, the IPCC figures quoted above only consider 'negative cost' opportunities (that is, those that yield financial benefits), that were found to be so abundant that higher cost opportunities were not considered. This figure is therefore known to underestimate the available opportunities. IPCC authors quote numerous published studies showing that energy savings of 50–75 per cent can be achieved in the commercial buildings sector through aggressive implementation of integrated sets of measures; savings in other sectors are estimated to be of this order as well (Levine et al., 2007, pp. 404–405).[2]

In its World Energy Outlook (2009), the International Energy Agency (IEA) concurs with the view that energy efficiency is the most important strategy

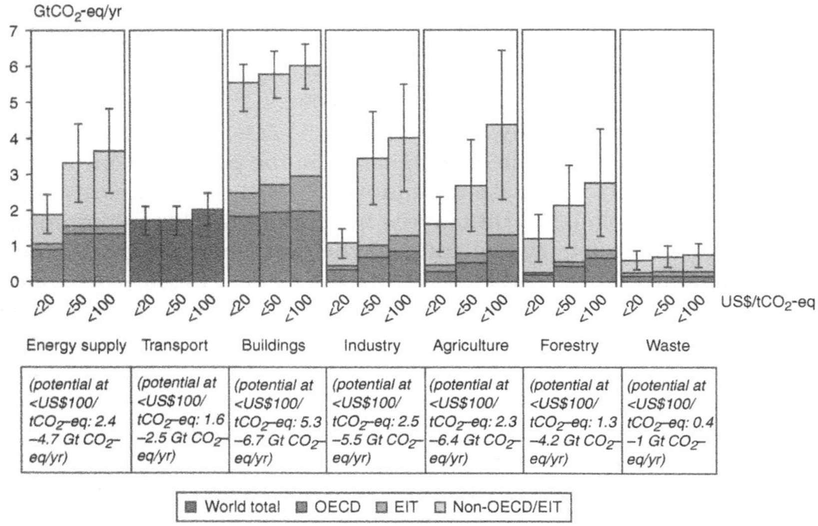

Figure 2.1 IPCC Fourth Assessment Report Working Group III estimates of abatement potential by sector
Source: IPCC (2007, p. 11).

for ensuring both emissions reductions and energy security of nations. The IEA has undertaken extensive work to consider future scenarios for meeting the world's energy demands and to project how global energy security can continue to be assured under various carbon constraints. One key scenario modelled by the IEA describes measures necessary to avert 'dangerous' climate change by restricting warming to less than 2°C. While a universal consensus on climate change science is notoriously difficult to reach, the majority of expert opinion holds that unacceptably dangerous and irreversible climate impacts can probably be avoided if global atmospheric carbon dioxide concentrations can be restricted to 450 parts-per-million.

In constructing its 450 parts-per-million scenario for global emissions reductions, the IEA assumes a hybrid policy approach, comprising a plausible combination of cap-and-trade systems, sectoral agreements and national measures, with countries subject to common but differentiated responsibilities. Under the scenario, end-use efficiency is by far the largest contributor to CO_2 emissions abatement in 2030 compared with the 'Reference Scenario' – in which it is assumed that the energy sector continues without carbon constraints on a 'business as usual' trajectory (Figure 2.2). Indeed, in the 450 parts-per-million scenario, energy efficiency accounts for more than half of total carbon dioxide savings. Early retirement of old, inefficient coal plants and their replacement by more efficient coal or gas-fired power plants

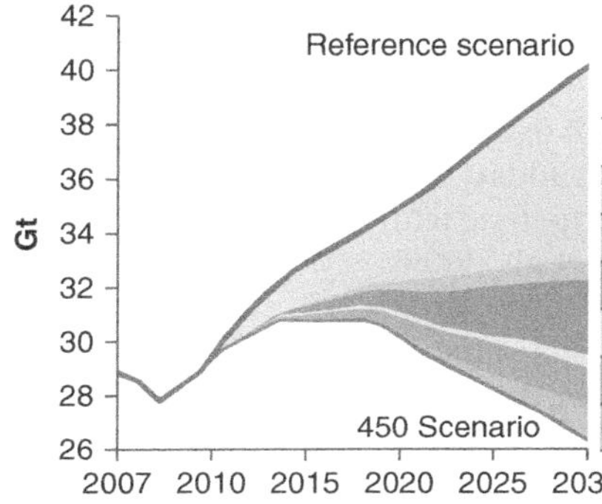

	Abatement (Mt CO_2)		Investment ($2008 billion)	
	2020	2030	2010–2020	2021–2030
Efficiency	2 517	7 880	1 999	5 586
End-use	*2 284*	*7 145*	*1 933*	*5 551*
Power plants	*233*	*735*	*66*	*35*
Renewables	680	2 741	527	2 260
Biofuels	57	429	27	378
Nuclear	493	1 380	125	491
CCS	102	1 410	56	646

Figure 2.2 Projected energy sector abatement contributions to a 450 ppm greenhouse scenario by 2030
Source: IEA (2009).

(see Chapter 10, p. 189), mainly in China (see Chapter 5, p. 66) and in the United States, account for an additional 5 per cent of the global emissions reduction under this scenario. The increased deployment of renewable generation capacity accounts for 20 per cent of CO_2 savings, while increased use of biofuels in the transport sector accounts for 3 per cent. Finally, additional carbon capture and storage (CCS) and nuclear each represent 10 per cent of the savings in 2030, relative to the Reference Scenario. From this, we can conclude that energy efficiency more than doubles the contribution of any other measure to emissions reduction targets, and its relative contribution increases as targets become more stringent. This is due to energy efficiency's immediate availability and deployability; energy savings are achievable using known techniques and readily available existing technologies.

These conclusions and studies regularly assume replacement of like-with-like technologies as a baseline for assessing the amount of energy savings available. What is less well considered is the efficiency opportunity that would be brought about by larger and more systemic change. Mims et al. (2009) consider this shortfall through analysis of the size of the electric productivity gap in the United States and show that electric productivity amongst US states varies dramatically. Electric productivity, a unit that measures how much gross domestic product is generated for each kilowatt-hour consumed, was calculated for each US state to determine which states use electricity most economically. The primary findings are as follows

- The electric productivity gap between the top-performing states and the rest of the United States is immense.
- There is a huge gap in the implementation of efficiency. If the rest of the country achieved the normalised electric productivity of the top

performing states, with 100 per cent adoption, the country would save a total of approximately 1.2 million gigawatt-hours (GWh) annually. This is the equivalent of 30 per cent of annual US electricity use, or 62 per cent of US coal-fired electrical power.
- In 2020, if the United States could, on average, achieve the electric productivity of the top-performing states today, a 34 per cent reduction in projected electricity demand is anticipated, while maintaining 2.5 per cent annual economic growth (Mims et al., 2009).

Of course, not even the top-performing states have exhausted all technical, economic or achievable efficiency. To the contrary, the authors concluded that these states still have the opportunity to greatly enhance their electric efficiency. It is difficult to engineer the sort of social and industrial changes that would be required to unlock energy efficiency potential at this scale, but the study points to the availability of order-of-magnitude changes in energy efficiency that could contribute to improved use of energy in the longer term.

Energy efficiency and energy security for Australia

The benefits of energy efficiency to Australia have been established by economic modelling carried out for the National Framework for Energy Efficiency.[3] In addition, recent Australian research completed under the auspice of the Australian Sustainable Built Environment Council (ASBEC, 2007, 2008) shows that, inter alia:

- The building sector accounts for approximately 23 per cent of national greenhouse gas (GHG) emissions, or approximately 130 Mt (2007, p. 3);
- By 2050, GDP could be improved by around A$38 billion per year if energy efficiency is adopted in the building sector (2008, p. 43);
- Energy efficiency in residential and commercial buildings could halve electricity demand by 2030, and reduce it by more than 70 per cent by 2050, on a cost-neutral basis (2007, pp. 29–30);
- Energy savings in the building sector could reduce the costs of GHG abatement across the whole economy by A$30 per tonne (or 14 per cent) by 2050 (2008, p. 41).

If these figures are accepted as accurate, then cost-effective building sector emissions reductions of 35 per cent by 2020 would see a reduction in Australia's emissions of approximately 45–50 Mt CO_2e, which would be delivered at zero net cost to the economy. If a figure of 50–70 per cent savings is possible, then this would result in a 65–95 Mt CO_2e reduction.[4]

Until recently, Australia's energy efficiency potential was unclear. In 2004 the National Framework on Energy Efficiency completed extensive work in this area which concluded that very substantial cost-effective savings could be made; however, the work was limited by its assumption that the cut-off of what was considered cost-effective was set at any measure which provided financial returns of more than 12.5 per cent per annum.

Recent analysis by ClimateWorks Australia (2010) takes this analysis further. ClimateWorks Australia undertook an extensive bottom up analysis of emissions reductions opportunities in its *Low Carbon Growth Plan*, the first economy-wide emissions reduction strategy developed for Australia. It clearly identifies that Australia can significantly reduce GHG emissions between now and 2020 at low cost. The report found that over 50 Mt CO_2e of abatement is available through energy efficiency measures across sectors at negative cost (see Figure 2.3). If this degree of savings was achieved, it would effectively mean no net growth in energy usage for Australia between now and 2020, and would obviate the need for a significant percentage of our investment in new energy network infrastructure (ClimateWorks, 2010, pp. 13–16).

Indeed the deferral and reallocation of network investment infrastructure is a key co-benefit of energy efficiency activity. It is now widely recognised that there are opportunities for substantial improvements in economic efficiency and environmental outcomes to be gained through the electricity industry reallocating some of the capital for tradition infrastructure investments into demand management and energy efficiency, and by supporting substantial increased usage of distributed generation.[5] This is now becoming urgent because the electricity industry needs to adjust to new imperatives resulting from government and market responses to climate change. The industry needs to provide increased distributed generation and local renewable sources and to facilitate the adoption of new technologies like electric vehicles, smart grids and smart meters. These changes place increased risks on network investments, as some traditional investment choices may be directed into assets that are later underutilised or stranded, resulting in consumers facing increased network charges to pay for poor investments.

A lower-risk and more secure strategy would better utilise demand management, to minimise allocation of resources to infrastructure that more or less only supplies the ongoing wasteful practice of energy consumers and avoidable escalating peak loads. This cannot be achieved by appending demand management into an existing regulatory structure that is skewed towards supply infrastructure investments. Demand management needs to become a primary planning tool and electricity industry regulations need to be changed to ensure that demand investments are made preferentially to infrastructure investments.

In a constrained supply system, the marginal cost of obtaining extra capacity to meet electricity demand is by far the lowest where waste demand is reduced and load is supplied through distributed high efficiency generation. Indications are that the cost saving could be very significant. For example,

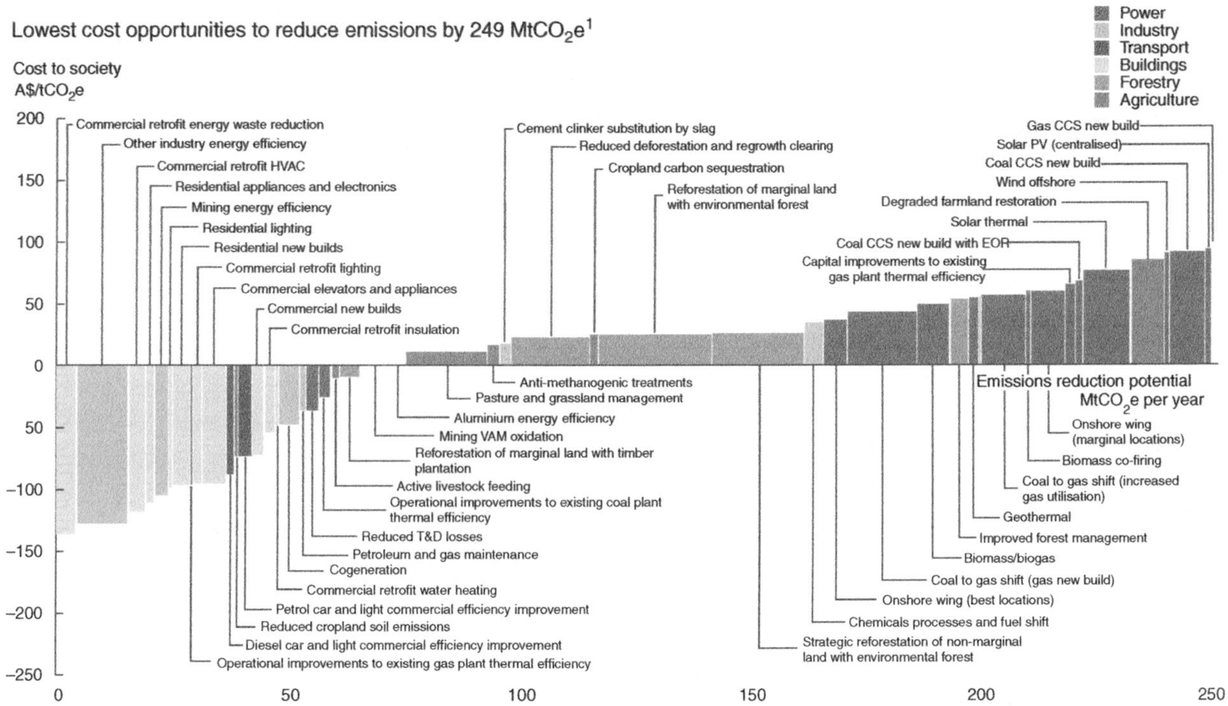

1 Includes only opportunities required to reach emission reduction target of 249 Mtpa (25% reduction on 2000 emissions): excludes opportunities involving a significant lifestyle element or consumption decision, changes in business/activity mix, and opportunities with a high degree of speculation or technological uncertainty

Figure 2.3 ClimateWorks Australia assessment of lowest cost abatement opportunities for Australia
Source: ClimateWorks Australia (2010, p. 10).

in California about one billion US dollars per year is spent on demand side programmes which, after 30 years of demand management programmes, now deliver two billion US dollars per annum of measured savings to the Californian economy (California Public Utilities Commission, 2008).

Rutovitz and Dunstan (2009) looked carefully at this issue in relation to the findings of the 2007 New South Wales Owen Inquiry into the need for new power generation in New South Wales (NSW). Their study considered alternative conclusions to the one reached by the Inquiry. At the time of the Owen Inquiry, a potential energy generation shortfall was identified of 2500 GWh in 2013/14. This shortfall was expected to rise to 11,600 GWh by 2020. However, due to changes in policy, anticipated introduction of new renewable generation during the period and lower economic growth than initially projected, the Owen Inquiry forecasts were later revised so the projected shortfall appears only in 2017, and by 2020 reaches only 3800 GWh (Rutovitz and Dunstan, 2009, p. 3).

However, even the revised energy shortfall disappears completely if moderate energy efficiency measures are put in place. Rather than an energy shortfall, there is the possibility of a surplus of electricity generation potential of more than 12,000 GWh by 2019/20 provided that:

- Energy efficiency measures including more efficient commercial lighting, and industrial and residential energy efficiencies, are adopted – these measures take the potential surplus supply to 3900 GWh;
- 700 MW of cogeneration is put in place, taking the potential excess supply to 9700 GWh;
- 50 per cent of the Snowy Mountains Hydro-Electric Scheme output is available to New South Wales, and a 12.5 per cent proportion of Australia's expected growth in scheduled renewable energy investment occurs in NSW, taking the surplus in generation potential to 12,800 GWh by 2020 (Rutovitz and Dunstan, 2009, pp. 5–6).

Rutovitz and Dunstan conclude that meeting the growth in peak demand with distributed energy is significantly cheaper than building a new coal-fired power station or meeting electricity growth needs with gas turbines. This is primarily because significant savings can be achieved by avoiding or deferring the need for expensive electricity network augmentation.

Based on submissions from utilities to the Australian Energy Regulator for the period 2011–2015, the combined total spend on electricity network infrastructure for the coming five years is in the order of A$42 billion, or approximately A$8 billion per year (Department of Climate Change and Energy Efficiency, 2010, p. 11). In the main, this cost is raised through levying charges on electricity consumers: as of July 2010, business customers in NSW were required to pay up to 60 per cent increases in network charges

(30 per cent overall increases in electricity costs), without notice. These customers were not given a chance to reduce these imposts through reducing their demand. Money raised by such levies could be diverted to energy-saving activities that achieve the same result at a substantial social benefit – reduced costs for consumers, reduced carbon emissions and in many cases better business outcomes through the more effective application of energy services.

Alongside the potential network infrastructure savings are savings in electricity transmission losses, which can be significant depending on the age and condition of existing infrastructure.

Energy security and Australia's supply-side bias

Despite the relative cost-effectiveness of demand management against supply as the best way to ensure energy security, at least for the short term, Australia is firmly fixed on supply-side solutions. A good indicator of this can be found in considering the stocks and flows of energy in Australia, as illustrated in Figure 2.4.

Figure 2.4 is a 'Sankey' diagram, a specific type of flow diagram in which the width of the arrows is shown proportionally to the flow quantity. Therefore, supply on the left of the diagram, augmented by imports from the top, flows to end uses at the right and exports at bottom.

This graphical representation makes it very clear that Australia's priorities in energy policy relate to both (a) the limited number of supply sources (at left), and (b) the export of energy, in particular coal and uranium. In contrast, the end use of energy, which evidence shows to be an important contributor to overall energy security and greenhouse reduction targets, is diffuse, disaggregated and difficult to target in a policy sense. This characteristic, along with the invisibility of energy efficiency as referred to in the title of this chapter, goes some way to explaining why Australia's energy security and greenhouse policy displays a clear supply-side bias – towards policies that ensure greater supply as the primary means of ensuring energy security, and towards policies that reduce emissions intensity of supply and/or promote investment into zero emissions energy supply sources. In recent years these investments have been growing, despite the availability of a cheaper, more abundant and more technologically available alternative. To some extent, this phenomenon is observable around the world, although Australia, which is rich in energy supplies, is an extreme example.

A supply-side bias is further demonstrated in the recent Federal Government Energy White Paper, the key policy document related to energy security in Australia (Department of Resources Energy and Tourism, 2009). While its headline statements suggest concern with both the supply and demand sides of the energy equation, there is a discernible bias in much of the language of the White Paper's terms of reference, towards increasing

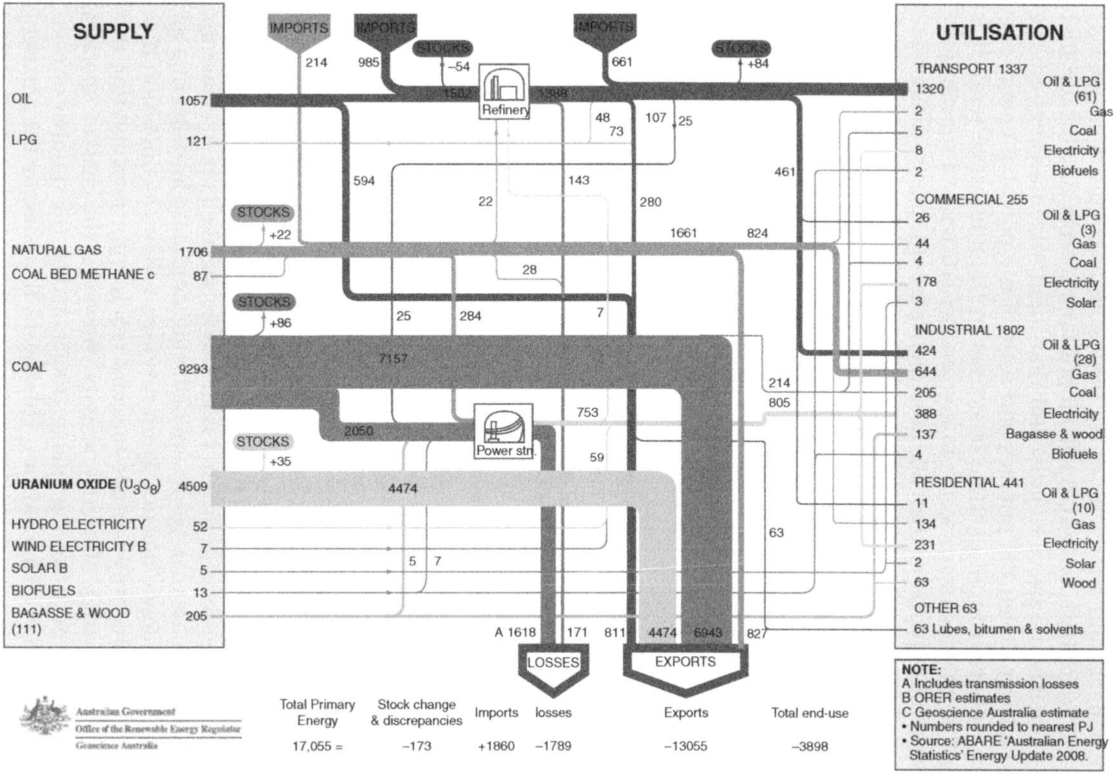

Figure 2.4 Australian energy flows (2006–2007)
Source: Office of the Renewable Energy Regulator (2009).

supply as the preferred option for obtaining energy security between now and 2030. For instance, public material concerning the White Paper's purpose reads that 'the Government intends to ensure the provision of clean, adequate, reliable and affordable *energy supplies* to meet Australia's *growing energy needs*' (emphasis added). Such proposition accepts uncritically that Australia's energy use needs to grow and that supply-side measures are the preferred answer. Given the primacy and scale of the potential energy efficiency contribution to all of these objectives in the immediate term, it is puzzling that the document seems to give energy efficiency a substantially lower degree of importance than all the evidence would suggest it deserves.

The social acceptability of energy efficiency as a means to achieving energy security

As discussed more directly in other chapters of this book, energy security can be defined in a range of ways. If we broadly accept the World Energy Council's millennium goals for achieving energy security set out in 2000, namely:

- *Accessibility* to modern, affordable energy for all;
- *Availability* in terms of continuity of supply and quality of service;
- *Acceptability* in terms of social and environmental goals[6];

then energy efficiency falters on the third of these goals. Its accessibility is widespread, immediate and is arguably technologically superior to other options, and its contribution to continuity of supply and reduced load on supply systems is well proven. While the environmental result of energy efficiency is appropriate, its social acceptance is less well understood and often the sticking point limiting widespread implementation.

Social unease concerning aggressive pursuit of energy efficiency promotes caution amongst policy makers. Doubts abound about the relative potential of energy efficiency, and whether it can live up to its claims. More pervasive, though, is the general view held by some economic theorists that the potential for cost-effective energy efficiency is already being taken up; in economic terms, this view holds that agents are behaving rationally in delivering an optimal level of energy efficiency. From this logic follows a conclusion that pricing carbon is the only sensible measure required for re-calibrating this optimal level of energy efficiency activity. However, the market operates less than perfectly in delivering energy efficiency due to a number of non-price-sensitive market characteristics. This means that, despite the apparent economic incentives, smarter energy use is often not taken up. A great deal of relevant work examines the dynamics of decision making concerning energy efficiency, and its non-rational behavioural aspects (Mullainathan and Thaler, 2000, pp. 1–27; IEA, 2005).

This work establishes that private actors face non-financial barriers, real or perceived, which inhibit better energy practice. As a result incremental increases in financial incentives by, for instance, attributing a price to carbon dioxide emissions through emissions trading will not in themselves unlock the energy savings potential. Complementary measures must instead be directed specifically at initiating smarter energy use. In relation to energy efficiency a case can be made for what Sunstein and Thaler (2003) called 'libertarian paternalism', that is, for attempting to steer people's individual choices in welfare-promoting directions without eliminating freedom of choice, to the achievement of broader societal goals.

Barriers to the uptake of smarter energy use practice have been well recognised in many studies including works by IPCC (2007), Garnaut (2008) and the Department of Climate Change and Energy Efficiency (2010), and broadly include:

- *Behavioural issues (for example, lack of priority, short-termism, cultural inertia, non-core business activity)* – electricity typically makes up a small percentage of business costs (estimated by Australia's National Institute of Economic and Industry Research) at under 3 per cent of total expenditure for most economic sectors. Further, there is a lack of understanding of potential cost-effective savings options and available expertise or mechanisms for financing and delivering them.
- *Split incentives* – in many cases the party incurring the capital cost of energy efficiency measures does not receive the saving benefits of the upgrade (e.g. split incentives between landlords and tenants of a building).
- *Transaction costs (especially measurement and/or verification)* – the recognition of savings often requires the aggregation of a large number of small energy-saving actions. In some cases this makes the transaction costs involved in realising the incentives prohibitive.
- *Network pricing (avoided infrastructure investment)* – due recognition is not currently given to the important role some technologies can play in reducing network costs and/or peak loads.
- *Administrative barriers* – the way that funding programmes are administered can themselves erect barriers to action. For example, where project funding needs to be approved according to a scheme of competitive bidding, on which eligibility rules can be at times unclear, efforts put into submitting bids for funding can deploy significant engineering resources for no discernible outcome and can create long delays or uncertainty for suppliers and customers.
- *High hurdle rates and incrementalism* – the selective implementation of opportunities that could be considered 'low hanging fruit' impedes implementation and cost-effectiveness of deeper savings programmes. Technology for energy savings cannot be applied on a purely incremental

basis. Often projects must be tackled in an integrated way to achieve synergies and greater energy savings.
- *Access to capital* – while energy efficiency can provide an attractive return there are many competing and better understood demands for investment capital.

It can be argued that many of these transaction costs and information asymmetries do not automatically and of themselves justify government intervention. However, the possible reduction in the overall cost of national abatement that can potentially be generated by overcoming non-financial barriers creates a clear role for government to provide incentives to accelerate uptake of energy efficiency over other abatement measures that would be pursued on a price signal alone.

This list of barriers outlines a highly theoretical approach to understanding how to scale up energy efficiency implementation. At issue is the assumption of economically rational actors, which is accepted more or less without scrutiny, other than as an acknowledgement under the first point about 'behavioural issues' related to economic decision making. However, this area warrants significant further attention. Many years of programmes in this area have demonstrated that a majority of energy efficiency decision making can be characterised as irrational. A more behavioural economic approach to energy efficiency decisions would see a different set of barriers targeted based on these irrationalities.

Rapid uptake of energy efficiency will require policies that understand both the market barriers and non-market or behavioural barriers that are faced. Typically, the focus of energy efficiency policy has been on overcoming market failures, though it is well understood that non-price barriers and behavioural aspects are strong determinants of energy choices: for example, social norms, habits, morality, formal and informal authority, non-monetary incentives, community expectations and the context in which choices are presented, all shape choices and social behaviour in various ways and are highly influential in determining outcomes.

Fuller (2009, p. 6) provides a useful list of irrational human behaviours and puts forward the idea that there are predictable patterns within them. In relation to the social acceptability of energy efficiency, some of the most important of these patterns include:

- *Excessive temporal discounting* – refers to the tendency for people to have excessively stronger preferences for immediate gains relative to future gains. Individuals routinely dismiss the future savings to be achieved from energy savings measures in favour of savings that they perceive may be achieved immediately. Rather than viewing energy efficiency action as an investment that yields returns comparable to any other investment, it is considered a cost to be avoided and/or recouped in full if at all possible.

- *Exposure effect* – refers to the tendency for people to like things simply because they are familiar with them. For example, the uptake of certain technologies such as solar photovoltaic cells and wind generation has been dramatic, despite them being vastly inferior cost propositions to energy efficiency. These technologies represent visible, tangible, understandable actions that can be taken as part of the climate change response.
- *Irrational escalation* – refers to the tendency to make irrational decisions based upon rational decisions in the past, or to justify actions already taken (Staw, 1976). For example, the regulatory framework of Australia's energy sector was built many years ago around the primacy of coal, and the historical subsidisation of infrastructure which facilitates its extraction and use. This leads to the somewhat self-evident conclusion that coal-fired energy is the cheapest way to meet our energy needs, without further assessment of this causation or the alternatives on a like with like basis. It also justifies an ongoing strong focus on 'clean coal' technologies, despite the obvious technological hurdles to their implementation (noting the evidence that some of the enthusiasm for these technologies is beginning to wane in recent times).

In addition, with specific reference to energy, there is an irrational growth and consumption orientation that springs from aspirations for individual potency and wealth. This is a characteristic that pervades much of society and culture in the developed world and which has implications for consumption other than energy (Hamilton, 2003); however, it is interesting to reflect on the fact that in the English language energy is synonymous with power – voluntarily relinquishment of power, therefore, is subconsciously unattractive, no matter how rationally justified it may be.

Therefore energy efficiency actions informed by a stronger understanding of realistic human behaviours and decision making will potentially lead to new approaches that are more successful at supporting transformational changes in energy efficiency uptake.

On this point, it is also worth noting that a major barrier (if not the major barrier) to scaled-up energy efficiency is expending the time and effort required to coordinate the existing morass of energy efficiency programmes. There has been widespread attention to energy efficiency policies in recent years; however, most have enjoyed limited success due to their piecemeal, small-scale and uncoordinated execution.

Conclusions and ways forward

Appropriate actions to acknowledge the potential for energy efficiency and scale up its implementation are, out of necessity, a slightly bewildering mix of legislative mandates and directives, market incentives and socio-cultural change. As this chapter has outlined, this is because the factors holding energy efficiency back from its potential are layered and complex. Some of these relate to pure economic intervention to improve allocatively efficient outcomes and overcome conventional market failures. Some, less well understood but at least as prevalent, relate to the nature of individuals and the societies and cultures in which they operate. These factors are difficult to address in the absence of broader narratives promoting the desirability of efficiency and a sense of collective responsibility. Rhetoric promoting energy security might provide a stronger basis for acceptance of energy efficiency than appeals to climate change responsibility alone. This certainly appears to have been the case in countries where energy security is less assured than in Australia.

If it is clear that a single energy efficiency policy is unlikely to release energy efficiency's potential, then it follows that a multi-dimensional approach is required, one that covers a range of sectors and approaches. Dunstan, Langham and Ison (2009) present the options for influencing energy efficiency and distributed generation in the form of a 'policy palette'. Types of policy options include the primary drivers of regulation, incentives and information which are complemented by the secondary drivers of targets, facilitation and pricing. In addition, coordination is a further crucial tool in ensuring an efficient policy response.

Additionally, support for energy efficiency and requirements for involvement are pervasive across all sectors of the economy. Similar to the disaggregated nature of the energy efficiency opportunity, political support for advancement of energy efficiency is disaggregated. That is not to say that it does not exist; on the contrary, if it can be harnessed and directed it is likely that a broad and powerful foundation of political support would be revealed.

This points to the importance of building coalitions of support behind energy efficiency rather than relying on a single industry or sector to promote its benefits. This is recognised through the recent formation of the Australian Alliance to Save Energy, which aims to bring together sector leaders across business, government and environmental groups to inform, influence and advance the efficient use of energy in Australia. Its activities keep energy efficiency central to the public policy debate and pave the way for the delivery of real, lasting, measurable action amongst businesses and consumers.[7] Rather than working as a traditional lobby group, the Alliance model involves a wide range of stakeholders from the outset to forge a robust consensus on action, resulting in multi-stakeholder advocacy for energy efficiency, not lobbying for sectoral interests. In a recent essay David Hetherington and Tim Soutphommasane (2010), argued that:

> [p]rogress on climate change policy in Australia now depends on a new approach to coalition building underpinned by a positive, pragmatic

argument about the benefits of reform. Relying on the moral urgency of climate change mitigation has proven not to be enough.

The authors go on to argue the importance of framing climate action as a nation-building exercise – in other words, that action 'must tap into a positive national story with which ordinary Australians can engage'. Interestingly, the national political stage is now set for this new task, with a new minority Federal Government elected in 2010, and the new Ministerial appointment describing his approach to the climate change portfolio as engaging in 'discussion, negotiation, consultation [and] building consensus'.[8]

Energy efficiency has the potential to bridge the gap by becoming a positive national story about climate change action. If energy efficiency is to throw off its tag of 'invisible giant' and become seen for the opportunity it is in creating energy security for Australia, then cross-sectoral coalitions, coupled with a nation-building agenda, will be critical to breaking down the bias favouring supply-side solutions within Australia's energy security policy making.

Notes

1. In this chapter, the sections of commentary describing the potential for energy efficiency in Australia and globally have been sourced from an earlier work by the author that was submitted to the Australian Senate Select Committee on Climate Policy, which finalised its work and tabled its report on 15 June 2009. For further detail, see: http://www.aph.gov.au/senate/committee/climate_ctte/index.htm; accessed 11 November 2010.
2. In this chapter, the sections of commentary describing the potential for energy efficiency in Australia and globally have been sourced from an earlier work by the author that was submitted to the Australian Senate Select Committee on Climate Policy, which finalised its work and tabled its report on 15 June 2009. For further detail, see: http://www.aph.gov.au/senate/committee/climate_ctte/index.htm; accessed 11 November 2010.
3. For instance, see publications available at: http://www.ret.gov.au/energy/efficiency/nfee/Pages/default.aspx; accessed 18 August 2010.
4. In this chapter, the sections of commentary describing the potential for energy efficiency in Australia and globally have been sourced from an earlier work by the author that was submitted to the Australian Senate Select Committee on Climate Policy, which finalised its work and tabled its report on 15 June 2009. For further detail, see: http://www.aph.gov.au/senate/committee/climate_ctte/index.htm; accessed 11 November 2010.
5. See, for instance, statements by the Queensland Office of Clean Energy, at: http://www.cleanenergy.qld.gov.au/demand_side_innovation.cfm; accessed 20 July 2010.
6. More detail about the goals as defined by the World Energy Council (2000) can be found at World Energy Council (2010).
7. For further background on the aims and activities of the Australian Alliance to Save Energy, see: www.a2se.org.au; accessed 13 September 2010.

8. These statements made by Minister for Climate Change and Energy Efficiency, the Hon Greg Combet MP, were quoted at http://www.theage.com.au/federal-election/no-carbon-copy-on-environment-policy-combet-promises-20100912-156zv.html; accessed 13 September 2010.

References

Australian Sustainable Built Environment Council (ASBEC) (2007), *Capitalising on the Building Sector's Potential to Lessen the Costs of a Broad based GHG Emissions Cut* (Sydney: Centre for International Economics).

Australian Sustainable Built Environment Council (ASBEC) (2008), *The Second Plank: Building a Low Carbon Economy With Energy Efficient Buildings* (Sydney: Centre for International Economics).

California Public Utilities Commission (2008), *California Long-Term Energy Efficiency Strategic Plan* (Sacramento: CPUC).

ClimateWorks Australia (2010) *A Low Carbon Growth Plan for Australia* (Melbourne: Monash University), ISBN 978-0-646-53123-6.

Department of Climate Change and Energy Efficiency (2010), *Prime Minister's Task Group On Energy Efficiency: Issues Paper*, March.

Department of Resources Energy and Tourism (2009), *Energy White Paper* [http://www.ret.gov.au/energy/facts/white_paper/Pages/energy_white_paper.aspx; accessed: 20 July 2010].

Dunstan, C., E. Langham and N. Ison (2009), *20 Policy Options for Developing Distributed Energy* (Sydney: Institute for Sustainable Futures).

Fuller, J. (2009), *Heads, You Die: Bad Decisions, Choice Architecture, and How to Mitigate Predictable Irrationality* (Melbourne: Per Capita).

Garnaut, R. (2008), *The Garnaut Climate Change Review* (Melbourne: Cambridge University Press).

Hamilton, C. (2003), *Growth Fetish* (Sydney: Allen and Unwin).

Hetherington, D. and T. Soutphommasane (2010), *What's the Story? Nation-building Narratives in Climate Politics* (Melbourne: Policy Network).

International Energy Agency (IEA) (2005), *The Experience with Energy Efficiency Policies and Programmes in IEA Countries: Learning from the Critics* (IEA Information Paper).

IEA (2009), *World Energy Outlook* (Paris: OECD/IEA).

Intergovernmental Panel on Climate Change (IPCC) (2007), 'Summary for policy-makers', in B. Metz, O.R. Davidson, P.R. Bosch, R. Dave and L.A. Meyer (eds): *Climate Change 2007: Mitigation. Contribution of Working Group III to the Fourth Assessment Report of the Intergovernmental Panel on Climate Change* (Cambridge-New York: Cambridge University Press).

Levine, M., D. Ürge-Vorsatz, K. Blok, L. Geng, D. Harvey, S. Lang, G. Levermore, A. Mongameli Mehlwana, S. Mirasgedis, A. Novikova, J. Rilling, and H. Yoshino (2007), 'Residential and commercial buildings', in B. Metz, O.R. Davidson, P.R. Bosch, R. Dave and L.A. Meyer (eds): *Climate Change 2007: Mitigation. Contribution of Working Group III to the Fourth Assessment Report of the Intergovernmental Panel on Climate Change* (Cambridge-New York: Cambridge University Press).

Mims, N., M. Bell and S. Doig (2009), *Assessing the Electric Productivity Gap and the U.S. Efficiency Opportunity* (Denver: Rocky Mountain Institute).

Mullainathan, S. and R. Thaler (2000), 'Behavioral economics' (Boston: Massachusetts Institute of Technology, Department of Economics Working Paper).

Office of the Renewable Energy Regulator (2009), *Australian Energy Flows 2006–07* [http://www.orer.gov.au/publications/energy-flows2006-07.html; accessed: 13 September 2010].

Rutovitz, J. and C. Dunstan (2009), *Meeting NSW Electricity Needs in a Carbon Constrained World: Lowering Costs and Emissions with Distributed Energy*, prepared as part of Project 4 of the CSIRO Intelligent Grid Research Program (Sydney: Institute for Sustainable Futures, University of Technology Sydney).

Staw, B.M. (1976), 'Knee-deep in the big muddy: A study of escalating commitment to a chosen course of action', *Organizational Behavior and Human Performance*, 16(1): 27–44.

Sunstein, C. and R. Thaler (2003), 'Libertarian paternalism is not an oxymoron' (AEI-Brookings Joint Center for Regulatory Studies, Working Paper No. 03-2).

World Energy Council (2000), *Energy for Tomorrow's World – Acting Now! WEC Millennium Statement* (London).

World Energy Council (2010), 'Energy policy scenarios to 2050' [http://www.worldenergy.org/publications/energy_policy_scenarios_to_2050/the_3_as/892.asp; accessed: 29 July 2010].

3

National Energy Security in a World Where Use of Fossil Fuels Is Constrained

Hugh Saddler

Introduction

This chapter focuses on the domestic energy policies of industrialised states and, in particular, those states which have been at the forefront in applying neo-liberal policies to the reform and restructuring of their energy supply industries. It examines the interactions between the neo-liberal and climate change mitigation agendas as they have been applied to energy policy, and the consequences these interactions are having for energy security, which is a core objective of energy policy for all states.

A case study approach is taken using two states, the United Kingdom and Australia, as examples. These countries, while markedly different in many respects, are alike in currently being largely, though not completely, self-sufficient in fossil fuel energy resources, having a high proportion of fossil fuels (including coal) in their primary energy supply and in having pursued liberalisation of their electricity and gas industries earlier and further than most other countries. The examination of the policies of the United Kingdom and Australia is framed by an initial discussion of the evolution of energy policy prescriptions recommended by the International Energy Agency (IEA), of which both the United Kingdom and Australia are long-standing members, together with the great majority of other industrialised states.

For the purpose of this chapter, the term energy security is used in what may be called its broadest sense. There is a variety of different broad definitions of energy security; the following, used by the Australian government in a 2009 publication, is a representative example: '[...] energy security is defined as the adequate, reliable and affordable supply of energy to support the functioning of the economy and social development, where:

Adequacy is the provision of sufficient energy to support economic and social activity;

Reliability is the provision of energy with minimal disruptions to supply; and

Affordability is the provision of energy at a price which does not adversely impact on the competitiveness of the economy and which supports continued investment in the energy sector.' (Department of Resources, Energy and Tourism, 2009, p. 5)

These words amount to a specification of the objectives of energy policy as a whole, that is, for the objectives of government actions relating to the provision of energy, both today and historically for as far back as governments, either national or sub-national, have taken such actions. The argument advanced in this chapter is that it is energy security in this broad sense that affects and is affected by policies directed towards mitigating the effects of climate change by reducing greenhouse gas (GHG) emissions, which requires the use of fossil fuels to be constrained. It is further argued that this is the case largely as a consequence of other energy policies implemented over the past 20 years or so, specifically the economic liberalisation of the supply of electricity and gas within the domestic markets.

At the outset it is worth defining the overall context, well known as this is. Firstly, industrial manufacturing processes, and the high levels of material consumption they facilitate, require the high intensity use of large quantities of energy. Until the last few decades, and with the limited exception of hydro-electricity, this could only be achieved by the use of fossil fuels. Economic activity today is still overwhelmingly dependent on the combustion of fossil fuels. Secondly, for all developed countries, and for the world as a whole, the combustion of fossil fuels to supply energy is by far the most important source of GHG emissions. Any effective action to achieve substantial reductions in emissions must involve large reductions in the combustion of fossil fuels.

The International Energy Agency

The IEA was established in late 1974 as an autonomous body within the framework of the Organization for Economic Co-operation and Development (OECD), and most OECD countries became members, either immediately or within a few years. Formation of the IEA was a direct response to the first oil shock one year earlier, which saw governments of the major oil-exporting countries seize control of their national oil production, the imposition of selective supply boycotts by some of these governments and a fourfold increase in the price of crude oil. This brought to the end a period of nearly three decades during which rapid developments in the technologies of finding, extracting, refining and transporting crude oil and petroleum products led to a steady reduction in the real price of petroleum and to the use of petroleum products, mostly replacing coal, in a far wider range of energy applications.

Nevertheless, and despite many new discoveries of crude oil, significant production remained confined to relatively few countries, and most countries, both developed and developing, remained heavily dependent on imports to meet their requirements for petroleum. The first oil shock exposed the resultant economic and social vulnerabilities in importing countries when petroleum supply was disrupted. The IEA's initial stated aims (1982) were as follows:

i) Co-operation among IEA Participating Countries to reduce excessive dependence on oil through energy conservation, development of alternative energy sources and energy research and development;
ii) An information system on the international oil market as well as consultation with oil companies;
iii) Co-operation with oil producing and other oil consuming countries with a view to developing a stable international energy trade as well as the rational management and use of world energy resources in the interest of all countries;
iv) A plan to prepare Participating Countries against the risk of a major disruption of oil supplies and to share available oil in the event of an emergency.

The strong emphasis on oil supply security is obvious in the second, third and fourth points. However, it is the first point, and in particular the prominence given to energy conservation (now called end-use energy efficiency), which is the most important change from the past. While the development of new energy supply sources, and support for the associated research and development activity, had previously been prominent features of national energy policies, end-use efficiency never had been. That end-use efficiency could make national energy systems less vulnerable to disruption and enhance overall economic welfare was a new idea for governments and a clear break with the pre-1973 energy policies of member countries.

Of course the policy positions advocated by the IEA partially reflect the collective position of member countries. By the early 1980s, following the second oil shock of 1979, most, including both the United Kingdom and Australia, had in place policies to promote greater end-use energy efficiency, to encourage fuel substitution away from petroleum to other established supply options, including coal, natural gas and nuclear energy (in Australia's case, not the latter), and to support the development of new energy supply options, including renewable energy. While many of these policy directions, such as promoting increased energy efficiency and the use of nuclear energy, had the incidental effect of curbing increased emissions of GHG emissions (although at the time these were not an energy policy concern), others, most notably promoting the substitution of coal for oil in electricity generation, had the opposite effect.

The official history of the first 20 years of the IEA notes that in 1974 'energy security [was] the paramount policy objective of the IEA' (Scott, 1994, p. 35). However, by the time that history was published, two years after the United Nations Framework Convention on Climate Change (UNFCCC) was signed, priorities had widened:

> The notion of energy security has [...] been broadened to include the need to strike the optimal balance among policies for energy security, environmental protection, and economic growth. It is clear that the environment element will continue as one of the driving forces of energy policy in the years to come. (Scott, 1995, p. 41)

This widening of priorities was formally embodied in the 'IEA Shared Goals', which were formally adopted by Ministers in 1993, effectively replacing the initial aims quoted above. The 'Shared Goals' emphasise enhanced energy use efficiency, diversified and efficient energy supply, and the liberalisation of both domestic and international energy markets (Scott, 1994, p. 41).

In the years since, the centrality of 'the environment element', most particularly climate change, to the policy research activities and the policy recommendations of the IEA has steadily increased. In 2004 the Agency took a further step by including in its annual 'flagship' publication, *World Energy Outlook* an 'Alternative Policy Scenario' for the global energy future, which, it said:

> [A]nalyses, for the first time, the global impact of environmental and energy-security policies that countries around the world are already considering, as well as the effects of faster deployment of energy-efficient technologies. In this scenario, global energy demand and carbon-dioxide emissions are significantly lower than in our Reference Scenario. (IEA, 2004, p. 30)

Every subsequent edition of *World Energy Outlook* has included both 'reference' and 'alternative policy' scenarios, and has consistently emphasised that enhanced energy efficiency and greater use of renewable energy sources are essential for achieving both energy security and emissions reduction goals.

Since 2005 the increase in climate change-related activity by the IEA has been strongly driven by the *Gleneagles Plan of Action on Climate Change, Clean Energy and Sustainable Development,* adopted by the leaders of the G8 at their 2005 summit in Gleneagles (Scotland). Under the *Plan of Action,* the leaders agreed on a range of activities to 'transform the way we use energy', by which was meant increasing the efficiency with which energy is used, and diversifying the energy supply mix, including greater use of renewables. The IEA was nominated as the lead body for supporting and promoting these changes and the detailed commitments under each of these two major headings amounted to a significant new work programme for the Agency. This work has examined details of the relationship between energy security and climate change policies, within the context of liberalised energy markets. Areas of research have included an examination of the factors affecting investment decisions in the electricity industry, and the development of quantitative indicators to measure trade-offs and synergies between energy security and climate change goals. Of particular note is the increased emphasis on ensuring energy security within domestic energy systems, particularly the electricity system.

Perhaps the most succinct summary of the position of the IEA on the relationship between energy security and climate change mitigation is found in *World Energy Outlook 2008* (pp. 3–4):

> It is not an exaggeration to claim that the future of human prosperity depends on how successfully we tackle the two central energy challenges facing us today: securing the supply of reliable and affordable energy and effecting a rapid transformation to a low-carbon, efficient and environmentally benign system of energy supply. What is needed is little short of an energy revolution. [...] Securing energy supplies and speeding up the transition to a low-carbon energy system both call for radical action by governments – at national and local levels, and through participation in co-ordinated international mechanisms. Households, businesses and motorists will have to change the way they use energy, while energy suppliers will need to invest in developing and commercialising low-carbon technologies. To make this happen, governments have to put in place appropriate financial incentives and regulatory frameworks that support both energy security and climate-policy goals in an integrated way.

It will be for national governments to determine what financial incentives and regulatory frameworks they consider appropriate. The remainder of this chapter examines the very different positions adopted by the United Kingdom and Australia.

United Kingdom

In 2008 the United Kingdom derived 40 per cent of its primary energy consumption from natural gas, just under 36 per cent from petroleum and 16 per cent from coal. Nuclear and renewables supplied the remaining 8 per cent. Imports supplied about three-quarters of coal and one-quarter of natural gas. Petroleum was both exported and imported in significant volumes, but in net terms imports exceeded exports by an amount equal to somewhat less than one-tenth of consumption (Department of Energy and Climate Change, 2010a). Until the early 1970s, the United Kingdom was amongst the world's largest coal producers, but production has declined steadily since then, to the present low level. During the 1980s and 1990s, when production of natural gas and petroleum from the North Sea was at its highest levels, the United Kingdom was a net exporter of energy. However, these resources are now in long-term decline, and, in the absence of decisive policy action, import dependence is expected to grow steadily (Department of Energy and Climate Change, 2009b). Security of supply of fossil fuels is thus a major concern for the United Kingdom. The main sources of primary energy for electricity generation are gas, coal and nuclear, accounting, respectively, for 46 per cent, 31 per cent and 13 per cent of total electricity supplied in 2008. Hydro supplied 1.4 per cent, other renewables 4.4 per cent and net imports 3 per cent.[1]

Total UK energy consumption has been near constant for some decades. Between 1990 and 2000 final energy consumption increased by 8 per cent, but from 2000 to 2008 it decreased by 5 per cent. GHG emissions from energy use accounted for 82 per cent of total national emissions in 2008, a significant increase since 1990, when they were 73 per cent of the total. Nevertheless, the absolute level of energy-related emissions in 2008 was 9 per cent below the 1990 level (Department of Energy and Climate Change, 2010c). Most of this decrease occurred in the early 1990s, when there was extensive substitution of gas for coal, particularly in electricity generation (the so-called 'dash for gas'). The decrease in energy-related emissions from 2000 to 2008 was 2.6 per cent.[2]

The United Kingdom led the world in the introduction of liberalised markets in the supply of electricity and gas. The state-owned monopoly gas supply business was privatised in the late 1980s. In 1990 the electricity supply business was privatised and competition introduced into the generation of electricity. Competition in the supply of both electricity and gas to consumers was introduced in the late 1990s. All elements of the UK energy supply industry are now privately owned.

The United Kingdom could be considered to have formally adopted an energy policy framework integrating climate change and supply security objectives when it issued its 2003 Energy White Paper. The White Paper (Department of Trade and Industry, 2003, p. 6) summarised what it called the three energy policy challenges facing the United Kingdom in the following terms.

> Our country needs a new energy policy. Despite the improvements we have made over the last five years, today's policy will not meet tomorrow's challenges. We need to address the threat of climate change. We must deal with the implications of reduced UK oil, gas and coal production, which will make us a net energy importer instead of an energy exporter. And

> over the next twenty years or so we will need to replace or update much of our energy infrastructure.

Both the second and third of these 'challenges' – reduced domestic fossil fuel production and the need for increased investment – represent threats to energy security in the medium to long term. Consistent with the approach advocated by the IEA, energy efficiency and renewable efficiency were seen as very important in addressing both climate change and security challenges. On the specific issue of long-term investment needs in electricity supply and distribution infrastructure, the White Paper was confident that the existing market structures, together with the various programmes to promote renewable generation, such as the 'Renewables Obligation', would provide adequate incentives for the required investment despite the impending decommissioning of most nuclear and coal-fired stations.

> There is inevitably a good deal of uncertainty as to the type and location of stations that will replace existing capacity as market participants respond to evolving price signals. But given current levels of capacity, including mothballed plant, and our expectations of growing renewables generation and energy efficiency improvements over the coming years, we are unlikely to need significant new investment in non-renewable power stations over the next five years or possibly longer. (Department of Trade and Industry, 2003, p. 86)

The 2003 White Paper, while defining 'goals' for energy policy, contained almost no new policy initiatives of any significance. It did, however, stress the potential importance of the impending European Emissions Trading Scheme.

> Central to the future market and policy framework will be a carbon emissions trading scheme [. . .] [F]rom 2005 electricity generators, oil refineries and other industry sectors are expected to be part of a much larger Europe-wide scheme. By setting caps on emissions the scheme will provide clear incentives for investment in energy efficiency and cleaner technologies at the lowest cost. (Department of Trade and Industry, 2003, p. 13)

Importantly, the White Paper went on to state:

> On its own emissions trading will not be enough to deliver our environmental goals. We will need additional measures, for example to stimulate further energy efficiency in business, in the public sector and in households. (Department of Trade and Industry, 2003, p. 14)

In 2005 the government announced that it would conduct a review of progress towards the goals set in the 2003 White Paper, and the process was initiated with release of a review report in 2006 (Department of Trade and Industry, 2006).

This document reduced the energy policy challenges to two: 'tackling climate change' and 'delivering secure, clean energy at affordable prices'. It identified achieving the right volume and type of investment in new electricity generation capacity as a key issue. Pointing out that up to 25 GW of new capacity would be required over the next two decades, mainly to replace closing coal and nuclear power stations, it noted that, on then current projections, much of this 'generation gap' would be met by gas-fired plants. This would increase the already high proportion of electricity generation fuelled by gas, with supply security implications, given the increasing dependence on imported gas. It would also lock in, for the life of the new plants, higher emissions than would be the case if renewables and/or nuclear were to supply more of the new capacity. The document emphasised that, in the UK context, 'It will be for private sector companies to make the necessary investment decisions within the regulatory framework set by the Government', and that the task for government is to ensure that the regulatory framework provides the right incentives (Department of Trade and Industry, 2006, p. 92 et seq.). It suggested a number of possible policy initiatives to reduce policy and regulatory uncertainty, to send stronger market signals relating to the value of low carbon investments, and to improve the quality of forward-looking market information. It also concluded, however, that the current electricity market framework would be capable of continuing to deliver the appropriate investments, and that 'the case for [government] intervention on grounds of security of supply has not been made' (Department of Trade and Industry, 2006, p. 95).

The review process effectively ended with the release of a second White Paper in 2007 (Department of Trade and Industry, 2007). It reached similar conclusions to the review regarding the risks to energy security arising from inadequate or inappropriate electricity supply investments, and saw no need to make major changes to the electricity market framework. Policy proposals were consequently aimed at reducing 'policy and regulatory uncertainties' by 'strengthening the EU ETS and the carbon market'; providing information to facilitate investment in new generating capacity; reform of the energy planning system; and clarifying policy on renewables, carbon capture and storage and nuclear power (Department of Trade and Industry, 2006, p. 158). In 2008 the government created a new Department of Energy and Climate Change, by combining energy policy, formerly in the business and industry portfolio, with climate change mitigation policy, formerly in the environment portfolio. In both symbolic and practical terms, this amounts to a clear statement of the intimate relationship between the two policy areas. The same year its *Energy Act 2008* implemented some of the changes contained in the White Paper. It also broadened the statutory duties of the Office of Gas and Electricity Markets (Ofgem), the body responsible for regulating the gas and electricity industries, to place greater emphasis on the achievement of sustainable development and to oblige the Office to consider the interests of future as well as current consumers in making its determinations.

The Climate Change Act 2008 requires the government to set mandatory, unconditional national emissions reduction targets over both the long term (2050) and over successive five-year periods, set three periods at a time. The first three five-year budgets, extending to 2022, will require the United Kingdom by 2020 to reduce its emissions by 18 per cent relative to 2008. The suite of measures which the (then) government proposes to achieve these emissions reductions are set out in the *UK Low Carbon Transition Plan*. There will be no net international transfers of emissions units, other than through the EU Emissions Trading Scheme (and these are expected to be small), meaning that the United Kingdom plans to achieve the emissions reduction targets entirely through reducing its own national emissions. Emissions relating to energy use are planned to contribute the great majority of the required emissions reductions (Department of Energy and Climate Change, 2009c).

Early in 2009 Ofgem launched what it called Project Discovery (Office of Gas and Electricity Markets, 2009, p. 2), with the objective of exploring 'whether current market arrangements are capable of delivering secure and sustainable energy supplies.' In early 2010 it released a consultation paper, setting out its conclusions from a year of study through Project Discovery (Office of Gas and Electricity Markets, 2010a). It states, contrary to the White Paper of three years earlier:

> We have identified a number of concerns with the current arrangements and have concluded that significant action will be called for given the unprecedented challenges facing the electricity and gas industries. We are keen to work with consumers, industry and government to find the best way forward. Prompt action will reduce the risk to energy supplies and environmental objectives, and can help reduce costs to consumers.

In a press release accompanying the publication of the consultant paper, Ofgem was more outspoken (Office of Gas and Electricity Markets, 2010b):

- Ofgem recommends far-reaching energy market reforms to consumers, industry and government;
- The unprecedented combination of the global financial crisis, tough environmental targets, increasing gas import dependency and the closure of ageing power stations has combined to cast reasonable doubt over whether the current energy arrangements will deliver secure and sustainable energy supplies;

- Prompt action will reduce risk to energy supplies, help lower costs to consumers and help progress towards climate change targets.

The body of the paper examines a number of different options for major changes to the UK gas and electricity markets, all of which involve substantial changes to both structure and operation, with a greater degree of government intervention. This could be seen as reversing the direction which UK energy policy had followed for the preceding 20 years and an acknowledgement that highly liberalised energy markets may not be capable of achieving major emissions reductions while maintaining supply security. Adding a price on emissions to these market structures may achieve marginal emissions reductions without endangering supply security. The large and rapid changes to the energy system, which achieving significant emissions reductions will necessitate, will in turn require more far-reaching changes to institutional structures and policy settings, if supply security is to be maintained. Consistent with the integrated energy and climate change policy approach, the options are assessed against criteria which include confidence of achieving supply security, confidence of achieving the 2020 emissions reduction targets through domestic reductions and confidence of achieving the 2020 renewables targets.

The new government, which took office following the election in May 2010, was no less committed than its predecessor to achieving deep cuts in emissions, and appeared to attach greater urgency to addressing the emissions reduction/supply security dilemma. In its first of a promised series of annual energy statements, released in July 2010, it strongly emphasised the need to ensure secure supplies of electricity, which it saw as being achieved both by increased energy efficiency and stronger incentives for private investment in new, low emissions electricity generation capacity (Department of Energy and Climate Change, 2010b). The centrepiece of its energy efficiency programme was a proposed Energy Security and Green Economy Bill, to place heavier obligations on energy companies to increase the efficiency with which their customers use energy. To support new generation investments, the Statement foreshadowed legislation and other actions to establish a higher and more certain carbon price, re-confirmed a previous commitment to establish what the government called a Green Investment Bank and committed itself to a comprehensive electricity market reform review, culminating in an Energy White paper in early 2011.

Australia

Relative to current and foreseeable domestic consumption, Australia has large resources of coal and natural gas (both conventional and coal seam gas) (Department of Resources, Energy and Tourism, 2010). It is currently the fourth largest producer and largest exporter of coal in the world (Australian

Bureau of Agricultural and Resource Economics, 2009) and is also about the tenth largest exporter of natural gas (as liquefied natural gas (LNG)) (BP, 2009). Its known resources of petroleum are far more limited and net imports currently account for about one-third of total consumption, a proportion which is expected to increase in coming years (Department of Resources, Energy and Tourism, 2010). Petroleum supplies about 34 per cent of total primary energy consumption. Emissions of greenhouse gases from fossil fuel extraction processing and use account for 71 per cent of Australia's total emissions. They have grown by 42 per cent since 1990, while all other emissions sources have decreased (Department of Climate Change and Energy Efficiency, 2010). Moreover, in per capita terms, Australia is amongst the highest emitting countries in the world. It has very high per capita energy consumption and a particularly heavy reliance on coal for electricity generation. Coal accounts for 40 per cent of total primary energy consumption, of which just under one-third is brown coal (lignite). This has very high moisture content and is an intrinsically inefficient source of combustion energy. Australia also has very large resources of uranium and solar radiation and, at least relative to domestic energy consumption, wind and wave energy.

Twenty years ago Australia embarked on a programme to introduce market liberalisation to both the electricity and gas industries. Vertically integrated statutory monopolies, owned by state governments, were turned into disaggregated businesses, competing in generation and retailing, and in some states were privatised. Starting in 1998, the National Electricity Market (NEM) was introduced, as an integrated wholesale market covering over 90 per cent of Australian electricity consumption in eastern and southern Australia (the geographically isolated electricity supply systems in Western Australia and the Northern Territory are excluded). This embraces full competition at both wholesale (between generators) and at retail (between suppliers of electricity to consumers). There is similar retail competition in the supply of gas and increasing competition at wholesale with the discovery and development of new gasfields and the construction of a more interconnected pipeline network.

The competitive market frameworks for electricity and gas are set, respectively, by the National Electricity Law and the National Gas Law. This framework is an agreement between the federal government and all state and territory governments, and its application extends to the whole country, not just those parts covered by the NEM. They are the key foundation documents for Australian domestic energy policy. Each contains succinct statements of the objective of the liberalisation policy, as follows:

7 – National electricity market objective

The objective of this Law is to promote efficient investment in, and efficient operation and use of, electricity services for the long term interests of consumers of electricity with respect to –

(a) price, quality, safety, reliability and security of supply of electricity; and

(b) the reliability, safety and security of the national electricity system.[3]

23 – National gas objective

The objective of this Law is to promote efficient investment in, and efficient operation and use of, natural gas services for the long term interests of consumers of natural gas with respect to price, quality, safety, reliability and security of supply of natural gas.[4]

It is noteworthy that neither of these objectives contains any reference to climate change or other environmental concerns. This was a conscious and deliberate decision of the Ministerial Council on Energy, the body responsible for the two laws, at the time when they were being reviewed and amended in 2004. In response to submissions arguing that environmental sustainability, including climate change mitigation, should be part of the NEM objective, the Council's response was: 'Environmental objectives are more appropriately dealt with in other policy instruments' (Ministerial Council on Energy, 2004a).

The objectives are very important because, under the respective Laws, the body responsible for making the market rules may only make rules which will or are likely to contribute to the achievement of the objectives and, more generally, must have regard to the objectives when performing its functions (Ministerial Council on Energy, 2004b).

The consequence of this framework is that, contrary to the approach advocated by the IEA and adopted by the United Kingdom, climate change mitigation is entirely external to the Australian domestic energy policy process and divorced from, rather than integrated with, the key energy policy objectives, including energy security. This approach to energy policy was fully reflected in the (then) government's energy policy White Paper of 2004 (Department of the Prime Minister and Cabinet, 2004).

The consequence of this energy policy approach for national emissions is seen in the most recent official projection of Australia's energy supply and demand. The modelling for this projection allowed for Australia's only major emissions mitigation programme, which is a renewable electricity mandate scheme, called the Renewable Energy Target (RET). The current version of the scheme requires renewable generation to increase by 2020 from the current level, of about 10 per cent of total electricity generated, to about 20 per cent. The modelling also allowed for the impact of the (now postponed) national emissions trading scheme, called the Carbon Pollution Reduction Scheme (CPRS). The design of the CPRS proposed very broad coverage, including all energy-related emissions, and some other emissions sources. Targets (caps) had not been set, but it was expected that a 2020 target would be a reduction from 2005 emissions levels of between 5 per cent and 15 per cent. Most importantly, there was absolutely no limit on the use of imported emissions units to meet domestic commitments under the CPRS. Accordingly, the modellers chose to represent the CPRS by a gradually increasing emissions price, which could be thought of as the international market price of Certified Emissions Reductions (CERs).

Projections prepared for the Department of Resources, Energy and Tourism indicate that, with these and other current policy settings, primary energy demand will increase by 35 per cent by 2030, relative to the 2008 level (figures for intermediate years, including 2010, are not published) (Syed et al., 2010). When generic emissions factors are applied to the projected mix of primary fuels, it is found that the projected growth in primary energy demand implies an increase in energy combustion emissions of about 21 per cent above 2008 levels and 38 per cent above 2000 levels. In other words, far from reducing energy emissions below current levels, the projection suggests that they will increase significantly, notwithstanding a price on emissions applied through the government's proposed emissions trading scheme. By implication emissions caps under the scheme could only be met by purchase on the world market of large volumes of CERs, or other internationally recognised credits. The official economic modelling undertaken as part of the design process for the emissions trading scheme, confirms that this was indeed the expectation of the schemes designers (Australian Treasury, 2008).

In designing its CPRS, the government considered the possible impact of the scheme on energy security, and took advice on the issue from the various agencies responsible for administering and operating the national electricity and gas markets. It also received submissions from owners of coal-fired power stations, which argues that imposition of a price on emissions would result in devaluation of their generation assets and reduced creditworthiness of their businesses, which could cause retirement of the plant before a replacement plant could be installed, with obvious negative effects on electricity supply security. In response, the government decided to provide the most severely affected generators with financial assistance, in the form of a quota of administratively allocated permits, with the quantity allocated depending on the emissions intensity of the individual generator (a more emissions-intensive plant would receive more permits) and extending over five years, provided that the plant continued to operate for that period (Australian Government, 2008). With that provision, the government then concluded that:

> Energy security can be maintained through the setting of a target range for emissions cuts that allows for a smooth transition to lower-emissions technology. Any minor amendments that are required to the energy market frameworks can be accommodated within the current rules amendment processes. (Australian Government, 2008, p. 48)

A separate official assessment of energy security concluded that this assistance, together with the detailed information about CPRS design provided by the government, would provide investors with the information and confidence they would require to make timely and appropriate investment decisions, thereby mitigating risks to electricity supply security (Department of Resources, Energy and Tourism, 2009).

Later in 2009 the Australian Energy Markets Commission, the body responsible for administration of the national electricity and gas markets, published the results of an extensive review of the adequacy of energy market frameworks to support efficient transition, in the light of the CPRS and the Renewable Energy Target. It concluded that the broad frameworks are capable of supporting an efficient transition and that no more than a few incremental improvements to the framework would be required (Australian Energy Markets Commission, 2009a).

Notwithstanding the conclusions about the adequacy of supply security under the arrangement proposed for the CPRS, electricity generation businesses continued to argue that they required more generous assistance if risks to supply security were to be avoided. It argued that the proposed Scheme did not:

> [A]dequately address the stranding of coal-fired generation assets. A measured transition to full auctioning (as proposed in most other schemes to date) would enable a greater volume of permits to be administratively allocated to affected generators to ensure there is no disproportionate loss of economic value on the sector's balance sheets or a rise in costs to such a level as to compromise both the ability to refinance, and/or re-invest in existing power plant. (National Generators Forum, 2009)

In a political compromise, made in an (ultimately unsuccessful) attempt to achieve parliamentary support for the passage of its CPRS legislation, the government proposed to increase the number of administratively allocated permits supplied to emissions-intensive generators and to extend the duration of such assistance, and hence the potential operating life of these generators, to ten years. Responding to a formal invitation to comment on these proposals, the Australian Energy Markets Commission (2009b) observed that 'there remains the potential risk that [the proposed assistance] may slow the transition away from carbon-intensive generation'.

There are several interesting aspects to this denouement. Firstly, the perceived risks to electricity supply security arise from possible damage to the financial integrity of the owners of emissions-intensive power stations. It has never been suggested that, in a hypothetical worst case situation (bankruptcy of an owner), the physical asset of the power station, under new ownership, would be incapable of continuing to operate. Secondly, the generation assets that it has been suggested might be at risk of closure are all privately owned.

It has never been suggested that any of the coal-fired generators which are publicly owned (by the state governments of New South Wales, Queensland and Western Australia) might be at risk of closure.[5] While the question of whether the benefits of liberalised energy markets can only be realised if all market participants are privately owned is a regular topic of public debate in Australia, it has received little attention in the particular context of energy security and climate change.

More generally, it is clear that, in the Australian policy context, responding to climate change is not only treated as external to and separate from energy policy, but that it is also seen as an issue of lower priority than preserving the economic benefits which are considered to flow from retaining and strengthening the liberalised market framework for the electricity and gas supply industries.

Conclusions

The risk of severely disruptive climate change cannot be reduced without making changes to energy systems, so as to reduce the consumption of fossil fuels, which in terms of both size and speed of the changes required are so large as to constitute, in the words of the IEA, an 'energy revolution'. Revolutionary changes are likely to be disruptive of established energy systems, and to the services they provide, of which energy security is amongst the most important. However, as the IEA has been arguing for over a decade, energy security and climate policy goals can and should be integrated because both are addressed by policies that emphasise increasing end-use efficiency and greater use of renewable sources of energy. That said, realising these synergies on a scale and at a rate which is 'revolutionary' is unlikely to leave unaffected the existing institutional structures and governance arrangements of the energy system. As the two national case studies presented here show, this is particularly true for states with a liberalised energy market framework.

In recent years, the United Kingdom, which has set itself relatively ambitious goals to reduce emissions by domestic action, has changed its policy framework so as to integrate energy security and climate policy goals, as advocated by the IEA. However, the United Kingdom faces a further challenge to maintain the security of electricity supply, in particular, while it transforms its energy system. With a liberalised market framework for the electricity supply industry, government options to affect the nature and level of energy system investments are necessarily indirect, and the outcomes of any particular government actions are uncertain, depending as they must on the decisions of multiple market participants. This problem was recognised by Ofgem in 2009 and, following the election of May 2010, the new Conservative–Liberal Democrat government has acknowledged the seriousness of the problem and committed itself to addressing it by changing the electricity market structure in ways which will necessarily be more interventionist.

In Australia, by contrast, the energy policy framework deliberately and explicitly treats climate change response as external to energy policy, making it effectively impossible to integrate energy security and climate-policy goals, and ensuring that climate policy presents no challenge to the pursuit of further market liberalisation. It is hardly surprising, then, that the national political process has failed to produce a commitment to strong emissions reduction goals or policies which will do more than curb the steady growth of energy-related emissions. What is more, both the government and the opposition parties expect purchasing international emissions units to play an important part in achieving, in accounting terms, more ambitious emissions reductions.

The overall conclusion is very simple. If states set themselves ambitious emissions reduction goals they will need to make radical changes to their energy systems, which, in the absence of decisive policy action, are likely to be deleterious to domestic energy security. By contrast, modest reduction goals will not require far-reaching energy system changes and will pose little threat to energy security, but will also do little to mitigate climate change.

Notes

1. Calculated from Tables 5.1.2 and 5.3 in Department of Energy and Climate Change (2010a).
2. All figures calculated from Table 1.4 in Department of Energy and Climate Change (2010a).
3. This definition appears in each separate Act, for example, National Electricity (South Australia) Act 1996.
4. This definition appears in each separate Act, for example, National Gas (South Australia) Act 2008.
5. It should be noted that these power stations use black, rather than brown coal, and thus are inherently less emissions intensive than the privately owned power stations in Victoria. Nevertheless, it is expected that they will suffer some loss of asset value.

References

Department of Climate Change and Energy Efficiency (Australia) (2010), *Australian National Greenhouse Accounts: National Greenhouse Gas Inventory* (Canberra: Department of Climate Change and Energy Efficiency).

Department of Resources, Energy and Tourism (Australia) (2009), *National Energy Security Assessment 2009* (Canberra: Department of Resources, Energy and Tourism).

Department of Resources, Energy and Tourism (Australia) (2010), *Australian Energy Resource Assessment* (Canberra: Department of Resources, Energy and Tourism).

Ministerial Council on Energy (Australia) (2004a), *Response to Key Issues Raised by Stakeholders on the Exposure Draft of the National Electricity Law* [http://www.ret.gov.au/Documents/mce/quicklinks/consultation.html; accessed: 29 November 2010].

Ministerial Council on Energy (Australia) (2004b), *Energy Market Reform: National Electricity Law and National Electricity Rules* [http://www.ret.gov.au/Documents/mce/quicklinks/consultation.html; accessed: 29 November 2010].
Australian Bureau of Agricultural and Resource Economics (2009), *Australian Commodity Statistics 2009* (Canberra: Australian Bureau of Agricultural and Resource Economics).
Australian Energy Markets Commission (2009a), *Review of Energy Market Frameworks in light of Climate Change Policies: Final Report* (Sydney: Australian Energy Markets Commission).
Australian Energy Markets Commission (2009b), *Letter to Department of Climate Change dated 23 November 2009* [http://www.climatechange.gov.au/government/initiatives/cprs/Proposed-CPRS-Negotiation.aspx; accessed: 29 November 2010].
Australian Government (2008), *Carbon Pollution Reduction Scheme: Australia's Low Pollution Future* [www.climatechange.gov.au; accessed: 29 November 2010].
Australian Treasury (2008), *Australia's Low Pollution Future: The Economics of Climate Change Mitigation* (Canberra: Australian Treasury).
BP (2009), *BP Statistical Review of World Energy June 2009* (London: BP).
Department of Energy and Climate Change (United Kingdom) (Report prepared by M. Wicks) (2009a), *Energy Security: A National Challenge in a Changing World* (London: The Stationery Office).
Department of Energy and Climate Change (United Kingdom) (2009c), *UK Low Carbon Transition Plan: National Strategy for Climate and Energy* (London: The Stationery Office).
Department of Energy and Climate Change (United Kingdom) (2009a, *Digest of UK Energy Statistics* (London: The Stationery Office).
Department of Energy and Climate Change (2010b), *Annual Energy Statement: DECC Departmental Memorandum* (London: The Stationery Office).
Department of Energy and Climate Change (2010c), *UK Emissions Statistics* (London: The Stationery Office) [http://www.decc.gov.uk/en/content/cms/statistics/climate_change/gg_emissions/uk_emissions/2008_final/2008_final.aspx; accessed: 29 November 2010].
Department of Trade and Industry (United Kingdom) (2003), *Our Energy Future – Creating a Low Carbon Economy* (London: The Stationery Office).
Department of Trade and Industry (United Kingdom) (2006), *The Energy Challenge: Energy Review Report* (London: The Stationery Office).
Department of Trade and Industry (United Kingdom) (2007), *Meeting the Energy Challenge: A White Paper on Energy* (London: Department of Energy and Climate Change).
Department of the Prime Minister and Cabinet (Australia) (2004), *Securing Australia's Energy Future* (Canberra: Department of the Prime Minister and Cabinet).
International Energy Agency (IEA) (1982), *World Energy Outlook* (Paris: Head of Publications Service).
IEA (2004), *World Energy Outlook 2005* (Paris: Head of Publications Service).
IEA (2008), *World Energy Outlook 2008, Executive Summary* (Paris: Head of Publications Service).
National Generators Forum (2009), *Submission to Department of Climate Change on Exposure Draft of the Carbon Pollution Reduction Scheme Legislation* [http://www.ngf.com.au/html//; accessed: 29 November 2010].
Office of Gas and Electricity Markets (OFGEM) (United Kingdom) (2009), *Project Discovery Energy Market Scenarios* (London: OFGEM).

OFGEM (United Kingdom) (2010a), *Project Discovery: Options for Delivering Secure and Sustainable Energy Supplies* (London: OFGEM).

OFGEM (United Kingdom) (2010b), *Action Needed to Ensure Britain's Energy Supplies Remain Secure* [http://www.ofgem.gov.uk/Media/PressRel/Pages/PressRel.aspx; accessed: 29 November 2010].

Scott, R. (1994), *The History of the International Energy Agency, Volume II: Major Policies and Actions of the IEA* (Paris: OECD/IEA).

Syed, A., J. Melanie, S. Thorpe and K. Penney (2010), *Australian Energy Projections to 2029–30*, ABARE research report 10.02, prepared for the Department of Resources, Energy and Tourism, Canberra.

4
Can Energy Security and Effective Climate Change Policies Be Compatible?

Mark Diesendorf

Introduction

There are arguably three principal threats to industrialised society and indeed to civilisation in the twenty-first century. All three are strongly linked to our current patterns of energy use and production. The first two threats are global climate change, that is, loss of climate security, and peak oil and gas, that is, loss of energy security. The third major threat, nuclear war, could be exacerbated by inappropriate responses to the other two threats.

Concerns about climate security arise from the scientific evidence for global warming resulting from the anthropogenic greenhouse effect. There is a large body of evidence – based on empirical observation, paleo-climatic data and computer models – that global warming is real and is caused primarily by the emission of greenhouse gases (GHGs) from the combustion of fossil fuels and, to a lesser degree, from changes in land use resulting from deforestation and agriculture. The impacts of global warming include heat waves, droughts, wild fires, floods, rising sea levels, loss of biodiversity, possibly an increase in the frequency of strong hurricanes and a general instability in climate (Parry et al., 2007; Allison et al., 2009).

Concerns about energy security arise primarily from the growing evidence that the global economy is very close to peak oil, the point in time when the maximum rate of global petroleum extraction is reached, after which the rate of production enters terminal decline (Aleklett et al., 2010). As a result, oil prices are likely to rise steeply as economies recover from the global financial crisis and growth in consumption resumes. Industrialised society is highly dependent upon oil for transportation, agriculture, plastics and chemicals. The problem is exacerbated by the situation that the principal substitute for oil, natural gas, is coming under increasing pressure for all these uses as well as for electricity generation, so it is possible that the world will reach a peak in gas production within a few decades. Long before that peak is reached, gas prices are likely to become high and could match those of oil (Laherrère, 2004). If coal production continues to increase, either as a result of governments ignoring climate security or as the result of carbon capture and storage becoming commercially available in the late 2020s and being implemented rapidly, then peak coal could be reached before 2050 (Mohr and Evans, 2009).

Apart from peak oil, gas and coal, other energy security issues include potential interruptions to trade in oil and gas and the need to provide stockpiles of these fuels to soften the impact of such interruptions. Countries that have few domestic energy resources (such as Japan) and those that are undergoing rapid economic growth (such as China and India) are particularly concerned about energy security.

This chapter explores the relationship between climate security and energy security. To do this, it first discusses various definitions of these concepts and their political implications. It offers an argument that neither energy security nor climate security should be pursued in isolation, because that would make the other issue much worse. I then discuss critically the respective strengths, limitations and risks of four different scenarios for a climate secure planet that could be potentially energy secure as well: conventional nuclear, new generation nuclear, so-called 'clean coal' and 'sustainable energy', that is, the efficient use of renewable energy. For many people, the latter scenario is linked, explicitly or implicitly, to a different vision of the kind of society to which people aspire.

While the four scenarios are stated in terms of different choices of technologies, other important aspects are political and involve ecological sustainability, social justice, industrialism and the notion of endless economic growth. These political issues are only mentioned in passing in this chapter. Some of them are discussed in more detail in Diesendorf (2009, 2011).

Basic concepts

To define climate security this chapter starts with the ultimate objective of the United Nations Framework Convention on Climate Change (UNFCCC), namely stabilising GHG emissions 'at a level that would prevent dangerous anthropogenic interference with the climate system' (UNFCCC website). Furthermore, 'such a level should be achieved within a time-frame sufficient to allow ecosystems to adapt naturally to climate change, to ensure that food production is not threatened, and to enable economic development to proceed in a sustainable manner'.

Although this broad statement is open to interpretation, many scientists now agree that the safe level has been well and truly exceeded. Leading climate scientists argue that the concentration of carbon dioxide (CO_2) in the atmosphere (which reached 389 parts per million in 2010) should be reduced to 350 ppm or lower as soon as possible (Hansen et al., 2008). For comparison, from 660,000 years before present up to industrialisation, CO_2 concentrations remained between 180 and 280 ppm (Solomon et al., 2007). This provided a relatively stable climate for the development of human societies.

Energy security is generally defined to be 'an adequate and reliable energy supply at a reasonable price'. Value judgements are inevitable in interpreting the adjectives 'adequate', 'reliable' and 'reasonable'. In practice, 'adequate' is often interpreted to mean 'having access to an energy supply system that can provide for any demand, including one that is exponentially increasing with a short doubling time'; reliability is often believed to be limited to fossil and nuclear energy; and 'reasonable price' is assumed to mean 'prices competitive with those existing in the early 2000s'. Is this 'business-as-usual' interpretation realistic or desirable, subject to the constraints of climate security and limited fossil fuel reserves? If we relax the demand for endless rapid growth in demand, can we develop a definition of energy security that also meets the requirements of climate security?

The relationship between the two securities

A conventional approach to energy security with respect to peak oil is to foster the development of unconventional fossil fuel resources: oil from tar sands, shale and coal. The extraction of oil from these resources requires high fossil energy inputs and results in much higher levels of GHG emissions than from conventional oil (Metz et al., 2007). Therefore it is incompatible with climate security.

Gas, in the forms of natural gas and coal seam methane, is also being fostered as a solution to peak oil in transportation. In some regions, gas is also the least-cost, and therefore the most favoured, substitute for coal as a fuel for base-load electricity. While the substitution would be a substantial improvement over the current situation in terms of climate security, it is unlikely to be sufficient, since combined-cycle gas power still emits about 40 per cent of the CO_2 of conventional coal power. Furthermore, these substitutions would fail to satisfy energy security, because of the concerns about peak gas mentioned in the introduction. While gas has potentially highly effective temporary roles to play in cutting GHG emissions – for example, in cogeneration of electricity and heating; trigeneration of electricity, heating and cooling; and as a back-up for solar hot water, solar thermal power and wind power – there is unlikely to be sufficient gas on a global scale for it to become a major fuel for transportation and electricity generation as well. Based on present trends, some experts suggest that global gas production may peak around 2030 (Laherrère, 2004).

Thus, energy security, taken in isolation from climate security, leads to climate insecurity, while one of the 'solutions' to climate security, gas, leads to both energy insecurity and, after a short delay, more climate insecurity.

Therefore, energy security and climate security must be considered together. Four energy scenarios, each allegedly satisfying the requirement of climate security, are now examined in turn.

Conventional nuclear

The conventional nuclear energy scenario includes the current generation of nuclear power stations, known as 'generation II', and a so-called 'new' generation called generation III by the nuclear industry. Since the latter comprises slightly improved versions of generation II, incorporating some limited passive safety features, it is treated together with generation II. As of 2010, no generation III reactor is operating. In western countries, there are two under construction, both behind schedule and over budget. Indeed, by the end of 2009 the Olkiluoto reactor, whose construction commenced in 2005 in Finland, was three years behind schedule and €1.7 billion over budget. Hence generation III reactors are classified as semi-commercial and may not become fully commercial for at least a decade.

Conventional nuclear power stations are characterised by their slow construction time, high and escalating capital costs, risk of nuclear weapons proliferation, absence of long-term nuclear waste repositories, risk of rare but catastrophic accidents and, in the longer term, significant CO_2 emissions from fossil fuels used to mine and mill low-grade uranium ore (Diesendorf, 2007, chap. 12; Schneider et al., 2009). Thus they have substantial environmental, health and safety risks, as well as high financial risks to investors. These risks are difficult to quantify.

Every stage of the nuclear fuel cycle except reactor operation involves the combustion of fossil fuels and hence the emission of CO_2. However, at present total emissions are small, typically about 60 g/kWh of electricity generated (Lenzen, 2008). While these emissions are lower than those of gas power (about 600 g/kWh), they are higher than those of large-scale wind power (10–20 g/kWh). At present nuclear power stations are fuelled either with uranium from high-grade ore (at least 0.1 per cent uranium oxide) or plutonium from retired nuclear weapons. However, both sources could be scarce within several decades, even at the current usage rate, and then low-grade ore (0.01 per cent uranium oxide) would have to be used. Then CO_2 emissions from mining and milling would increase by a factor of 20 and emissions from the whole nuclear fuel cycle would increase to 130 g/kWh (Lenzen, 2008, table 18) or 437 g/kWh (Storm van Leeuwen and Smith, 2005), depending upon which study is quoted. Based on the different assumptions of the two studies, I suggest that the intermediate value of about 220 g/kWh is credible.

Thus, on the basis of climate security, conventional nuclear energy is an unsatisfactory long-term solution to energy security and, on the basis of its long construction times, it cannot be a significant short-term solution.

Generation IV nuclear scenario

A new generation of nuclear power stations, promoted as 'generation IV' by the nuclear industry, is on the drawing board or operating as demonstration plants. The type of generation IV reactor that is of interest in this chapter is the fast (neutron) reactor. If operated as a breeder reactor, it can produce much more plutonium than conventional reactors and so can potentially have much lower CO_2 emissions per unit of electricity generated than conventional reactors.

The principal system of interest is known as the 'integral fast reactor', comprising a fast neutron reactor and, on the same site, a new type of chemical reprocessing plant that uses a method known as 'pyroprocessing'. Still at the R&D stage, pyroprocessing can separate the long-lived wastes (actinides) from the medium-lived wastes (fission products), without separating the plutonium from the other actinides. The actinides can be fed back into the reactor as fuel. Thus, in theory, the large quantities of plutonium produced by the fast reactor could be used for fuel and not for nuclear weapons. Another potential advantage is that the high-level wastes remaining after the actinides have been recycled as fuel, the fission products, would only have to be managed for about 500 years instead of the hundreds of thousands of years required for the actinides in the waste from a conventional reactor. However, in practice there is little to stop the governments or corporations who own the integral fast reactors from extracting the plutonium using conventional reprocessing (the Purex process) and using it in nuclear weapons (McFarlane, 2002). Indeed, after pyroprocessing, the remaining actinides will be much less radioactive than the original mix of actinides and fission products, and so it would be easier and less expensive to apply conventional reprocessing to separate the plutonium.

Fast reactors have been stuck at the demonstration stage for decades, because they have performed so poorly, and pyroprocessing is still at the experimental stage. Therefore, the integral fast reactor is unlikely to be commercially available before 2030. It would be very risky to base an energy security and climate security policy upon its future development.

'Clean fossil' scenario

The so-called 'clean fossil' technologies considered in this chapter involve carbon capture and storage (CCS), more precisely the separation and geosequestration of CO_2 from large point sources such as power stations, steel works, cement works and oil refineries. For countries highly dependent upon coal (for example, China, Poland, South Africa and Australia), there are strong political pressures to develop CCS if possible.

However, CCS is an unproven technological system, still at the R&D stage. The separation of CO_2 is expected to be particularly difficult, expensive and energy-intensive in the case of coal power. Even proponents of CCS from the International Energy Agency (IEA, 2009) and coal industry (Coal Utilization Research Council website) estimate that advanced systems could not be deployed before 2025–2030; independent authors and the IEA (2008) 'blue map' scenario suggest that large-scale production at the commercial stage is unlikely before 2030. It is also unclear whether sufficient underground storages exist in some regions of the world.

The cost and energy intensity of CCS increase with the percentage of CO_2 captured. While capture of over 90 per cent is technically possible, it is likely that economic pressures will make 80–85 per cent the norm in commercial systems. This corresponds to CO_2 emissions from coal power with CCS in the range of 120–200 g CO_2/kWh for black coal and 160–300 g CO_2/kWh for brown coal. These emissions levels are similar to those expected for conventional nuclear power fuelled by uranium from low-grade ore. In a context of rapidly increasing electricity demand and supply under the shadow of climate change, these levels may well prove to be unacceptable.

While it is probable that coal power with CCS will eventually be technically proven as a whole system, there is doubt as to whether it will be able to compete in 2030 with renewable electricity systems that are currently at the commercial and pre-commercial stages. The prices of these systems are declining rapidly as their markets expand. Thus the whole CCS enterprise has considerable financial risk in addition to the health and environmental risks of the escape of a large quantity of CO_2 from an underground storage. This is not an argument against attempting to develop and commercialise CCS technologies, but rather a warning that the CCS scenario is risky and that we cannot assume that it will be the principal means of CO_2 avoidance in the energy sector. Indeed, even the 'blue map' scenario of the IEA (2008), a strong proponent of CCS, envisages that CCS will make a smaller contribution to global GHG reductions (19 per cent) in 2050 than each of efficient energy use (36 per cent) and renewable energy (21 per cent) (IEA, 2008).

Sustainable energy scenario

The only energy technologies that are very low in GHG emissions, can provide energy security for millions of years, and are either commercially available or semi-commercial are efficient energy use and certain renewable energy technologies.

For at least the next decade, the principal commercial renewable energy technologies will be solar hot water, hydro-electricity, wind, the production of electricity and heat from biomass combustion and geothermal heat. Conventional tidal power, with large dams across estuaries, and conventional geothermal power are commercially available, but very limited in terms of suitable sites. More expensive, but rapidly becoming less so, are commercial solar photovoltaic (PV) modules and, at a semi-commercial stage, concentrated solar thermal power with thermal storage. These solar technologies could be already making significant contributions during the 2020s. New sources of marine power (wave; ocean current) and hot rock geothermal power are at the demonstration stage and are not yet ready for commercial mass production. However, they have medium potential and are likely to be commercially available on a small scale before 2020 (Boyle, 2004; Diesendorf, 2007).

All the renewable energy technologies listed above work well. Most have the advantage that they can be constructed and disseminated much more rapidly than nuclear or coal power stations. This is because these renewable energy technologies are manufactured in factories and can be installed quickly, while coal and nuclear power stations are gigantic construction projects that are very difficult to mass produce. (Large hydro and conventional tidal power stations are also big construction projects and hence slow to install.)

Renewable energy technologies at the commercial and semi-commercial stages are experiencing declining prices as their markets expand, apart from occasional spikes when demand temporarily overtakes supply capacity, as occurred for wind and PV in 2006–2007. Therefore, these technologies are of low risk to investors, provided appropriate government policies and programmes are in place to bridge temporarily the gaps between their prices and those of fossil energy. With the possible exception of large hydro, renewable energy technologies have very low physical risks.

There is ample renewable energy available for global demands projected to 2050, without compromising food production (Sørensen and Meibom, 2000). However, like fossil fuels and uranium, renewable energy is not distributed equitably across the earth and so trade will be necessary, by transmission line, pipeline and ship. Solar energy is widely distributed, with high potential in south-west United States, Mexico, Peru, northern Chile, Central Asia, northern and southern Africa, southern Europe, the Middle East and much of Australia. Biomass is available in many parts of the world, even after excluding native forests on environmental grounds. Although wind energy resources are more limited globally, there are excellent regions in the United States, northern Europe, southern Australia, New Zealand, coastal and north-west China and coastal north-west Africa. Conventional geothermal power follows the boundaries of tectonic plates, but only a few regions have been partially developed so far (Iceland, California and New Zealand). The full potential of global hot rock geothermal power still has to be evaluated; nevertheless, there already appears to be large potential in the United States, Europe and Australia.

For comparison, oil and gas are highly concentrated geographically, with most of the remaining oil in the Middle East and most natural gas in Russia, Iran and Qatar (Lefèvre, 2010). A common fallacy fostered by greenhouse polluters and the nuclear industry is that renewable energy cannot provide base-load (24-hour per day) electricity. To the contrary, bioelectricity, geothermal, solar thermal with thermal storage, and wind power with intermittent back-up from peak-load plants can each substitute for conventional base-load power (coal and nuclear), while energy efficiency, energy conservation and solar hot water can reduce the demand for base-load. Intermediate-load (demand in daytime and early evening) could be supplied by combined-cycle power stations burning biomass residues, solar photovoltaics and solar thermal power with short-term thermal storage. Peak-load would be supplied, as at present, by existing hydro and gas turbines, as well as solar thermal power with short-term storage. As gas becomes scarce, gas turbines would be fuelled by either biogas or liquid biofuels (Diesendorf, 2010a).

Compared with the present mix of base- and peak-load, initially there would be a larger proportion of peak-load plant in the 100 per cent renewable electricity system, in order to handle the fluctuations in wind and solar PV power. However, due to geographic dispersion of wind farms, large fluctuations in total wind power output would be infrequent and the back-up would only be used intermittently (Diesendorf, 2007, chap. 6). Eventually peak-load back-up could be reduced as less expensive forms of electrical storage become commercially available. In addition to existing pumped hydro, promising new storage technologies include compressed air, flow batteries such as vanadium redox and, as electric vehicles become prevalent, batteries that can operate in vehicle to grid mode. Temporarily shedding demand that does not have to be met continuously (for example, aluminium smelting, refrigeration, water pumping) is already practised and could be greatly increased in a 'smart' grid (Smart Grid Australia website).

Although most renewable energy sources do not suffer the same constraints as fossil and nuclear energy, some have their own constraints:

- Wind and biomass plantations require sufficient land area in appropriate locations. However, wind power is highly compatible with agriculture and the use of biomass *residues* does not entail any additional land use.
- There may be insufficient areas of land and shallow coastal waters available to meet the energy demand of some regions (for example, the United Kingdom and continental Europe) (MacKay, 2009).
- Large contributions from the subset of renewable electricity sources that fluctuate need either some intermittent back-up, or storage, or additional transmission links, in order to facilitate system integration.
- Large hydro and conventional tidal power may have large impacts on biodiversity and sometimes involve shifting large numbers of people off the land to be flooded.
- Although most renewable energy technologies are very low in GHG emissions, there are exceptions: dams covering large areas of vegetation become large emitters of the GHG methane for many years after flooding,

and bioenergy fuelled by clearing native forests is responsible for both CO_2 and methane emissions.

None of these limitations on individual renewable electricity sources in particular circumstances need to diminish the viability of a mix of different renewable electricity sources. Technological advances could also open up other options: for instance a recent study found that, if floating wind turbines (currently at the early demonstration stage) are included in scenarios, the United Kingdom could become a net exporter of renewable electricity within a few decades (Offshore Valuation Group, 2010).

Discussion

Table 4.1 summarises the four scenarios for energy and climate security. Of the four options, sustainable energy is the only one that has sufficient commercial and semi-commercial technologies to make a large contribution by 2020. These sustainable energy technologies have the lowest financial risk, as well as the lowest physical risk. Sustainable energy technologies currently at the demonstration stage (for example, hot rock geothermal) have greater financial risk.

It is clear that, on a finite planet, growth in energy demand and hence the concept of energy security are inevitably constrained. Therefore, in this chapter, energy security is defined to be the provision of energy use patterns and quantities and types of energy supply that are sufficient for a good life for all, without subjecting the planet and its people to high risks of major environmental and health damage including global warming and nuclear war, social inequity and loss of food production. A global energy system based mostly or even entirely on energy efficiency, energy conservation and renewable sources of energy is technically feasible by 2050 (Sørensen and Meibom, 2000; Peter and Lehmann, 2008; Teske et al., 2010; WWF, Ecofys and OMA, 2011).

At present it is not possible to cost the 'Clean Fossil' or the Generation IV Nuclear scenarios, because the technologies are not commercially available. Even the Conventional Nuclear scenario is difficult to cost, because the industry ceased to grow around 2005, there is limited economic data available and cost estimates in studies conducted for the United States have exhibited very rapid cost escalations from 2002 to 2009 (Schneider et al., 2009; Diesendorf, 2010b). The Sustainable Energy scenario relies on several technologies that are commercially available or semi-commercial and also has the advantage over the other scenarios that the economic savings from reducing demand can pay for a large fraction of the increased cost of renewable energy (McKinsey & Co., 2009; ClimateWorks, 2010). Prices of the more expensive renewable energy technologies are expected to continue to fall as their markets expand. Although it is too early to expect detailed costing for

Table 4.1 Comparison of different electricity scenarios for achieving both climate security and energy security

Technological scenario	Year to contribute 30% of electricity	Comments on technological status and risks
Conventional nuclear (generations II and III)	2030	Generation II is commercial and generation III semi-commercial; escalating cost and hence financial risk; proliferation and safety risks; CO_2 emissions 130 kg/MWh when low-grade uranium used
Generation IV nuclear	2035	Still in R, D & D stages and hence high financial risk; requires reprocessing; costs unknown but greater than conventional nuclear; proliferation and safety risks, despite claims to the contrary by some supporters; negligible CO_2 emissions
'Clean fossil' (i.e., fossil with carbon capture and storage)	2035	Technologically unproven, hence high financial risk; CO_2 emissions about 120 kg/MWh; risk of CO_2 escape
Sustainable energy	2020	Key technologies are commercial (energy efficiency; solar hot water; hydro; wind; some bioenergy) or pre-commercial (concentrated solar thermal with thermal storage; off-shore wind) and are low financial risk. However, hot rock geothermal, wave and ocean current energy are at the demonstration stage and hence have high financial risk. Most have low CO_2 emissions and low physical risks

N.B.: The scenario timescales in column 2 are based on the assumption that governments implement effective policies to disseminate the technology rapidly.

100 per cent renewable energy, there are grounds for arguing that it will be the least-cost of the four and in the long run may even be cheaper than the direct costs of business as usual. If the indirect costs of business as usual are taken into account (for example, climate change, air and water pollution, land degradation), then it is likely that its costs will exceed those of climate mitigation (Stern, 2006).

Energy security in a socially just society

A 'good life for all' requires more than an ecologically sustainable energy system. It also requires social justice. Social justice may be defined as equal opportunity for all people to access their basic needs. Many authors agree that these needs include sufficient nutritious food, clean water, housing, warmth in cold weather, personal security, education and health services, social support and an unpolluted environment.

In a socially just society, energy security involves the provision of energy use patterns and quantities and types of energy supply that are sufficient for a good life for all. The 'centralised renewable energy' scenario developed by Sørensen and Meibom (2000) has low land use and hence does not compete with food production, yet it provides for all from renewable energy sources used efficiently.

While social justice is determined by a wide range of government policies (industry, tax, education, health, transport, etc.), it is likely that a renewable energy system would be more compatible with social justice than an energy system based on large fossil or nuclear power stations. This is because the renewable energy system would be composed of a mix of centralised and local energy sources, allowing households at least partial energy independence. Furthermore, there are likely to be more local jobs in such an energy system (MacGill et al., 2002; Hatfield-Dodds et al., 2008).

Political implications

The differences between the scenarios are not simply differences in technologies. They may also involve different visions of a future society and economy, different political stances and different values. The connections between energy technology and opposing social and political orientations make it very difficult to gain political and community agreement on the way forward to address the two urgent issues of climate security and energy security.

Many supporters of the 'clean fossil' and nuclear scenarios follow the 'hard energy path' discussed by Lovins (1977). They have a vision of a highly industrialised society with an endlessly growing capitalist economy, which is nominally democratic but where decision-making is centralised and made by an elite group of 'expert' power-holders. They tend to have faith in technological solutions in general and large centralised technologies in particular, and find it difficult to envisage an energy supply system based on distributed sources. They are reluctant to acknowledge the risks of the relying on the future development of the 'clean fossil' and nuclear scenarios. They tend to favour the continued dominance of large industries and multinational corporations.

The supporters of sustainable energy scenarios are more diverse. Many hold the same general vision as outlined above for the fossil and nuclear scenarios, but with a change of technologies. They see renewable energy feeding the growth society and economy. Others recognise that the drivers of an unsustainable society, including energy insecurity and climate insecurity, are not only inappropriate technology, but also economic growth (Jackson, 2009) and population growth (Diesendorf, 2009, pp. 21–23; 119). Even Lord Nicolas Stern, former chief economist of the World Bank and author of the Stern Review on the economics of climate change (Stern, 2006), was quoted as saying that the rich countries would have to consider reining in economic growth from 2030 (Watts, 2009). Another eminent economist, Herman Daly (1977), who is a strong supporter of sustainable energy, argues on much broader grounds that 'a steady-state economy is a necessary and desirable future state of affairs and that its attainment requires quite major changes in values, as well as radical, but non-revolutionary, institutional reforms'. Still other supporters of sustainable energy envisage a society that is less centralised and less industrialised than at present, with more local decision-making. This diversity of socioeconomic visions amongst supporters of renewable energy weakens the campaign to build renewable energy in competition with fossil fuels and nuclear energy.

Conclusions

Are energy security and effective climate change policies necessarily contradictory? The answer depends on the definition of 'energy security' we choose, the kind of society we aspire to, globally and nationally, and the level of risks we are prepared to take. As seen from the age of fossil fuels, energy security was 'an adequate and reliable energy supply at a reasonable price', where the adjectives are all interpreted within the paradigms of endless economic growth and the externalisation of environmental and social costs. Within that framework the key issues were peak oil and gas and interruptions to trade in these and other vital commodities.

However, looking forward from the end of the age of fossil fuel to a future ecologically sustainable and socially just age, energy security involves energy use patterns and quantities and types of energy supply that are sufficient for a good life for all, including future generations, other species and the planet as a whole. Within this context, energy security must also satisfy the requirements to prevent the principal ecological threat of the twenty-first century, anthropogenic climate change.

Within the energy sector, climate security involves the provision of energy use patterns and quantities and types of energy supply that are very low in GHG emissions. In this context, specific climate security needs are as follows:

- Immediate rapid implementation of commercially available and precommercial efficient energy use and renewable energy technologies;
- Behavioural change to foster energy conservation activities;

- Research, development and demonstration (R, D & D) of carbon capture and sequestration and those energy efficiency and renewable energy technologies that still need further improvement; and possibly
- R, D & D to try to develop a safe, low-cost form of nuclear energy that could be rapidly constructed and disseminated.

Different technologies involve different types and magnitudes of risk. This preliminary examination suggests that energy security and climate security could be achieved together at very low risk with an ecologically sustainable, socially just energy system and economy. The only energy system satisfying these requirements is one based on the efficient use of renewable energy. Therefore, implementation of the sustainable energy scenario should receive the greatest priority and support by government, business and the community at large. With international trade in renewable energy, such a system could reliably provide sufficient energy for a good life for all. Key changes to the economic system are also needed to shift emphasis to broader indicators of socio-economic progress than gross domestic product and to foster substantial reductions in the use of energy, materials and land.

Compared with the above sustainable energy scenario, the nuclear energy scenario involves greater risks, which arise from the proliferation of nuclear weapons, the absence of long-term nuclear waste dumps, terrorism, rare but devastating accidents, and financial risk associated with rapidly escalating capital costs and the physical risks. Nuclear energy, based on existing technologies, is also problematic because it is inherently slow to construct and is likely to become a medium-level CO_2 emitter within several decades as high-grade uranium reserves are used up. Generation IV reactors would avoid the latter problem, but since they are about two decades away from commercial operation, it would be very risky to rely upon their future development.

Coal power with carbon capture and storage is also likely to be a medium-level CO_2 emitter, in this case as the result of economic pressures. This energy supply system is unproven and, like generation IV nuclear energy, at least 20 years away from large-scale commercial operation. Therefore it would be very risky to rely upon its future development. A corollary is that existing coal-fired power stations should be phased out as soon as possible, starting with the oldest and most greenhouse-intensive.

To conclude, energy security and climate security need not be contradictory objectives. They can and must be addressed together by developing a very low-carbon energy system based primarily upon the efficient use of renewable energy. However, we have to accept that neither renewable energy nor nuclear energy nor coal power with CCS will be as cheap as fossil energies were in the early 2000s. Nevertheless, it is likely that several renewable energy sources will be economically competitive with fossil fuel use combined with CCS by the time the latter eventually becomes commercially available.

References

Aleklett, K., M. Höök, K. Jakobsson, M. Lardelli, S. Snowden and B. Söderbergh (2010), 'The peak of the oil age: Analysing the world oil production Reference Scenario in World Energy Outlook 2008', *Energy Policy*, 38(3): 1398–414.

Allison, I. et al. (2009), *The Copenhagen Diagnosis: Updating the World on the Latest Climate Science* (Sydney: Climate Change Research Institute, UNSW) [http://www.copenhagendiagnosis.org/default.html; accessed: 05 August 2010].

Boyle, G. (ed.) (2004), *Renewable Energy: Power for a Sustainable Future* (Oxford: Open University and Oxford University Press).

ClimateWorks Australia (2010), *Low Carbon Growth Plan for Australia* (Melbourne: ClimateWorks Australia).

Coal Utilization Research Council (undated), *Carbon Capture and Storage: Technology Status, Cost, Deployment Timing* [http://www.coal.org/briefs; accessed: 05 August 2010].

Daley, H.E. (1977), *Steady-State Economics: The Economics of Biophysical Equilibrium and Moral Growth* (San Francisco: WH Freeman & Co.).

Diesendorf, M. (2007), *Greenhouse Solutions with Sustainable Energy* (Sydney: UNSW Press).

Diesendorf, M. (2009), *Climate Action: A Campaign Manual for Greenhouse Solutions* (Sydney: UNSW Press).

Diesendorf, M. (2010a), *The Base-Load Fallacy*, Briefing Paper No. 16, EnergyScience [http://www.energyscience.org.au/factsheets.html; accessed: 05 August 2010].

Diesendorf, M. (2010b), 'Comparing the economics of nuclear and renewable sources of electricity', Solar 2010 conference, proceedings (Canberra: Australian Solar Energy Society).

Diesendorf, M. (2011), 'Lost energy policy opportunities', in K.J. Walker and K. Crowley (eds): *Environmental Policy Failure: Learning from Australian Studies* (Melbourne: Tilde University Press).

Hansen, J., M. Sato, P. Kharecha, D. Beerling, R. Berner, V. Masson-Delmotte, M. Pagani, M. Raymo, D.L. Roya and J.C. Zachos (2008), 'Target atmospheric CO_2: Where should humanity aim?', *Open Atmospheric Science Journal*, 2: 217–31.

Hatfield-Dodds, S., G. Turner, H. Schandl and T. Doss (2008), *Growing the Green Collar Economy: Skills and Labour Challenges in Reducing Our Greenhouse Emissions and National Environmental Footprint*, Report to the Dusseldorp Skills Forum (Canberra: CSIRO Sustainable Ecosystems).

International Energy Agency (IEA) (2008), *Energy Technology Perspectives 2008* (Paris: IEA/OECD).

IEA (2009), *Technology Roadmap: Carbon Capture and Storage* [http://www.iea.org/publications/free_all_papers.asp; accessed: 05 August 2010].

Jackson, T. (2009), *Prosperity without Growth: Economics for a Finite Planet* (London: Earthscan).

Laherrère, J. (2004), *Future of Natural Gas Supply*, Conference of Association for the Study of Peak Oil & Gas (Berlin, 25 May) [http://www.peakoil.net/JL/JeanL.html; accessed: 05 August 2010].

Lefèvre, N. (2010), 'Measuring the energy security implications of fossil fuel resource concentration', *Energy Policy*, 38(4): 1635–44.

Lenzen, M. (2008), 'Life cycle energy and greenhouse gas emissions of nuclear energy: a review', *Energy Conversion & Management*, 49: 2178–99.

Lovins, A.B. (1977), *Soft Energy Paths: Toward a Durable Peace* (Harmondsworth, UK: Penguin).

McFarlane, H.F. (2002), *Proliferation Resistance Assessment of the Integral Fast Reactor*, Argonne National Laboratory [www.ipd.anl.gov/anlpubs/2002/07/43534.pdf; accessed: 05 August 2010].

MacGill, I., M. Watt, and R. Passey (2002), *The Economic Development Potential and Job Creation Potential of Renewable Energy: Australian Case Studies*, commissioned by Australian Cooperative Research Centre for Renewable Energy Policy Group, Australian Ecogeneration Association and Renewable Energy Generators Association.

MacKay, D.J.C. (2009), *Sustainable Energy – Without the Hot Air* (Cambridge: UIT Cambridge Ltd).

McKinsey & Company (2009), *Pathways to a Low-Carbon Economy*, Version 2 of the global greenhouse gas abatement cost curve [http://www.mckinsey.com/clientservice/ccsi/pathways_low_carbon_economy.asp; accessed: 05 August 2010].

Metz, B. et al. (eds.) (2007), *Contribution of Working Group III to the Fourth Assessment Report of the Intergovernmental Panel on Climate Change, 2007* (Cambridge-New York: Cambridge University Press).

Mohr, S.H. and G.M. Evans (2009), 'Forecasting coal production until 2100', *Fuel*, 88(11): 2059–67.

Offshore Valuation Group (2010), *The Offshore Valuation: A Valuation of the UK's Offshore Renewable Energy Resource*, Study by Boston Consulting Group (Machynlleth, Wales: Public Interest Research Centre) [www.offshorevaluation.org; accessed: 05 August 2010].

Parry, M.L. et al. (eds.) (2007), *Contribution of Working Group II to the Fourth Assessment Report of the Intergovernmental Panel on Climate Change, 2007* (Cambridge, UK-New York: Cambridge University Press).

Peter, S. and H. Lehmann (2008), *Renewable Energy Outlook 2030: Energy Watch Group Global Renewable Energy Scenarios* (Bonn: Energy Watch Group) [www.energywatchgroup.org?Studien.4+M5d637be38d.0.html; accessed: 05 August 2010].

Schneider, M., S. Thomas, A. Froggatt and D. Koplow (2009), *The World Nuclear Industry Status Report 2009: With Particular Emphasis on Economic Issues*, Commissioned by German Federal Ministry of Environment, Nature Conservation & Reactor Safety.

Smart Grid Australia, [http://www.smartgridaustralia.com.au/index.php?page=about; accessed: 05 August 2010].

Solomon, S. et al. (2007), *Contribution of Working Group I to the Fourth Assessment Report of the Intergovernmental Panel on Climate Change, 2007*, Technical Summary (Cambridge, UK-New York: Cambridge University Press).

Sørensen, B. and P. Meibom (2000), 'A global renewable energy scenario', *International Journal of Global Energy Issues*, 13(1/2/3): DOI: 10.1504/IJGEI.2000.000869.

Stern, N. (2006), *Stern Review: The Economics of Climate Change* [http://www.webcitation.org/5nCeyEYJr; accessed: 05 August 2010].

Storm Van Leeuwen, J.W. and P. Smith (2005), *Can Nuclear Power Provide Energy for the Future; Would It Solve the CO_2-Emission Problem?* [www.stormsmith.nl; accessed: 05 August 2010].

Teske, S. et al. (2010), *Energy [R]evolution: A Sustainable World Energy Outlook*, 3rd ed. Greenpeace International and European Renewable Energy Council [http://www.energyblueprint.info/1201.0.html?PHPSESSID= df26d3ac1e7b98e2fd903e9dec1a0ca4; accessed 05 July 2011].

UNFCCC, [www.unfccc.int/2860.php; accessed: 05 August 2010].

Watts, J. (2009), 'Stern: Rich countries will have to forget about growth to stop climate change', *guardian.co.uk*, 11 September [http://www.guardian.co.uk/environment/2009/sep/11/stern-economic-growth-emissions; accessed: 05 August 2010].
WWF, Ecofys and OMA (2011), *The Energy Report: 100% Renewable Energy by 2050,* [http://wwf.panda.org/what_we_do/footprint/climate_carbon_energy/energy_solutions/renewable_energy/sustainable_energy_report/; accessed: 05 July 2011].

Part II

Climate Change and Energy Policy Formulation in Asia-Pacific

5
Energy and Environmental Challenges in China

Xu Yi-chong

Energy is central to human survival and development. Energy is therefore not only a development issue but also a political one as it has implications for social justice and equity. No government can ignore energy issues, whether they are related to availability, reliability, affordability, or increasingly, sustainability. However, all four components of 'energy security' are interpreted differently across countries and by different players.

Oil – more than other energy sources – generally dominates discussions of global energy security. Oil is at the centre of debate partly because it 'is a global commodity that can be shipped at a cost that is low relative to its value [and] the price of oil is essentially determined by the world market regardless of where it is produced' (Bordoff et al., 2010, p. 212). Oil often grabs the global headlines because of its importance for rich countries, which, in aggregate, supply nearly 40 per cent of their energy needs from oil. Amongst less fortunate countries, the energy security story is by and large a domestic one. This story concerns providing citizens with access to modern energy, rather than focusing on the 'obsession with energy independence'. In turn, this dynamic defines these countries' interpretations of the following components of energy security:

a) Making energy available to the majority of people at an affordable price – which requires development of all energy sources, of which oil is only a small proportion;
b) Investment in energy infrastructure – which is often considered a public good in which private investors have little interest; and
c) Providing energy without sacrificing the livelihood of people, the majority of whom are engaged in agrarian activities.

China sits between the two stories as it is both increasing usage of oil and expanding access to modern energy. Most energy security issues that emerged in the past decade highlighted the challenges China is facing in the processes of industrialisation and urbanisation. These processes have inevitably demanded increasing consumption of all energy sources (oil, coal, natural gas, hydro and the modern energy, electricity and heat generated by primary energy sources). This challenge is particularly acute for China, which has about 20 per cent of the world's population, but holds 1.1 per cent of the world's oil reserves, 1.3 per cent of the world's natural gas reserves and 14 per cent of global coal reserves (BP, 2010). Given the size of its population, China has to find a way to meet most of its energy demands domestically: as Indian Prime Minister Manmohan Singh had noted in relation to food supplies, 'if India and China cannot feed themselves, no one could'. This means that while coal will remain the most important energy source for China, other sources – including domestic hydro, nuclear and renewable energy as well as overseas coal and oil – must be developed to meet rising demand.

Struggling to meet its rising energy demand, the government in Beijing has expanded its definition of 'energy security' beyond oil. In the first three decades of the reform (1978–2008), expanding electricity access was the top priority of China's energy policies, partly because social and economic development was unattainable without modern energy and partly because the country as a whole suffered greatly from environmental pollution – including high emissions of dust and particles in cities and widespread acid rain, a direct consequence of coal burning. Consequently, electricity generation capacity expanded from 66 GW in 1980 to 316 GW in 2000 (Xu, 2002, p. 47). Coal-fired generation plants represented over 70 per cent of such increased capacity, mainly as a consequence of the interaction of three factors. Firstly, construction of thermal power plants was cheaper and faster than hydro or nuclear power plants. Secondly, China lacked the technological, financial and human capital to build other modern renewable generation capacity. Finally, China did not have foreign exchange or access to the purchase of oil and natural gas on global markets.

Entering the twenty-first century, China faced a quite different set of challenges in terms of energy security and energy-related environmental problems. Between 1980 and 2010, more than 200 million people had moved from rural to urban areas. Energy consumption for urban citizens is now three or four times higher than it is in rural areas, where over half of energy consumption is from biomass. To meet rising energy demand from industrialisation and urbanisation, China expanded its generation capacity at an unprecedented rate, adding 400 GW capacity in only eight years. This has brought new challenges to all four components of 'energy security' in China: its abundant coal reserves – especially that of good quality and with easy access – have been depleting fast, and its heavy reliance on coal has resulted in both air pollution and greenhouse gas (GHG) emissions-intensive economic growth.

Since 2002, while global attention might have been on rising oil prices and threats of climate change, the Chinese government defined its energy security in a much broader sense – exploring and expanding low-carbon and 'unlimited' energy sources to ensure adequate energy supplies. Bound by climate change considerations, its emphasis has been on energy efficiency, conservation and development of low-carbon energy. A series of policies were adopted:

- The 11th Five Year Plan (FYP) (2006–2010), which set 'an ambitious target of a 20 per cent reduction in energy intensity' by 2010, while incorporating, for the first time, 'quantitative indicators for energy efficiency' (World Bank, 2008b, p. 35);
- The Medium and Long-term Energy Development Plan (2004–2020);
- The Medium- to Long-term Energy Conservation Plan, both of which were released in 2004;
- The Medium- to Long-term Nuclear Energy Development Plan, released in 2005.

In 2005, the government enacted the Renewable Energy Law, which provided mandates for provinces and industries to develop renewable energy in terms of investment, pricing, connection and regulation. In response to the global financial crisis, China, like many other states, quickly put together a large financial stimulus package (US$586 billion), in which a third of total expenditure was devoted to energy efficiency and low-carbon energy development – development of low-carbon vehicles, rail transportation, a more flexible and sophisticated electricity grid infrastructure that enables greater use of renewable energy sources and energy efficiency in buildings. Together, these overarching economic policies were designed to achieve:

1. A clean-energy standard – 15 per cent of primary energy from non-fossil sources by 2020;
2. An efficiency target – 20 per cent reduction of energy intensity below 2005 level by 2010;
3. A carbon target – 40–50 per cent carbon intensity below 2005 level by 2020 (UNEP, 2009; World Bank, 2010a, 2010b).

Despite these serious measures, a complex demographic balance – a 400 million-strong 'middle class' scattered in a sea of over 800 million people who live very much in 'developing-country conditions' (Lieberthal, 2009, p. 7) – and competing environmental concerns, some of which could not be dealt with without access to adequate and reliable supply of modern energy, remain the extremely fundamental forces in China's development. It is difficult to ensure adequate and reliable supplies of modern energy to its citizens while bringing growth in carbon emissions under control, but both prongs of this strategy are indispensible for human development. This challenge is not uniquely limited to China; it represents a common one for most developing countries, where the interpretation of the four components of energy security – availability, reliability, affordability and sustainability – is markedly different from those formulated in developed countries. Availability and reliability are really about accessibility; while affordability is about a wider population whose gross domestic product (GDP) per capita represents only a fraction of that in the Organization for Economic Co-operation and Development (OECD) countries (China's is 6.8 per cent of that in the United States) (World Bank, 2010c). Sustainability for large developing countries including China and India is about ensuring sustainable domestic energy supplies.

Dealing with issues of energy security requires governing capacity. As in most developing countries, 'China's leaders lack the institutional and technical capabilities to achieve many of the improved energy outcomes that they seek' (Lieberthal, 2009, p. 7). That is, political will does not necessarily equate with the capacity to govern. This is particularly problematic for a transition economy where economic growth is much faster than the development of operational, legal or regulatory regimes or a governing capacity. If it is difficult for a small-sized developed country – as it is in the case of Australia – to reach agreement on how to cut CO_2 emissions in energy production and consumption, the challenges facing China would have to multiply these difficulties by the size of the population and square them with the gap between urban and rural, industry and agriculture, coastal and inner areas, elite and the masses. Taking size into consideration is hence crucial for us to understand the scale of China's challenges.

This chapter discusses the changes in energy policies in China in the past three decades, by focusing in particular on the post-2002 era. Its aims are to provide explanations as to why specific policies were adopted, how climate change shaped recent policies and why some important policies on sustainable development have failed to be implemented. It is possible to divide the challenges facing China vis-à-vis energy security and climate change into three types: structural, technical, and political. Addressing the challenges of energy-related climate change requires a fundamental change in our approach to producing and consuming energy. In turn, this requires structural changes in the economy in general and the way of life of its citizens. Such changes are central to facing the intertwined challenges of energy security and climate change. To these ends, this chapter discusses briefly:

a) Structural challenges regarding energy security and environmental pollution;
b) Policies and measures undertaken by the Chinese government in order to deal with these challenges;
c) The politics of policy development and implementation.

This chapter will argue that addressing these twin challenges requires not only short-term and immediate adjustment in China's economic development but, more importantly, long-term structural changes in its economy – which appear much more difficult to accomplish. While suggesting that policies that offer new opportunities can be implemented more easily than those requiring structural changes, the chapter concludes that the Chinese government – which is to all intents and purposes aware that climate inaction will lead to its own economic undoing – has limited capacity to push through the necessary measures for sustainable development.

Structural challenges

After three decades of high economic growth, China is simultaneously facing structural challenges and opportunities, primarily located in the processes of industrialisation and urbanisation. China's industries are the largest consumer of energy and the largest contributor to GHG emissions. Since 1990, about 15 million people every year have moved to urban areas: this trend is projected to continue for another 20 years (Lieberthal, 2009). The combination of industrialisation and urbanisation means that energy demand, both per capita and as a whole, will continue to rise. Given that energy resources are depleting quickly and energy production and consumption contribute to the lion's share of GHG emissions, the introduction of structural changes in China's economy is indispensible to ensure energy security and environmental protection. Alongside these challenges, there are a number of opportunities, of which some large enterprises in China have decided to take advantage.

China's industrialisation process has three basic implications for energy consumption. First, in the case of China, industrial energy consumption as a share of total energy consumption is much higher than in most countries. Over 70 per cent of China's energy demand comes from industries, comparing with 49 per cent in India, 35 per cent in Russia, 25 per cent in the United States and 39 per cent in Japan. To be more specific, in 2008, agriculture and fishery contributed to 11.3 per cent of the country's total GDP while accounting for 3.1 per cent of total energy consumption. Industries (including mining, manufacturing, energy and construction) contributed 48.6 per cent of GDP and consumed 73.1 per cent of total energy. Services contributed 40.1 per cent of GDP and consumed only 5.9 per cent of the total energy. While residential and commercial use of energy accounted for 43 per cent of total energy demand in the United States, China's figures in this regard do not exceed 19 per cent. China's manufacturing industry is the country's largest energy consumer (58.9 per cent of total consumption) (IEA, 2007, 2010b).

Secondly, data from the International Atomic Energy Agency (IAEA) (2006) shows that in 2006 China produced 34 per cent of the world's total steel, 47.1 per cent of cement, 49 per cent of flat glass, 15.9 per cent of paper and pulp and 27.7 per cent of aluminium. These industries are not only energy-intensive but also much more polluting than many others. Their production is not only destined for domestic but also for foreign markets. Several studies have shown that, since the late 1990s, exports have been a main driver of the rise in Chinese CO_2 emissions. As Weber et al. (2008, p. 3572) explain:

> In 2005, around one-third of Chinese emissions (17,000 Mt Co_2) were due to production of exports, and this proportion has risen from 12 per cent (230 Mt) in 1987 and only 21 per cent (760 Mt) as recently as 2002.

In 2008, China produced 660 million tonnes of steel, on which only 500 Mt (76 per cent) was consumed domestically, while the rest was exported. Total cement production amounted to 1870 Mt with domestic consumption reaching about 1400–1500 Mt (approximately 75–80 per cent of the total). This makes China one of the largest virtual energy exporters in the world.

Thirdly, Chinese industries fell far behind other countries in energy efficiency, measured by energy use per unit of GDP (see Table 5.1). In 2004, overall primary energy intensity (energy use per unit of GDP) in China was over six times that in Japan, and more than three times that in the United States. According to some analyses, energy use per unit of output across eight sectors was about 48 per cent higher than the best practice in the world (IEA, 2007).

If these three features – an industry-centred economy, export-oriented industries and low energy efficiency – are at the core of China's problems of energy security, the problems with rising energy demands and a worsening environment in China 'are not the usual complaints: an overabundance of cheap coal or a reckless disregard for the environment' (Chandler and Gwin, 2008, p. 6). These reflect the fundamental structure of the economy. Coal provides nearly 70 per cent of China's primary energy mix and nearly half of coal is used to produce electricity. The coal sector is also where the main problems are located. Coal is an expensive and difficult-to-deliver

Table 5.1 China's energy intensity vis-à-vis international best practice in specific industries

	Steel	**Cement**	**Fertiliser**	**Paper**	**Electric motors**	**Coal-fired boilers**	**Heavy tracks**	**Coal-fired power**
Best practice	1.00	1.00	1.00	1.00	1.00	1.00	1.00	1.00
China good practice	1.21	1.45	1.31	2.20	1.11	1.15	2.25	1.19

Source: NDRC (2004).

energy source not only because coal mining is becoming increasingly difficult (remaining coal reserves are very deep underground), but the vast distances between coal reserves and the load centres has placed tremendous pressures on transport (over 50 per cent of rail capacity is used for transporting coal in China) (IEA, 2006; World Bank, 2008a). The rapid depletion of coal has become a serious energy security threat (Shealy and Dorian, 2010). China's problems with accessing sufficient coal supplies only reflect larger world trends in coal availability.

The obvious options to deal with these twin challenges are to change the economic structure from an energy-intensive, industry-based and export-oriented one to that of a service-led economy. Switching from industries to services without involving large-scale unemployment will in turn require (a) an increase in consumption and (b) a highly skilled labour force, both of which imply a process of urbanisation, which, as we have seen, also represents a primary factor behind China's rising energy demand.

What has China been doing?

Energy shortages and their associated environmental problems have been discussed in policy making ever since China's reform started in the late 1970s. In their first two decades, the reforms' focus was on increasing modern energy production and consumption – primarily electricity – because direct coal burning at the time had not only very low energy efficiency rates but also produced a large quantity of ashes and particulates. For example, in the early 1980s, the concentration of particulates of sulphur dioxide (SO_2) and nitrogen oxide (NO_x) in the air in the centre of Beijing exceeded the national standard by two to four times, and Beijing's average dust (total suspended particulate) levels were about seven times greater than the US air quality standard (Xu, 2010). In rural areas, biomass fuel users caused serious hillside soil erosion, excessive water runoff, deforestation and declines in soil fertility (UNDP, 2000; World Bank, 1989). To prevent further increases in already unacceptably high levels of urban air pollution, as well as to economise on fuel, China has invested heavily to replace decentralised and uncontrolled burning of coal in households and enterprises with centralised, large-scale, environmentally controlled combustion in order to produce cleaner forms of energy (gas, electricity, steam, hot water) for distribution to final users (World Bank, 1985). Its total primary energy supplies more than doubled between 1979 and 2000 (236 per cent) and then almost doubled again between 2000 and 2007 (193 per cent). Electricity consumption grew four and a half times between 1979 and 2000 (532 per cent) and then one and a half times between 2000 and 2007 (245 per cent).

Before 2000, few talked about GHG emissions in China. The World Bank shared policy makers' view that poverty alleviation, economic and social development could not have been accomplished without people gaining access to modern energy. The Bank greatly assisted China in its expansion of electricity generation capacity by providing financial assistance, facilitating investment by multinational companies in China and pushing and advising electricity reforms. During this period (1980–2000), energy intensity (energy consumption per unit of GDP) improved significantly 'by default' – that is, China had started the reform from a very low base in terms of living standards and economic performance. Technology change was the most important contributor to the reduction in energy intensity – in two decades, China's economy quadrupled while its energy consumption only doubled. By 2000, energy intensity had declined by 65 per cent compared to 1980.

The year 2002 ushered in a new era that surprised everyone, both within China and in the wider international community. Growth in energy demand exceeded GDP growth. It was not simply that the decline in energy intensity had slowed, but, from 2003 onwards, energy intensity began to go upwards instead. This can be partly explained by economic structural changes. The primary industries – agriculture, fishery and forestry – are the least energy-intensive industries and their share of GDP declined steadily. The share of industries that include mining, manufacturing, energy and construction remained stable in 1980–2000 and rose from 45.9 per cent in 2000 to 48.6 per cent in 2008 (Sinton et al., 1998; Sinton and Fridley, 2000; Wu et al., 2005). The structural change in industries has contributed most to the rise in energy intensity in the 2000s. This structural change was not anticipated at the end of the 1990s when the government was quite optimistic in setting up a target of quadrupling its GDP by 2020 while only doubling its energy consumption.

The reality was that in China, GDP tripled with industries growing 321 per cent between 2000 and 2008 while total energy consumption doubled (World Bank, 2009). When energy shortages, especially power shortages, re-emerged after a three-year decline in late 2002, there was a widespread concern about energy security in China as well as in the world. Rising energy demand in China came in an era where many Chinese enterprises had become international players. They had been freed from the planning system, yet had not learned how to behave as market players with long visions. They expanded domestically and into the international market. To mitigate the impact of rising prices, Chinese energy companies sped up their overseas investment in energy resources. This, in turn, prompted concern in many developed countries about their own energy security.

Meanwhile, as energy production and consumption rose faster than anticipated, with over 80 per cent of electricity generated from coal-fired capacity, the consequences of environmental pollution and climate change became apparent and began to attract widespread criticism inside and outside China. While in 2000 China contributed to 12.9 per cent of global CO_2 emissions, by 2007 its share had reached 21 per cent, surpassing that of the United

States (20 per cent). Electricity production alone contributes to over 70 per cent of CO_2 emissions and 40 per cent of GHG emissions in China (IEA, 2010a). The growing economic and health costs of pollution and energy shortages combined with citizen protests and non-governmental organisation (NGO) activism forced many Chinese officials to change their 'pollute first clean up later' philosophy. Since 2002, China has enacted a series of policies to ensure adequate and sustainable energy supplies. Its 'green' initiatives were boosted by the US$586 billion stimulus package that included at least US$221 billion in green spending, making it the largest green stimulus package in the world (UNEP, 2009).

In 2007, the State Council adopted 'China's Energy Conditions and Policies', based on two underlining assumptions:

- Development is the only path to survival; and it cannot take place without energy;
- China does not have adequate energy endowments; priority must be hence given to conservation, efficiency, technological break-through and international cooperation.

The adopted policy framework did strive to 'build a stable, economical, clean and safe energy supply system, so as to support the sustained economic and social development with sustained energy development' (State Council, 2007, p. 11). In other words, measures to deal with climate change threats are part and parcel of the broad efforts to secure energy supplies. Three economy-wide policies are behind the 'green initiatives':

1. A *clean energy standard* mandating that 15 per cent of China's primary energy will come from non-fossil sources by 2020. China currently acquires around 9 per cent of its energy from these sources;
2. An *efficiency target* mandating a reduction in energy intensity of 20 per cent below 2005 levels by the end of 2010. China had reduced energy intensity by around 13 per cent by July 2009;
3. A *carbon target* mandating a reduction in carbon intensity of 40–50 per cent below 2005 levels by 2020.

These economy-wide policies are reinforced by an array of sector- and technology-specific policies, targets and incentives. Most policies and measures designed to achieve the target of 15 per cent of non-fossil energy sources have been implemented more successfully than those designed to achieve energy efficiency and carbon reduction. Those concerning the first set of policies include specific measures to encourage development of non-fossil energy sources – wind, solar and nuclear.

The World Bank (2005, p. 19) observed that 'China has long had one of the world's largest renewable energy programs, leading to the development of more than 30 GW of small hydropower and large-scale installation of improved woodstoves and biogas plants'. The Renewable Energy Law was adopted in 2005, setting a target of 15 per cent of the total energy consumption from renewable sources – wind, biomass, solar and hydro – by 2020. In September 2007, a target was set for the five major power generation companies so that, by 2010, at least 3 per cent of their generation capacity would have to be from renewable resources (World Bank, 2009, 2010a, 2010b). In September 2009, the Chinese President, Hu Jintao, in remarks at the United Nations General Assembly meeting, promised the world that China would expand its renewable energy to 20 per cent by 2020. Since then, a large amount of investment has been made in all renewable sources.

Wind generation capacity, for example, doubled each year between 2005 and 2009. In 2005, China had wind capacity of only 1.27 GW; it doubled to 2.6 GW a year later, and then doubled again to 5.9 GW in 2007. By the end of 2009, its wind generation capacity had expanded to 24 GW, which had exceeded the expected target of 20 GW wind power capacity by 2010. Nevertheless, only 16 GW out of 24 GW is currently connected to grids (GWEC, 2010). China is also the world leader in installed solar hot water systems: about 70 per cent of the world's solar heating system is located in China. About 10 per cent of Chinese households use solar water heaters, with 30 per cent targeted by 2020. For large developing countries – including China and India – the International Energy Agency (IEA), IAEA and the World Bank have all suggested that electricity generation has to shift dramatically from coal to renewable and nuclear to face energy security challenges (IEA 2007, 2009; IAEA 2009; World Bank 2010a, 2010b).

China started its nuclear energy programme quite late. Its first nuclear power plant went into operation only in 1991. Since then, China has added ten plants, which produce about 2 per cent of the total electricity supply. Nuclear power has been promoted as a clean base-load energy supply, as it has zero CO_2 emissions and near-zero emissions of other GHGs. The initial target to 40 GW by 2020 has recently been revised to 60–70 GW. As of 2010, 23 nuclear reactors (40 per cent of the world's total) were under construction in China (Xu, 2010).

The central government has also issued other taxation and fiscal policies to facilitate renewable and low-carbon energy development (Eighth Senior Policy Advisory Council, 2005). Value-added tax reductions and rebates for wind generators and imported materials used in wind turbine manufacturing were the major incentives for many firms to invest in wind generation capacity. The expansion of renewable and nuclear generation capacity as a supplement to coal-fired generation capacity has been quite successful. These are the relatively easy policies to implement because they represent opportunities for job creation, economic growth, energy security, pollution reduction and health protection. For each nuclear project, for example, the minimum investment is about US$4 billion which includes a large amount of investment on roads, water and other facilities. Local governments are appreciative of these projects because of the opportunities created by this level of direct investment (Xu, 2010).

The construction of large, cleaner and more efficient power generation plants and the establishment of advanced ultra-high voltage transmission grids represent two additional important measures to deal with the challenges of energy security and climate change. By the end of 2007, 74 per cent of newly ordered thermal capacity was 600 MW and above. By 2010, beside the 24 units already in operation within China, 64 supercritical power plants with a capacity of 1000 MW each were under construction. These figures made China the globe's largest operator of supercritical power generation plants (IEA, 2010b). The State Grid Corporation, China's largest utility company, has also installed its first 1000 kv ultra-high voltage line from coal-rich Shanxi to Hubei, in the proximity of the Three-Gorges Dam. The idea is to send electricity from North to South in dry seasons, with a South–North inversion planned for the raining season. Such a strategy might also balance the demand and supply amongst those provinces with those without equivalent energy resources. The Chinese government was planning to invest US$44 billion through 2010 and US$88 billion through 2020 on these grids. If 400 miles of these advanced ultra-high voltage grids will be in place by 2020, the country could afford to decrease its projected capacity of 20 GW. International organisations have encouraged the construction of large power plants and high voltage lines to improve energy efficiency. Furthermore, both types of projects offer new economic opportunities.

In addition, since the early 2000s, subsidies to energy have been dramatically reduced and energy prices in China are increasingly reflective of actual costs (IEA, 2007). Coal prices have been opened to the market since 1996, when electricity prices were also adjusted upwards. Between 2004 and 2006, power tariffs went up by nearly 20 per cent. The Energy Bureau of the National Development and Reform Commission (NDRC) put forward a plan to implement a differential electricity pricing system for different categories of end-users, and, in 2010, another plan to allow different pricing for peak and off-peak consumption. As observed by Zhou, Levine and Price (2010, p. 15): '[T]hree tax-related measures – corporate income tax, deductions, vehicles and fuel taxes, and export taxes – have been used to promote energy efficiency in China in recent years'.

Other taxation and fiscal policies were also adopted to encourage investment in low-carbon energy resources and to reduce energy consumption of those energy-intensive sectors. Together these constitute what the Chinese have called a 'recycling' industrialised economy. Richerzhagen and Scholtz (2008, p. 312) observed that:

> The aim of these measures is to increase energy efficiency and the share of renewable energies in order to cut energy costs, increase energy security

> [...] [and] overcome the negative effects of energy scarcity on economic growth.

These policies, if implemented accordingly, could have significant impacts on energy security and the environment.

The other two sets of policies – reduction in energy intensity and carbon intensity – were not as successful. It is difficult to translate these policies into action because they require structural changes. As the World Bank (2008, p. 36, emphasis in the original) stated, to achieve these two reductions, China would have to adopt structural, technical and managerial changes:

> (i) *structural*, resulting from rebalancing the economic and industrial structure, particularly reducing the share of energy-intensive industries; (ii) *technical*, through technical progress to reduce energy consumption per unit of product; and (iii) *managerial*, by reducing energy waste during energy production, transportation and consumption through strengthening regulatory and administrative institutional capacity.

Restructuring its economy – especially moving away from energy-intensive industries (steel, aluminium or petrochemical) to service sectors – is a long-term process that involves heavy social, economic and even political costs. As the experiences of other countries seem to suggest, it has never occurred without radical changes (Lin et al., 2006).

Energy conservation, therefore, is a long and arduous strategic task, requiring the leadership of the government and participation of enterprises and the public as a whole, while involving structural changes in the economy and society. China's 11th FYP (2006–2010) was formulated in 2003–2005 when it had become clear that capital-intensive and industry-led growth had placed tremendous pressures on energy, natural resources and the environment. The FYP gave priority to rebalancing the economic structure and to environmental and social objectives. Structural changes meant shifting out of some energy-intensive industries. The growth rate of some of these energy-intensive industries in 2006 and 2007, however, exceeded that of the average of 2000–2005, as indicated by Table 5.2.

Much of the increased production of these energy-intensive products was exported. For example, exports of flat glass increased 37.9 per cent in 2005, 32.6 per cent in 2006 and 17 per cent in 2007 (Rosen and Houser, 2007). There was no sign that these industries would reduce production in the near future.

Energy conservation required closing some highly energy-intensive enterprises, such as small-scale steel plants and power generation plants. To improve energy production efficiency, the government decided to close

Table 5.2 Growth of key energy-intensive products

Name	Production (Mt, 2005)	Growth (%, 2000–2005)	Production (Mt, 2010 planned)	Production (Mt, 2007)	Growth (%, 2006)	Growth (%, 2007)
Steel	397	24.7	414	567	25.3	21.3
Nonferrous	16.3	15.5		23.5	17.2	22.7
Cement	106.4	13.0	1305	1360	15.5	9.9
Main	140.8	11.9		158.7	13.5	11.4
Chemicals and paper	56	12.9		77.9	16	18
Flat glass	420.3	18		497.5	12.5	13

Source: World Bank (2008a, p. 44).

small power plants with a total capacity of 50 GW by 2010. The swift implementation of this policy is illustrated by the successful closure of 533 small coal-fired power plants with a total capacity of 21.6 GW in 2007 – an effort that doubled the projected target. Small coal-fired thermal power plants (6–300 MW) still account for 43 per cent of the total number of units while those with capacity of 300 MW and above account for 39 per cent. Amongst recently built power plants, small-sized ones still account for the largest number of units but large and super-large plants account for the larger share of generation capacity (World Bank, 2008a). The government also closed small-sized steel and iron mills with a capacity of 84 billion tonnes, again exceeding the planned 65 billion tonnes target (World Bank, 2008, p. 45). It also required the closure, by 2010, of cement factories with a capacity of 250 Mt and steel factories with a capacity of 55 Mt. These represent difficult political tasks, as most small and inefficient steel mills and power generation plants are located in areas with limited investment and limited opportunities for employment.

In the final analysis it seems that the probability of achieving a 20 per cent reduction in energy intensity by 2020 depends on the pace of economic growth – that is, the higher the growth rate, the lower the probability; the higher the economic growth, the higher the contribution from technical progress is needed to achieve the target. Further, if GDP growth rate continues at an average annual rate of 9.5 per cent or more, stronger actions and policies are required.

The global financial crisis initially seemed to provide an opportunity for China to achieve its targets, as energy consumption declined in the initial stage of the crisis. However, the huge stimulus package put in place by the Chinese government, although potentially benefiting the global economy, exacerbated energy- and environment-related problems. In particular, according to officials from the Ministry of Environmental Protection (MEP) the stimulus packages that encouraged rural consumption kept economic growth rates high and brought environmental problems to rural areas.

Politics in balancing energy and environment

'To its credit', stated the World Bank (2009, p. 4), the Chinese government 'fully recognises that [its development] trends cannot continue indefinitely and therefore is committed to building a resource-saving and environmentally friendly society as a stated national policy'. The government in Beijing has expressed its desire to move away from being the world's factory to becoming an economy with larger high-tech and services sectors. It has invested heavily in developing low-carbon energy sources and improving energy efficiency as a way to ensure sustainable energy and environmental security. As Kenneth Lieberthal (2009, p. 6) stated before the US Senate Foreign Relations Committee:

> China's rate of growth of carbon emission, especially since 2002, has been extremely steep, and pollution problems in China, I think, are rightly viewed as severe. Most Americans seem to believe that China is, therefore, ignoring its carbon emissions while pursuing all-out economic growth. But [...] the reality is that the leaders in Beijing have adopted serious measures to bring growth in carbon emissions under control, even as they have tried to maintain rapid overall expansion of GDP.

Acknowledging the importance of climate change and energy security is the first necessary step towards the adoption of proper policies and measures to deal with the twin challenges. However, to translate these policies and measures into actions and produce immediate and desired results requires more than an acknowledgement of the problems or even of the right diagnoses of the problems. It requires that the government has the capacity to develop one set of consistent policies and to implement them accordingly. Such capacity first of all needs an institutional structure that can prescribe 'the rules of the game', provide both incentives and restrictions for economic players, and can facilitate cooperation amongst various energy sub-sectors, between the central and provincial government, and amongst enterprises and the public.

In China, as the World Bank (2009, p. 4) has concluded, 'institutional and policy failures are a major cause of these environmental and resource-use problems'. China is regarded as a centralised state, at least in theory, with a hierarchical relationship between the central, provincial, municipal and other levels of governments. The Chinese Communist Party dictates this 'party-controlled government' in whichever way it sees fit (Dumbaugh and Martin, 2009). In practice, however, the government has never enjoyed the perceived levels of unity. It is fragmented with ministries and agencies competing for influence and for expanding their turfs. The central government has far less influence on the provinces than one would expect – even in a country with a formally federalist division of power. Governments and their policies are challenged and contested by non-state players, particularly powerful large state-owned corporations. Crucially, there is no central voice on energy or climate change issues.

In both energy and environment policy making, it is difficult to see who is in the driver's seat – government agencies are competing for control within ministries and organisations of the central government. This represents the main obstacle blocking the central government's adoption of sound national policies. Indeed, for two decades, the Chinese central government unsuccessfully tried to create one central ministry in charge of all energy sectors. As it has been noted, '[u]nclear distribution of responsibilities and weak coordination amongst various government organisations is becoming an issue undermining the effective implementation' of policies designed to deal with both energy security and climate change threats (World Bank, 2009, p. 26).

Responsibility for energy policy making was distributed amongst more than 12 different government departments and bureaux. The establishment of the NDRC in 2003 intended to centralise responsibility for energy coordination. This control, however, was diluted across a wide spectrum of government bureaucracies: the State Council National Energy Leading Group (created in 2005), the Ministry of Finance, the Ministry of Land and Resources, the National Environmental Protection Administration (now the MEP), the Ministry of Water Resources, the State Administration of Coal Safety and the other NDRC departments in charge of pricing and investment. In addition, all major energy companies in China are state-owned, and thus placed under the supervision of the State-owned Assets Supervision and Administration Commission (SASAC). SASAC has wanted to consolidate energy firms and minimise their numbers, while the NDRC, for over a decade, planned to break up the energy companies' monopoly in the name of encouraging competition. As remarked by Cunningham (2008):

> The energy corporation initially served as a vehicle to resolve increasingly blurred rights and claims between central and local government control over energy assets, and also to attract foreign technology and financing to develop domestic resources under tight credit market conditions.

When those corporations were formed, the NDRC's energy bureaucracy lost much of its expertise to the companies and its influence in coordinating energy production.

Chaotic energy investment and energy production and the conflicts amongst several energy sub-sectors alarmed the government to such a degree that it repeatedly called for greater coordination and more centralised policy making. In March 2008, at the 11th National People's Congress, the State Council created two new energy policy-making organisations: the State Energy Commission – in replacement of the National Energy Leading Group, entitled with setting policy priorities, and the National Energy Administration (NEA). With a total staff of 112 employees, the NEA is a vice-ministerial organisation under the authority of the NDRC. Starting in July 2008, the NEA has been responsible for governing and planning the activities of the oil, gas, coal and power industries. In addition, it plays a role in proposing changes to energy prices and approving overseas energy investment projects. The creation of the NEA is a compromise between the NDRC – that did not want to give up control over the energy sectors – and the supporters of a mega-ministry of all energy sectors. Since the NEA is not a full ministry, it is unable to coordinate actions of all relevant government agencies. It also lacks human capital, authority and instruments to coordinate the actions of all state-owned energy corporations.

Energy-related environmental policy making has suffered similar institutional weakness and lack of capacity. In March 2008, the State Council upgraded the State Environmental Protection Administration into a full-ministerial agency, namely the MEP. This ministerial establishment represented a clear indication that environmental concerns have attracted serious interest within the central government. Nonetheless, compared to the US Environmental Protection Agency (EPA), the MEP has limited manpower of 2600 with only 300 employees working out of the headquarters in Beijing. In contrast, the US EPA has 17,000 employees with nearly 9000 working in Washington, DC. In dealing with large energy corporations and local governments, the MEP seems to be dwarfed by both; for them making profits and maximising local development are the first priority, and both have many more resources at hand in dealing with the MEP. Finally, MEP is not as heavy-weight a player in economic decision making as, for example, the NDRC or Ministry of Finance. The best example is that, frustrated by the spread of environmental pollution, the Chinese Minister for Environmental Protection was recently recorded criticising 'the lack of respect for the environment as the country carries out its economic stimulus plan'.

Moreover the government agencies in charge of macroeconomic performance, those interested in energy security and those responsible for climate change often send conflicting signals. The Ministry of Commerce wants to see continuing export growth, while the MEP and the NEA call for changing the export-oriented economic structure. Whereas the Ministry of Science and Technology would like to see the development of domestic low-carbon energy technologies, the MEP and the NEA push for adoption of the most advanced technologies, domestic and international. While the NEA would like to see China's energy companies invest overseas to ensure direct access to energy resources, the Ministry of Foreign Affairs issues cautions about the diplomatic impacts of Chinese investments in certain countries and regions. The policy gap between the central and provincial governments is even larger. In sum, as the World Bank (2009, p. 28) pointed out, it would be very difficult to adopt a set of coherent energy strategies and to implement a national approach towards energy security and climate change 'if different arms of government send conflicting signals'.

In addition to the fragmented government agencies, 'weak government capacity is reflected in lack of adequate policy research to assist the government in making sophisticated policies' (World Bank, 2009, p. 23). Without adequate research, policies and measures issued by the government could be quickly undermined by actions taken by enterprises that have accumulated substantial financial wealth. This can be seen in both solar and wind energy development. Less than 2–3 years after the government adopted policies to encourage renewable energy, both sectors suffered over-capacity as the result of over-investment and inadequate development in other facilities. For example, in 2008–2009, over 30 per cent of the wind generation capacity laid idle while solar photovoltaic (PV) panels went into overproduction. Even after the central government proposed a feed-in tariff for solar and announced that it would pay for up to 70 per cent of the cost of solar PV projects selected by provincial governments, solar PV panels were still primarily produced for exports. However, when European economies went through difficult times, their demands for Chinese solar PV experienced corresponding decline.

In contrast with fragmented government agencies, large state-owned enterprises enjoyed oligopolistic positions in their respected fields, obtained substantial financial wealth and had significant political influence in shaping the policies in their favour. They are modern corporations seeking to expand their profits by taking advantage of the market. Such enterprises, many of which are in monopolised or oligopolistic positions, can be real obstacles to green energy development as they seek to protect their existing interests.

In sum, current developments in Chinese energy security and environmental policy are neither all good nor all bad. The complete picture is so complex as to defy comprehension. For example, after a year of fieldwork a team from the Massachusetts Institute of Technology (Steinfeld et al., 2008, p. 31) concluded:

> Several changes – almost revolutions in some cases – are occurring simultaneously. New energy infrastructure is being added at a torrid rate. Fuel allocation is shifting rapidly toward a market footing, with prices responding accordingly, if chaotically. Myriad new transactions are taking place [...], often in the context of imperfect information and ambiguous product standards. Power plants, like mines, have increasingly come to be treated as commercial entities, autonomously pursuing and financing a range of long-term investment and day-to-day operational strategies. Meanwhile, as the central state has increasingly removed itself from direct control over production... it has become ever more focused on regulation, particularly in new areas like environmental management. As a result, all manner of new rules have been put into play, even as the state scrambles to build the capacity needed to ensure that those rules get enforced.

In China, environmental and climate issues have been incorporated in energy policies and development. Indeed, China has expanded its low-carbon energy sources significantly since 2003 and such sources are entirely developed in the name of ensuring adequate energy supplies and minimising environmental and climate change threats. Meanwhile, fundamental structural changes in its economy are difficult to come by because of (a) fragmented government agencies with competing agendas, (b) the government lacking the capacity to adopt coherent and consistent policies and to implement them accordingly, and (c) slow creation of an operational legal and regulatory system. Policy makers in China are struggling simply to figure out what is unfolding on the ground while looking for points of leverage to achieve their desired changes. Given that the two issues cover a wide range of economic and social implications, actions taken on one issue may or may not have positive results on the other. Addressing energy-related, environmental and climate change threats requires the political commitment of governments, wide participation of enterprises and the public and technological innovation. It has been a great challenge for leaders in Beijing to balance (1) long- and short-term development and (2) the diverse interests of urban and rural population, coastal and interior regions, and the elite and the masses.

References

Bordoff, J., P. Noel and M. Deshpande (2010), 'Understanding the interactions between energy security and climate change policy', in C. Pascual and J. Elkind (eds): *Energy Security: Economics, Politics, Strategies and Implications* (Washington, DC: The Brookings Institution Press).

British Petroleum (BP) (2010), 'BP statistical review or world energy', June 2010.

Chandler, W. and H. Gwin (2008), *Financing Energy Efficiency in China* (Washington, DC: Carnegie Endowment).

Cunningham, E.A. (2008), 'Testimony before the U.S.-China economic and security review commission' (Hearing on China's Energy Policies and Their Environmental Impacts, 13 August: http://www.uscc.gov/hearings/2008hearings/hr08_08_13.php; accessed: 01 November 2010).

Dumbaugh, K. and M.F. Martin (2009), *Understanding China's Political System* (Congressional Research Service, R41007, 31 December).

Eighth Senior Policy Advisory Council (2005), 'Tax and fiscal policies to promote clean energy technology development', Beijing, 19 November.

Global Wind Energy Council (GWEC) (2010), 'China wind power report' [http://www.gwec.net/uploads/media/wind-power-report.pdf; accessed: 26 October 2010].

International Atomic Energy Agency (IAEA) (2006), *Nuclear Power and Sustainable Development* (Vienna: IAEA).

IAEA (2009), *Climate Change and Nuclear Power* (Vienna: IAEA).

International Energy Agency (2007), *World Energy Outlook 2007: China and India Insights* (Paris: OECD).

IEA (2006), *China's Power Sector Reforms* (Paris: OECD).

IEA (2009), *World Energy Outlook 2009* (Paris: OECD).

IEA (2010a), *Key World Energy Statistics* (Paris: OECD).

IEA (2010b), *World Energy Outlook 2010* (Paris: OECD).

Lieberthal, K. (2009), *US-China Clean Energy Cooperation: The Road Ahead* (Washington, DC: The Brookings Institution Press).

Lin, J., N. Zhou, M.D. Levine and D. Fridley (2006), *Achieving China's Target for Energy Intensity Reduction in 2010* (Ernest Orlando Lawrence Berkeley National Laboratory, LBNL-61800, December).

NDRC (2004), *Mid- to Long-Term Energy Conservation Plan* (Beijing: NDRC).

Richerzhagen, C. and I. Scholtz (2008), 'China's capacities for mitigating climate change', *World Development*, 36(2): 308–24.

Rosen, D.H. and T. Houser (2007), *China Energy* (Washington, DC: Centre for Strategic and International Studies and Peterson Institute of International Economics).

Shealy, M. and J.P. Dorian (2010), 'Growing Chinese coal use: Dramatic resource and environmental implications', *Energy Policy*, 38(5): 2116–22.

Sinton, J.E. and D.G. Fridley (2000), 'What goes up: Recent trends in China's energy consumption', *Energy Policy*, 28(10): 671–87.

Sinton, J.E., M.D. Levine and Q.Y. Wang (1998), 'Energy efficiency in China: Accomplishments and challenges', *Energy Policy*, 26(11): 813–29.

State Council, (2007), *China's Energy Conditions and Policies* (Beijing: Information Office of the State Council of the People's Republic of China, December).

Steinfeld, E.S., R.K. Lester and E.A. Cunningham (2008), 'Greener plants, greyer skies: a report from the frontlines of China's energy' (MIT China Energy Group, August).

UNEP (2009), 'Global green new deal: an update for the G20 Pittsburgh Summit', September.

UNDP (2000), *World Energy Assessment: Energy and the Challenge of Sustainability* (New York: UNDP).

Weber, C.L., G.P. Peters, D. Guan and K. Hubacek (2008), 'The contribution of Chinese exports to climate change', *Energy Policy*, 36(9): 3572–7.

World Bank (1985), *China: Long-Term Development, Issues and Options* (Washington, DC: The World Bank).

World Bank (1989), *Energy Sector Management Assistance Program No.101/89* (Washington, DC: The World Bank).

World Bank (2005), 'Project appraisal document on a proposed loan for the first phase of the renewable energy scale-up program', *Report No. 30698-CN*, 19 May.

World Bank (2008a), *Economically, Socially and Environmentally Sustainable Coal Mining Sector in China* (Washington, DC: The World Bank).

World Bank (2008b), 'Mid-term evaluation of China's 11th five-year plan', *Report No. 46355-CN*, 18 December.

World Bank (2009), 'Developing a circular economy in China: Highlights and recommendations', World Bank technical assistance program, 48917, June.

World Bank (2010a), *Winds of Change: East Asia's Sustainable Energy Future* (Washington, DC: The World Bank).

World Bank (2010b), *World Development Report 2010: Development and Climate Change* (Washington, DC: The World Bank).

World Bank (2010c), 'World development indicators' [http://data.worldbank.org/; accessed: 26 November 2010].

Wu, L., S. Kaneko and S. Matsuoka (2005), 'Driving forces behind the stagnancy of China's energy-related CO emissions from 1996 to 1999', *Energy Policy*, 33(3): 319–35.

Xu, Y. (2002), *Powering China* (Dartmouth: Ashgate).

Xu, Y. (2010), *The Politics of Nuclear Energy in China* (Basingstoke: Palgrave Macmillan).

Zhou, N., M.D. Levine and L. Price (2010), 'Overview of current energy efficiency policies in China', *Energy Policy*, 38(11): 6439–52.

6

Energy Security and Climate Change Challenges: India's Dilemma and Policy Responses

Tulsi C. Bisht

Introduction

Development, energy security and climate change are closely linked issues. Since India gained independence in 1947, policy making has prioritised economic development with the aim of eradicating widespread poverty. This emphasis on economic growth and a long neglect of environmental issues have resulted in a polluted and degraded environment, in which deforestation, desertification, soil degradation, water and air pollution, growth of urban slums and unhygienic living conditions have featured prominently. Effects of climate change on various sectors will further compound these problems.

Economic development is directly linked to the availability of energy resources. In the Indian context, sustained availability of energy resources is vital to achieving economic growth leading to poverty alleviation. However, a sharp rise in energy demand, dwindling access to energy resources and enhanced competition for available reserves have the potential to threaten the current upward trends of economic growth. At the same time, unrestrained use of fossil fuels for energy generation could further degrade the environment.

To ensure energy security and environmentally sustainable development, India needs to take concrete measures. In recent years, government policy responses to energy security and climate change threats have taken a pragmatic turn. India's policy makers are realising the necessity of dealing with issues of economic development, energy security and environmental sustainability from a perspective that underlines the linkages between the three. This pragmatism is evident in two recent major policies – the 2006 Integrated Energy Policy (IEP) and the 2008 National Action Plan on Climate Change (NAPCC).

Although marking a significant shift, these policy frameworks still remain anchored in traditional economic growth paradigm. However, the two policies do unambiguously recognise the centrality of both energy security and climate change concerns to the pursuit of sustainable growth. This chapter argues that the IEP and the NAPCC have the potential to act as complementary policies to help India strike a balance between energy security and successful response to climate change challenges.

The chapter begins by offering a background of India's energy scenario and the way energy security has been re-conceptualised in recent years, marking a significant – though not paradigmatic – shift from the traditionally held approach. Analysis of the way global and local constraints play a role in reformulating and re-conceptualising the notion of energy security follows. The chapter further explores the issues of climate change and India's response to these threats, especially the emergent realisation that these concerns can no longer be relegated to secondary importance. The role of global and local factors in reshaping the country's policy response to climate change is outlined and analysed. Finally, the chapter draws linkages between the two policies, by arguing that there is room for convergence to achieve an energy secure and environmentally sustainable path of development.

A synchronised approach from the central and various state governments has been an important aspect of this policy discourse. During the meeting of the National Development Council on 9 December 2006, the Prime Minister of India, Manmohan Singh, impressed upon the Chief Ministers of all states the need to achieve developmental goals in a sustainable manner. He emphasised that although economic development remained the first priority at both central and state levels, it should not lead to 'negative externalities for humankind' and attempts should be made to make the country's economy less energy-intensive in the interest of energy security and environmental sustainability.

Analysing India's energy mix

As India inherited a stagnant and impoverished economy from the colonial era, economic development became a major challenge for post-independence policy makers. The Planning Commission – India's apex planned economic development body – identified raising the people's standard of living as the central objective of planning. Despite the rapid economic growth of recent years, a large section of India's population still lives below the poverty line. It is envisaged that to meet its development goals and to eradicate poverty, the country will require a sustained annual economic growth of 8–10 per cent for the next two decades. To achieve this growth rate, India will require its energy supply to grow by '3 to 4 times and electricity generation/capacity supply by 5 to 6 times of their 2003–2004 levels' (Planning Commission, 2006, p. xiii). A constant and secure supply of energy is, therefore, vital for India to achieve economic growth.

Traditionally, India has been heavily reliant on non-commercial fuels. In 1953–1954, non-commercial sources met 68 per cent of energy requirements (Monga and Sanctis, 1994). During the 1960s, the industrialisation process fuelled demand for energy. In the early 1970s, use of commercial energy overtook use of non-commercial energy, even though reliance on biomass remained high. Since the early 1900s, as a result of liberalisation, the Indian economy has gained momentum and the demand for energy has been rising. It is estimated that India's energy consumption will grow at an annual rate of 3.2 per cent until 2025 (EIA, 2006).

Energy requirements and consumption patterns in India have also changed drastically. Population growth, a rising middle class, increasing urbanisation and changing household and kinship patterns (Sudarshan and Noronha, 2009) have increased energy demand. India is the world's fifth largest consumer of energy, accounting for 3.7 per cent of total global consumption. However, India's per capita energy consumption remains amongst the lowest in the world. In 2003, per person consumption of primary energy was 439 kgoe, compared to the world average of 1688 kgoe (IEA, 2004). Under the business as usual scenario, the situation is not going to change much and, by 2030–2032, India's per capita energy consumption will equal that of China in 2005, while representing 16 per cent of 2005 US per capita consumption (Sethi, 2009). Moreover, a large section of the Indian population has no, or very little, access to commercial sources of energy and continues to rely upon bio-energy sources such as wood, cow dung and agricultural waste, raising the issue of internal equity of energy demand and consumption.

To meet its growing and diversified energy needs, India has adopted a complex energy mix. Coal, which accounts for about 53 per cent of primary commercial energy consumption, dominates India's energy mix. It is followed by oil, accounting for 31 per cent, natural gas at 8 per cent, hydroelectricity at 6 per cent and nuclear energy at 1 per cent (EIA, 2006). India lacks indigenous resources, with the exception of coal. If production continues to grow at the current rate (5 per cent per annum), India's coal reserves are expected to last for only the next 40 years (Planning Commission, 2006). Moreover, the quality of Indian coal is low and the country continues to rely on coal imports to meet growing demand.

Domestic oil and gas reserves are limited, making India heavily reliant on the import of these commodities. In 2006, 70 per cent of oil requirements were met through imports: this figure is likely to grow to 85 per cent by 2012 (EIA, 2006). Over-reliance on oil imports not only raises energy security concerns; it also imposes a heavy burden on the country's exchequer.

Natural gas is growing as an important source of energy. India's known reserves of natural gas are greater than its oil reserves (Monga and Sanctis,

1994). There has been a steady growth of this sector in recent years and natural gas consumption is expected to grow over 5 per cent per annum in coming years.

Hydroelectricity has vast potential, but only a small part of this potential source is currently used (Kashyap, 1990). Large multi-purpose hydroelectric projects not only have long gestation periods, but they also have adverse environmental and social implications, often resulting in environmental degradation and large-scale population displacement (Cernea, 1999).

Finally, India is in the process of developing its nuclear energy programme and has recently signed agreements with the United States and other partners on transfer of technologies and nuclear fuel. Non-conventional sources of energy play a very limited role in India's energy consumption. Solar, wind and other renewable sources remain untapped. Use of biomass continues to play an important role in meeting the energy requirements of a vast number of people.

Energy security and the IEP

India relies on a diverse mix of energy resources to meet an extremely varied demand structure. Such complexity makes it difficult to define energy security in the Indian context. The World Energy Assessment Report defines energy security as 'the continuous availability of energy in varied forms in sufficient quantities at reasonable prices' (Khatib, 1999, p. 112). This definition is driven by market principles of demand and supply and fails to take into account the complexities of energy requirements of a developing country like India. The definition also fails to clarify the term 'sufficient' (Sethi, 2009). In the Indian context – in which a significant part of the population does not have any access to commercial energy – what quantity of energy at what price would be treated as sufficient? Energy security – when related to the specific case of India – needs therefore to be assessed from a perspective that takes into account economic growth, energy equity, environmental and climate changes (Sudarshan and Noronha, 2009).

Economic growth has been one of India's major concerns in order to alleviate poverty and improve the living standards of large sections of the population. In the last two decades, India has witnessed rapid economic growth that has resulted in both rising living standards and sharp increases in energy demand. To maintain this momentum, the country needs an uninterrupted supply of various energy resources. India's dependence on imports to meet its energy requirements is only going to grow in coming decades. Uncertainty therefore surrounds the availability of energy resources and the Indian government will have to meet its requirements in a constantly competitive and constrained market. Energy supply could be interrupted by various factors which are largely beyond India's control. Factors such as geopolitics of global energy supplies, price volatility, political upheavals, stiff and rising competition for scarce energy resource bases and other security concerns can adversely impact energy supply and impede economic growth.[1] As a result of these economic concerns or 'traditional threats' (Sudarshan and Noronha, 2009), securing energy supply has gained significance and 'energy security' has become a buzzword in India's political and bureaucratic circles. These economic concerns about energy security are regularly expressed at both federal and state level.

In order to ensure an inclusive economic growth path, energy equity remains a critically important factor in conceptualising energy security. The linkage between energy availability and economic development is therefore a key dynamic in contemporary Indian politics. Poverty alleviation remains one of the main goals of India's emphasis on sustained economic growth: 30 per cent of India's population still lives in conditions of poverty (Planning Commission, 2006). Statistics concerning access to affordable, adequate and safe energy are even less promising. In spite of the steady rise in India's energy consumption, 86 per cent of rural and 20 per cent of urban residents still depend on biomass energy – and approximately two-thirds of India's population lives in rural areas (National Sample Survey of India, 1999; Urban et al., 2009). This widespread lack of access to clean energy not only perpetuates poverty; it also exacerbates health risks and educational deprivation, especially for women and young girls (ESMAP, 2004).[2] This widespread 'energy poverty' (Pachauri et al., 2004; Sudarshan and Noronha, 2009) has the potential to undermine India's economic progress. Excessive use of bio-fuels, at the same time, can adversely impact the environment. Hence, ensuring energy equity is a necessary prerequisite for energy security and environmental sustainability.

Finally, challenges related to climate change may also destabilise India's energy security. Climate change has two main implications for India's energy security. On the one hand, multi-sectoral impacts of climate change (IPCC, 2007) will adversely affect India's livelihood systems – specifically rural livelihood systems that are dependent on the environment to meet their energy requirements. On the other, various global regimes – including the climate change regime – could hinder India's access to energy resources. As the campaign for cleaner technologies gains momentum within global climate negotiations, India's heavy dependence on fossil fuels, especially the continued dependence on coal, could leave it vulnerable to increased energy costs. Other multilateral global regimes also have the potential to scuttle energy resource supplies. Australia, a major supplier of uranium for nuclear power plants, has refused uranium supply to India on the pretext that India is a non-signatory to the Nuclear Non-Proliferation Treaty (Dodd, 2008).

India therefore needs to take a broader perspective to achieve the future energy security on which inclusive and environmentally sustainable economic growth will depend. The IEP 2006 is one such step in this direction. The new policy's first positive contribution is to bring together diverse, sector-based energy policies under the ambit of one single policy that emphasises their inter-linkages.[3] The policy further underlines the key importance of energy equity to allow vulnerable households access to cleaner forms of energy. Emphasising the need to attain economic growth in an environmentally sustainable manner, the policy defines energy security as follows:

> We are energy secure when we can supply lifeline energy to all our citizens irrespective of their ability to pay for it as well as meet their effective demand for safe and convenient energy to satisfy their various needs at competitive prices, at all times and with a prescribed confidence level considering shocks and disruptions that can be reasonably expected. (Planning Commission, 2006: 54)

The IEP makes a wide range of proposals at macro and micro levels to achieve energy security. With its increased emphasis on risk prevention, reduction and response, the policy aims to ensure lifeline energy to all citizens at all times. It emphasises increasing energy efficiency, reducing import dependency, diversifying fuel choices, expanding the domestic energy resource base as well as enhancing India's ability to import energy and withstand supply shocks. Oil diplomacy to tap energy resources is seen as an important strategy and substantial investments are being made in various parts of the globe.

In recognition of the adverse environmental impacts of fossil fuel-based energy supply, the IEP does seem to emphasise the needs for (1) a growing use of renewable energy sources – including hydroelectric power; (2) reduction of carbon emissions through the Clean Development Mechanism (CDM) as proposed under the Kyoto Protocol; and (3) the introduction of a tax system on environmentally unsustainable use of energy. Recognising that coal is going to remain the mainstay of energy production, the policy calls for use of improved technologies in this area. The IEP, however, remains open to criticism for its mostly market- and growth-oriented approach with a gross national product (GNP)-maximising focus (Sharma, 2010), and for its continued emphasis on coal as the major source of energy (Badrinarayana, 2010). Policy responses to climate change, especially concerning carbon emissions, therefore remain constrained by the traditional approach of measuring emissions on a per capita basis.

Climate change and India

Natural environment plays a distinctive role in the life of a large section of the Indian population. It does not simply refer to the natural surroundings; rather it is closely integrated with the culture and livelihood patterns of the people and is directly related to the subsistence and survival of many.

Poor environmental health and climate change threats are, therefore, particularly detrimental to those who live close to the margins. The First Citizens' Report on the State of India's Environment (Agarwal et al., 1982) pointed out that the poor in the country do not always benefit from GNP growth and emphasised the necessity of creating a balance between environment and development.

Environmental issues have traditionally played a secondary role in India's policy formation. Although various Five Year Plans have frequently highlighted the notion of 'harmony with nature', in reality environmental issues have remained neglected. At the Stockholm United Nations (UN) Conference on Human Environment (1972), then Indian Prime Minister Indira Gandhi underlined that poverty was the worst polluter, indicating economic development and poverty alleviation as India's key priorities. The emergence of climate change as a global phenomenon has raised new challenges for India. The Fourth IPCC Assessment Report lists multi-sectoral impacts of climate change (IPCC, 2007). Some of the major sectors that will be adversely affected are coastal ecosystems, agriculture, water resources, natural habitat and biodiversity, human health and wellbeing including the possibility of large-scale displacement of communities (Rajan, 2008).

As it is rising to the rank of 'global polluters' and its traditional emphasis on measuring emissions on a per-capita basis is coming under increasing scrutiny, India faces mounting pressure to take more concrete measures when dealing with the threats of climate change. These measures are required not only to respond to impending climatic threats but also to deal effectively with the challenges faced within various multilateral climate negotiation processes. The recently announced NAPCC is one step in this direction, as it attempts to integrate environmental degradation and climate change issues with those of economic development, including energy security.

Evolution of India's climate change policy and the NAPCC

India's climate change policy has been constrained by both internal and global factors. Internally, India needs to negotiate climate change with priorities set within the contexts of development and poverty alleviation. However, India can no longer afford to neglect climate change issues on the pretext of development, as climate change will have a substantially adverse economic impact (Parikh et al., 2009). Globally, India needs to defend its position as an emerging 'polluter', while also taking responsibility for mitigation of climate change threats.

Although the Indian government has taken a number of initiatives to deal with environmental degradation and atmospheric pollution, its response to climate change has reflected 'traditional concerns about sovereignty, equity and the importance of economic development' (Rajan, 1997, p. 104). India holds industrially developed countries responsible for climatic changes and has attempted to rally support from other developing nations to establish a united front in various multilateral negotiations.

The notion of 'global equity' has been at the forefront of India's policy response within the global climate change regime. It has received a strong support from civil society organisations working in areas of environment and climate change (see Bisht, 2009). For example, in the 1980s, the Centre for Science and Environment (CSE) – a Delhi-based non-governmental organisation (NGO) and research think tank – published two citizens' reports that were scathing about the perilous state of India's environment. However, the CSE strongly opposed the propositions included in a World Resources Institute (WRI) report on the state of greenhouse gas emissions (GHGs). The report suggested that the emissions contributions of developing countries were almost equal to those of developed nations, indicating that developing countries – including India – ought to share part of the blame for global warming. In calculating national emissions, the report heavily emphasised emissions production on the basis of deforestation, rice fields and livestock while underplaying emissions resulting from burning of fossil fuels. Pointing to the WRI report's prejudiced methodologies, the CSE termed it as an example of 'environmental colonialism' (Agarwal and Narain , 1991). The CSE presented its own comparative data indicating that industrialised nations contributed to almost two-thirds of global GHG emissions. This stand was subsequently vindicated in later studies, which reported that developed nations contributed to almost 70 per cent of GHG emissions.

Indian policy makers adopted the CSE rhetoric to support their demand for an equitable response to climate change challenges (Rajan, 1997; Gupta, 2001). This was evident in India's initial response to the United Nations Framework Convention on Climate Change (UNFCCC). The Indian government welcomed the convention outcomes on the basis of the principle of 'differentiated responsibilities' (Rajan, 1997; Gupta, 2001) outlined in its Preamble and Article 3. India also sees the UNFCCC as a mechanism that could thwart the possibility of the Organization for Economic Co-operation and Development (OECD) nations imposing 'technological emission standards through the multilateral financial bodies' (Rajan, 1997, p. 151) such as the World Bank and International Monetary Fund (IMF) by linking emissions standards with financial assistance.

Three underlying reasons seem apparent in the Indian government's insistence on 'differentiated responsibilities' to reflect states' differing historical responsibility for anthropogenic climate change. First – from the 'stock' perspective – India argues that the accumulation of GHGs is a result of the industrialisation process in developed nations. As the data reveal, India's contribution of the cumulative CO_2 emissions between 1850 and 2000 has been 2 per cent, compared to a combined 57 per cent of the United States and the European Union (Baumert and Pershing, 2004). India therefore calls on developed nations to fulfil their 'historical responsibility' to mitigate emissions. Second – on the 'flow' perspective – India ranks fifth in the category of major polluters, contributing 5 per cent of total present-day global emissions. Its per capita emissions are below the world average – and much below the advanced western economies. As indicated by the GRID-Arendal (2002) figures, India's per capita CO_2 emissions in 2002 were 1.1 tonnes compared to 20 tonnes in the United States. Third, the Indian government sees that developed nations' reluctance to unconditionally transfer green technologies and funds will ultimately result in dependency relationships that will undermine the sovereignty of developing countries like India.

India's cautious approach to multilateral negotiations was evident in its response to the Kyoto Protocol. The protocols' implementation of the norm of 'common but differentiated responsibilities' via targets that were only applicable to developed countries was a sufficient concession to allow India's ratification of the Protocol in 2002. Moreover, the Protocol did not require India to make any voluntary commitment towards future emissions reduction and was seen as opening opportunities to benefit from the transfer of technology and additional foreign investments in areas of renewable energy and afforestation through the protocol's Clean Development Mechanism.

The Indian government approached the UNFCCC Copenhagen Conference (2009) cognisant of the impending pressure – coming from developed countries in general and the United States in particular – to commit to binding emissions limits. Responses to such pressures were discussed during pre-conference deliberations that India held with the other BASIC countries – Brazil, South Africa and China. Following China's commitment to cut CO_2 emissions per gross domestic product (GDP) unit by 40–45 per cent below 2005 levels by 2020, India announced a goal of reducing CO_2 emissions per GDP unit by 20–25 per cent of 2005 levels by 2020. Like China, India insisted that these limits should be voluntary rather than legally binding. The outcomes of the UNFCCC Copenhagen Conference remain debatable. Shyam Saran, the Prime Minister's Special Envoy on Climate Change, described it as 'more a statement of intent rather than a charter of action. It fails to address, in a comprehensive manner, the agenda set forth by the Bali Action Plan' (Saran, 2010). Outlining the significance of the Conference for India, Saran (2010) pointed out that:

> For us, most importantly, the conference decided, by consensus, to continue multilateral negotiations on both the Bali track as well as the Kyoto Protocol track with no change in their mandates. This means that the UNFCCC continues to be the basis for negotiations... we can take satisfaction from the fact that we have successfully forestalled the relentless effort on the part of certain developed countries to renegotiate the UNFCCC and to abandon the Kyoto Protocol. Despite enormous pressure generated

> by developed countries, particularly the U.S., we managed to uphold the clear distinction between the responsibilities of the developed countries, on the one hand and developing countries, on the other. We were able to obtain a categorical reaffirmation of the important principle of 'common but differentiated responsibilities and respective capabilities.' There is also an unambiguous endorsement of the right to development of developing countries, including the recognition that our developmental goals and poverty eradication are first and overriding priorities.

Within the global climate change regime, India has so far been able to successfully negotiate its traditional position of measuring emissions on per capita basis while stressing the need for differentiated responsibilities.[4] However, growing climate change threats and India's ability to effectively deal with these threats are becoming a cause of concern. These concerns are also being linked to the country's energy security (Pachauri, 1998). Furthermore, cracks are emerging in India's armour of 'equity', based on per capita emissions. A recent report by Greenpeace (2007) has raised the issue of India's internal climate injustice: a relatively small wealthy class is responsible for very high emissions which are masked in the per capita average by the very low emissions of the poor.

Various internal and external constraints compelled the Indian government to make substantial changes to its climate change policy. The NAPCC released in June 2008 is one such effort that is being promoted as a 'directional shift in the development pathway (Government of India, 2008)' that does not compromise the country's economic growth. It visualises 'sustainable and inclusive development' with the use of 'appropriate technologies' to address rising concerns about economic growth and climate change. The Action Plan will be implemented under eight National Missions to achieve the goals of climate change adaptation. These eight missions are as follows:

1) National Solar Mission – promoting development and use of solar energy for power generation;
2) National Mission for Enhanced Energy Efficiency;
3) National Mission on Sustainable Habitat – promoting energy efficiency as a core component of urban planning;
4) National Water Mission– for improvements in water use efficiency;
5) National Mission for Sustaining the Himalayan Ecosystem;
6) National Mission for a 'Green India' – aiming at afforestation of degraded forest lands and expanding forest cover;
7) National Mission for Sustainable Agriculture;
8) National Mission on Strategic Knowledge for Climate Change.

The NAPCC is the first systematic attempt to build a comprehensive policy road map to deal with the challenges of climate change. It is, at the same time, an acknowledgement of the significance of climate concerns by Indian policy makers. However, the plan continues to prioritise economic and developmental concerns over climate change concerns, while endorsing India's support for 'differentiated responsibility' it remains silent on the issue of domestic mitigation. The one undertaking made by the NAPCC is that India's per capita emissions will at no point surpass those of developed counties. These considerations led some critics to highlight the plan's unsustainability (e.g. Thakkar, 2009). In spite of a number of drawbacks, the plan should be read in the light of its attempt to address the problems faced by the sectors that are most vulnerable to the impact of climate change. Its significance for the energy sector, as outlined in the following section, is especially noteworthy.

IEP and NAPCC – A space for convergence

There is a close relationship between India's need for economic development, the country's energy security and its ability to deal with the challenges of climate change. India's responses to both energy security and climate change are furthermore constrained by internal and external factors. In order to realise its development goals, the Indian government needs to take measured steps and the two policies described above – IEP and NAPCC – need to play complementary roles.

The IEP is a comprehensive document. In keeping with the view that India needs a sustained high growth of over 9 per cent per annum for the next 25 years, the policy outlines an energy mix facilitating the attainment of these goals without threatening the environmental and climatic balances. Examining the existing energy scenario in detail the IEP seeks an integrated approach to various energy sectors that have hitherto been functioning either independently or without any communication. The policy also seeks to provide an institutional mechanism that brings various energy sectors within one single ministry. Treating energy as a 'lifeline' for economic development, the IEP seeks to achieve energy security through various measures, including power sector reforms, reducing cost of power, rationalising fuel prices, augmenting resources, enhancing hydro and nuclear power contributions and developing renewable energy. The policy takes into account the fact that severe energy poverty is affecting the wider Indian population and that, without widespread household energy security, the country can neither develop the national economy nor alleviate poverty. Under the Rural Electrification Scheme, the IEP prescribes completion of household and village electrification in a five-year timeframe with special preference to Dalit, tribal and other weaker sections of the society. Towards this end, the policy envisages providing capital subsidies to the different states. Climate change concerns also feature prominently in the policy document that endorses maintenance of environmental balance. The policy, therefore, envisages a future growth that is equitable, resource efficient and environmentally sustainable.

The NAPCC is not exclusively directed at the challenges of climate change; it also has the potential to play a complementary role in meeting India's energy security goals. The policy plan highlights the necessity of developing renewable energy sources and diversifying the existing energy mix, granting great importance to solar power generation – India envisages installing up to 20 GW of solar power capacity by 2022. The National Solar Mission forecasts increased use of solar photovoltaic in urban areas and commercial and industrial establishments and aims to achieve parity with coal-based thermal power by 2030. Substantial sums of money are being invested in this programme, which aims to establish India as a global leader in solar power generation.

The policy emphasis on enhancing energy efficiency is expected to result in substantial energy savings. Targeting industry – a primary consumer of energy and emitter of CO_2 – the plan emphasises enhancing energy efficiency by introducing various measures including fiscal incentives. Two key components of the plan – the 'Mission for sustaining the Himalayan Ecosystem' and the 'Mission for a Green India' – could play complementary roles in dealing with the issues of climate change and in strengthening energy security by meeting the biomass energy requirements of the household energy sector.

Although there are some drawbacks in both policies and economic development still remains their main focus, the IEP and NAPCC mark a defined shift away from the traditional viewpoint that more or less neglected environmental and climatic concerns. Both policies underline the linkage between development, energy security and climate change and create the potential for convergence between the two policies.

Conclusions

The world remains heavily dependent on carbon-based energy systems. Globally, per capita carbon emissions are roughly proportionate with each state's level of economic development. Given the present state of technology it is not yet feasible to completely delink economic development from carbon emissions. In particular, India is expected, in the next few decades, to be heavily reliant on fossil fuels, including coal. The challenges that India faces are how to limit carbon emissions without compromising economic growth for the betterment of masses. The rationale for interlinking energy, environment and development policies has therefore become more compelling than ever.

In the Indian context, issues of energy security, climate change and economic development are closely interlinked. As economic development is necessary for poverty alleviation, the cumulative impact of growing energy consumption along with a growing population can threaten energy security and the ecosystem. India has long kept these domains separate. In the present scenario, this separation has become increasingly unsustainable. Indian stakeholders have finally realised that an integrated approach is required to tackle the issues of development, energy security and climate change. The two policies, IEP and NAPCC are amongst the most prominent indicators of these efforts.

Notes

1. The Iran–Pakistan–India gas pipeline is one example of the ways in which geopolitical and security concerns can be detrimental to India's efforts to gain access to energy resources. The pipeline negotiations have come under pressure from the United States, which seeks to isolate Iran globally. The pipeline has also been subject to security concerns as it passes through the volatile areas of western Pakistan. The tense relationship between India and Pakistan is also a stumbling block for the conclusion of an agreement. Finally, there has been growing concern about the pricing of natural gas by Iran. All these factors together have thus almost throttled the implementation of the pipeline project.
2. A UNDP Report (2004) illustrates various adverse impacts of clean energy deprivation on women's life in rural India including health, education, economic independence and leisure time.
3. India currently has five separate ministries – Coal; Petroleum and Natural Gas; Atomic Energy; Power; and Non-conventional Energy sources. Each ministry develops its own policy with little synergy with the policies of other sectors of energy.
4. The first such official measurement was undertaken as a part of India's initial national communication to the UNFCCC in 2004 (Ministry of Environment and Forests, 2004).

References

Agarwal, A., R. Chopra and K. Sharma (1982), *The State of India's Environment: The First Citizen's Report 1982* (Delhi: Centre for Science and Environment).

Agarwal, A. and S. Narain (1991), *Global Warming in an Unequal World: A Case for Environmental Colonialism* (Delhi: Centre for Science and Environment).

Badrinarayana, D. (2010), 'India's integrated energy policy: A source of economic nirvana or environmental disaster?', *Environmental Law Reporter*, 40 (10708) (Washington, DC: Environmental Law Institute).

Baumert, K and J. Pershing (2004), *Climate Data: Insights and Observation* (Working paper prepared for the Pew Center on Global Climate Change; http://www.pewclimate.org/docUploads/Climate%20Data%20new.pdf; accessed: 04 November 2010).

Bisht, T.C. (2009), 'Climate change and India's response', *Asian Currents*, 62 [http://asaa.asn.au/publications/ac/2009/asian-currents-09-11.html; accessed: 04 November 2010].

Cernea, M. (1999), 'Development's painful social costs', in S. Parasuraman (ed.): *The Development Dilemma: Displacement in India* (The Hague: Institute of Social Studies).

Dodd, M. (2008), 'No uranium sales until India signs NPT', *The Australian*, 16 January [http://www.theaustralian.com.au/business/mining-energy/no-uranium-sales-until-india-signs-npt/story-e6frg9df-1111115327126; accessed: 09 November 2010].
ESMAP (2004), *The Impact of Energy on Women's Lives in Rural India* (Washington, DC: The World Bank).
EIA (Energy Information Administration) (2006), *Country Analysis Briefs India* [http://www.eia.doe.gov/emeu/cabs/India/Background.html; accessed: 10 June 2010].
Government of India (2008) *National Action Plan on Climate Change* [http://pmindia.nic.in/Pg01-52.pdf; accessed: 18 August 2010].
Greenpeace (2007), *Hiding Behind the Poor: A Report by Greenpeace on Climate Injustice* [http://www.greenpeace.org/india/fungames/animations/india-hiding-behind-the-poor; accessed: 06 June 2010].
GRID-Arendal, 2002, *National Carbon Dioxide (CO_2) Emissions Per Capita* [http://maps.grida.no/go/graphic/national_carbon_dioxide_co2_emissions_per_capita; accessed: 25 September 2009].
Gupta, J. (2001), 'India and climate change policy: between diplomatic defensiveness and industrial transformation', *Energy and Environment*, 12(2–3): 217–36.
International Energy Agency (IEA) (2004), *World energy outlook 2004* [http://www.worldenergyoutlook.org/2004.asp; accessed: 04 November 2010].
Intergovernmental Panel on Climate Change (IPCC) (2007), *Climate Change 2007: Synthesis Report* [http://www.ipcc.ch/publications_and_data/ar4/syr/en/contents.html; accessed: 04 November 2010].
Kashyap, S.C. (1990), 'National energy policy', in S.C. Kashyap (ed.): *National Policy Studies* (Delhi: Tata McGraw-Hill).
Khatib, H. (1999), 'Energy security' in: *World Energy Assessment: Energy and the Challenges of Sustainability* (New York: UNDP).
Ministry of Environment and Forests, Government of India (2004), *India's Initial National Communication to the United Nations Framework Convention on Climate Change* [http://unfccc.int/resource/docs/natc/indnc1.pdf; accessed: 09 June 2010].
Monga, G.S and V.J. Sanctis (1994), *India's Energy Prospects* (Delhi: Vikas).
Pachauri, R.K. (1998), 'Global climate change: science and sustainable policies', *Environmental and Development Economics*, 3: 381–4.
Pachauri, S., A. Mueller, A. Kemmler and D. Spreng (2004), 'On measuring energy poverty in Indian households', *World Development*, 32(12): 2083–104.
Parikh, K.S., V. Karandikar, A. Rana and P. Dani (2009), 'Projecting India's energy requirements for policy formulation', *Energy*, 34(8): 1–14.
Planning Commission (2006), *Integrated Energy Policy: Report of the Expert Committee* [http://planningcommission.nic.in/reports/genrep/rep_intengy.pdf; accessed: 04 November 2010].
Rajan, M.G. (1997), *Global Environmental Politics: India and the North-South Politics of Global Environmental Issues* (Delhi: Oxford University Press).
Rajan, S.C. (2008), *Climate Migrants in South Asia: Estimates and Solutions* (Bangalore: Greenpeace India).
Saran, S. (2010), 'India at Copenhagen', *Seminar*, 606 [http://www.india-seminar.com/semsearch.htm; accessed: 04 November 2010].
Sharma, S. (2010), *Shadow Integrated Energy Policy* [National Alliance for Movement against Coal; http://www.scribd.com/doc/35913056/2010-August-Shadow-IEP-Revised-Draft-by-Shankar-Sharma; accessed: 02 September 2010].
Sethi, S. (2009), 'India's energy challenges and choices', in L. Noronha and A. Sudarshan (eds): *India's Energy Security* (London-New York: Routledge).

Sudarshan, A. and L. Noronha (2009), 'Contextualizing India's energy security', in L. Noronha and A. Sudarshan (eds): *India's Energy Security* (London-New York: Routledge).

Thakkar, H. (2009), *There Is a Little Hope Here* (Delhi: South Asia Network on Dams, Rivers and People).

Urban, F., R.M.J. Benders and H.C. Moll (2009), 'Energy for rural India', *Applied Energy*, 86(supplement): S47–S57.

7
Conflicting Policies: Energy Security and Climate Change Policies in Japan

Akihiro Sawa

Introduction

On 11 March 2011, the Fukushima Daiichi nuclear power plant was struck by one of the largest earthquakes and tsunamis in history. The tsunami washed away the emergency power supply systems of four reactors at the plant, impairing thereby their cooling functions. Consequently, the fuel rods were damaged and a significant amount of radioactive material was discharged into the surrounding area. The Fukushima plant had supplied electricity to Japan's capital, Tokyo, where scheduled blackouts have been imposed after the plant ceased operation. Faced with suspended lifeline networks owing to energy supply disruptions for the first time in the 30 years since the second oil shock, the Japanese people have re-awakened to the importance of energy security.

Nuclear power had been counted upon as the main player in realising a low carbon-oriented society given its advantage over other energy sources in terms of energy security underpinned by abundant uranium reserves located in politically stable regions, and its climate friendliness. However, this serious accident will inevitably hinder the future development of nuclear power. Future energy policy might be reviewed based on the three following options:

1) Renewable energy will play a central role, but will require acceptance of rigid demand management based on lower standards of economic activity and livelihood provoked by the absolute shortage of power and high costs.
2) Despite projections of the carbon dioxide emission increases entailed, a priority should be set on restoring the economy and daily life through the intensive use of thermal power generation fired with coal or liquefied natural gas (LNG), which promise increased supply in the short term and which can be more stably supplied compared with oil, thus better serving energy security purposes.

3) Once the recent accident has been resolved, the causes of the accident should be analysed for the preparation of renewed nuclear power development plans featuring higher safety standards.

As I update the introduction to this chapter (in early April 2011), the situation in Fukushima remains unstable and no clear direction has been provided for either an energy policy review or for associated climate change policy. In the following paragraphs which were written prior to the Fukushima incident, I will reflect upon how Japan struggled to balance energy security and climate change policy before it approached its turning point on 11 March.

Japan's level of energy self-sufficiency has traditionally been low. With limited fossil fuels, mineral resources and land, Japan relies on imports for the greater half of the resources required to support its national economy and the livelihood of its citizens. Japan's reliance on imported petroleum in the post-Second World War era left it highly vulnerable to the 1973 oil crisis and the Organization of the Petroleum Exporting Countries (OPEC) trade embargo. Rather than creating a real physical oil shortage, these events primarily caused a sharp rise in oil prices, growing public fear and a sense of impending doom *vis-à-vis* major disruptions of energy imports. As petroleum accounted for approximately 70 per cent of Japan's power generation at the time, the Japanese public panicked that their lifeline system – electricity – might be cut off through loss of access to petroleum imports. The widespread sense of crisis that took root amongst the Japanese public ensured that energy security policy became a key priority for Japan.

After the second oil crisis in 1978, Japan sought to lower its oil dependency (approximately 77 per cent in 1973) and to decrease its dependency on energy supplies from politically unstable regions, such as the Middle East. These ends were achieved through an energy security policy framework that involved enhanced national contingency measures (including stockpiling oil) and the numerous mid- and long-term policies that will be described in this chapter. Although the weighting given to different policy components has shifted with changing circumstances, when it comes to energy security, Japan's policy direction has remained essentially unchanged.

Demand

In order to maintain a balance with economic growth, rather than curbing total energy demand, there is a need to introduce energy conservation and efficiency measures to improve energy consumption intensity. All economic entities in all sectors, including the industrial, residential and transport sectors, should engage in energy-saving actions, while at the same time, the government provides policy support for the introduction of products and production methods with improved energy intensity, as well as investments in technological research and development for higher energy efficiency.

Supply

Promoting strategies for a petroleum-free energy-mix

In the wake of the oil shocks, nuclear power was widely viewed as the alternative energy source that was most likely to replace petroleum. However, nuclear power generation was always bound to trigger political debate in Japan, on the basis of the public intolerance of nuclear energy which was deeply rooted in Japan's unique experience of atomic warfare, and the anti-nuclear campaigns launched by left-wing and Communist-influenced political forces during the Cold War. The shock of two oil crises left the Japanese public in fear of blackouts and increased public acceptance of the need for nuclear power. Consequently, nuclear power – which, in 1973, had only sourced 2 per cent of the electricity generated in Japan – accounted for almost 30 per cent by 1995, and continued to hold a share of 23 per cent in 2008 (IEEJ, 2010).

In terms of fossil fuels, fuel conversion from petroleum to LNG was generally encouraged and, on the basis of the provisions contained in the decisions made at the third board meeting of the International Energy Agency (IEA) (May 1975), the installation of new oil-fired units in Japan was prohibited. As a result, the share of petroleum-based power generated by Japan's major power companies dropped drastically from approximately 75 per cent in 1973 to less than 10 per cent in 1998.

Diversifying energy import sources and promoting independent development of natural resources

Geographical proximity has meant that Japan has traditionally been reliant on Middle Eastern countries for crude oil; its oil supply has therefore been vulnerable to political instability. In order to overcome such circumstances, the Japanese government has taken measures to diversify its crude oil import sources by increasing imports from Southeast Asian countries and also to diversify its fuel source from oil to coal and LNG, the reserves of which are geographically less concentrated. However, in the 1990s, as the international oil market developed and oil prices stabilised, oil imports from Southeast Asian countries decreased, enhancing yet again Japan's dependency on the Middle East. With increasingly larger imports of coal from Australia, Japan's dependency on the Middle East for fossil fuel resources has resumed a downward trend, but still stood at 47 per cent in 2008 – a significant dependency level, especially if compared to those experienced by the United States (18 per cent) and France (13 per cent) (IEA, 2010).

In 1967, the Agency for Natural Resources and Energy under the Ministry of Economy, Trade and Industry and its advisory council, the Advisory Committee on Energy and Natural Resources, submitted their first report, which, amongst other things, outlined the first Long-term Energy Supply and Demand Outlook (Agency for Natural Resources and Energy, 1967). The report based Japan's energy supply policy on low-cost oil imports and pointed out that stabilising its oil supply was a top governmental priority. After the two oil crises, the third Long-term Energy Supply and Demand Outlook (1975) and succeeding Outlooks emphasised the need to introduce and promote nuclear power and alternative energy sources and called for energy conservation and efficiency measures. Nevertheless, the successive Outlook's energy supply and demand forecasts, which were intended to serve as quantitative targets, did not diverge significantly from the business as usual scenario (RIST, 2010).

Against the backdrop of global developments directed towards the United Nations Framework Convention on Climate Change (UNFCCC), the 1990 Outlook introduced the government's concept that global environmental issues needed to be addressed, consequently giving the Long-term Energy Supply and Demand Outlook the additional role of presenting a non-binding target for Japan's long-term energy policy (Agency for Natural Resources and Energy, 1990). In light of the expansion of policy goals to be covered in energy policy, the Basic Act on Energy Policy was adopted in 2002. This law identified energy policy as a fundamental national priority and required the implementation of energy-related measures addressing both supply and demand dimensions in response to circumstantial changes (Basic Act on Energy Policy, 2002).

Three key principles of energy policy – securing stable supply; environmental adaptation; and utilising market principles – were stipulated in the law and became underpinning elements of the Basic Energy Plan. The current Energy Basic Plan (METI, 2010), adopted by the Japanese Cabinet on 18 June 2010, exemplifies the focal points of recent energy policy debate, which are summarised in the following three points.

First, an increasingly serious problem of resource scarcity jeopardises the secure and stable supply of energy and resources in Japan. World energy demand continues to follow a surging trend, especially in Asia, intensifying competition over resource-related interests. On the other hand, producer nations are confronted with geopolitical risks, and are therefore driven towards resource nationalism. Consequently, energy prices continue to be highly volatile and are predicted to rise in the mid- and long-term. Furthermore, with continuing risks from terrorism and earthquakes, demand for 'security' in terms of energy transport and supply as well as nuclear power has risen. Energy security in its traditional sense will continue to constitute the primary axis of Japan's energy policy.

Second, there are stronger pressures to address global climate change issues more robustly and comprehensively through energy policy. The First Commitment Period of the Kyoto Protocol began in 2008, after the G8 Hokkaido Toyako Summit. At this summit meeting, it was agreed that global greenhouse gas (GHG) emissions would be mitigated by a minimum of 50 per cent by the year 2050 (MOFA, 2010a). At the ensuing G8 Summit meeting held in L'Aquila in 2009, this target was reconfirmed and taken further: by 2050, developed countries would collectively reduce emissions by at least 80 per cent from 1990 or more recent years (G8, 2010). At the UNFCCC Copenhagen Conference (December 2009), Japan pledged a '25 per cent reduction, [from 1990 levels,] which is premised on the establishment of a fair and effective international framework in which all major economies participate and on agreement by those economies on ambitious targets' (Embassy of Japan, 2010). Japan registered the same target in the Copenhagen Accord, which although not formally adopted was the key outcome of that meeting. Considering that approximately 90 per cent of Japan's GHG emissions are generated by energy production, energy policy must play a relatively large role in emissions reduction, especially if we compare the Japanese case with the European Union and the United States, where methane and other GHGs continue to represent a comparatively large share of total emissions.

A third key characteristic of Japan's energy policy is that the energy and environmental sectors are looked on as the drivers of economic growth. After the Lehman Shock in 2008 and the ensuing global economic downturn, the world economy has been faced with one of the worst depressions in history and many countries are confronted with the challenge of re-establishing industrial structure and growth strategies. Many countries are now focusing their national strategies on development of new markets and creation of new employment through developing and deploying energy- and environment-related technologies and products. There is already fierce competition over global market shares in the areas of nuclear energy, smart grid technologies and energy-saving technologies, with the active engagement of government. In Japan, the New Growth Strategy (Basic Policies) – approved in a Cabinet meeting in December 2009 – laid out a set of industrial policies that draw on Japan's advantage in these areas (Prime Minister of Japan and His Cabinet, 2010a).

Discrepancies between energy security and climate change policies

The following sections discuss the different impacts that the incorporation of climate change issues into the governmental agenda has had on Japan's energy security measures. I argue here that energy security and climate change can share the same policy direction in many dimensions. For example, from the perspectives of both coping with climate change and enhancing energy security, the following are commonly suitable measures:

a) Proactive deployment of nuclear power plants;
b) Promotion of energy conservation and efficiency;

c) Increased supply of renewable energy for the purposes of reducing Japan's dependency on imported energy resources and decreasing the impact that oil imports from politically unstable areas might have on Japan's energy balance.

Two main factors contributed to the considerable amount of friction that has emerged between Japan's environmental and energy policies. Firstly, the reduction target that Japan has pledged in international climate change negotiations is too strict in relation to Japan's realistic domestic reduction potential. Japan's commitment under the current Kyoto Protocol to reduce emissions by 6 per cent compared to 1990 levels is domestically understood to be an impractical compromise, which was made in the Kyoto negotiations under the pressure of Japan's host country responsibilities. Japan's original stance was to resume 1990 levels, or if necessary to compromise by accepting emissions reductions of up to 2.5 per cent. Approximately 90 per cent of total GHG emissions in Japan represent CO_2 emissions of energy origin. In the Japanese case, mitigating GHG emissions has therefore had more of a direct impact on economic activities than it would in a country where methane accounts for the larger ratio of emissions. As a consequence, the promised 6 per cent reductions cannot be imposed upon the industrial or household sectors, as additional reductions have to be achieved domestically through further constraints on energy consumption. For this reason, the Kyoto Protocol Target Achievement Plan assumes that 1.6 per cent of reductions can be achieved by purchasing emissions rights from overseas.

Furthermore, after the Democratic Party of Japan (DPJ) seized power, then Prime Minister Hatoyama Yukio announced in September 2009 that Japan would reduce emissions by 25 per cent from 1990 levels by 2020 (MOFA, 2010b). As the former Liberal Democratic Party (LDP) government had based its policy on 15 per cent reductions compared to 2005 levels in 2020 (or, reductions by 8 per cent from 1990 levels) (Prime Minister of Japan and His Cabinet, 2010b), the DPJ's policy demanded a significant leap in reduction requirements. Later, under the Copenhagen Accord, the government registered the new target announced in the Hatoyama Initiative with the UNFCCC as Japan's mid-term target, conditional on the establishment of a fair and effective international framework and agreement setting ambitious targets amongst all major economies (UNFCCC, 2010). There is an ongoing heated debate between the Ministry of Economy, Trade and Industry (METI) and the Ministry of the Environment regarding Japan's technological potential to achieve the mid-term target and the costs incurred. METI, on behalf of Japan's industrial sector, contends that the aforementioned precondition must be strictly met as similarly large reductions cannot be achieved at a reasonable cost in Japan, which is the world's leader in energy conservation and efficiency. On the other hand, the Ministry of

Environment, with the ultimate view to take climate change measures forward, has announced a draft roadmap towards the achievement of this goal (MOE, 2010).

The other factor contributing to the emergence of friction between Japan's environmental and energy policies relates to the nature of the country's environmental activism. Many green activists come from factions that campaigned in opposition to the introduction of nuclear power plants in Japan and still firmly oppose nuclear power, which would enable Japan to pursue both climate change and energy security goals. At the same time, Japan's nuclear power supporters are represented by conservatives, including politicians from the LDP, electric companies and other industries. Consequently, any discussion of promoting nuclear power as a policy means for solving environmental issues while simultaneously achieving economic growth is likely to develop into ideological controversy, hence obstructing progress.

Renewable energies – such as wind and solar power – remain the preferred energy options of Japanese green activists. Nevertheless, these energy sources still lack the capacity required to meet Japan's growing demand. However, considering the domestic resistance against nuclear power plants, the Japanese government has been unsuccessful in increasing nuclear capacity, and has instead relied on expanding LNG and coal-fired power generation. Increased dependence on fossil fuels would, needless to say, generate larger amounts of GHG emissions. Nevertheless, in order to maintain a stable power supply – a crucial element of energy security – government decision makers and electric companies could not have avoided such choices.

As a result of their strenuous efforts to ensure energy security after the oil crises, the Japanese public has ironically become impervious to energy security risks. Although price fluctuations can still impose a threat, the wider public is no longer overcome by the fear that electricity and other energy supplies might suddenly be suspended. Environment, economy and energy are closely intertwined and cannot be individually dealt with in policy making. Remarkably though, Japanese public opinion does not seem to share this conclusion. Consequently, nuclear power and coal-fired power generation have failed to win wide public support and, moreover, they are considered to be 'environment-unfriendly'. Therefore, it has been a frustrating time for LDP politicians, energy-related bureaucrats and electricity companies who have long been the target of public criticism but still take pride in having successfully maintained Japan's energy security.

The advantages of nuclear power and coal in energy security

In 2001, the Energy Security Working Group under the Advisory Committee on Energy and Natural Resources submitted a major report to the METI's Agency for Natural Resources and Energy (METI, 2001). This report was designed to analyse the contribution made by different energy sources towards Japan's energy security. Ten years after the announcement, the report's fundamentals have retained much of their relevance. The report concluded that:

1) If environmental constraints were to be ignored, shifting from oil to nuclear power and coal – and increasing their share in Japan's energy mix – would most effectively serve to mitigate mid- and long-term energy supply risks;
2) Even in the event that environmental constraints would stand in the way of a substantial shift to coal, supply risks could be lowered by further increasing nuclear power or converting to natural gas.

The emergence of an international (and globalised) oil market strengthened the prevalent belief that oil was on the verge of becoming a procurable market commodity. Nevertheless, the METI report did not depart from the conservative approach according to which oil was viewed as a politically strategic product and, in this sense, advocated for the energy security strategy outlined above. Today, with China and other emerging economies obviously rushing to strategically enclose the resources required for their own economic development, this report's conclusions have become even more relevant.

It is worth noting that Japan has a relatively long history of using natural gas, which is imported as LNG and utilised in power generation and gas supply. From a security perspective, natural gas represents a favourable energy source, as it can be procured from neighbouring regions and its import is widely based on long-term contracts. Furthermore, its carbon emissions coefficient is approximately half that of coal, thereby giving it an environmental advantage in the climate change context. These characteristics have served as grounds for the Japanese government to promote the wider use of natural gas as an important agenda. Nevertheless, natural gas appears to involve higher security risks than coal, as it is largely imported from developing countries and the Middle East. Also, given the decline of major gas fields nuclear power and coal seem likely to occupy increasing shares in Japan's future energy security.

Nuclear power

A technical feature of nuclear power is that the fuel's energy density is higher than that of other energy sources, facilitating in turn stockpiling. Uranium, the fuel source, is widely located in politically relatively stable countries and regions, such as Canada and Australia, thus promising a stable supply. Japan has secured mainly long-term contracts for natural uranium with a number of countries in order to diversify import sources (Agency for Natural Resources and Energy, 2010b). This represents an advantage over oil and renewable energies, which can be procured domestically but for which the issue of energy fluctuations – resulting from dependence on natural conditions – cannot be ignored.

Although part of Japan's uranium is enriched at the Rokkasho Enrichment Plant (north-eastern Japan) and then used as fuel in nuclear power plants, most of Japan's imported uranium is enriched in the United States or Europe prior to its import (Agency for Natural Resources and Energy, 2010b). As a global oversupply of uranium enrichment services is projected to continue in the immediate future, supply risks for Japan are expected to diminish. In terms of costs, given the status of supply and demand for uranium enrichment services, it is unlikely that fuel prices will surge. Nevertheless, even if fuel prices do eventually rise, such price increases will not have a great impact as the ratio of fuel costs against total generation costs remains small. Japan has no special stockpiling facilities for enriched uranium, but possesses sufficient domestic resources to fuel at least two years of operation, including stock at fuel-processing plants (Tokyo Electric Power Company, 2010). Fuels contain still usable uranium and newly generated plutonium, which can be chemically separated and processed into mixed oxide (MOX) fuel (a blend of oxides of plutonium and uranium) to be reused in nuclear plants. MOX fuel has already been introduced in a number of Japanese plants. Based upon these considerations, nuclear power can be considered a quasi-domestic resource for Japan, in so far as it represents a remarkable energy source that promotes national energy security.

Coal

Since global coal reserves and supply sources are not geographically concentrated, coal has a much lower supply risk than other energy sources. Japan's coal is procured relatively easily from neighbouring countries. In 2006, 64 per cent of Japan's imported coal came from Australia and Canada (IEEJ, 2010). From an energy security perspective, coal, both in terms of volume and costs, is generally more advantageous than other fossil fuels. Furthermore, from the standpoint of maintaining international price negotiation power for other fossil fuels, coal – along with nuclear power – remains the leading option for energy security in Japan, which possesses minimal fossil fuel reserves.

Between the end of the Second World War and through the 1960s – when it could be mined domestically on an economic basis – coal accounted for 40 per cent of Japan's primary energy supply. However, reflecting the energy shift to oil, the share of coal in the primary energy supply mix dropped to below 20 per cent in the 1970s. As it continued to follow a declining trend, domestic coal completely disappeared from Japan's energy mix after 2000.

After the two oil crises, Japan sought to diversify energy sources in policy, employing imported coal as the backup power source in case of suspensions of operation that have occasionally occurred at nuclear power plants. This strategy increased in turn coal's share in Japan's primary energy supply mix to exceed 20 per cent since 2005 (Agency for Natural Resources and Energy, 2010a, 2010c).

Conflict between energy security and climate change policies

Regular controversies have surrounded Japan's debates on the roles of nuclear power and coal in energy security and climate change policy. In this context, the draft roadmap towards the 2020 mid-term target – which the Ministry of the Environment announced in March 2010 – continues to be discussed within the government just as the Basic Energy Plan is under review at the METI. Efforts to seek compromise are underway but, at the time of writing, no decision has been reached.

Insight into Japan's current energy security policy can also be gained by referencing the Long-term Energy Supply and Demand Outlook announced in August 2009 (METI, 2009). Having reviewed Japan's energy policy from the supply side, it should be noted that energy conservation and efficiency policies are the most effective measures in achieving both economic growth and improved energy security. The Long-term Energy Supply and Demand Outlook not only includes macro framework indicators – GDP growth rate and population – in its economic activity indices, but, while forecasting energy demand, it also accumulates semi-macro elements – projected production in energy-intensive industries, such as material industries; energy demand forecasts in the household and office sector based on projected office floor area and number of households; assumptions of the diffusion rate of various energy-saving equipment; and predicted traffic volume of passengers and freight in the transportation sector. Moreover, the Outlook not only contains business as usual (BAU) forecasts, but it also presents policy targets promoting various measures – for example, the projected energy efficiency improvements to be achieved by introducing state-of-the-art technology and the wide promotion of energy-saving equipment – in order to improve the energy intensity of the entire Japanese economy. Therefore, the Long-term Energy Supply and Demand Outlook can be considered a 'policy target' rather than an 'outlook'. Finally, as regards energy supply, the Outlook assumes that nine nuclear power plants will be newly constructed by 2020, and establishes quantitative targets for renewable energies, including photovoltaic power, wind power and biomass. As demonstrated by Table 7.1, such figures represent policy targets rather than forecasts – they are numerical expressions of an appropriate future primary energy mix, that also serve as targets based upon which policy inducement measures are considered.

Table 7.1 Japan: Long-term energy supply and demand outlook (million kl, crude oil equivalent)

Sources of final energy consumption	**FY1990**		**FY2005**		**FY2020 (prospected)**					
	Actual		**Actual**		**Technology frozen case**		**Continuous effort case**		**Maximum introduction case**	
		Composition ratio (%)		**Composition ratio (%)**		**Composition ratio (%)**		**Composition ratio (%)**		**Composition ratio (%)**
Industry	181	50	181	44	180	43	180	45	177	47
Residential and commercial	95	26	134	32	149	35	134	33	121	32
Residential	43	12	56	14	61	14	56	14	52	14
Commercial	52	14	78	19	88	21	78	19	68	18
Transportation	83	23	98	24	92	22	86	21	78	21
Total	**359**	**100**	**413**	**100**	**421**	**100**	**401**	**100**	**375**	**100**
Sources of primary energy supply										
Oil	265	52	255	43	227	36	215	36	190	34
LPG	19	4	18	3	18	3	18	3	18	3
Coal	85	17	123	21	128	20	120	20	107	19
Natural gas	54	11	88	15	114	18	103	17	89	16
Nuclear	49	10	69	12	99	16	99	17	99	18
Hydro	22	4	17	3	19	3	19	3	19	3
Geothermal	0	0	1	0	1	0	1	0	1	0
New energy, etc.	13	3	16	3	22	3	22	4	22	5
Renewable energies total	*35*	*7*	*34*	*6*	*42*	*6*	*42*	*7*	*50*	*8*
Total	**508**	**100**	**588**	**100**	**627**	**100**	**596**	**100**	**553**	**100**

N.B. New energy includes utilisation of unutilised energy such as blast furnace top gas pressure recovery power generation as well as new energy.
Source: *The Handbook of Energy & Economic Statistics in Japan* (edited by The Institute of Energy Economics, Japan, 2010)

The Long-term Energy Supply and Demand Outlook assumes three scenarios for 2020,[1] which can be summarised as follows:

1) The *Technology Frozen Case* sets the benchmark at 2005 (status quo), assuming that a) no new energy technologies are introduced in the future; b) the current level of energy efficiency of equipment is maintained; and c) outdated equipment that has approached the end of its service life is replaced with equipment of current energy efficiency levels;
2) The *Continuous Effort Case* assumes that a) current energy efficiency improvement efforts are continued for equipment and facilities for which such improvements have been pursued to date and b) outdated equipment which has approached the end of its service life is replaced with more energy efficient equipment;
3) The *Maximum Introduction Case* assumes that dramatic improvements will be achieved by implementing policy measures that amount to legal enforcement requiring individuals and companies to renew outdated equipment in order to maximally deploy state-of-the-art technologies which entail high costs but are ready for practical use and promise enormous energy efficiency improvements.

On the demand side, large reductions cannot be expected from the industrial sector, for which only slight reductions from 1990 levels are forecast in all cases. This indicates that Japan has made so much progress in deploying existing energy efficiency technologies that there are no energy-conserving opportunities left for its production process. In the household, office and transportation sectors, the Outlook seeks to reduce absolute consumption amounts by installing generous subsidies for the diffusion of energy-saving equipment and facilities (household appliances and automobiles, housing, etc.).

In terms of supply, the Outlook draws a picture where oil dependency is dramatically reduced with expectations that it will be replaced with nuclear energy and new energy sources. Nuclear power accounts for 18 per cent of total primary energy supply in the Maximum Introduction Case (12 per cent in 2005), where new energies will have a share of 5 per cent (3 per cent in 2005) by policy inducement. However, Japan's dependency on coal will decrease from 21 per cent in 2005 to 19 per cent in 2020, revealing the government's intention to shift from coal to natural gas (which will increase from 15 per cent in 2005 to 16 per cent in 2020) in terms of fossil fuels.

As previously stated, reflecting recent trends towards laying more emphasis on climate change issues than on energy security, the policy focus has moved to reducing fossil fuel use. However, as we have seen earlier, nuclear power embraces difficulties concerning the construction of new plants as well as risks of shutdowns due to force majeure events, including earthquakes. Therefore, envisioning an energy mix that is highly dependent on nuclear power entails potential hazards. Acknowledging that nuclear power possesses an advantage in energy security, the Japanese government should also have a backup plan in case nuclear power cannot actually be increased. Fossil fuel-fired plants using coal and natural gas will become essential in the face of such unpredictable events. Moreover, with the increased introduction of solar and wind power, backup thermal power plants will be required in order to maintain the stability of the power system. If such dynamics impose problems in mitigating GHG emissions, the reduction target should be lowered to flexibly meet security requirements. The target announced in the Hatoyama Initiative – that is, to reduce emissions by 25 per cent with respect to 1990 levels – lacks feasibility from both technological and cost aspects, casting a shadow upon the energy security debate.

International reconciliation of interests

At the UNFCCC Copenhagen Conference, developed countries and emerging developing countries clashed over reduction obligations and financial support levels and methods. An increasing number of countries questioned the validity of the United Nations as a forum for negotiation adopting the consensus decision-making approach. Intense diplomatic negotiations on the establishment of a post-Kyoto framework are likely to develop in rough waters. Under these circumstances, is it really possible to envisage a developed country/developing country cooperation model that can effectively serve climate change purposes without interfering with national energy security? In prior work (21ppi, 2009), I have suggested that the Japanese government ought to conclude a bilateral agreement for mutual cooperation in preventing climate change with an emerging economy in Asia, and promote substantial GHG reductions through cooperation in the areas of renewable energy and nuclear power. The elements of such an agreement might be:

1. The two governments ought to identify and decide on projects related to energy efficiency, renewable energy and nuclear power that can be promoted through bilateral cooperation. Relevant industries should simultaneously engage in cross-border discussions on details of how to take endorsed projects forward;
2. The governments should establish: (a) GHG mitigation targets – for example, 0.5–1 billion tons – respective of BAU reductions or (b) an intensity-based target to be achieved by such projects. A study should be conducted to see if the projects contribute to improving the energy security of the developing country;
3. Offset credits that are generated by achieving a target should be jointly 'accredited' by a measurable, reportable and verifiable (MRV) method bilaterally agreed upon and allocated according to the degree of financial

> and technological contribution. The offset credits generated in this manner shall be valid in domestic schemes. For example, in countries where emissions trading schemes have been introduced, they can be employed as offset credits to meet requirements in emissions trading schemes.

A promising option under this scheme is the diffusion of supercritical coal-fired power plants and technology. Possessing an advantage in energy security, coal is considered an important future energy source in all Asian countries. Therefore, a win–win policy that could satisfy both energy security and climate change mitigation would involve promoting the wide use of coal by employing Japanese technologies that can achieve power generation with the highest efficiency. This strategy can only prove successful by mobilising both public and private funding to cover the required costs. The key here is to make it an attractive investment by incorporating an offset credit scheme, which, unlike the Clean Development Mechanism (CDM) can be implemented flexibly and speedily without dissipating time and energy on international negotiations over procedures and additionality.

Conclusions

With the experience of two oil crises and very limited domestic resources, Japan has promoted the introduction of nuclear power, coal and natural gas with the aim of lowering its oil dependency. As a result, government policy has successfully maintained a well-balanced energy mix in terms of energy security. However, climate change measures have become increasingly important since the 1990s – when the UNFCCC and Kyoto Protocol came into effect – revealing obvious contradictions with and inconsistencies within Japan's energy policy. On the demand side, energy conservation arouses little policy conflict, whereas on the supply side, the introduction of nuclear power, which could actually achieve both policy goals, has been delayed due to resistance from environmentalists. The other alternative, coal-fired generation, has also been the subject of criticism. Renewable energy, which is favoured by environmentalists, cannot be expected to fully cover Japan's massive energy demand. Limited land area is a natural circumstance that poses another high bar for Japan in the wide-scale introduction of renewable energy. The simultaneous pursuit of both energy security and environmental goals is still under debate between advocates on both sides.

On the other hand, by transferring and disseminating Japan's highly efficient energy technology and facilities to other countries, the Japanese government can contribute to curbing the growth of GHG emissions in other countries – developing countries, in particular – while improving energy security. This will prevent explosive increases in GHG emissions at the global level while enhancing Japan's energy security. Possessing the world's highest technology level, Japan should take the initiative in presenting an international model for developed country–developing country energy cooperation.

The Japanese government has recently decided to officially adopt this scheme for a number of reasons. A major policy issue for the Japanese government is to achieve the mid-term target of 25 per cent reductions from 1990 levels with minimal negative economic impact. Yet, estimates have revealed that marginal mitigation costs for relying exclusively on domestic measures could be as much as US$500/tonne.[2] In order to achieve the target with minimal costs, it will be important to acquire emissions allocations from overseas. However, just purchasing emissions allowances generated by hot air will provoke political criticism, as the Japanese public will feel that their tax money is being spent on 'mere pieces of paper', or emissions certificates. On the other hand, environmentalists in Japan have demanded that energy-intensive industries relocate overseas so that GHGs can be mitigated. Industry also became increasingly sceptical of the DPJ Administration, which is seen as being inclined towards environmentalist views since its ambitious target was determined without any consultation with industry. The government's intentions were to eliminate any industrial concerns over leakage of energy-intensive industries, while achieving its mid-term target by securing credits and revitalising the Japanese economy by exporting technologies and facilities. The scheme described above is innovative in comparison to conventional CDMs, in the sense that if credits are secured by an MRV method agreed upon bilaterally, they will have the effect of providing substantive mitigation of global GHGs despite possible rejection as credits that are defined in the Kyoto Protocol framework. Furthermore, by transferring technologies that enable the efficient use of energy, energy consumption will decrease in the recipient country and domestic pressures towards energy supply will thus be mitigated, contributing indirectly to Japan's energy security.

METI has launched a programme to promote this scheme by providing financial support towards overseas transfer of climate change technologies. On 10 August 2010, 15 out of 32 projects subscribed by private companies were granted support.[3] Selected technologies include high-efficiency coal-fired power plants; geothermal power plants; iron and steel production technologies; and energy conservation in plants. Remarkably, these are all competitive areas for Japan. The Japanese government selected different locations, mainly in Asia, for deploying the projects – while four projects will be implemented in Indonesia alone, the Philippines, Thailand, India and Vietnam will host two projects each. In order to mitigate business risks for private companies, the Japanese government is due to conclude agreements with other governments on conditions for grants and measures to protect intellectual rights related to technology transfer.

In the UNFCCC forum, as a result of fierce conflict between developed and developing nations, climate change measures have not made the advances expected. However, if countries can begin to consider ways to promote climate change policy, energy policy and economic policy in harmony, they can take a significant step forward with these dormant measures. In the future, a post-Kyoto framework could be materialised by combining bilateral agreements, which are themselves the building blocks of multilateral agreements.

Notes

1. The actual analysis extends to 2030, but only projections for 2020 are discussed here due to space constraint.
2. Comparative studies of national mid-term targets can be found at Research Institute of Innovative Technology for September 2010).
3. Press release can be found at: http://www.meti.go.jp/information/data/c100810aj.html (accessed: 06 September 2010; only available in Japanese).

References

Agency for Natural Resources and Energy (1967), *The First Long-term Energy Supply and Demand Outlook* (Tokyo).

Agency for Natural Resources and Energy (1990), *The Long-term Energy Supply and Demand Outlook* (Tokyo).

Agency for Natural Resources and Energy (2010a), *The Current Situation of Coal* [http://www.enecho.meti.go.jp/energy/coal/coal02.htm; accessed: 08 November 2010].

Agency for Natural Resources and Energy (2010b), *The International Situation and the Main Issues about the Nuclear Power* [http://www.meti.go.jp/committee/materials2/downloadfiles/g81030a05j.pdf, accessed: 08 November 2010].

Agency for Natural Resources and Energy (2010c), *The Primary Energy Trend* [http://www.enecho.meti.go.jp/topics/hakusho/2008energyhtml/2-1-3.htm; accessed: 08 November 2010].

Embassy of Japan (2010), 'Note Verbale dated 26 January 2010 from the Embassy of Japan in Germany to the Secretariat of the United Nations Framework Convention on Climate Change in Bonn' [http://unfccc.int/files/meetings/application/pdf/japancphaccord_app1.pdf; accessed: 06 September 2010].

G8 (2010), 'L'Aquila Summit' [http://www.g8italia2009.it/static/G8_Allegato/Fact%20Sheet%20-%20Climate%20Change%20(ENG).pdf; accessed: 08 November 2010].

Institute of Energy Economics (IEEJ) (2010), *The Handbook Energy & Economic Statistics in Japan* (Tokyo: IEEJ).

International Energy Agency (IEA) (2010), *IEA Oil Market Report* [http://omrpublic.iea.org/; accessed: 08 November 2010].

METI (2001), 'Report of the security working group under the advisory committee on energy and natural resources' [Energy Security Working Group, Advisory Committee on Energy and Natural Resources; http://www.meti.go.jp/report/downloadfiles/g10628bj.pdf; accessed: 06 September 2010, in Japanese].

METI (2009), 'Recalculation for the long-term energy supply/demand outlook' [Energy Supply and Demand Subcommittee, The Advisory Committee for Natural Resources and Energy; http://www.meti.go.jp/report/data/g90902aj.html, accessed: 08 September 2010, in Japanese].

METI (2010), 'Basic energy plan' [http://www.meti.go.jp/committee/summary/0004657/energy.pdf; accessed: 10 September 2010, in Japanese].

Ministry of Environment (MOE) (2010), 'A draft roadmap against the global warming problem' [http://www.env.go.jp/earth/ondanka/mlt_roadmap/shian_100331/main.pdf, accessed: 08 November 2010].

Ministry of Foreign Affairs of Japan (MOFA) (2010a), 'Hokkaido Toyako Summit' [http://www.mofa.go.jp/policy/economy/summit/2008/info/theme.html; accessed: 08 November 2010].

MOFA (2010b), 'Statement by Prime Minister Yukio Hatoyama' [http://www.mofa.go.jp/policy/un/assembly2009/pm0922.html; accessed: 08 November 2010].

Prime Minister of Japan and His Cabinet (2010a), *New Growth Strategy* [http://www.kantei.go.jp/jp/kakugikettei/2009/1230sinseichousenryaku.pdf; accessed: 08 November 2010, in Japanese].

Prime Minister of Japan and His Cabinet (2010b), *The Press Launch of the Former Prime Minister Aso* [http://www.kantei.go.jp/jp/asophoto/2009/06/10kaiken.html; accessed: 08 November 2010, in Japanese].

Research Institute of Innovative Technology for the Earth (RITE) (2010), 'Systems analysis' [http://www.rite.or.jp/Japanese/labo/sysken/systemken.html; accessed: 06 September 2010].

Research Organization for Information Science & Technology (RIST) (2010), *Long-term Energy Supply and Demand Outlook* [http://www.rist.or.jp/atomica/data/dat_detail.php?Title_No=01-09-09-05; accessed: 08 November 2010].

The 21st Century Public Policy Institute (21ppi) (2009), 'New Climate Policy Agenda: Verifying the 25 per cent mitigation initiative and a new proposal for substantive reductions' [http://www.21ppi.org/pdf/thesis/091211.pdf; accessed: 30 June 2010, in Japanese].

The Basic Act on Energy Policy (2002) [http://law.e-gov.go.jp/htmldata/H14/H14HO071.html; accessed: 08 November 2010].

Tokyo Electric Power Company (2010), *The Stability for Supply of a Nuclear Power* [http://www.tepco.co.jp/nu/knowledge/merit/merit02/index-j.html; accessed: 08 November 2010].

UNFCCC (2010), 'Appendix I – Quantified economy-wide emissions targets for 2020' [http://unfccc.int/home/items/5264.php, accessed: 08 November 2010].

8

Russia's Energy Security and Emissions Trends: Synergies and Contradictions

Anna Korppoo and Thomas Spencer

Energy policy drives Russian emissions

The dramatic post-1990 restructuring of the Russian economic and political system led to a collapse of Russia's greenhouse gas (GHG) emissions, which, in 2007, were 34 per cent below 1990 levels. A further slump in total GHG emissions is thought to have followed the economic recession of 2008–2009 (see for instance Novikova et al., 2009). As Russia's commitment under the Kyoto Protocol of limiting emissions to the 1990 level can be achieved without the introduction of targeted measures, very few mitigation policies have been introduced in Russia to date. Climate policy remains a marginal political concern, and there is a history of scepticism within domestic scientific, social and policy discourses (Rowe, 2009). There is also a widespread perception that Russia has already 'sacrificed' much to reduce its emissions since 1990 (Tynkkynen, 2010). These factors make it unlikely that Russia will implement any economically disruptive climate policies in the foreseeable future.

The Russian economy is dominated by the energy sector. As the world's largest producer and exporter of natural gas (2008) and second largest exporter of oil (2007) (IEA, 2009a), the fuel and energy complex accounted for 31 per cent of Russian gross domestic product (GDP) and 58 per cent of the budget's tax revenues in 2005 (UNECE, 2010, p. 236). Maintaining the export capacity of energy resources is a high priority of the government, whereas reducing energy wastage and rationalising the fuel mix are becoming increasingly important factors in maintaining Russian export capacity and security of domestic supply, due to declining production capacity, the expense and technical difficulty of bringing new capacity on line, and the projected growth in GDP and energy demand (Russian Federation, 2009a, pp. 40, 62; Sutela, 2009). Energy efficiency measures account for 90 per cent of Russia's projected economically attractive GHG savings to 2020 (McKinsey, 2009, p. 12). Energy efficiency thus provides the primary link between energy security and climate mitigation in the Russian context, although, in this regard, policies influencing the fuel mix have become increasingly relevant.

Oil or hydrocarbon exporting states are often economically highly dependent on export revenues, and hence prioritise the security of demand for their energy exports, or more simply *the security of export revenues* (see Lesage et al., 2010, p. 38). However, energy-exporting states with a functioning 'social contract' must also ensure conditions for adequate supplies of energy to the domestic economy. Thus for energy exporters like Russia, the concept of energy security is double-edged, as it includes both the security of export revenues and the security of adequate supply for the domestic economy. When defined in terms of security of export revenues, energy security can be further broken down into several facets:

1. Availability of surplus resources for export;
2. Access to markets;
3. Security of demand;
4. Profitability of exports to international markets.

Energy security as seen from the perspective of energy exporters has certain parallels with the more multifaceted conception of energy security elaborated by energy importers and consumers, which is often defined – as it is in the case of the European Union (EU) – in terms of security, competitiveness and sustainability of supply (see Commission of the European Communities, 2008, p. 3). Although the Russian Energy Strategy until 2030 (Russian Federation, 2009a, p. 28) does recognise similar elements – namely sufficiency, economic availability, environmental and technical acceptability of energy supplies – the actual practice of Russian energy policy reflects a more complex interaction of synergies and trade-offs between the sectional interests expressed by different economic, political and social actors and the imperative of supplying domestic and international energy markets.

Russian energy policy is thus driven by the imperative to maintain export capacity while ensuring sufficient domestic supply. It is in the context of this dialectic that the key link to climate policy emerges, in so far as it may incentivise improved energy efficiency or changes in the fuel mix. However, other energy policies – such as market reform and liberalisation or policies related to investment and modernisation of the energy sector – could also have a material impact on Russian energy consumption and the fuel mix. Hence, it is also necessary to give consideration to broader issues in domestic and foreign energy policy when analysing linkages between energy security and climate policy in the Russian context. This chapter seeks to identify the elements of energy security policies that drive GHG emissions trends; review the status of implementation of these policies; and highlight the problems tackled so far in order to provide a 'reality check' of the prospects for mitigation. This chapter is structured as follows: firstly, we review key issues in Russia's domestic and foreign energy policy. Then we identify potential synergies or trade-offs between Russian energy security and climate policy to finally review the status of implementation of the identified policies.

Domestic energy policy

Energy market and investment needs

As Russia is extremely dependent on the export of energy resources, maintaining existing export capacity represents the number one priority for the national economy. However, production from existing gas fields is in decline, and future capacity will come from remote, expensive and technically difficult fields (Figure 8.1). Russia's oil fields are widely believed to have peaked, although a 10 per cent increase in production is predicted by the Ministry of Energy for 2008–2030 (Russian Federation, 2009a, p. 145).

Before the economic crisis, a number of analysts were predicting a supply crunch in Russian gas, with potential consequences for Russian and international markets. In 2006, due to a lack of available gas, Russia cut supplies to Serbia, Bosnia and Herzegovina, Croatia, Italy, Romania and Poland (Fredholm, 2008). The economic crisis and recent progress in the initial development of the Bovanenko field (Yamal Peninsula, north-western

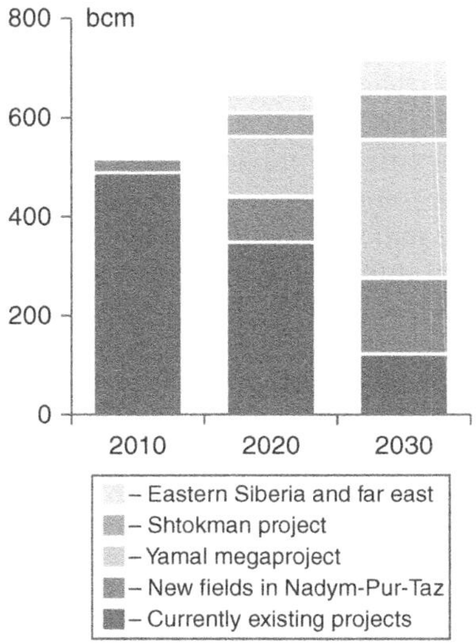

Figure 8.1 Gazprom's production to 2030
Source: Gazprom (2011).

Siberia) may have mitigated some of these concerns in the medium term (compare Stern, 2009a with Stern, 2009b). Nonetheless, as indicated by Stern (2009a, p. 11), the development of Russian energy demand remains 'a very important energy [security] issue in its own right' for Russia, and, arguably, for its export customers too.

Russia's energy strategy to 2030 identified the high degree of fixed asset depreciation, low level of investments, technological obsolescence and general inefficiency as the main threats to energy security (Russian Federation, 2009a, pp. 28–29). The energy strategy foresees a massive investment programme in the energy sector of some US$2.1 trillion over the next 20 years. Interestingly, 90 per cent of these investments are projected to come from Russian energy companies. These figures have been considered unrealistic due to the lack of incentives for Foreign Direct Investment (FDI) or domestic investment in the energy sector, which remains very much dominated by state-controlled companies and regulators (Blagov, 2009).

The trajectory of Russian energy demand is hence not just dependent on energy efficiency policy *per se*, but also on broader economic and energy market reforms. As production and utilisation were strongly subsidised, energy prices in the Soviet Union did not reflect production costs or resource scarcity (Nove, 1977, p. 266). This established the tradition of cheap energy and wasteful energy consumption in Russia. A central theme of Russian energy policy from the mid 2000s onwards has therefore been the beginning of processes of restructuring and liberalisation of the domestic energy market.

In the electricity sector, the formerly state-owned holding company RAO UES – which owned 72.4 per cent of generating capacity (the rest came from the state-owned nuclear energy sector) and 96.1 per cent of the transmission lines (Petersen, 2009, p. 174) – was broken up into seven major regional wholesale generating companies and 14 independent generating companies. In addition, transmission and generation were unbundled with the creation of the state majority owned Federal Grid Company. The energy market restructuring was intended as a large-scale privatisation with the aim of attracting massive investment in the ageing electricity sector (Øverland and Hjærnet, 2009). The need for such investments is truly dire: depreciation of capital stock is over 46 per cent in the natural resource extraction sector; 70 per cent in the thermal power sector; and about 80 per cent in hydropower (quoted in Charap and Safonov, 2010, p. 140).

In the gas sector the situation appears different. Russia's gas sector remains dominated by Gazprom, which controls 60 per cent of the country's proven gas reserves and 84.7 per cent of production; it has a legal export monopoly and owns and operates Russia's transmission pipelines, which it effectively deploys to squeeze the market share of third parties (Heinrich, 2008; Mitrova, 2009, p. 23). Nevertheless, the relative weight of independent producers in Russian gas production is expected to increase in the next decade. The extent to which this actually takes place is closely related to the progression of reforms on the domestic gas market, that is, raising domestic gas tariffs and conditions around third-party access to the pipeline network. In 2006, the Russian government outlined a plan to increase domestic gas tariffs to European 'net-back'[1] levels by 2011. However, the economic recession has led the government to grant a three-year extension, and tariff reform is now touted to be completed by 2014.

Russian laws on foreign investment – introduced in 2008 – heavily limit the involvement of foreign investors in strategic sectors, including the energy sector. In the extraction sector, these limitations reach beyond the possession of 50 per cent or more of voting rights by the state: in the case of subsoil exploitation, foreign investors are allowed a 10 per cent maximum share of voting rights. The continental shelf can only be exploited by companies with at least five years of experience in Russian continental shelf exploration and production, and which are at least 50 per cent owned by the Russian Federation: in practice, this limits the field to only Gazprom, Rosneft and their subsidiaries (Seliverstov, 2009). The Putin era trend towards renationalisation of the oil industry – with the bankruptcy of Yukos and the expansion of state-owned Rosneft – is directly connected with the state's interest in retaining control of the strategically important energy sector.

A number of factors help explain the rationale behind policies limiting the involvement of foreign investors and domestic third parties in the energy sector – which could deliver much-needed investments to update the obsolete energy infrastructure. The first is the desire to keep this strategic sector under close state control. As described by Heinrich (2008, p. 1542), Prime Minister Vladimir V. Putin has 'emphasized the importance of the resource sector for Russia's economic and geo-strategic revival and asserted the primacy of state interests in major decision about energy and natural resources'. The second factor may be related to Hellman's theory of 'state trap', whereby private individuals that obtain substantial rents from the initial reforms of the post-Communist transition have a stake in maintaining or normalising the new *status quo* (Hellman, 1998).

Saving up for export

Russia's domestic energy market exhibits a contradictory hybrid structure, in which free-market and statist trends appear to coexist (Mitrova, 2009, p. 50). The former is related to the need to improve efficiency, attract investment and modernise capital stock, while the latter derives from the Russian government's desire to maintain control over strategic aspects of the energy sector and the interests of rent-seeking incumbents to maintain their position. In addition to market structuring, a number of specific domestic policies aim at limiting energy consumption, as well as reducing the consumption of high value added fuels demanded on the export market. This section reviews the policies on energy efficiency, renewable energy and the coal strategies implemented by the Russian Federation.

In Soviet times, energy was viewed as a social right provided for by generous public subsidies. Russia's huge energy resources shielded the Soviet population and economy at large from the energy security concerns that were sparked by the oil crises of the 1970s (Nove, 1977, p. 266; Cooper and Schipper, 1991, p. 344). As a result, today's Russian economy is, on a purchasing power basis, 2.1 times more energy intensive than China's, and 2.41 times more energy intensive than the Organization for Economic Development and Cooperation (OECD) average (IEA, 2010a, p. 438, 2010b, p. 201). Significant improvements in domestic energy efficiency would facilitate Russia's efforts to maintain domestic economic growth and export margins. The country's size, climate, economic structure and economic scale help to explain the magnitude of Russia's energy wastage: nevertheless, approximately 25 per cent of Russia's energy consumption cannot be justified by these factors (IFC, 2008, p. 30).

President Dmitrii A. Medvedev has made energy efficiency a (rhetorical) priority of his administration. In November 2009, the Russian government passed a comprehensive legislative framework on energy efficiency (Federal Law No 261-F3), which laid the legal foundations for initiatives to improve the country's energy efficiency. Specifically this law requires energy labelling of appliances; new buildings to conform to energy efficiency guidelines; the installation of energy meters for gas, water, heat and electricity; and mandatory energy audits for government agencies, state companies, utilities and big energy users. Further, the law establishes municipal programmes for energy efficiency; rules for energy-efficient public procurement; energy service contracts as a civil-service contract under the Civil Code; and fiscal incentives for investments to improve efficiency, including accelerated depreciation and tax credits.

In addition to the law on energy efficiency, the Russian government approved further legislation to cut associated gas flaring by 95 per cent by 2012, with the ultimate view to save resources and cut emissions. Penalties for breaches of this law were also increased (N7, 8 January 2009) (Russian Federation 2009c).

Estimates of the total associated gas flared by Russia from oil production fluctuate between 20 and 38 bcm per year. This is approximately the same quantity as is exported to Germany, the largest buyer of Russian gas. The magnitude of these figures can be fully appreciated through comparison with the annual planned capacity for the Nabucco gas pipeline, which is 31 bcm.

In an example of the contradictions of Russian energy policy, commentators have identified the lack of third-party access to the Gazprom-owned pipeline network as the most significant barrier to the utilisation of associated gas (IEA, 2006, p. 145).

The International Energy Agency (IEA) has estimated that the annual commercial potential of renewable energies in Russia is approximately 270 mtoe. In 2007, Russia's total primary energy supply amounted to 672 mtoe (IEA, 2010c), while in 2005 the actual share of renewable energy sources and waste was only 1.1 per cent of total primary energy supply, or 7.2 mtoe (IEA, 2008b, p. 187). The IEA has suggested that renewables could be used to enhance the energy security of the Russian periphery, which has to rely on expensive imports of fossil fuels and electricity from other regions. According to a study by O.C. Popel' (2008, p. 98), two-thirds of the country – and one-seventh of the total population – is not connected to the central grid, while more than 50 per cent of the Russian regions are reliant on energy exports originating elsewhere in the country. Renewable energy technologies and 'green' electricity exports could also be used to diversify the fossil fuel export dependent economy (IEA, 2003, pp. 98, 101–103). Towards these ends, there has been talk of producing hydropower in Siberia for export to China (Moscow Times, 2010b). There is significant potential for hydropower: the technical hydropower resources in Siberia and the Far East have been estimated at 1441 TWh per annum (86 per cent of total), while their economically feasible potential has been estimated as 690 TWh (81 per cent of total) in comparison to the 1038 TWh total generation in 2008 (IEA, 2003, p. 39, 2010c, p. 27).

The current renewable energy policy was first launched in 2009 (Decree 1-r, 8 January 2009) (Russian Federation, 2009b). Its main goal was to generate 4.5 per cent of the country's electricity demand from renewable resources by 2020, up from around 1 per cent today. According to the International Centre for Sustainable Development, legislative measures that would establish a feed-in premium for renewable energy sources while earmarking money from the federal budget for connecting renewable energy projects to the grid have been drafted (UNECE, 2010, p. 249). There are nevertheless a number of serious obstacles to the expansion of renewables, including the lack of economic incentives due to the low price of energy and regulatory uncertainty regarding grid connection; the low level of awareness amongst government agencies, business and society; the lack of experience with demonstration projects; and insufficient financing for research and development and concrete asset financing (Popel', 2008, p. 98).

Dependence on domestic gas does impact on Russia's energy security. The 2003 'Energy Strategy of the Russian Federation until 2020' established that, in order to save more gas for export, domestic coal ought to replace gas in the energy balance. Given the significantly higher carbon content of coal in comparison to gas (102 versus 62 grams of CO_2 per MJ of energy), implementation of this policy would inevitably lead to higher emissions.

In this context, Russia's nuclear industry has been kept under state control and funding, as the government has been eager to sustain the activities of Russia's nuclear power industry. The Energy Strategy predicts that the share of nuclear combined with hydropower and renewable electricity will grow from 10 per cent of the total fuel balance in 2008 to some 12–14 per cent by 2030. This forecast diverges from the 2006 federal nuclear programme, which projected the share of nuclear of the total electricity generation to increase from 15.7 per cent to 18.6 per cent in 2007–2015 (Federal Programme, 2006).

Energy foreign policy

Certainty of export revenues

The 2003 Energy Strategy (p. 21) recognises the increasing uncertainty and price volatility in future world energy markets. In order to finance the massive investments required to secure future energy exports and consolidate the long-term certainty of its export markets, Russia has been seeking to insulate itself from market and non-market volatilities, while securing a competitive price for its exports. Towards these ends, Russia's energy foreign policy has followed a number of strategies.

A number of commentators have considered the progression of Russia's energy foreign policy during the 2000s, in particular concerning gas, as one in which economic interests have been systematically prioritised vis-à-vis political ones. It is in this context that we have to place the ultimate end of raising prices for Russian gas exports to neighbouring Commonwealth of Independent States (CIS) countries: the reduction – if not the complete termination – of a lasting Soviet legacy and a more recent form of Russian hegemony, namely the implicit energy subsidies enjoyed by CIS countries (Ürge-Vorsatz et al., 2006, p. 2280). In the 2000s, this strategy in turn favoured the eruption of a series of so-called 'gas wars' involving disputes over prices with CIS countries, which led some analysts to accuse Russia of using the energy trade for political ends (see for instance Hedenskog and Larsson, 2009, ff. 45). While geopolitical considerations seem likely to have played a role in certain individual incidents, the desire to secure the profitability of these markets cannot be discounted as a major factor influencing the Russia–CIS energy relationship (Mitrova, 2009, ff. 34). Nonetheless, the continuing confluence of foreign policy concerns and Russia's energy trade was recently exemplified by an explicit exchange with Ukraine, which granted gas price concessions in return for an extension of the Russian navy's lease of the key strategic Black Sea port of Sevastopol. Prime Minister Putin drily described this deal as 'anything but a simple decision for us. Anything but simple, because it is expensive' (Moscow Times, 2010a).

A primary factor driving the price increases for Russian exports was increasing competition from the EU and China for Central Asia's gas resources. Russia has traditionally relied on exporting cheap Central Asian gas to Europe in order to fulfil its export contracts. The margin charged has been utilised in support of lower gas prices from Gazprom, as in the case of

Ukraine. With the entry of China into the Central Asian market, Russia has been forced to pay more for Central Asian gas in order to remain competitive. Russia is also trying to keep the EU out of this market. This was a main reason behind Russia's official rejection in 2009 of the EU-driven Energy Charter Treaty, which included non-discriminatory, third-party access to transport networks that would facilitate direct export by the Central Asian energy producers to the EU, effectively cutting out Russia's lucrative business as a middle-man (Belyi, 2009, p. 4; Morozov, 2009, p. 47; Norton Rose, 2009). Russia has also been contracting gas that could supply the EU's Nabucco pipeline, by pushing its rival project South Stream (Romanova, 2010). Finally, Moscow is trying to secure demand by gaining a foothold in the downstream market, via asset swaps or joint ventures with established European firms.

Russia's pursuit of transit infrastructure, diversified transit routes and downstream assets highlights a key concern, namely the difficulty of securing future demand for its energy exports. Four factors greatly complicate this concern:

1. The process of liberalising the EU gas market has to date promoted spot trading and undermined the long-term contracts upon which Gazprom has sought to build its business (Locatelli, 2008);
2. Continuing uncertainty over the global economic recovery and future demand levels;
3. The shale gas revolution in the United States and its potential to occur in other countries, including those located in Russia's immediate neighbourhood (e.g. Poland);
4. The impact of climate policy on future gas demand, predominantly although not exclusively that originating in the EU. For example, the IEA's projection of how global GHG emissions could be restrained to '450 ppm' anticipates that in this scenario gas consumption in the EU (Russia's largest export market) would decline by 18 per cent below business as usual (IEA, 2009b, p. 218).

This brief discussion has a double-edged implication for the link between Russia's energy security and climate policy. Firstly, it has attempted to highlight the extent to which security of export revenues remains a driving concern for Russian energy policy. Secondly, it has indicated that the reduction of domestic energy wastage and the optimisation of the domestic fuel mix are by no means the only factors in the balancing act of Russia's foreign and domestic energy policy. The prospects for significant improvements in energy efficiency and changes to the fuel mix need therefore to be analysed within the broader context of Russia's domestic and foreign energy policies.

Synergies between energy security and mitigation?

Common goals and contradictions

The IEA (2007, pp. 38–39) argues that potential synergies between energy supply security and climate policy are mostly located in the insecurities generated by resource concentration, as they create incentives promoting movement away from fossil fuels use and improvements in energy efficiency. Although the issue of revenue security for energy exporters was not explicitly addressed by the IEA, the above discussion indicated that, in the Russian context, the need to save energy for export may incentivise similar policies and have similar synergies with climate mitigation.

The CO_2 emissions scenarios developed by Novikova et al. (2009) demonstrate this link. The scenarios indicate that successful implementation of Russia's headline goals in its Energy Strategy – (i.e. an energy efficiency target of 40 per cent improvement by 2020 and an increase in the share of renewable energy to 6.6 per cent by 2020) – would have a significant impact on Russia's emissions. The difference between the policies' success (achieving both targets) and failure (no policy implementation, only autonomous energy efficiency improvement) – assuming an annual GDP growth of 4 per cent – is some 220 Mt CO_2 or a 15 per cent circa difference in the emissions trends by 2020 (Figure 8.2). Analogous conclusions might

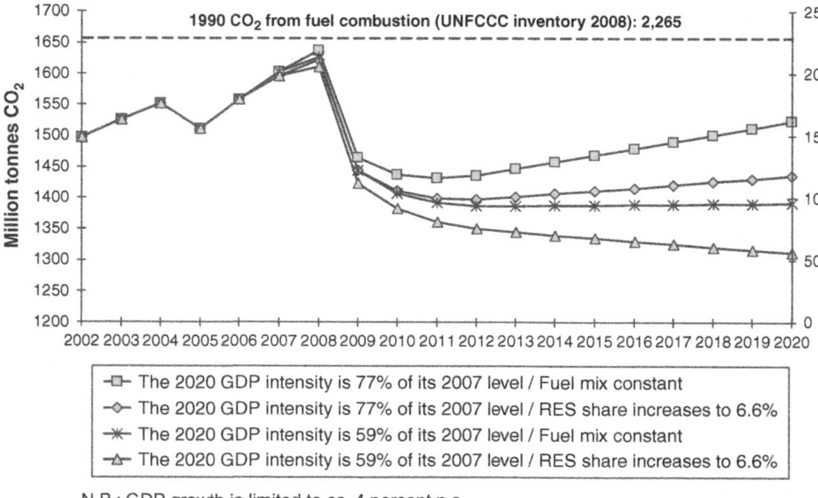

Figure 8.2 Russian Federation: Scenarios of CO_2 emissions to 2020 for different efficiency and fuel mix cases
Source: Novikova et al. (2009).

be drawn by relating successful implementation of the policy to associated gas flaring cuts and increasing nuclear power share.

The two obvious contradictions between energy security policies and mitigation are linked to changes in energy balances (switch from gas to coal), and incomplete implementation of energy market reforms. The former would increase emissions due to the higher carbon concentration of coal in comparison to gas, but would enhance the security of export revenues by freeing up additional gas for export. The latter would reduce the investment incentives provided by tariffs which reflect the costs of production (let alone environmental externalities), but may be motivated by the government's desire to shield domestic energy consumers from higher prices and retain control over the domestic energy sector. The importance of market reform for energy efficiency is highlighted by Stern (2005, p. 55), who calculated that domestic price reforms would cause a 1 per cent per annum reduction in gas demand from 2010 to 2020. Lack of energy sector reforms could also hinder the entrance of third parties and foreign corporations into the energy sector, preventing de facto initiatives that might increase production capacity, modernise capital stock and potentially diversify the energy mix. Nevertheless, the successful implementation of the announced policies ultimately remains the main factor defining the real synergies or contradictions between energy security policies and mitigation.

Success of policies

Many of the policies outlined above are currently under implementation. As a result, it is difficult to assess their future impact on energy security or climate mitigation. This section discusses the implementation prospects of some of these policies.

In 2009, Russian *wholesale gas prices* averaged US$66.70/1000 m^3, compared to the almost US$300 charged in Europe. The plan to increase gas tariffs to European net-back levels has been endangered by the high price for oil, to which EU gas prices are indexed, and, on the other hand, by the economic recession, which hit the Russian economy particularly hard. These two factors led the Russian government to concede a three-year extension to its plans for net-back price parity between domestic and export markets, which will now be tentatively achieved in 2014 with gas prices continuing to increase annually.

Although the policy to *switch from gas to coal* has been operating since the early 2000s, Figure 8.3 illustrates that the share of coal has actually been steadily decreasing while the share of gas has increased. The IEA (2002, p. 47) recognised that such a large-scale change of fuel balance would put pressure on the energy transportation system, and rail more in particular. To date, this policy – and emissions growth caused by it – has not encountered much success. However, increasing gas prices are currently beginning to facilitate

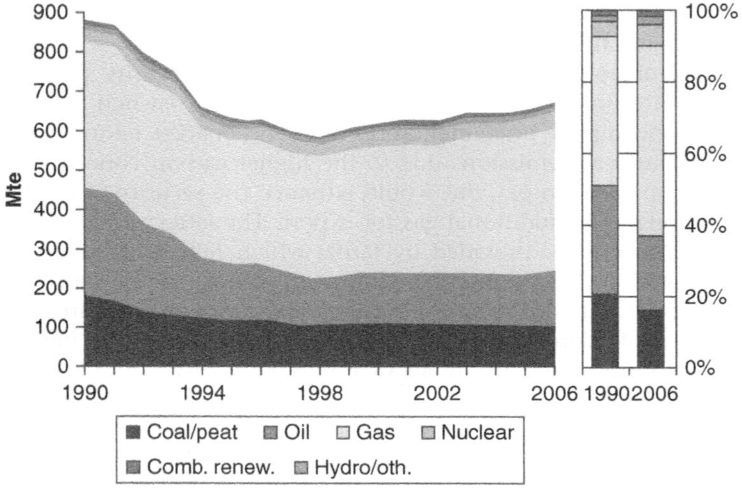

Figure 8.3 Russian Federation: Total primary energy supply
Source: IEA (2008b, p. 187).

such a shift: while many facilities are already completing the switch in spite of technical fixes, coal resources remain easily available for power and heat producers.

Restructuring in the Russian electricity sector compressed a sweeping reform agenda into a relatively short time. It seems that reform has facilitated some (foreign) investment in the energy sector, with private foreign companies like E.ON, RWE, Inel and Fortum now participating in the Russian electricity market. However, there is a risk of de facto monopoly situations in the six regional wholesale markets, competition between which is precluded by the country's huge size. The restructuring and liberalisation processes aim to prevent similar occurrences by creating 'guaranteeing suppliers', who are obliged to supply consumers who request a change of supplier, and may charge a regulated supply premium in addition to the wholesale price. In this fashion, the liberalisation process aimed to create at least a minimum competition between suppliers, even though a number of commentators have pointed out that the Russian government continues to retain 'tremendous discretion in the field of electricity regulation', that is, in tariff setting (Tompson, 2005, p. 22). However, the capacity market auctioning system – based on prices regulated by the state – appears to incentivise the introduction of new capacity while providing longer-term certainty of return for investors.

At the time of writing, *energy efficiency policies* are in their early implementation stages. Initial analyses of the legislation and interviews with Russian experts highlight a number of problems. Economic incentives for energy efficiency are still considered weak; energy prices remain too low to motivate energy savings amongst consumers; the tax break system envisaged by the legislation requires further development; the Energy Saving Companies' (ESCOs) capacity and general experience with energy saving contracts remain underdeveloped and their envisaged roles seem to depart from commonly adopted energy saving-based profit-oriented approaches. Also, current legislation does not introduce heat tariff increases which could mobilise significant energy saving potential. Finally, the ongoing policy-formation process continues to be plagued by administrative delay. Nonetheless, the approval of the framework law on energy efficiency does signal a step forward.

The law on *renewable energy* can be considered merely aspirational, and the further legislative process could be protracted. There are many barriers to the introduction of renewable energy in Russia: although independent power producers are legally able to operate in the country, they commonly experience problems with the tariff structures and in gaining access to the grid (IEA, 2003). Further, the 2009 law listed the lack of competitiveness against fossil fuels, statutory acts on renewables, and infrastructure such as information and public resources as barriers to the development of renewables.

A substantial amount (8.6 GW) of new *nuclear* capacity is currently under construction while a further 14.5 GW is planned to be built by 2020. This increase is significant in comparison to the existing 23 GW capacity; however, large portions are scheduled to be decommissioned (3.5 GW by 2015, and altogether 7.8 GW to approximately 35 per cent of the existing capacity – by 2020) (World Nuclear Association, 2010). While capacity under construction could replace the capacity to be decommissioned, the potential extension of lifetime of the existing capacity could radically change this equation. Plans to make the main actor of the nuclear sector, *Energoatom*, self-sufficient of funding based on its export activities, may limit the investment available for new capacity.

Utilising *associated gas* as required in the legislation is not a straightforward undertaking. To begin with, oil extraction often takes place in remote areas where there is little local demand for gas. Second, the composition of associated gas requires generation capacity adjustment to allow utilisation. Third, oil companies lack access to the Gazprom-controlled gas pipeline network, and they have also been reluctant to invest in the gas utilisation infrastructure due to its small-scale and complex collection technology. In this context, associated gas has been estimated to be 4–5 times more expensive than natural gas. Instead, many oil companies have chosen to use associated gas for local power production, including their own consumption (Kristalinskaya, 2010). In March 2010, the Russian government granted electricity generated from associated gas a priority access to the grid (Federal Law N26-F3, 9 March 2010). It can be anticipated that this legislation may meet with some success, given (1) the penalties and independent status of many oil companies required to cut flaring and (2) the government's legal support to the companies' market-based implementation choices. However, due to the lack of good-quality statistics on flaring, it will be difficult to verify whether the required cuts have actually taken place.

Limited impact of specific climate policies

Russia is eligible to participate in the Kyoto emissions trading mechanisms, which could channel investments in the refurbishment of the national energy sector and, at the same time, increase energy security. However, the impacts of 'Joint Implementation' and 'Emissions Trading' on energy security and emissions trends have been very limited, mainly due to the lack of policy priority given to their implementation by the Russian government. As the future of the global climate regime and the role of the Kyoto Protocol remain uncertain – the first commitment period of the Kyoto Protocol ends in 2012 – the Russian Federation has already run out of time to fully utilise the mechanisms.

Russia first introduced a Joint Implementation (JI) project approval system in 2007 (Decree 332, 28 May 2007), but was forced to introduce substantial revisions in 2009 (Order 884-r, 27 June 2009; Decree 843, 28 October 2009) as the original system proved to be dysfunctional. The first tender for project selection opened only in February 2010, and the first projects planned to reduce 30 Mt CO_2 were endorsed in July 2010. However, instead of providing a full approval of the selected projects, the operator of JI in Russia, Sberbank, has subjected the endorsements to the sale price of emissions allowances and the terms and conditions of payments. This may reduce the future attractiveness of Russian JI projects to foreign buyers. There is also some interest in facilitating international emissions trading by establishing a Green Investment Scheme (GIS) – a bilateral arrangement between buyer and seller aimed at guaranteeing the reinvestment of assigned amount units (AAUs) transaction revenues to emissions reduction projects. Although some legislation has been passed, there are few prospects for the establishment of a functional GIS in Russia by 2012, due to transparency problems, related lack of trust by buyers and the limited demand for AAUs given the competition from other analogous schemes introduced in the EU, Ukraine and within the Kyoto mechanisms.

Conclusions

Two main trends seem therefore to characterise Russian energy policy: the emergence of a hybrid domestic market with elements of liberalisation and state control and a dialectic of economisation and politicisation of the state's energy foreign policy. We have argued that Russian energy policy, both domestically and abroad, displays a multilayered conception of energy security. It emphasises security of demand for Russia's exports, comprising the sub-objectives of availability of surplus resources, access to markets and profitability of markets. At the same time, Russian energy policy has been guided by the need to ensure adequate resources to the domestic economy, comprising the traditional triangle of security, competitiveness and sustainability of supply.

While GDP growth is the main political priority in Russia, climate change remains a marginal policy issue. Therefore, the introduction of economically disruptive climate policies is not realistic in the short term, and energy policies are continuing to define Russia's emissions trends. Based on the synergies identified between climate and energy security policies, energy security policies, if successful, are likely to limit emissions trends. We also identified a number of mitigation interests that, to different extents, appear to contradict energy security policies. However, due to the weaknesses of the Russian administrative system, the success of the identified policies remains uncertain, and in some cases difficult to predict.

As power sector reform is ongoing, elements of regulation and lack of competition remain an essential part of the system. Due to the economic downturn, gas price reform slowed down in comparison to the original plan. Quite strikingly, prices have been increasing steadily. The share of coal is yet to increase in comparison to gas, but gas price reforms will soon incentivise switching to coal, a move which will work against mitigation interests. Projects to construct new nuclear capacity have been delayed, and the government is now likely to replace existing capacity – soon to be decommissioned – rather than provide additional low-carbon generation capacity in the mid term. Several independent policies to incentivise energy efficiency improvements – whose degree of success is nevertheless difficult to determine – have been recently introduced.

Although energy efficiency legislation is not designed to achieve the full potential of energy efficiency improvements, existing policies appear likely to deliver some emissions cuts. Renewable energy policy (beyond hydropowder) is virtually absent in Russia, and for now it has only been embraced rhetorically. When it comes to the flaring of associated gas, the ambitious limitations introduced are likely to suffer from both practical problems and the lack of data to monitor independently the progress of implementation. It is therefore virtually impossible to estimate the potential mitigation effect of this policy. Due to the late start, JI and GIS are likely to have only minor impacts on emissions, at least until 2012.

The gap between energy security and mitigation *policies* and the *actual measures* to improve energy security and emissions cuts illustrate the importance of a 'reality check' when estimating potential synergies and contradictions between policies in the Russian context. Although many powerful interests in the Russian energy sector have appeared to be supportive of mitigation, the future prospects for mitigation efforts remain uncertain. However, it is positive that major contradictions within energy security policy are limited, and that even in the absence of a fully successful implementation of policies, synergies can be expected to deliver emissions limitations in the future.

Acknowledgements

Preparation of this chapter was supported by the Finnish Institute for International Affairs and the NORKLIMA programme of the Research Council of Norway.

Note

1. The retail price on European markets minus transport costs and taxes.

References

Belyi, A.V. (2009), *A Russian Perspective on the Energy Charter Treaty* (Madrid: Real Instituto Elcano, ARI 98/2009, 16 June).

Blagov, S. (2009), 'Russia Seeks to Sustain Its Energy Security', *Eurasian Daily Monitor,* 6(221), 2 December.

Charap, S. and G. Safonov (2010), 'Climate change and role of energy efficiency', in A. Åslund, S. Guriev and A. Kutchins (eds): *Russia after the Global Economic Crisis* (Washington: Peterson Institute for International Economics and the Center for Strategic and International Studies).

Commission of the European Communities (2008), 'Second strategic energy review: an EU energy security and solidarity action plan', COM(2008) 781 [http://eur-lex.europa.eu/LexUriServ/LexUriServ.do?uri= COM:2008:0781:FIN:EN:PDF; accessed: 01 September 2010].

Cooper, C. and L. Schipper (1991), 'The Soviet energy conservation dilemma', *Energy Policy,* 19(4): 344–63.

Fredholm, M. (2008), 'Natural Gas: An Expensive Trickle', in: *TOL Special Report: Energy* (Prague: Transitions Online).

"Gazprom (2011), *All You Need Is Gas: Gazprom Investor Day February 2011* (Moscow: Gazprom). [http://gazprom.ru/f/posts/37/219660/2011_02_15_investorday_final.pdf; accessed: 7 July 2011].

Hedenskog, J. and R.L. Larsson (2009), *Russian Leverage on CIS and the Baltic States* (Stockholm: Swedish Defence Research Agency).

Heinrich, A. (2008) 'Under the Kremlin's Thumb: Does Increased State Control in the Russian Gas Sector Endanger European Security of Supply?', *Europe-Asia Studies,* 60(9): 1539–74.

Hellman, J.S. (1998), 'Winners Take All: the Politics of Partial Reform in Post-Communist Transitions', *World Politics,* 50(2): 203–34.

International Energy Agency (IEA) (2002), *Russia Energy Survey* (Paris: The International Energy Agency).

IEA (2003), *Renewables in Russia: From Opportunity to Reality* (Paris: The International Energy Agency).

IEA (2006), *Optimising Russian Natural Gas: Reform and Climate Policy* (Paris: The International Energy Agency).

IEA (2007), *Energy Security and Climate Policy: Assessing Interactions* (Paris: International Energy Agency).

IEA (2008a), *Natural Gas Market Review 2008* (Paris: The International Energy Agency).
IEA (2008b), *Energy Balances of Non-OECD Countries: 2008 Edition* (Paris: The International Energy Agency).
IEA (2009a), *Key World Energy Statistics 2009* (Paris: The International Energy Agency).
IEA (2009b), *World Energy Outlook* (Paris: The International Energy Agency).
IEA (2010a), *Energy Balances of Non-OECD Countries* (Paris: The International Energy Agency).
IEA (2010b), *Energy Balances of OECD Countries* (Paris: the International Energy Agency).
IEA (2010c), *Key World Energy Statistics 2010* (Paris: the International Energy Agency).
International Finance Corporation and the World Bank (2008), *Energy Efficiency in Russia: Untapped Reserves* (Washington: The International Finance Corporation and the World Bank).
Kristalinskaya, S. (2010), 'Russia Tackles Associated Gas Flaring', *Oil&Gas Eurasia*, 3 [http://www.oilandgaseurasia.com/articles/p/115/article/1143/#; accessed: 26 May 2010].
Lesage, D., T. Van de Graaf. and K. Westphal (2010), *Global Energy Governance in a Multipolar World* (Hampshire and Burlington: Ashgate).
Locatelli, C. (2008), 'EU Gas Liberalization as a Driver of Gazprom's Strategies' (Paris and Brussels: Institut Français des Relations Internationales and Russia/New Independent States Centre).
McKinsey and Co. (2009), 'Pathways to an Energy and Carbon Efficient Russia: Opportunities to Increase Energy Efficiency and Reduce Greenhouse Gas Emissions' [http://www.mckinsey.com/clientservice/sustainability/pdf/CO2_Russia_ENG_final.pdf; accessed: 19 August 2010].
Mitrova, T. (2009), 'Natural gas in transition: systemic reform issues', in S. Pirani (ed.): *Russian and CIS Gas Markets and their Impact on Europe* (Oxford: Oxford University Press).
Morozov, V. (2009), 'Energy dialogue and the future of Russia: Politics and economics in the struggle for Europe', in P. Aalto (ed.) (2009): *The EU-Russian Energy Dialogue. Europe's Future Energy Security* (Aldershot: Ashgate).
The Moscow Times (2010a), 'Putin: Ukraine Deals "Anything But Simple" ... ', 23 April.
The Moscow Times (2010b), 'RusHydro Building New Plant', 30 August.
Nove, A. (1977), *The Soviet Economic System* (London: G. Allen & Unwin).
Novikova, A. A. Korppoo and M. Sharmina (2009), 'Russian pledge vs. business-as-usual: Implementing energy efficiency policies can curb carbon emissions', UPI Working Paper 61, 4 December 2009 [http://www.upi-fiia.fi/fi/publication/97/; accessed: 25 May 2010].
Øverland, I. and H. Kjærnet (2009), *Russian Renewable Energy: The Potential for International Cooperation* (Hampshire and Burlington: Ashgate).
Petersen, M. (2009), 'Restructuring the Electricity Sector in the EU and in Russia', *European Energy and Environmental Law Review*, 18: 171–9.
Popel', O.S. (2008), 'Vozobnovlyaemye Istochniki Énergii: Rol' i Mesto v Sovremennoĭ i Perspektivnoĭ Energetike', *Rossiĭskiĭ Khemicheskiĭ Zhurnal*, 52: 95–106.
Romanova, T. (2010), 'Energobezopasnost' bez paniki: Dialog Rossii i ES vozvrashajetsa k ekonomitseskim osnovam', *Russia in Global Affairs*, 9: 151–63.
Norton Rose (2009), 'Russia's Withdrawal from the Energy Charter Treaty', (London: Norton Rose) [http://www.nortonrose.com/knowledge/publications/2009/pub22691.aspx?lang=en-gb; accessed: 24 July 2010].

Rowe, E.W. (2009), 'Who Is to Blame? Agency, Causality, Responsibility and the Role of Experts in Russian Framings of Global Climate Change', *Europe-Asia Studies*, 61(4): 593–619.

Russian Federation (2006), 'Development of Nuclear Energy Sector in Russia 2007–2010 with prospects until 2015, Federal Programme #605 from 6 October 2006'.

Russian Federation (2009a), 'Energy Strategy of Russia for the Period up to 2030' from 13 November 2009 (Moscow: The Ministry of Energy of the Russian Federation).

Russian Federation (2009b), Federal Law no. 261-F3 from 23 November 2009 'On Energy Efficiency and Energy Savings and on Introducing Amendments to Certain Laws of the Russian Federation'.

Russian Federation (2009c), Decree no. N7 from 8 January 2009 'On measures to stimulate limits to polluting atmosphere by burning associated gas at flaring installations'.

Seliverstov, S. (2009), *Energy Security of Russia and the EU: Current Legal Problems* (Paris: Institute Français des Relations Internationales).

Stern, J. (2005), *The Future of Russian Gas and Gazprom* (Oxford: Oxford University Press).

Stern, J. (2009a), *Future Gas Production in Russia: Is the Concern about Lack of Investment Justified?* (Oxford: The Oxford Institute for Energy Studies).

Stern, J. (2009b), 'The Russian Gas Balance to 2015: Difficult Years Ahead', in S. Pirani (ed.): *Russian and CIS Gas Markets and their Impact on Europe* (Oxford: Oxford University Press).

Sutela, P. (2009), 'Links Between Economic Growth and Energy Consumption in Russia', Presentation at the Finnish Institute of International Affairs, 'Energy Efficiency and the Russian Economy – Trends and Links to Climate Policy', 16.10.2009 [http://www.upi-fiia.fi/assets/events/pekka_sutela.pdf, accessed: 19.08.2010].

Tompson, W. (2005), 'Russia's Power Sector Reform: Creating Robust Competition or a Potemkin Market?', *Russian/CIS Energy and Mining Law Journal*, 3 (1–2).

Tynkkynen, N. (2010), 'A Great Ecological Power in Global Climate Policy? Framing Climate Change as a Policy Problem in Russian Public Discussion', *Environmental Politics*, 19(2): 179–95.

United Nations Economic Commission for Europe (2010), *Policy Reforms for Energy Efficiency Investments* (Geneva: United Nations Economic Commission for Europe).

Ürge-Vorsatz, D. Miladinova, G. & L. Paizs (2006), 'Energy in Transition: From the Iron Curtain to the European Union', *Energy Policy*, 34(15): 2279–97.

World Nuclear Association (2010), 'Nuclear Power in Russia' [http://www.world-nuclear.org/info/inf45.html#Electricity_Supply; accessed: 28.09.2010].

9
Energy Security in Indonesia

Budy P. Resosudarmo, Ariana Alisjahbana & Ditya Agung Nurdianto

Introduction

Indonesia, which spreads over more than 17,000 islands and has a population of approximately 230 million, is the world's largest archipelago and the fourth most populous nation. It stretches along the equator for about 6000 kilometres – approximately the same distance as from San Francisco to New York. The territory extends roughly from 6° N to 10° S and from 95° E to 142° E, between the Indian and Pacific oceans and links the continents of Asia and Australia. While the country's territory covers an area of approximately 7.9 million km^2 (including the coastal Exclusive Economic Zone area), only approximately 1.9 million km^2 is land. Indonesia is the largest member state of the Association of Southeast Asian Nations (ASEAN) and accounts for nearly 40 per cent of its population and 36.5 per cent of its gross domestic product (GDP) (ASEAN, 2010).

Indonesia consumes the equivalent of 191 million tons of oil annually. This figure is projected to increase as a product of economic growth (World Bank, 2010). The Indonesian government has made energy security a policy priority. The Indonesian Ministry of Energy and Mineral Resources states that one of its missions is to provide energy security and ensure energy independence, as well as increase energy efficiency and take into account environmental issues in a way that maximises the welfare of the people (ESDM, 2010). Article 3 in the recently enacted law on energy (Law No. 30/2007) states that the ethos behind managing energy in Indonesia is to support the country's sustainable development and energy security. However, the law does not define energy security exactly. Nevertheless, the law does mention the goals of energy management energy, which are as follows:

a) Achieving independent energy management;
b) Guaranteeing the availability of energy in the country, both through domestic and foreign sources. Such availability is for:

- Supplying domestic energy demand;
- Supplying intermediate inputs of domestic industries;
- Increasing foreign reserves;

c) Guaranteeing optimal, integrated and sustainable management of energy resources;
d) Efficient use of energy in all sectors;
e) Improving energy access for low-income people and those living in remote areas to improve their welfare in an equal and just way by:

- Providing support to make energy available to people on low incomes;
- Building energy infrastructure in undeveloped regions and thus reducing regional disparity;
- Developing autonomous energy industries and services and improving human professionalism;
- Protecting the environment.

Based on the energy management goals stated in Law No. 30/2007, most Indonesian policy makers and energy analysts talk in terms of the '4 As' (availability, accessibility, affordability and acceptability), indicating the availability of energy at all times in various forms, in sufficient quantities, that can be accessible by most people at affordable prices, and obtained in a way that is not environmentally destructive (Indriyanto, 2010).

The issue of energy security has been the subject of discussion in Indonesia for a long time. However, until the end of the 1990s, it had never been central to the country's policy debates. The turning points were the depreciation of the rupiah, particularly in relation to the US dollar, during the 1997/98 Asian financial crisis and the increasing price of crude oil in the early 2000s, which made it very expensive to control the domestic price of fuel and electricity through energy subsidies. At that time, with approximately 43 per cent of its energy sources derived from crude oil,[1] the amount of government spending on energy subsidies increased from almost nothing in 1996 to approximately 21 per cent of total government expenditure in 2005 (ESDM, 2009). Whether the government could guarantee Indonesia's energy needs at an affordable price, and how to achieve it, became one of the hottest policy debates.

The issue of energy security became even more complex in 2005 when, for the first time in several decades, Indonesia became a net importer of oil. Since Indonesia is amongst the top 3–5 emitters of CO_2 globally, mostly as a result of deforestation and forest degradation, the increasing prominence of climate change concerns in the first decade of the twenty-first century also increased attention on energy concerns (Sari et al., 2007).

The Indonesian government reacted by developing policies and programmes to overcome the challenges associated with meeting energy security targets. This chapter will review some of the main challenges and provide some understanding of the basis for Indonesia's current energy security policies. To achieve these goals, we first review Indonesian economic trends and development patterns since the 1970s, to provide background information on the main drivers of energy demand. Second, the chapter discusses energy supply and demand trends, which have been influenced by different issues, including declining oil and gas production and rapidly increasing domestic demand. Third, the Indonesian government's energy policies, including petroleum and electricity subsidies, are examined. Fourth, we discuss climate change issues and how concerns regarding the energy sector's greenhouse gas (GHG) emissions are influencing current energy security policies. We conclude with some final remarks related to energy security issues in Indonesia.

The Indonesian Economy

For the sake of simplicity, Indonesia's 17,000 islands can be roughly divided into five major island-groups: Java-Bali, Sumatra, Kalimantan, Sulawesi and Eastern Indonesia. Indonesia shares the islands of Kalimantan with Malaysia, and Papua with Papua New Guinea (Resosudarmo et al., 2000). The Java-Bali island group dominates much of the Indonesian economy, accounting for 61 per cent of the total population and 61 per cent of GDP (Hill et al., 2008) while only occupying 7 per cent of the total land area.

Indonesia has 33 provinces, with the capital province Jakarta leading the regional income per capita. Inequality amongst provinces is widespread, with 50 per cent of the national GDP contributed by the three big provinces of Java: Jakarta, West Java and East Java. In 2004, the ratio of per capita gross regional domestic product (GRDP) of the richest to poorest province was 15.9 and 11.3 for household expenditure (Hill et al., 2008). Jakarta and the wider Java-Bali region is the centre for service-based, industrial economic activity, while the rest of the country relies heavily on mining and natural resource extraction.

In the 1970s, Indonesia grew at an average rate of above 7 per cent with earnings from oil exports as the main source of income. Indonesia was a net exporting country for oil until 2005 and the only Southeast Asian member of the Organization of the Petroleum Exporting Countries (OPEC) until 2008. Indonesia benefited from high oil prices in the 1970s but then suffered from the world oil price drop in the 1980s. Prices went from US$37 per barrel in 1981 to US$14 per barrel in 1986. To cope with the declining revenue and economic crisis at the time, the Indonesian government decided to diversify its economy by developing non-oil sectors. Relying too much on the oil and gas sector for economic revenue was considered not sustainable given the volatile nature of world markets. Indonesia adopted policies with the goal of liberalising trade, providing incentives for increasing exports, and conducting structural changes within the local economy. This reform was a trendsetter that instigated Indonesia's current direction, that is, developing the industrial and services sector that are mainly concentrated in the Java-Bali island group (Resosudarmo and Kuncoro, 2006).

The 1997–1998 Asian financial crisis was a significant blow to the Indonesian economy. The Indonesian rupiah collapsed from 2300 to the dollar in June 1997 to more than 17,000 by January 1998. Inflation rose to 78 per cent and overall GDP growth was approximately minus 13 per cent. Since Indonesia controlled domestic fuel prices and wanted to maintain the pre-crisis price, the energy subsidy increased from almost nothing to approximately 17 per cent of total government expenditure, creating a significant fiscal burden on the government (Hartono & Resosudarmo, 2008).

The economic reforms following the Asian crisis focused mainly on strengthening the banking system, liberalising trade and foreign investment and promoting a better, more transparent government (Resosudarmo and Kuncoro, 2006). Reforms included an attempt to reduce the energy subsidy, which triggered huge riots, arson and mass looting in Jakarta. In May 1998, in the aftermath of the riots, under the threat of impeachment from no longer compliant leaders of parliament, Soeharto resigned from the presidency after 32 years in power. An important shift from Soeharto's authoritarian regime towards democracy took place. In 2001, the government enacted a new policy of political decentralisation, by vowing to increase the power of regional governments and change the centrist system of the Soeharto era. Before this decentralisation policy, the central government had the final say on nearly every issue, with regional powers exerting only limited authority in their own provinces. The system was also economically centrist, as most revenues from the mining and natural resource extraction went to Jakarta. Only non-resource revenue streams were distributed to regions. Under this model, high-earning regions saw only a fraction of their revenue contribution redistributed back to them. Decentralisation aimed to increase regional authority and the economic autonomy, so that high-earning regions could enjoy their revenue and manage their own budgets. These positive impacts, however, were not without their negative counterparts. The decentralisation policy caused increasing conflict between the central government and the regions; unprepared regional institutions caused more widespread corruption. These problems continue to affect Indonesia's investment sector (Resosudarmo and Kuncoro, 2006).

During the early 2000s, the increasing world price of crude oil increased the cost of the energy subsidy and placed the question of energy security on the political agenda. Various policy fora addressed the issue of whether Indonesia would be able to provide its people with the energy they need, and whether or not there would be enough energy to boost the country's industrial growth.

Despite these problems, including those regarding the energy sector, the Indonesian economy was able to recover. Since 2004, Indonesian per capita

Table 9.1 Indonesia: Main macroeconomic indicators

	Unit	2000	2002	2004	2006	2008
GDP at 2000 prices	*Trillion Rp*	1390	1506	1657	1846	2082
Growth rate	%	4.93	4.38	5.03	5.5	6.06
Population	*Million*	206	212	218	222	229
Growth rate	%	1.12	1.61	1.2	1.52	1.28
GDP per capita	*Thousand Rp*	6753	7104	7606	8308	9111
Growth rate	%	3.77	2.71	3.83	3.85	4.73

Source: ESDM (2009).

income has returned to pre-crisis levels, the rupiah has stabilised, inflation has been under two digits, foreign reserves have been relatively abundant and the economy has been able to grow by more than 5 per cent annually (Kuncoro and Resosudarmo, 2006). Table 9.1 shows that Indonesia's GDP has been growing at an average annual rate of approximately 5 per cent in the last ten years. Furthermore, it is projected that Indonesia will be growing at close to 6 per cent throughout the next decade.

Besides the economy, the population has also been growing at an average rate of approximately 1.3 per cent in the last decade, which is slightly higher than the world average, mainly due to the improvement in general health conditions. The infant mortality rate, as an important variable indicating general health conditions, dropped from 145 deaths per 1000 births in 1971 to 47 in 2000. In general, people's welfare has improved significantly since the 1970s. Average schooling years rose from only 1.9 in 1971 to 5.4 in 2000 (Hill et al., 2008). Poverty, measured by the percentage of people living below the official poverty line, dropped from approximately 30 per cent in 1984 to 17 per cent in 2004. Indonesia's Human Development Index (HDI) has been rising since the 1970s and continues to do so in the 2000s; HDI has risen by approximately 1.26 per cent annually, from 0.673 in 2000 to 0.734 in 2007 (UNDP, 2009).

The growing economy, increasing population and improvement of welfare are the main drivers of Indonesia's increasing consumption of energy. This is not surprising given that the United Nations Developments Programme (UNDP) (2004) has shown that there is a positive correlation between a country's HDI and its per capita energy consumption. In this sense, energy security has become central to Indonesia's policy debate.

Energy Demand and Supply in Indonesia

Indonesia consumed the equivalent of approximately 191 million tons of oil in 2007, making it the 13th largest total energy consumer in the world and

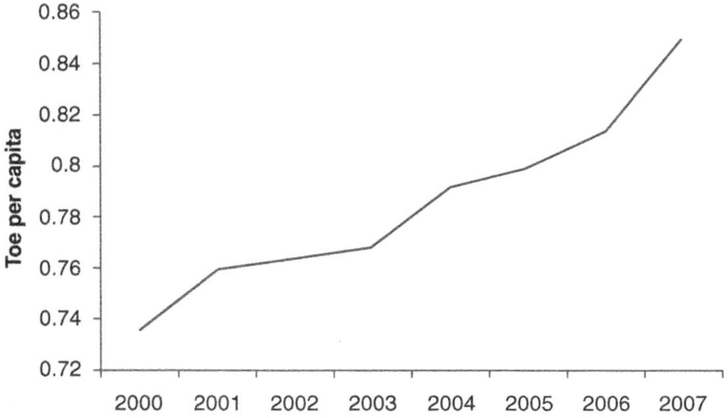

Figure 9.1 Indonesia: Final energy consumption per capita
Source: NCCC and UNFCCC (2009).

the biggest in ASEAN. When calculated on a per capita basis, Indonesians consumed 0.85 toe per capita in 2007, far below the world average of 1.82 toe per capita and even below the ASEAN average of 2.22 toe per capita (World Bank, 2010). The energy consumption trend, however, has been increasing. From the year 2000 until 2008, the final energy consumption per capita has seen an increase of more than 15 per cent, or approximately 2.1 per cent annually, from the equivalent of 0.74 toe per capita in 2000 to 0.85 toe per capita in 2007 (Figure 9.1).

Analysed by sector, the end-users are categorised into industrial, household, commercial, transportation, and other sectors, with the industrial sector leading Indonesia's energy consumption with nearly half the total. Transportation is second, followed by the household sector (Figure 9.2). It can be inferred that the increase in energy consumption in the last two decades is mostly due to industrial sector growth.

Another characteristic of the high growth rate of Indonesia's energy consumption is that its consumption is not efficient, measured by the amount of energy used per GDP. Due to a technological gap, most developing countries have a higher energy intensity rate (i.e. less efficient use of energy) than developed countries. Industrialised countries tend to have access to better, more efficient technologies and cleaner fuel sources. However, Indonesia's energy intensity is also high when compared with several other developing countries, as shown in Figure 9.3. It must nevertheless, be noted that Indonesia's energy intensity started to decline from 2001 onwards, after increasing in the period 1996–1999.

While strong demand side growth reflects Indonesia's economic growth – mainly due to the growth of the industrial sector – the domestic supply side

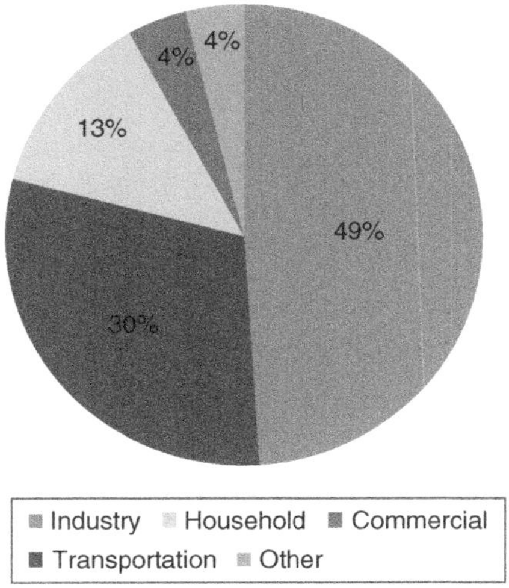

Figure 9.2 Indonesia: Share of total final energy consumption by sector (2008)
Source: ESDM (2009).

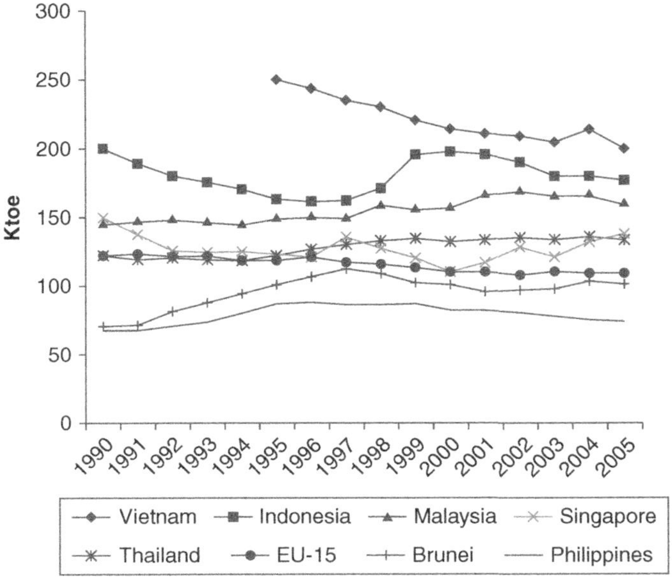

Figure 9.3 Energy intensity for selected Southeast Asian countries and EU-15
Source: IEA (2007a, 2007b).

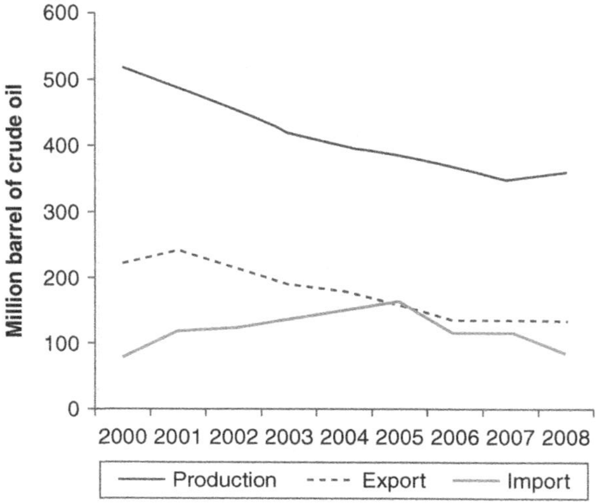

Figure 9.4 Indonesia: Crude oil production, export and import
Source: ESDM (2009).

has not seen a similar trend. Crude oil production – on which Indonesia has traditionally relied for its energy needs and domestic oil reserves – has been consistently declining since 2000 (IIEE Research Team, 2006). In 2000, Indonesia's crude oil production was 517 million barrels, whereas in 2008 it dropped to only 357 million barrels (Figure 9.4). One of the main factors contributing to this decline is the location of new reserves, mostly in far-flung areas where exploration is technically challenging. In addition, there is relatively flat exploration expenditure by oil companies, lack of investment in new technologies and no significant increase in refining capacity over the past decade (IIEE Research Team, 2006).

Flowing from production decline, Indonesian crude oil exports have also declined in the last decade. In 2005, Indonesia was a net-importer of crude oil as the government decided to prioritise domestic crude oil consumption over exports. As a result, the government enacted the Presidential Decree no 5/2006 on National Energy Policy in 2006 – a policy that explicitly pushes the country to reduce its reliance on crude oil and seek other energy sources – and decided to withdraw from OPEC in 2008.

Imports, on the other hand, increased along with increasing consumption and decreasing production in between 2000 and 2005. The Presidential Decree no 5/2006 prioritised a shift away from oil towards increased coal and natural gas consumption. This strategy might help to explain the more recent decline in crude oil imports. While the Indonesian government is trying to rely less on oil, it is still the main fossil fuel used throughout the country and, as with energy consumption, there is increasing demand for refined petroleum products such as gasoline. Lack of investment in additional domestic refineries made way for increases in imported refined fuels, thus increasing Indonesia's vulnerability to international oil price fluctuations (IIEE Research Team, 2006).

While oil is Indonesia's main energy commodity, coal and natural gas have also played an important role, especially in the last decade. As of January 2007, Indonesia held the 10th largest proven natural gas reserves in the world and, in 2004, was the second largest net coal exporter in 2004 (EIA, 2007). Figure 9.5 illustrates Indonesia's various primary energy sources and their percentage share of the total energy supply. Petroleum products outstrip other sources, but its share is decreasing. Coal, on the other hand, has seen a sharp increase, as it is increasingly used in electricity generation. Coal soared from virtually zero in 1984 to 47 per cent of the state-owned power line networking's (PLN) fuel sources in 2008 (Resosudarmo et al., 2008; ESDM, 2009).

By 2007, coal had probably become the profitable mining sector. Coal-mining operations accounted for approximately 70 per cent of around US$6 billion that mining contributed to government revenue in that year (US Commercial Service, 2007). Furthermore, since 2003, the export value of coal has been the highest amongst other mining commodities, reaching approximately US$6 billion. As the government has set a target of increasing coal's share of primary energy supply to more than 33 per cent by 2025, up

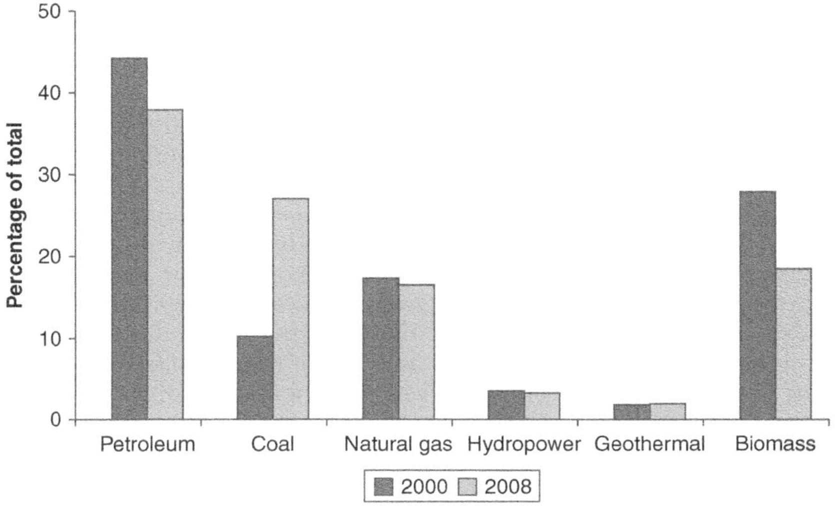

Figure 9.5 Indonesia: Primary energy supply
Source: ESDM (2009).

from 26 per cent in 2008, Indonesia's coal production is expected to increase. At the same time, revenues from exporting coal have become increasingly important for the Indonesian government.

Energy Security and Development Policies

Since the mid 2000s, energy security has been a priority for the government of Indonesia. The strategies adopted by the government to manage its resources and the policies enacted to balance domestic use and supply have become critically important issues, given Indonesia's rapidly developing economy. The state plays a prominent role in regulating and managing the country's energy and natural resources, as stipulated by the 1945 Constitution. The Ministry for Energy and Mineral Resources defines its first priority as ensuring energy security and independence, with an emphasis on domestic supply of energy sources.

Recent key energy security policy legislation consists of: Presidential decree No. 5/2006 on National Energy Policy, Law No. 30/2007 on Energy, Law No. 17/2007 on the Long-term National Development Plan 2005–2025 Rencana Pembangunan Jangka Panjang Nasiona (RPJPN) and Law No. 5/2010 on the Medium-term National Development Plan 2010–2014 Rencana Pembangunan Jangka Menengah Nasional (RPJMN). All four of them present programmes and policies connected to the availability of energy, development and people's welfare (Indriyanto et al., 2007). The main goal of these recently introduced policies is to diversify energy sources for Indonesia in order to reduce its dependence on oil. As previously mentioned, Indonesia is vulnerable to the dynamics of the international oil market, juggling declining domestic production with increasing consumption and refined imports. The main challenge, however, is Indonesia's controversial but popular energy price subsidies. Domestic energy prices are controlled by the government and they are below both supply cost and world prices, with the heaviest subsidies in place for kerosene, one of the nation's main cooking fuels and 'premium' gasoline (a non-subsidised version, 'pertamax', exists). According to the revised 2010 state budget, this fuel subsidy is projected to cost the government approximately US$9.78 billion for 2010. In addition to petroleum products, the Indonesian government also controls the end-user price of electricity, which is currently lower than the production cost, and so subsidises electricity prices too. The state-owned National Electricity Company has a monopoly on electricity generation and distribution. The main energy source for power plants is oil. Hence, both fuel and electricity subsidies place a heavy burden on the government when crude oil prices are high (Indriyanto, 2008). For example, during the period of high world prices of crude oil (see Figure 9.6), the total government subsidy of fuel and electricity amounted to approximately 23 per cent of total government expenditure in 2008. In 2009, the world price of crude oil declined and so the total subsidy

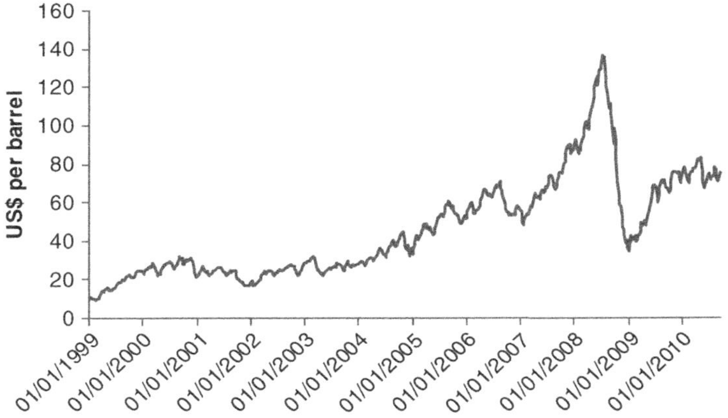

Figure 9.6 Crude oil: Average world price (1999–2010)
Source: US Energy Information Administration [http://www.eia.doe.gov/dnav/pet/pet_pri_wco_k_w.htm; accessed: 28 September 2010].

on fuel and electricity went down to 10 per cent. Increasing the domestic price of fuel and electricity typically creates social and political unrest and so it can only be implemented progressively. Other options are to increase energy intensity and divert the source of energy from oil to other sources.

The Presidential Decree no 5/2006 explicitly lists two priorities for the national energy policy: reduce energy elasticity to lower than 1 by 2025, and supply the optimal primary energy mix by 2025. Energy elasticity refers to energy intensity per GDP, which is currently higher in Indonesia than in most other ASEAN countries. The optimal energy mix policy aims to diversify the country's energy sources, with less reliance on oil and more on natural gas, coal and renewable energy. As Table 9.2 clearly indicates, the decree lists the optimal primary energy portfolio that needs to be achieved by 2025. In comparison to the 2008 primary energy consumption, the

Table 9.2 Indonesia: Primary energy consumption

2008		2025 Target	
Petroleum	37%	Coal	33%
Coal	26%	Natural gas	30%
Biomass	18%	Petroleum	20%
Natural gas	16%	Biofuels	5%
Hydropower	2%	Geothermal	5%
Geothermal	1%	Other renewables	5%
		Other fossil fuels	2%

Source: Republic of Indonesia (2006), Presidential decree No. 5/2006.

Indonesian government will have to increase the share of natural gas and coal, and decrease the share of petroleum and biomass. Some experts have expressed concern that the targeted share of geothermal energy is too small, given the country's abundant potential in this area.

With this policy in place, it is clear that the government is trying to steer the nation away from oil dependence. Another regulation attempting to divert Indonesia energy sourcing is Law 5/2010 on the Medium-term National Development Plan 2010–2014 released by Indonesia's National Planning and Development Agency (*Badan Perencanaan dan Pembangunan Nasional* or Bappenas). This law – which identifies energy as the 8th National Development Priority – aims to attain national energy security and to ensure the continuity of national growth through institutional restructuring, while optimising the widest possible utilisation of alternative energy. Therefore, developing renewable energy is now a greater priority, assuming that the policy is fully implemented (Bappenas, 2010). Article 3 of the legislation targets an increase in electricity generation capacity by an average of 3000 MW per year starting in 2010. The ultimate target is to increase the spread of electricity, from an electrification ratio of 62 per cent at present to 80 per cent in 2014.

Despite the attempt to diversify energy sources, Indonesia still has to address the problem of how to eliminate its energy subsidies. It is true that the main goal of the subsidies is to enable low-purchasing power people to consume fuel, but the negative implications of this policy seem to be obvious. Indriyanto et al. (2007) argued that subsidies tend to cause overconsumption, since the market price does not reflect the actual cost of producing one unit of petroleum product. Subsidies also discourage energy efficiency measures and the development of alternative or renewable energy sources by way of low electricity tariffs. The state budget is heavily burdened by this policy and, in order to provide low-priced electricity, a little less than half the population are denied access to electricity. This policy mostly favours the urban population or those who are privileged enough to have access to electricity while forgoing the development of necessary new infrastructure needed to deliver electricity to those without it.

The issue of subsidies needs to be dealt with prudently. It has in fact become a highly political process as confirmed by past riots in response to price reforms. To this end, the Ministry of Energy and Mineral Resources has developed a strategy to reduce the petroleum subsidies gradually. The ultimate goal of this strategy is to eliminate petroleum subsidies entirely by 2025 (Sutijastoto, 2006). Whether or not the Indonesian government will succeed in implementing necessary reforms remains to be seen.

Climate Change Issues

As an archipelagic developing country located on the equator, Indonesia is quite vulnerable to the effects of anthropogenic climate change. Sea-level rise brought on by melted glaciers and expanding seawater will affect Indonesian coastal areas greatly, and precipitation and rainfall pattern changes will hinder agricultural productivity, amongst other problems (Bappenas, 2010). As the globe continues to warm, increasing volatility of seasonal patterns, and water shortage and flood problems are amongst the worst climate change effects on Indonesia.

Although it is a developing country, Indonesia's GHG emissions are significant. In the mid 2000s, although Indonesia ranked in the top five national emitters of GHGs, it would have ranked 16th or lower globally if emissions from deforestation and forest degradation were excluded (Sari et al., 2007). The forestry sector gained most government and international public attention, since it contributed more than 85 per cent of Indonesia's CO_2 emissions.

Emissions from the energy sector, however small, are rapidly growing. As mentioned, Indonesia is a fast emerging economy with an increasingly affluent population which aspires to better living conditions and, as a consequence, energy consumption per capita is increasing. As the population continues to grow and becomes richer, energy use will also grow. It is expected that, at the current rate of consumption and fossil fuel use, emissions from the energy sector will at least triple from 0.3 Gt CO_2e in 2003 to more than 1 Gt CO_2e in 2030 (Sari et al., 2007). CO_2 emissions from the energy sector must be managed, as this sector is crucial to the development of the Indonesian economy, both for earning export/foreign exchange revenue and for fulfilling the need for domestic energy (Bappenas, 2010).

In line with the above concerns and the national development planning priorities, the Indonesian government will focus on a set of priority sectors. These priority sectors are divided into mitigation and adaptation priorities, with the energy sector falling into the mitigation category. In order to reduce emissions from the energy sector Indonesia needs to properly address its heavy reliance on fossil-based fuels. More than 79 per cent of Indonesia's energy comes from fossil fuels, with 26 per cent of the total coming from coal. Heavy reliance on coal for power generation sector is the main contributor to Indonesia's high energy intensity rate (Resosudarmo et al., 2009). Coal is the dirtiest of the three main fossil fuels as it releases twice as much carbon dioxide per unit of energy as natural gas (EIA, 1993).

During the 2009 G-20 meeting in Pittsburgh, Indonesia announced its national target of reducing GHG emissions by 26 per cent below the Business As Usual (BAU) scenario by 2020 without the financial assistance of other countries, and by 41 per cent with international assistance. Figure 9.7 illustrates Indonesia's sectoral emissions in 2005. Quite obviously peatland, forestry and energy make up the largest sectoral emitters of CO_2 in Indonesia. Under the BAU scenario, this composition will not change much by 2020. With continuing deforestation, the forest area in Indonesia will naturally decline by 2020 with a corresponding declining growth rate of CO_2

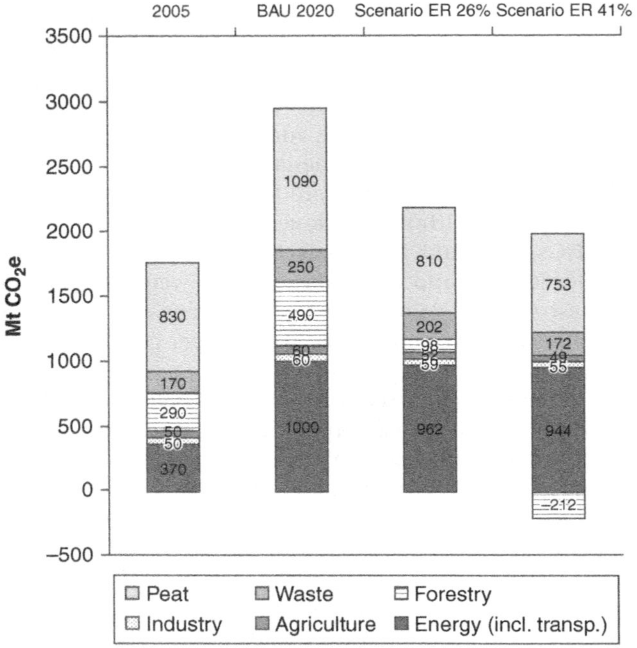

Figure 9.7 Indonesia: Projection of 2020 GHG emissions under BAU and emissions reduction scenarios
Source: NCCC (2009).

emissions from forest fires and less land clearing. The energy sector, on the other hand, is expected to grow continuously during this period, and thus its CO_2 emissions will rapidly grow from approximately 375 Mt CO_2e in 2005 to approximately 1 Gt CO_2e in 2020.

Looking at the 26 per cent reduction scenario, the forestry sector's emissions share declines significantly. But under this scenario, Indonesia is able to maintain the size of its forest cover, as the primary reduction of CO_2 emissions will come from the prevention of deforestation. This in turn will make the energy sector the largest sectoral emitter of CO_2 by 2020.

Table 9.3 lists Indonesia's overall plan of action to reduce CO_2 emissions by 2020. With regard to the energy sector, the Indonesian government opted to focus on three aspects, namely demand-side management, energy efficiency and developing renewable energy. Demand-side management primarily deals with end users and their energy consumption patterns. High fuel consumption coupled with low energy prices due to government subsidies are pressing concerns. On the supply side, the emissions intensity of electricity generation must also be improved. The possibility of using

Table 9.3 Indonesia: Emissions reduction plan

Sector	Action plan
Peatland	Improve peatland management, peatland mapping and law enforcement, generate alternative economic activities and strengthen peat fire management
Forestry	Improve programmes in forest fire management, combating illegal logging, preventing deforestation, local community involvement as well as land and forest rehabilitation
Agriculture	Improve water management programmes and plant rice varieties with less methane
Waste	Implement municipal solid waste law, enhance 3Rs (reuse, recycle, recovery), encourage private sector investment and develop landfill improvement programmes
Industry	Increase energy efficiency and access to better technologies
Transportation	Implement fuel efficiency standards, enhance public transportation infrastructure and implement traffic demand management
Energy	Improve programmes in energy conservation, demand-side management, geothermal energy and other renewable energy development

Source: NCCC and UNFCCC (2009).

cleaner and more efficient – though potentially more expensive – energy sources should be explored. Aside from gas, renewable energy sources such as micro-hydro and geothermal provide feasible alternatives to coal and oil. For Indonesia to be able to implement this, of course, requires reforms in the energy sector, though political willingness does not appear to be embedded in this policy.

Indonesia's ongoing energy security strategy seems to conflict with the goal of mitigating climate change. On the one hand, diversification policies aim to reduce oil reliance. Without taking into account environmental considerations, the logical alternative to oil is coal. By using coal, Indonesia achieves domestic energy security by utilising domestic reserves, so there is no, or limited, reliance on imports. Since coal is more of a local commodity than oil, it also enjoys fewer price fluctuations on the international market. Ready-to-use technologies and government incentives make coal mining an even more financially viable choice as Indonesia's main energy source.

When climate change is taken into consideration, the solution for diversification needs to be different. The coal-favouring situation conflicts with the solutions necessary to reduce energy sector emissions. The solutions currently considered by the government to resolve this conflict are as follows:

- Electricity reforms: To promote a significant shift away from coal and oil as primary fuel choices and utilise more natural gas, geothermal and other renewable energy sources such as hydropower;
- Carbon tax: A comprehensive tax that mainly targets the carbon-intensive coal industries. The carbon tax would be designed to have a larger impact on heavy industries and less on ordinary Indonesians, since most of the population still has low levels of energy consumption;
- Eliminating fuel subsidies: A far more serious attempt to eliminate or decrease subsidies on kerosene, gasoline and other refined fuel products remains a potential solution to drive down consumption and provide incentives to develop alternative energy sources. Decreasing subsidies for end user consumers, however, will affect ordinary Indonesians, who are still struggling with low purchasing power, the most.

Therefore, with climate change taken into consideration, the direction of the ongoing energy security strategy has to be re-orientated to take into account the energy reforms mentioned above.

Again, however, how far Indonesia will be diverted from its ongoing energy strategy remains to be seen. First, Indonesia is currently implementing its crash programme to build 10,000 MW of coal power plants within the next five years or so. One power plant has been finished and two more should be completed by the end of 2010. Implementation of this programme is certainly complicating Indonesia's attempt to redirect its energy security strategy towards one that takes the climate change issue into consideration. Second, in an attempt to gain popularity, President Susilo Bambang Yudhono decided to lower the domestic price of fuel. It is true that world crude oil prices, throughout 2010, have been low; however, the president's attitude really shows how reluctant the government is to adjust the domestic price of fuel in line with world prices.

Concluding Remarks

This chapter sought to describe ongoing energy security policies in Indonesia and to explain the underlying reasons for these policies, while showing how climate change issues might affect the direction of these policies. From the discussion presented here, it can be concluded that the main drivers of increasing energy consumption in Indonesia are, as in many other countries, the steady growth of its economy and of the population's welfare. While there is generally nothing wrong with this trend, it must be remarked that energy intensity in Indonesia is relatively high – even when compared with other developing countries in the region – and that the main source of energy in Indonesia has to date been oil, with its wildly fluctuating prices. Indonesia currently sets its domestic price of fuel and electricity much lower than world prices in an attempt to support the purchasing power of its people. Consequently, when the world price of oil increases, the subsidies inflate and become a great burden on the government. Such considerations notwithstanding, these subsidies remain popular. Whenever it tries to level domestic prices to the world price, the Indonesian government receives much criticism, in many cases followed by social unrest. On the other hand, it enjoys higher public support each time it reduces the price of domestic fuel. Hence, even if the government really wants to adjust the domestic price of fuel and electricity in line with the world price, it can only do so gradually. The other way to reduce the burden of this subsidy would be to diversify the country's energy source away from oil. Towards this end, the initial obvious option is coal. Indonesia's coal reserve is abundant and the technology needed to build coal power plants is relatively cheap.

Since the 1990s, climate change due to GHG – mostly CO_2 emissions – has rapidly emerged as the top environmental problem worldwide. Indonesia recognises that it has been amongst the top CO_2 polluters around the world, and has reacted by committing to reduce its level of CO_2 emissions. The current plan is to reduce total emissions by as much as 26 per cent compared to BAU by 2020 without the financial assistance of other countries, and by 41 per cent with international assistance. Though this commitment mostly affects the Indonesian forestry sector, it significantly forces the Indonesian government and economy at large to rethink their energy sector policy, and more precisely its energy security policy. First, Indonesia needs to actually implement its plan to reduce and eliminate its energy subsidies and, if possible, to reduce the time taken to eliminate these subsidies. Second, diverting its source of energy from oil to coal will increase Indonesia's CO_2 emission, since coal is a dirtier source of energy than oil. Indonesia needs to redirect this path away from oil, not to coal, but to much cleaner energy sources, such as geothermal, gas or other renewable energy sources. Indonesia has started developing plans to more seriously reduce and eliminate its energy subsidy as well as to create incentives for investments in utilising much cleaner energy sources. The devil will be in the details when it comes to implementation of this policy. It is clear, however, that a successful outcome will require a much stronger commitment to reform than the Indonesian government has shown to date.

Notes

1. Indonesia's energy sources also include gas (16 per cent of the total), coal (10 per cent), and other sources, predominantly wood (31 per cent).

References

Association of Southeast Asian Nations (ASEAN) (2010), *ASEANSTATS: Building Knowledge on the ASEAN Community* [http://www.aseansec.org/22122.htm; accessed: 20 June 2010].

Energy Information Administration (EIA) (1993), *Emissions of Greenhouse Gases in the United States 1985–1990* (Washington, DC: Department of Energy).

EIA (2007), *Country Analysis Briefs: Indonesia* [http://www.eia.doe.gov/cabs/Indonesia/Background.html; accessed: 30 June 2010].

Hartono, D. and B.P. Resosudarmo (2008), 'The Economy-wide Impact of Controlling Energy Consumption in Indonesia: An Analysis Using a Social Accounting Matrix Framework', *Energy Policy*, 36(4): 1404–19.

Hill, H., B.P. Resosudarmo and Y. Vidyattama (2008), 'Indonesia's Changing Economic Geography', *Bulletin of Indonesian Economic Studies*, 44(3): 407–35.

Indonesian Institute for Energy Economics Research Team (IIEE Research Team) (2006), 'Overview 2005: Energy Challenges', *Indonesian Energy Economics Review*, 1: 1–17.

Indriyanto, A.R.S, B. Wittimena, H. Batih, I. Sari and Triandi (2007), 'Policy and Regulatory Perspectives on Energy Security', *Indonesian Energy Economics Review*, 2: 1–10.

Indriyanto, A.R.S. (2008), 'Subsidi dan Ketahanan Energi', paper presented at the Seminar on Energy Security, Financial Sector and Funding Alternatives (Jakarta, 23 October).

Indriyanto, A.R.S. (2010), 'Kebijakan Energi dan Implementasinya: Tinjauan dari sisi Ketahanan Energi', paper presented at the Kelompok Diskusi Sore Hari-LPEM (Faculty of Economics, University of Indonesia, Jakarta, 5 August).

International Energy Agency (IEA) (2007a), *Energy Balances of Non-OECD Country: Documentation for Beyond 20/20 Files* (Paris: Head of Publications Service).

IEA (2007b), *Energy Balances of OECD Country: Documentation for Beyond 20/20 Files* (Paris: Head of Publications Service).

Kuncoro, A. and B.P. Resosudarmo (2006), 'Survey of Recent Development', *Bulletin of Indonesian Economic Studies*, 42(1): 7–31.

National Planning and Development Agency (Bappenas) (2010), *National Medium-Term Development Plan 2010–2014* (Jakarta: Bappenas).

National Council on Climate Change (NCCC) and United Nations Framework Convention on Climate Change (UNFCC) (2009), 'National Economic, Environment and Development Study (NEEDS) for Climate Change: Indonesia Country Study' (Jakarta: National Council on Climate Change).

Ministry of Energy and Mineral Resources (ESDM) (2009), *Handbook of Energy and Economic Statistics of Indonesia 2009* (Jakarta: Kementerian Energi dan Sumber Daya Alam).

Ministry of Energy and Mineral Resources (ESDM) (2010), 'Peraturan Menteri Energi dan Sumber Daya Mineral No. 4/2010: Rencana Strategis Kementrian ESDM 2010–2014' [http://www.esdm.go.id/prokum/permen/2010/; accessed: 22 June 2010].

Republic of Indonesia (2006), *Presidential Decree no 5/2006 on National Energy Policy* (Jakarta: Pemerintah Indonesia).

Resosudarmo, B.P., N.I. Subiman and B. Rahayu (2000), 'The Indonesian Marine Resources: An Overview of Their Problems and Challenges', *Indonesian Quarterly*, 28(3): 336–55.

Resosudarmo, B.P. and A. Kuncoro (2006), 'The Political Economy of Indonesian Economic Reform: 1983–2000', *Oxford Development Studies*, 34(3): 341–53.

Resosudarmo, B.P., F. Jotzo, A.A. Yusuf and D.A. Nurdianto (2008), 'Challenges in Mitigating CO2 Emission: The Importance of Managing Fossil Fuel Combustion', paper presented at the Workshop on 21st Century Indonesia: Challenges Ahead (ISEAS, Singapore, 13–14 November).

Resosudarmo, B.P., I.A.P. Resosudarmo, W. Sarosa and N.L. Subiman (2009), 'Socioeconomic Conflicts in Indonesia's Mining Industry', in R. Cronin and A. Pandya (eds): *Exploiting Natural Resources: Growth, Instability, and Conflict in the Middle East and Asia* (Washington, DC: The Henry L. Stimson Center).

Sari, A.P., M. Maulidya, R.N. Butarbutar, R.E. Sari and W. Rusmantoro (2007), 'Working Paper on Indonesia and Climate Change: Current Status and Policies' (Jakarta: PEACE – Pelangi Energi Abadi Citra Enviro).

Sutijastoto, F. (2006), 'Energy Efficiency Policy of Indonesia', paper presented at the 2nd International Center for Environmental Technology Transfer (ICETT) (Tokyo, 31 July–4 August 2006).

United Nations Development Programme (UNDP) (2004), *World Energy Demand: Overview 2004 Update* (New York: Bureau for Development Policy).

UNDP (2009), *Human Development Report 2009* [http://hdrstats.undp.org/en/countries/country_fact_sheets/cty_fs_IDN.html; accessed: 27 June 2010].

US Commercial Service (2007), 'Indonesia: Coal Mining Equipment' [http://commercecan.ic.gc.ca/scdt/bizmap/interface2.nsf/vDownload/IMI_8691/$file/X_4867069.PDF; accessed: 30 June 2010].

World Bank (2010), *The World Bank Data: Indonesia* [http://data.worldbank.org/country/indonesia; accessed: 23 June 2010].

10
Energy Governance and Climate Change: Central Asia's Uneasy Nexus

Luca Anceschi

Introduction

Since the collapse of the Soviet Union the international community has looked at Central Asia's energy resources with increasing interest. The substantial hydrocarbon reserves of Kazakhstan, Turkmenistan and Uzbekistan and, to a lesser extent, the abundant yet untapped hydropower capacities held by Kyrgyzstan and Tajikistan, have been the main factors behind the region's growing relevance in international affairs.

At the end of 2009, Kazakhstan's proven oil reserves were estimated at 39.8 tmb, representing 3 per cent of global reserves. Mainly due to the magnitude of Turkmenistan's natural gas reserves (estimated at 8.10 tcm at the end of 2009), Central Asia holds a 6 per cent share of the world's total gas reserves (BP, 2010). In 2008, Tajikistan's hydropower resources – estimated at 527 billion kWh per year – ranked eighth in the world (Valamat-Zade, 2008, p. 89). Accurate estimates report that the potential of Kyrgyzstani hydropower production oscillates between 140 and 160 billion kWh per year (Peyrouse, 2007, p. 144). It must nevertheless be noted that neither Kyrgyzstan nor Tajikistan are currently able to use more than 3 per cent of their respective hydropower resources, remaining as a consequence net energy importers.

Due to the diversified nature of its energy potential and its geostrategic location, Central Asia has become a key component in the energy security strategies devised by neighbouring states – including the Russian Federation (see Chapter 8, p. 150–151) and the People's Republic of China – and more distant actors (the European Union).

In Central Asia, assessing prospects for resource export has been a critical factor in the crystallisation of national energy security perceptions. In the cases of Kyrgyzstan and Tajikistan, a complex set of factors – small stateness, widespread political instability, declining economic performance and inadequate technological know-how – prevented the transformation of national energy potentials into exportable commodities, leaving energy issues at the margins of the two economic foreign policy systems. On the other hand,

Central Asia's hydrocarbon-rich republics have been able to place energy at the core of their external polices. Facilitating the access of resources to global energy markets represented a key element in the energy policies formulated by the leaderships of Kazakhstan, Turkmenistan and Uzbekistan. To this end, the three governments finalised a significant number of transit and exploration deals with Russian, Western and, more recently, Chinese firms.

The different structural roles assigned to energy in the foreign economic policies of the Central Asian republics led to the emergence of two distinct conceptualisations of energy security in the region. Central Asia's energy importers – Kyrgyzstan and Tajikistan – have placed safe and regular access to energy resources at the core of their energy security concepts. Several factors – including political mismanagement of the national energy systems, and the impact of climate change on regional water resources – made the achievement of this end a rather challenging undertaking for the leaderships in Bishkek and Dushanbe. As a consequence, regular energy deficits – which have become more acute in the winter months – have affected Kyrgyzstan and Tajikistan in the last decade. The severe electricity shortages experienced since 2007–2008 have forced the Kyrgyzstani government to schedule six-hour-long blackouts for central Bishkek for the greater part of the winter season, while planning longer interruptions for rural areas (AKI Press, 2008). Similarly, major Tajikistani centres experienced daily interruptions of electricity, with protracted blackouts (often longer than 15 hours) affecting the country's rural areas (Medrea, 2009).

In spite of their destabilising potential, the repeated collapses of the national electricity infrastructure did not spark popular unrest in Tajikistan. The International Crisis Group reported that only a small number of demonstrations – which were to all intents and purposes 'efforts to obtain information or help rather than to protest' (ICG, 2009, p. 5) – were organised during the energy shortages of 2007–2008. In Kyrgyzstan, on the other hand, widespread energy insecurity had a detrimental impact on the political stability of the ruling regime. The population's grievances as regards safe access to electricity – particularly those framed in relation to rising heat and power prices – were regularly expressed in the lead-up to the popular uprising that, in mid April 2010, led to the demise of the regime headed by Kurmanbek Bakiyev (Daly, 2010; ICG, 2010, p. 9).

Mutatis mutandis, energy security is also critical to the political stability of Kazakhstan, Turkmenistan and Uzbekistan – Central Asia's energy exporters. Identifying energy security as the acquisition of 'adequate, reliable supplies of energy at reasonable prices and in ways that do not jeopardize major national values and objectives' (Yergin, 1988, p. 111) is of little help if we are to understand how priorities, issues and dynamics associated with energy security are perceived, absorbed and re-elaborated by the leaderships in Astana, Ashgabat and Tashkent. In these contexts, where large resource endowments are sufficient to address the domestic energy demand, national energy security strategies are more closely related to the states' ability to ensure a regular flow of revenues from the exploration, processing and, ultimately, export of large hydrocarbon reserves. In most cases – with the notable exception of Uzbekistan – hydrocarbon revenues do represent the main source of income for the regimes, and thus constitute an essential component in the survival mechanisms devised by the national leaderships. In Kazakhstan, the petroleum industry accounts for 'more than 30% of the country's GDP and more than half of its export revenues' (*Kazakhstan Oil & Gas Report*, 2010, p. 11). Gas revenues – estimated at US$14.22 billion for 2010 (*Turkmenistan Oil & Gas Report*, 2010, p. 39) – occupy a similarly central role in the Turkmenistani national budget. Although representing only a minor percentage of the national gross domestic product (GDP), hydrocarbon revenues are equally crucial to regime maintenance in Uzbekistan: President Islam Karimov is allegedly using the country's gas revenues to lubricate his patronage network and forge alliances with alternative centres of power (ICG, 2007, p. 24). Lack of transparency in relation to revenue use also features prominently in the Kazakhstani and Turkmenistani political contexts (Hayman and Mayne, 2010, p. 140–145).

The energy security of Central Asia's energy exporters is therefore closely connected with the ability to guarantee a regular flow of revenues through the export of energy resources at a convenient price. This has to be consistent with regime objectives and values, which, in the three cases in question, are associated with extreme forms of authoritarian governance. It is in this sense, we are led to believe, that energy security is critical to regime maintenance in Kazakhstan, Turkmenistan and Uzbekistan.

The establishment of a direct correlation between energy security and regime stability in Central Asia does raise a number of questions about the leaderships' perceptions of and responses to the challenges that climate change is posing to energy policy at both national and regional level. In general terms, the Central Asian leaderships, when formulating and implementing their energy policies, have opted to prioritise their respective political interests and limited their commitment to adaption or mitigation initiatives to a purely rhetorical exercise. Within the two different energy security concepts described above, the Central Asian leaderships adapted the fuel mixes chosen to power the five national economies in line with the different compositions of their respective resource endowments. In turn, this choice favoured the emergence, throughout the region, of two different emissions trends.

The region's hydrocarbon-dependent states – Kazakhstan, Turkmenistan and Uzbekistan – are regularly included amongst the world's 12 most carbon-intensive economies, reporting extremely large shares of greenhouse gas (GHG) emissions per dollar of GDP (Olshanskaya and Slay, 2008, p. 19). On the other hand, Kyrgyzstan and Tajikistan have systematically reported below average GHG emissions rates, with emissions structures largely dominated by the residential sector. Nevertheless, it is the combination of declining industrial production and massive reliance on hydropower that contributed most decisively to the collapse of Kyrgyzstani and Tajikistani emissions.

The last proposition is critical to defining the central purpose of this chapter, which intends to look at the intersection of energy governance, energy security and environmental problems – especially those connected to climate change – in the Central Asian context. It is through exploring the dense linkages between energy exports/imports and regime stability, we are led to believe, that it is possible to shed light on the systemic failures encountered by the Central Asian states when fronting the numerous challenges posed by climate change. Post-Soviet Central Asia is particularly vulnerable to the environmental problems induced by climatic change: raising temperatures will exacerbate the regional tendency towards desertification (Lipovsky, 1995), while aggravating the melting of the region's glaciers, and reducing water flow in the Syr-Darya and Amu-Darya basins (Perelet, 2008, p. 8).

This chapter will identify, outline and discuss three key facets of the Central Asian leaderships' policy responses to climate change. Initially, this chapter will focus on Central Asia's fuel mix and emissions structure. Extreme emphasis on coal and hydrocarbons – as experienced in Kazakhstan, Turkmenistan and Uzbekistan – has to date led to systemic failures in exploring future prospects for producing cleaner energy. This trend will be observed in conjunction with an analysis of the Kyrgyzstani and Tajikistani energy structures and their environmental impact.

Our analysis will then move to the placement of environmental concerns within Central Asia's energy policy making. While, in most cases, dependence on unclean energy sources has not decreased in any significant way, the five leaderships have failed to promote a thorough coordination of their respective energy policies. A survey of regional energy policy initiatives will reveal an underlying tension between the interests of the national regimes and adoption of coordinated responses to regional environmental problems.

An unclean fuel mix

Ensuring continuity with practices consolidated during the Soviet era has been a common strategy adopted by the Central Asian leaderships when formulating and implementing their respective national energy policies. Central Asia's energy mix has therefore remained substantially unchanged throughout the post-Soviet era. While Kyrgyzstan and Tajikistan have continued to depend on hydropower resources, the economies of Kazakhstan, Turkmenistan and Uzbekistan are still predominantly powered by hydrocarbons and coal, as the extraction, use, transportation and export of fossil fuels remained matters of critical concern for national leaderships. Surveying the different primary energy supply structures of the Central Asian republics is hence indispensible to understanding the nature of the region's emissions trends.

Kazakhstan is Central Asia's main producer and exporter of hard coal – predominantly anthracite and bituminous coal. In 2009, Kazakhstan's total production of coal was estimated at 96.2 Mt, registering a decrease of 10.7 per cent from the 2008 levels (IEA, 2010a, p. II.6). In spite of declining production, total consumption increased by 15.2 per cent in 2009 (IEA, 2010a, p. II.9), reducing significantly the amount of hard coal available for export. Approximately 70 per cent of Kazakhstan's coal production is consumed domestically (Esenova, 2008, p. 111): in 2009, 70.3 per cent of total Kazakhstani electricity was produced through coal conversion (IEA, 2008a). In addition to its key role *vis-à-vis* domestic demand – it constitutes 42.9 per cent of Kazakhstan's Total Primary Energy Supply (TPES) – Kazakhstani coal is also a critical resource for the energy security of the wider Central Asian region; it is, for instance, regularly exchanged for Kyrgyzstani electricity (Dorian, 2006, p. 549). With coal satisfying much of the internal energy demand, the leadership assigned oil a crucial role within Kazakhstan's external energy trade system and, as we have seen earlier, within the wider Kazakhstani economy, which remains oil-dominated. A sharp increase in oil production – whose share in Kazakhstani industry increased by more than 200 per cent between 1996 and 2006 (Esenova, 2008, p. 112) – was the main driver of Kazakhstan's economic growth during the decade preceding the global financial downturn of 2008.

Analogous patterns can be detected within the Turkmenistani energy system, whose balance is essentially linked to the availability of hydrocarbon products, particularly gas. Gas represents over 85 per cent of total energy production and accounts for 72.9 per cent of the national TPES (IEA, 2008d). As it constitutes the bulk of the national exports, gas is also crucial to the Turkmenistani income generation process. At the same time, increasingly substantial amounts of Turkmenistani gas are being converted into electricity, in line with the national leadership's plans to increase Turkmenistan's share in electricity markets located beyond the Commonwealth of Independent States (CIS) (*Internet Gazeta Turkmenistan.ru*, 2010). The share of oil in the powering of the Turkmenistani economy is expected to grow, especially as the regime headed by Gurbanguly M. Berdymukhammedov continues to limit access to onshore oil reserves to international companies. Estimates for the 2010–2019 decade forecast a 55.1 per cent increase in Turkmenistan's domestic oil consumption (*Turkmenistan Oil & Gas Report*, 2010, p. 6). Coal does not play any significant role in the current energy security strategy.

In Uzbekistan – which in 2006 ranked as the world's second GHG-intensive economy (CAIT website) – dependence on hydrocarbons acquires even more extreme tones. The country's modest oil production – estimated for 2009 at 4.9 million tonnes (BP, 2010) – is almost entirely allocated for domestic consumption (IEA, 2008e). Similar usage patterns can be detected within the Uzbekistani gas sector: approximately 80 per cent of total production – which in 2009 amounted to 64.4 tcm (BP, 2010) – is used domestically. Further, a large portion of Uzbekistani electricity is generated through coal conversion (World Energy Council, 2007, p. 18). As a consequence, the Uzbekistani TPES – in which hydropower and coal account for minimal shares (1.9 and 2.4 per cent, respectively) – is overwhelmingly made up by hydrocarbons.

The complex nature of Central Asia's fuel mix is further unveiled by an observation of the energy profiles of Kyrgyzstan and Tajikistan. In these two contexts, vast hydropower potentials have to date failed to ensure self-sufficiency, and both states remain net electricity importers. This proposition is all the more puzzling when considering total electricity production in Kyrgyzstan and Tajikistan. In the latter case, figures for 2008 were 7.7 per cent larger than that of Turkmenistan, which, as we have seen earlier, is exporting electricity to its non-CIS neighbours (IEA, 2008c, 2008d). So far as Kyrgyzstan, total generated electricity (11,877 GWh in 2008 – IEA, 2008b) appears to be sufficient to meeting internal demand, although imports are needed for system stability and balancing purposes. As Kyrgyzstan's and Tajikistan's energy insecurity is by no means caused by generation capabilities, it is the dismal status of the two hydro-electric infrastructures that continues to play a major role in the energy deficits regularly experienced by the national populations.

In the case of Tajikistan, the national grid is virtually split in two disconnected segments: as the connection between the northern and the southern parts of the Tajikistani electricity grid is extremely poor, the electricity produced in southern Tajikistan can only reach the northern part of the country via the export of hydropower through Afghanistan and Uzbekistan (Peyrouse, 2007, p. 140). In Kyrgyzstan, the energy policies implemented by successive regimes have failed to meet the rising electricity demand originating in the residential sector, which, following the inexorable contraction of the national industrial sector, represents 95 per cent of total registered electricity accounts in Kyrgyzstan (Zozulinsky, 2010, p. 2). At the same time, significant portions of the annual generated capacity – 45 per cent in 2007 (World Energy Council, 2007) and 28 per cent in 2009 (Zozulinksy, 2010, p. 3) – are lost each year due to distribution inefficiency, illegal diversion or major leakages.

In assessing the impact of alternative energy sources upon the regional fuel mix, it must be noted that Central Asia's renewable sector does not represent a significant contributor to the powering of the regional economies. Development prospects for clean energy technologies in Central Asia seem to be affected by a fundamental contradiction: in most cases, the region's potential in terms of renewable energy remains untapped, as the national governments have to date failed to engage in wide-ranging initiatives to develop the sector. While large portions of Kyrgyzstan's and Tajikistan's generating capacity already come from clean sources, only minor percentages of the generation capacity in Kazakhstan, Turkmenistan and Uzbekistan originate in the renewable sector.

Kazakhstan is the only Central Asian state to have introduced a legislative framework for renewable energy sources (Law No 165-IV, 4 July 2009, «O podderzhke ispol'zovaniya vozobnovlyaemykh istochnikov energii»). This law provides a relevant framework to regulate the national renewable sector, whose expansion will be carried out – predominantly although not exclusively – through to the attraction of private investment. In determining that clean sources (mostly wind energy) will amount by 2024 to 5 per cent of the Kazakhstani energy balance, the law intends to develop Kazakhstan's substantial renewable potential, which national estimates have set at 1 trillion kWh per annum (Lemeshev, 2010). So far as Turkmenistan and Uzbekistan, their respective renewable energy potentials – solar and wind in the Turkmenistani case, with the Uzbekistani solar energy potential estimated to be one of the more significant within the CIS (EBRD, 2009) – remain substantially undeveloped, as the two governments have so far failed to establish relevant legislative frameworks to regulate the production of clean energy.

The different sizes of the five national economies have to be taken into account. Due to the small size of the hydropower-based economies (Kyrgyzstan and Tajikistan), clean energy sources are reduced to have a minimal impact on the regional energy balance. Central Asia's energy mix is therefore dominated by the usage patterns of the region's main economic actors, and particularly Kazakhstan, whose economy is larger than the sum of the other four (World Bank website). In this sense, the regional energy mix is essentially based on fossil fuels. The latter proposition is further validated by observing coal usage patterns at regional level: while total coal supply represents only one-fifth of Central Asia's TPES, coal consumption constitutes a larger share (38 per cent) of total fuel consumption for heat and power, with 65 per cent of the region's total heat and electricity production being the result of coal conversion (World Bank, 2010, p. 52). It is the economic performance of the main regional actors that has driven Central Asia's emissions trends, whose fluctuations in the period 1990–2005 are illustrated by Table 10.1 and discussed in the next segment of the chapter.

Delaying the energy switch

The data presented in Table 10.1 identify the two diverging trends that have characterised GHG emissions in Central Asia since 1990: while some actors have consistently reported declining emissions rates, significant increases can be detected within the total emissions of other regional economies. These two trends are essentially associated with the two different energy security conceptualisations outlined before. Between 1990 and 2005, GHG

Table 10.1 Central Asian Republics: Total GHG emissions (1990–2005, Tg CO_2e)

	1990	1991	1992	1993	1994	1995	1996	1997	1998	1999	2000	2001	2002	2003	2004	2005
Kazakhstan	330.0	–	345.0	–	308.0	–	–	–	156.0	145.0	172.0	178.0	195.0	205.0	228.0	243.0
Kyrgyzstan	30.2	29.3	21.2	16.0	11.7	10.7	11.5	11.2	11.5	10.5	11.0	10.7	11.5	11.7	12.3	12.0
Tajikistan	23.2	23.1	19.4	16.8	10.9	8.4	6.6	6.6	5.8	5.5	5.5	5.7	6.0	6.5	–	–
Turkmenistan	–	–	–	–	52.1	–	–	–	–	–	56.9	–	69.9	–	–	109.4
Uzbekistan	181.3	184.4	177.1	205.5	185.6	185.4	190.0	179.0	177.4	183.3	200.1	203.1	207.3	204.7	201.5	200.2

Source: Government of the Kyrgyz Republic (2009); Government of the Republic of Kazakhstan (2009); Government of the Republic of Tajikistan (2008); Government of the Republic of Turkmenistan (2006); Government of the Republic of Uzbekistan (2008).

emissions in Kyrgyzstan and Tajikistan reduced substantially, Kyrgyzstani GHG emissions decreased by 60.6 per cent, while Tajikistan's – between 1990 and 2003 – have declined even more significantly (72.9 per cent). On the other hand, Turkmenistan and Uzbekistan reported ascending emissions trends, which were more substantial (+109 per cent on the 1994 baseline in 2005) in the case of Turkmenistan.

The trajectory of Kazakhstani emissions reflects both trends described above. Kazakhstan's total GHG emissions halved between 1994 and 1999, when the rate of decrease was similar to that in Tajikistan. Such declining trends reversed between 2000 and 2005, when the Kazakhstani government reported average annual increases of 5–10 per cent.

Data in Table 10.1 also indicate that, as they represent the region's largest economies, Central Asia's hydrocarbon-rich states remain the biggest emitters. The sum of total GHG emitted by Kyrgyzstan and Tajikistan is less than 5 per cent of total regional emissions, of which almost half are produced by Kazakhstan. Central Asia's emissions trends have oscillated in line with fluctuations in the economic performances of the regional states. Declining emissions trends reported by Kyrgyzstan and Tajikistan throughout the post-Soviet era and by the government of Kazakhstan in the 1990s occurred in the context of when systemic failure in introducing economic reforms resulted in sharply declining industrial production (Spechler, 2008). In Kazakhstan, the combination of revised utilisation patterns for the country's natural resources (Pomfret, 2005, pp. 867–869) and the post-2000 increase in world oil prices, reversed the negative economic cycle. As the Kazakhstani economy boomed on the back of an export-oriented oil industry, coal-fired power plants became increasingly crucial to domestic production of heat and electricity (World Bank, 2010, p. 18), leading in turn to a significant increase in Kazakhstan's total GHG emissions. Rising emissions rates for the period 1990–2005 have also been reported by Turkmenistan and Uzbekistan. In parallel with the Kazakhstani context, improved economic performance due to expansion of the hydrocarbon industries appears to be the main driver behind increasing emissions rates in Turkmenistan and Uzbekistan. As a consequence, the 2005 per capita rates of GHG emissions in Turkmenistan and Uzbekistan were well above the global average (Perelet, 2008, p. 9).

Energy activity represents therefore the main source of GHG emissions in Central Asia. As the regional fuel mix has not substantially changed since the achievement of independence, and usages of unclean fuels have increased in most parts of Central Asia, the energy sector's share of Central Asia's emissions has remained substantial throughout the post-Soviet era. In 2005, energy activity represented 80 per cent of total GHG emissions in Kazakhstan, 74 per cent in Kyrgyzstan and 87 per cent in Uzbekistan (Government of the Republic of Uzbekistan, 2008, p. 8; Government of the Republic of Kazakhstan, 2009, p. 13; Government of the Kyrgyz Republic, 2009, p. 59). The Tajikistani emissions structure represents the exception to the regional norm: the share of emissions from fuel combustion decreased from 67 per cent of total GHG emissions in 1990 to an astonishingly low – at least by regional standards – 27 per cent in 2005, leaving the agricultural sector as the main national emitter (Government of the Republic of Tajikistan, 2008, pp. 20–21).

Carbon dioxide (CO_2) remains the greatest contributor to Central Asia's total emissions. In the cases of Kazakhstan and Kyrgyzstan, CO_2 continues to represent well over two-thirds of total emissions (Government of the Republic of Kazakhstan, 2009, p. 14; Government of the Kyrgyz Republic, 2009, p. 60). The aggregate structure of Uzbekistani emissions is on the other hand more composite, as substantial increases in methane emissions – due to massive growth of volumes of gas recovery – reduced the CO_2 share to approximately 50 per cent of the total (Government of the Republic of Uzbekistan, 2008, p. 43). Table 10.2 presents a more detailed breakdown of aggregate CO_2 emissions in Central Asia.

Poor energy efficiency continues to negatively affect Central Asia's energy activity, impacting decisively on national emissions rates. Investments in energy efficiency – as remarked by the World Bank (2010, p. 47) – might contribute to achieve 'three goals, simultaneously and at least cost: lower greenhouse gas emissions, better energy security, and more sustainable economic growth'. Boosting energy efficiency therefore offers the potential to harmonise national energy and climate policies. The outdated technology that supports Central Asia's production, transportation and distribution infrastructures is amongst the main causes of the region's highly inefficient use of energy. In this sense, the region's inefficient use of energy is a Soviet legacy: a great part of the technology supporting Central Asia's energy industry predates the achievement of independence, when efficient energy activity did not play any role in the energy agendas of Soviet administrators.

A mix of internal and external measures is currently adopted in Central Asia to increase energy efficiency. External loans are frequently sought by the national governments to improve different facets of their energy activity: Uzbekistan, for instance, obtained in April 2010 a US$350 million loan from the Asian Development Bank to build Central Asia's first 800 MW combined cycle gas turbine power plant, which will improve power generation efficiency to 50 per cent (ADB, 2010). Kyrgyzstani efforts to reduce energy inefficiency have moved along similar lines: in November 2009, the Bakiyev regime – in cooperation with the United Nations Developments Programme (UNDP) – introduced new construction regulations, with a view to reduce energy consumption within the residential sector (Biggar, 2010). As early as 1997 the Kazakhstani government introduced a law on energy savings, in which obsolete technologies and a high-energy intensity GDP were identified as two key hindrances to achieving the national energy savings potential. In spite of the establishment of a relatively tight legal framework, the overall efficiency of the Kazakhstani energy system declined,

Table 10.2 Central Asian Republics: Total CO_2 emissions (2008)

	TPES[a]	Total CO_2 emissions[b]	Electricity and heat production	Other energy industries	Manufacturing industry and construction	Transport	Other sectors	Sectoral approach			CO_2 emissions/ TPES[c]	CO_2 emissions/ population[d]
								Coal/ peat[b]	Oil[b]	Gas[b]		
Kazakhstan	2969	201.6	83.6	12.0	44.9	14.2	46.9	110.4	32.6	58.6	67.9	12.86
Kyrgyzstan	120	5.9	1.4	–	1.7	1.4	1.4	2.2	2.2	1.5	49.4	1.12
Tajikistan	104	3.0	0.5	–	–	0.3	2.2	0.4	1.6	1.0	29.0	0.44
Turkmenistan	788	47.3	13.6	7.0	–	2.8	24.0	–	15.2	32.1	60.0	9.41
Uzbekistan	2114	114.9	34.1	4.2	21.8	9.0	45.8	5.1	11.9	97.9	55.4	4.21

N.B.: CO_2 emissions from fuel combustion only
[a]PJ.
[b]million tonnes CO_2.
[c]tonnes CO_2/terajoule.
[d]tonnes CO_2/capita.
Source: IEA (2010b).

and significant losses – particularly in heat distribution networks in urban areas – are reported by official sources (Government of the Republic of Kazakhstan, 2009, p. 163). Energy production and transmission waste are also significant emissions sources. Kazakhstan is ranked fifth in the world in terms of gas flaring and gas venting. In 2005, the Kazakhstani energy industry flared and vented 8.8 bcm, while the total of associated gas flared or vented by Turkmenistan, Uzbekistan and Azerbaijan accounted for 7 bcm, making the Caspian energy industry one of the most flaring intensive in the world (World Bank, 2010, pp. 43–44).

A largely unclean fuel mix, which is produced, transported and distributed through highly obsolete infrastructures, is the main driver of Central Asia's GHG emissions. Rising emissions trends, sporadic use of renewable energy sources and the poor energy efficiency of the region's carbon-intensive economies suggest that the individual energy policies implemented by the Central Asian governments have achieved effective emissions abatement. At the same time, analogous failures have been replicated at regional level, as energy policy coordination amongst the regional actors has to date failed to take off. It is precisely to the observation of this dynamics that our attention now turns.

Coordinating the national energy policies

In the era of climate change, Central Asia's environmental crises are distinctively transnational. A common thread connects the region's main environmental emergencies, including the ecological disaster of the Aral Sea, the progressive deterioration of Caspian Sea ecosystems and the predicted degradation of regional glaciers (Perelet, 2008). Their ramifications are in fact not confined within the borders of a single state, as more than one regional actor is affected by each of the crises mentioned above: the Aral Sea catastrophe has a critical impact on Uzbekistan and Kazakhstan, the ecological degradation of the Caspian littoral area has serious repercussions on specific economic sectors of western Turkmenistan and south-western Kazakhstan, while the reduction of the Central Asian glaciers will first impact Kyrgyzstan and Tajikistan, before hitting the agricultural systems of Uzbekistan and Turkmenistan.

As Central Asia's environmental crises have a regional raison d'être, the key to their solutions lies in shared initiatives to be advanced at regional level. Are the Central Asian states implementing coordinated measures to face this task? Given energy's decisive impacts upon Central Asia's emissions trends and the wider environmental balance, are the regional actors implementing a common agenda to adapt the respective energy policies to the environmental emergencies set into motion by climate change?

So far as Central Asia's biggest emitters, the energy policies formulated by Astana, Ashgabat and Tashkent are yet to take environmental matters into full consideration. The legislative framework supporting Kazakhstan's power industry (Law No 588-II, 9 July 2004, «Ob elektroenergetike») does not include specific environmental recommendations, while the national adaptation measures framed by the Kazakhstani leadership are mostly focused on sectors other than energy (Government of the Republic of Kazakhstan, 2009, pp, 121–125). In spite of recent progress – including the 2009 law on renewable energy sources – the Kazakhstani government is yet to frame a wide-ranging national strategy on climate change. The extent of Turkmenistan's deficiencies is even larger, as the Turkmenistani government has so far failed to elaborate an explicit energy efficiency strategy (Government of the Republic of Turkmenistan, 2006), with the designation of the national authority for the Clean Development Mechanism (CDM) occurring as late as 2010. Further, the Uzbekistani climate change action appears to have only reached its embryonic stages: the establishment of a Designated National Authority on CDMs (2006) allowed the launch of over 60 CDM-related projects, with an even larger number expected to be implemented after 2008 (Government of the Republic of Uzbekistan, 2008, p. 57).

In spite of cosmetic commitment to international initiatives against climate change – the three states are signatories of the Kyoto Protocol and as non-Annex I countries to the United Nations Framework Convention on Climate Change (UNFCCC) carry out periodic emissions inventories – not much has been done by the leaderships of Kazakhstan, Turkmenistan and Uzbekistan to perform the energy switch necessary to instigate a reverse into GHG emissions trends.

In addition to limited individual commitment from the state actors, the responses to climate change formulated at regional level have to date been uncoordinated. The five Central Asian states acknowledged that environmental crises have indeed a transnational impact, but have so far failed to frame a coordinate response to such crises (Blank, 2010, p. 106). Simply put, a Central Asia-wide mitigation plan is yet to be formulated, let alone implemented. The main determinant for this lack of coordination seems to be connected with the single energy policies of the states, which are moved by conflicting interests and hence pursuing clashing objectives. On paper, the five regional states appear to be well suited *vis-à-vis* energy cooperation, due to highly compatible energy structures. In practice, the national energy policies remain largely uncoordinated. The following examples substantiate the latter proposition.

For most of the post-Soviet era, Kazakhstan, Turkmenistan and the other littoral states (Russia, Iran and Azerbaijan) have shown little concern for the Caspian Sea's environmental health. Inshore and offshore sources of pollution, particularly those associated with the energy industry, are one of the major anthropogenic threats to the Caspian ecosystem (EnvSec, 2008, pp. 142–149). The International Energy Agency (IEA) reported consistent increases in oil and gas production in the Caspian areas, in further confirmation of the increasingly central role played by Caspian reserves in the energy systems of the littoral states, and Kazakhstan and Turkmenistan more in particular (IEA, 2008f, pp. 7–11). In addition to increasing hydrocarbon production, the Caspian region acquired key relevance within the Eurasian transportation system, as safe transit routes are needed to export Central Asia's oil and gas to lucrative Western markets. Pollution resulting from hydrocarbon production (including flaring) and transportation, and the ubiquitous danger of oil spills (Blua, 2010) constitute direct threats to the maritime Caspian environment, and particularly to local biodiversity, including the critically endangered Beluga sturgeon and the Caspian seal populations. The future of Caspian fisheries is especially at risk: while production of hydrocarbons is entering the peak stage, the fishing industry has the potential to last for centuries (EnvSec, 2008, p. 38). While for much of the 1990s environmental considerations remained at the margins of energy policy making in the Caspian context, from 2000 onwards the environmental management activities of the Caspian Environment Programme (CEP) have intensified (Akiner, 2004, p. 357). To date, nevertheless, the programme has achieved little coordination amongst the energy activities of the littoral states: in this sense, CEP has prioritised hydrocarbon extraction over environmental protection (TDH, 2010).

Water management is another area where the lack of coordination amongst the Central Asian states has negatively affected formulation of efficient responses to climate change challenges. Renat Perelet (2008, pp. 9–10) rightly placed water issues at the epicentre of Central Asia's energy security dynamics in the era of climate change. In general terms, the five states have not reached an agreement on the best possible use for regional water resources: will these be used for irrigation in summer or to produce electricity for heating in the winter? Further disagreement has emerged in relation to water payments to the upstream states, namely Kyrgyzstan and Tajikistan, which have in turn denounced the inflated prices imposed on fuel exports by the leaderships of hydrocarbon-rich neighbouring states (Pannier, 2009). Water governance in Central Asia is hence a highly contested issue, whose resolution is further complicated by the systematic violations of the several inter-state agreements regulating regional hydro-energy cooperation (Mirimanova, 2009).

The diverging approaches adopted by the Central Asian leaderships in relation to regional water management have been replicated *vis-à-vis* power transmission arrangements, thus preventing the establishment of a unified power system in the region. Turkmenistan withdrew in 2003 from the regionally integrated power grid – the Central Asia Power System (CAPS) – to integrate with the Iranian grid and expand its role within the extra-CIS electricity market. More detrimental to the future of the CAPS – and to Central Asia's energy balance more generally – were the withdrawals announced by

Kazakhstan and Uzbekistan in late 2009. With the relevance of CAPS now rapidly declining, Central Asia's electricity transmission is currently regulated by an odd combination that includes bilateral energy agreements and emerging national power grids (Toralieva, 2010).

The leaderships' lack of domestic and regional accountability, according to Erica Marat (2008), constitutes the underlying cause of Central Asia's dual crises of water governance and power transmission. It is the implementation of inward-looking energy policies that has further complicated the process of transnationalisation of the regional water management system and the preservation of the unified regional electricity grid inherited from the Soviet Union. Prioritising the pragmatic interests of the different leaderships during energy policy making has not only polarised national attitudes in relation to regional energy cooperation, but it also resulted in the formulation of inadequate responses to the challenges that climate change has to date posed to Central Asia.

Concluding remarks

The uneasy nature of the nexus connecting national energy security dynamics and regional action against climatic change is the main conclusion of this analysis. The transnational nature of the region's environmental security has not represented a major consideration in the energy security strategies formulated by different national leaderships. In this sense, this chapter has identified a remarkable tension between energy policy making at domestic level and regional energy governance (see Chapter 13, p. 245).

Central Asia's failure in formulating effective responses to climate change – as demonstrated by the lack of regional cooperation concerning the Caspian Sea or water management – is entrenched in two distinct yet interconnected tiers of governance. At the national level, the main emitters – which incidentally also represent the region's principal economic actors – have to date persisted in the development of carbon-intensive economies, mainly as a consequence of the systemic failures experienced in relation to fuel mix diversification and energy efficiency enhancement. Such energy strategies have ultimately led to the significant increases in GHG emissions recently reported by Kazakhstan, Turkmenistan and Uzbekistan. In these non-democratic contexts national disinterest in regional energy policy coordination can be explained by looking at the main determinants of energy policy and, perhaps most decisively, their interconnection to regime stability.

At the regional level, on the other hand, the contrasting ends of the various domestic energy policies and the clashing interests of national leaderships have prevented the regional states from coordinating and enhancing supra-national energy cooperation, in spite of the recognition that, so far as post-Soviet Central Asia, the impact of climate change will continue to be felt regionally.

Acknowledgements

The author wishes to thank Dr Sébastien Peyrouse (Central Asia and Caucasus Institute, Johns Hopkins University School of Advanced International Studies) for his insightful comments on prior versions of this chapter.

References

Akiner, S. (2004), 'Environmental Security in the Caspian Sea', in S. Akiner (ed.): *The Caspian – Politics, Energy and Security* (Abingdon-New York: RoutledgeCurzon).

Asian Development Bank (ADB) (2010), 'ADB to Help Uzbekistan Build Efficient and Clean Power Plant', *ADB News Release*, 20 April.

AKI Press (2008), 'Targeted Blackouts in Bishkek to Last No More Than 6 Hours in Night Time', 12 November, 17:10 pm.

Biggar, H. (2010), 'Kyrgyzstan Goes Green with New Construction Codes', UNDP Feature Article [http://europeandcis.undp.org/environment/kyrgyzstan/show/11A5395D-F203-1EE9-BC154BF7C9ED5DBC; accessed: 25 November 2010].

Blank, S. (2010), 'Energy and Environmental Issues in Central Asia's Security Agenda', *China & Eurasia Forum Quarterly*, 8(2): 65–108.

Blua, A. (2010), 'History, BP Oil Spill Haunt Caspian Sea', *RFE/RL Feature Article*, 25 May.

British Petroleum (BP) (2010), *BP Statistical Review of World Energy* [http://www.bp.com/statisticalreview; accessed: 09 November 2010].

Climate Analysis Indicators Tool (CAIT) website, [http://cait.wri.org/cait.php?page=carbecon&mode=view; accessed: 30 October 2010].

Daly, J.C.K. (2010), 'The Impact of Energy Issues on the Kyrgyz Upheaval', *Central Asia-Caucasus Institute Analyst*, 23 June.

Dorian, J.P. (2006), 'Central Asia: A Major Emerging Energy Player in the 21st Century', *Energy Policy*, 34(15): 544–55.

EBRD (2009), 'Renewable Development Initiative: Uzbekistan Country Profile' [http://ebrdrenewables.com/sites/renew/countries/Uzbekistan/profile.aspx; accessed: 24 November 2010].

Environment and Security Initiative (EnvSec) (2008), *Transforming Risks into Cooperation – The Case of the Eastern Caspian Region* (UNEP).

Esenova, G. (2008), 'Kazakhstan's Fuel and Energy Complex: Reforms, Problems, and Prospects', *Central Asia & the Caucasus*, 5(53): 105–120.

Government of the Kyrgyz Republic (2009), *Second National Communication of the Kyrgyz Republic to the UN Framework Convention on Climate Change* (Bishkek: Poligrafoformlienie).

Government of the Republic of Kazakhstan (2009), *Kazakhstan's Second National Communication to the Conference of the Parties to the United Nations Framework Convention on Climate Change* (Astana: Ministry of Environmental Protection).

Government of the Republic of Tajikistan (2008), *The Second National Communication of the Republic of Tajikistan under the United National Framework Convention on Climate Change* (Dushanbe: State Administration for Hydrometeorology).

Government of the Republic of Turkmenistan (2006), *Initial National Communication of Turkmenistan under United Nations Framework Convention on Climate Change* (Ashgabat: Research-Production Center of Ecological Monitoring).

Government of the Republic of Uzbekistan (2008), *Second National Communication of the Republic of Uzbekistan under the United Nations Framework Convention on Climate Change* (Tashkent: Centre of Hydrometeorological Service under the Cabinet of Ministers of the Republic of Uzbekistan).

Hayman, G. and T. Mayne (2010), 'Energy-related Corruption and Its Effects on Stability in Central Asia', *China & Eurasia Forum Quarterly*, 8(2): 134–148.

International Crisis Group (ICG) (2007), 'Central Asia's Energy Risks', *Asia Report* 133, 24 May.

ICG (2009), 'Tajikistan: On the Road to Failure', *Asia Report* 162, 12 February.

ICG (2010), 'Kyrgyzstan: A Hollow Regime Collapses', *Asia Briefing* 102, 27 April.

International Energy Agency (IEA) (2008a), 'Kazakhstan – 2008 Energy Balance' [http://www.iea.org/stats/balancetable.asp?COUNTRY_CODE= KZ; accessed: 15 November 2010].

IEA (2008b), 'Kyrgyzstan – 2008 Energy Balance' [http://www.iea.org/stats/balance table.asp?COUNTRY_CODE= KG; accessed: 15 November 2010].

IEA (2008c), 'Tajikistan – 2008 Energy Balance' [http://www.iea.org/stats/balancetable. asp?COUNTRY_CODE= TJ; accessed: 15 November 2010].

IEA (2008d), 'Turkmenistan – 2008 Energy Balance' [http://www.iea.org/stats/balance table.asp?COUNTRY_CODE= TM; accessed: 15 November 2010].

IEA (2008e), 'Uzbekistan – 2008 Energy Balance' [http://www.iea.org/stats/balance table.asp?COUNTRY_CODE= UZ; accessed: 15 November 2010].

IEA (2008f), 'Perspectives on Caspian Oil and Gas Development', International Energy Agency Working Paper Series, December.

IEA (2010a), *Coal Information 2010* (Paris: IEA).

IEA (2010b), *Co_2 Emissions from Fuel Combustion – 2010 Edition Highlights* (Paris: IEA).

Internet Gazeta Turkmenistan.ru (2010), 'V 2010 godu naselenie Turkmenii bezvozmzedno poluchilo 1,4 mlrd. kVt. Ch elektroenergii', 13 September.

Kazakhstan Oil & Gas Report (2010), Q4 (London: Business Monitoring International).

Lemeshev, S. (2010), 'Razvitie energetiki – zalog ekonomicheskogo rosta', *Kazakhstanskaya Pravda*, 11 November.

Lipovsky, I. (1995), 'The Deterioration of the Ecological Situation in Central Asia: Causes and Possible Consequences', *Europe-Asia Studies*, 47(7): 1109–123.

Marat, E. (2008), 'Towards a Water Regime in the Syr Darya Basin', *Central Asia-Caucasus Institute Analyst*, 12 November.

Medrea, S. (2009), 'Energy Update – Tajikistan: An Eye for An Eye?', *Central Asia-Caucasus Institute Analyst*, 28 January.

Mirimanova, M. (2009), 'Water and Energy Disputes of Central Asia: In Search of Regional Solutions?', *EUCAM Commentary*, February.

Olshanskaya, M. and B. Slay (2008), 'Carbon Finance in Europe and the CIS', *Development & Transition*, 1: 18–20.

Pannier, B. (2009), 'Battle Lines Drawn in Central Asian Water Dispute', *RFE/RL Feature Article*, 19 April.

Perelet, R. (2008), 'Climate Change in Central Asia', *Development & Transition*, 10: 8–10.

Peyrouse, S. (2007), 'The Hydroelectric Sector in Central Asia and the Growing Role of China', *China and Eurasia Forum Quarterly*, 5(2): 131–48.

Pomfret, R. (2005), 'Kazakhstan's Economy since Independence: Does the Oil Boom Offer a Second Chance for Sustainable Development?', *Europe-Asia Studies*, 57(6): 859–876.

State News Agency of Turkmenistan (TDH) (2010), 'Constructive partnership in Caspian region based on friendship and good neighbourliness', 20 November [http://www.turkmenistan.gov.tm/_en/?idr=1&id=101120a; accessed: 30 November 2010].

Toralieva, G. (2010), 'Destruction of Central Asian Electricity Grid: Causes and Implications', *EUCAM Commentary*, 8 January.

Turkmenistan Oil & Gas Report (2010), Q4 (London: Business Monitoring International).

Spechler, M.C. (2008), 'The Economies of Central Asia: A Survey', *Comparative Economic Studies*, 50(1): 30–52.

Valamat-Zade, T. (2008), 'Tajikistan Energy Sector: Present and Near Future', *Central Asia & the Caucasus*, 49: 89–97.

World Bank (2010), *Lights Out? The Outlook for Energy in Eastern Europe and the Former Soviet Union* (Washington, DC: The World Bank).

World Bank website, [http://data.worldbank.org/; accessed: 23 November 2010].

World Energy Council (2007), *Electricity in Central Asia: Market and Investment Opportunity Report* (London: World Energy Council).

Yergin, D. (1988), 'Energy Security in the 1990s', *Foreign Affairs*, 67(1): 110–132.

Zozulinsky, A. (2010), 'Kyrgyzstan: Power Generation & Transmission', [www.photos.state.gov/kyrgyzrepulic/Kyrgyz%20Power%20Industry%20Report%20_2_.pdf; accessed: 15 November 2010].

11
More Fossil Fuels and Less Carbon Emissions: Australia's Policy Paradox

Leigh Glover

Introduction

Energy is critical to contemporary Australian life as the country's wealth and prosperity is built on fossil fuel use. Securing energy supply has been largely a routine technical and engineering challenge to date and, through extensive mineral extraction, oil production and importation, and investment in energy supply infrastructure, Australia has enjoyed high levels of energy security through the modern era. Responding to the advent of climate change and peak oil will see this era of carbon-based economic prosperity draw to a close. Australia's future understanding of energy security and what this means will be necessarily changed from the prevailing position. This has broad implications for Australian society, economic production and environmental protection, as well as for governance and political life.

Arguably, Australian energy and energy security policy conflicts with its climate change policy, with the former encouraging growth in fossil fuel development and the latter requiring 'de-carbonisation' of the national energy system. Officially, such conflicts are recognised and reconcilable. In introducing the National Energy Security Assessment (NESA), the federal Minister for Resources and Energy, Martin Ferguson, stated (DETR, 2009a, p. 1):

> Maintaining secure energy supplies requires careful balancing of many policy objectives: facilitating timely and appropriately sized investment in the energy sector; moves to a lower carbon economy; providing internationally competitive frameworks for Australian industry; and delivering reliable, adequate and affordable energy to Australian households.

Given these essential conflicts, there must be a question concerning how much 'balance' is possible. Australians have amongst the highest, if not the highest, per capita greenhouse gas (GHG) emissions in the world, at around 25 tonnes CO_2e (in 2007–2008). Growth in GHG emissions has been high: excluding land use emissions, Australia was the fifth-highest United Nations Framework Convention on Climate Change (UNFCCC) Annex I nation in its increases in GHG emissions over 1990–2007 (being some 30 per cent higher) (UNFCCC, 2009). National energy sector emissions alone were 44 per cent above the 1990 baseline by 2008 (DCEE, 2010, p. 29). Achieving even modest GHG emissions abatement will necessitate significant changes to Australia's energy system, given that most emanate from fossil fuel combustion (see DCCEE, 2010). Of Australia's 550 Mt CO_2e total annual GHG emissions in 2008 (excluding land use), some 76 per cent were from energy sources (as combustion and fugitive emissions) (DCCEE, 2010, p. 24). Energy security has become a central plank in an energy policy that has supported the supply of fossil fuels for Australia's energy needs. So if there is a paradox in the national policy positions regarding the future of fossil fuel energy use, then energy security policies are an important component.

This chapter aims to examine the main issues of Australia's current energy policies, its climate change policies relating to GHG emissions, its position on international climate change negotiations and expectations, and some key relationships between these matters. Specifically, it explores the proposition that there is paradox in Australia's national policy regarding energy and climate change, and the place of energy security policy.

Energy resources, production and consumption

Australia has considerable energy resources, meeting a significant proportion of domestic energy needs and providing a major source of export income. In 2007–2008, of the 17,360 PJ of energy production, 76 per cent (net) was exported and 33 per cent consumed domestically (ABARE, 2010, p. 1). This activity makes Australia the world's ninth-largest energy producer (ABARE, 2010, p. 1). Coal dominates total production (54 per cent), followed by uranium (27 per cent), and natural gas (11 per cent) (ABARE, 2010, p. 1). Australia is the world's largest coal exporter, earning A$55 billion in 2008–2009 and comprising Australia's largest commodity export (ABARE, 2010, p. 37). One-third of all export income in 2008–2009 was derived from energy (ABARE, 2010). These energy export earnings had increased by an order of magnitude higher than the previous decade: with its current mineral and energy resource exports, Australia is in the midst of a 'mining boom' and the 2009 deal to sell A$50 billion worth of Australian natural gas to China prompted Minister Ferguson to dub Australia a 'global energy superpower'.

Australian society uses a great deal of energy, with a primary energy consumption of 5772 PJ in 2007–2008 (ABARE, 2010, p. 13), equating to an annual per capita rate of 277 GJ. This places Australia in the top ten developed nations on this indicator, according to the International Energy Agency (IEA). Fossil fuels dominate fuel consumption: for 2007/2008 the major sources were black coal (1701 PJ), brown coal/lignite (611 PJ), natural gas (1,262 PJ) and petroleum products (2036 PJ) (ABARE, 2010, Table 5). Broadly speaking, brown and black coal account for 40 per cent, petroleum 43 per cent, natural gas 22 per cent and renewable energy, some 5 per cent (ABARE, 2010). National energy consumption has more than doubled since the mid-1970s (it was 2695 PJ in 1974–1975), but growth rates have slowed. A recent government study projected total primary energy consumption to grow 1.5 per cent annually, amounting to a 35 per cent increase over the period 2007/2008–2029/2030 (Syed et al., 2010). Over this time, transport energy demand is projected to increase annually by 0.9 per cent; renewable energy grows by 8 per cent and accounts for 8 per cent of total consumption by 2029/2030 (Syed et al., 2010).

Renewable energy plays a small role in meeting Australia's energy services, accounting for 2 per cent of national energy production and for 5 per cent of energy consumption in 2007–2008 (ABARE, 2010: 31). Bagasse (from sugar production), wood and wood waste, and hydroelectricity provide the bulk of renewable energy production (87 per cent), with wind, solar and biofuels (including landfill and sewage gas) making up the balance of the 2007–2008 total renewable energy production of 290 PJ (ABARE, 2010, p. 31). Renewable energy production increased 6 per cent over 2002/2003–2007/2008. Over the year ending 2007–2008, growth was notable in biogas (80 per cent) and wind energy (55 per cent over the same period) (ABARE, 2010, p. 32). Solar hot water supplied 6.5 PJ of energy in 2007/2008 and solar electricity supplied 0.4 PJ (ABARE, 2010, p. 31).

Australia has considerable fossil fuel energy resources in coal, moderate resources in gas and quite modest petroleum resources. Based on demonstrated economic reserves, the reserves:production ratio is 490 years for lignite, 140 years for uranium, 90 years for black coal, 63 years for conventional gas, 20 years for liquefied petroleum gas (LPG) and only ten years for oil (ABARE, 2010, p. 4). Australia also has considerable renewable energy resources, particularly solar, wind and geothermal. As large-scale hydropower potential has been largely developed, the potential for growth is only in smaller-scale facilities (e.g., Geoscience Australia and ABARE, 2010).

An overview of national energy consumption highlights key energy and climate change issues. Of the 5772 PJ of energy consumed in 2007–2008, the following sectors had the highest consumption levels: electricity generation 1760 PJ, transport 1338 PJ, manufacturing 1301 PJ, mining 436 PJ, residential 426 PJ, commercial 268 PJ, agriculture 93 PJ and construction 26 PJ (ABARE, 2010, p. 15). Electricity generation is primarily fuelled by brown and black coal (76.3 per cent) and gas (15.9 per cent), reflecting low prices and relative abundance, especially on the East Coast (ABARE, 2010, p. 21). Petroleum supplies most transport energy (over 90 per cent). Australia both exports and imports oil and oil products; while it is a net LPG exporter, it relies on oil imports to satisfy demand and is currently about 50 per cent self-sufficient. There is no peak oil debate over Australia's resources: peak production occurred in 2000 and, under current trends, future net importation will increase. Stationary energy consumption by manufacturing is dominated by relatively few energy-intensive industries, notably those of iron and steel, non-ferrous metals, basic chemicals, wood and paper, and cement and associated industries.

Energy policy

Energy policy is diverse and fragmented: in Australia's federal system of government, the Commonwealth, eight states and territories, and over 700 local governments, together with multiple departments and agencies, all have a role in formulation and delivery. Therefore, although national energy policy occupies a primary position and provides overall national direction, it only constitutes part of a complex policy field. Australia's last major energy policy statement was the government's 2004 *Securing Australia's Energy Future.* Its stated strategy was to, amongst other things (Australia, 2004, p. 2):

- Attract investment for resource discovery and development;
- Ensure economic prosperity and meeting environmental protection goals;
- Encourage cleaner technologies;
- Develop more efficient energy markets;
- Minimise supply disruptions.

The document's chapter 7 dealt with energy security; its major findings were as follows (Australia, 2004):

1. Energy security is high because of abundant coal, gas, and oil reserves; extensive delivery infrastructure; and access to world markets;
2. Investment in sustainable supply systems will be a long-term challenge;
3. Transport fuels are secure because of access to global markets.

A new energy policy is under development and a White Paper – originally due for release at the end of 2009, but now delayed – is in preparation. Its proposed principles are (DETR, 2009b, p. 3):

1. Economic development is sustainable and efficient;
2. Effective operation of competitive energy markets is promoted;
3. The need and scope for government intervention on the basis of market failure is identified;
4. International and national interests and obligations are met.

Further, the consistency of themes and directions in these recent energy policy initiatives closely resembles those of the nation's early energy policies (Saddler, 1981). Primarily energy policy is directed at securing national economic growth and a stream of economic benefits arising from energy exports and ensuring low-cost and abundant domestic supplies. Relatively little interest has been shown in energy efficiency or the energy system's social and environmental externalities. One persistent feature has been public subsidies of various kinds to fossil fuel energy producers and retailers, including tax arrangements for company-owned cars, research and developments funds, automotive and aluminium industry assistance, fuel tax rebates, road and freeway construction funding and others (see, for example, Reidy and Diesendorf, 2003).

Despite this emphasis on conventional energy, there have been efforts to promote alternative energy through national energy policy. Prominent amongst these is the national renewable energy target scheme that has undergone several revisions. Essentially, the original goal was to have 20 per cent of Australia's electricity met by renewable energy sources by 2020. Following problems, the original scheme has been modified and, most recently, the federal government divided it into small- and large-scale schemes, which it expects to exceed the original target (of 45,000 GWh by 2020). Considerable effort has gone into the Clean Energy Initiative, including major federal funding to develop technologies for carbon capture and storage, a solar energy programme (including a solar schools programme and a national home insulation programme), and creation of an institution to further renewable energy development.

Support for improved national energy efficiency through national policy has generally been weak, although there have been quite a number of federal and state programmes for many years. Recently, the former Department of Climate Change became the Department of Climate Change and Energy Efficiency and a task group and advisory group were established. However, there is no national energy efficiency strategy and national policies are not highly developed. For example, while there are energy performance standards for some appliances and equipment in Australia, no mandatory standards currently apply. Further, while some state jurisdictions require disclosure of the energy performance of building facilities, these do not apply uniformly across the country and, more importantly, do not apply to buildings. There remain price incentives in energy charging that encourage increased consumption. Overall, it appears that energy efficiency measures have had only very minor impacts on reducing Australia's national energy consumption (ABARE, 2009).

Energy security policy

Industrial societies have always had, and must have, policies for the assured supply of energy on which production depends. Energy security policy is part of the energy policy specialisation that occurred in the 1970s with the rise of the broader notion of energy policy. With this development, global energy trade issues became part of the practice and scholarship of international relations. After the Organization of the Petroleum Exporting Countries' (OPEC's) demonstration of market power produced the 1970s oil crises, in most developed nations national energy policy co-joined with national security agendas: in the United States, for example, this linkage created the 'Carter Doctrine' (Randall, 2005).

Australia's 2009 NESA defines 'energy security' conventionally as the 'adequate, reliable and affordable supply of energy to support the functioning of the economy and social development' (DETR, 2009a, p. 5). NESA's listing of factors for evaluating energy security includes the 'conditions in the domestic economy' and 'international factors and vulnerabilities'. Australia's energy security assessments comprise, therefore, both technical assessment and policy appraisal.

Although in popular imagination energy security is the national security dimension of energy supply, it more properly embraces domestic and imported energy, as in the NESA. In essence, the NESA expresses:

1. A confidence that the global oil market will provide for increasing national oil imports at acceptable prices;
2. Greater investment in electricity and gas supply infrastructure is needed to serve expanding markets;
3. A commitment to low energy prices through federal discipline on taxation (on electricity, natural gas and petroleum);
4. A commitment to public subsidies for oil and gas exploration and development.

Nevertheless, it should be noted that there have been some dissenting views within government, including those expressed in *Australia's Future Oil Supply and Alternative Transport Fuels* – a federal Senate committee report that questioned future oil availability (Australia, 2007).

Climate change policy

International policy responses

It can be useful to consider Australia's climate change policy as having an international relations dimension and a domestic dimension, with greatest scholarly attention given to the former. Australia has been involved throughout the international response to climate change, which began with scientific meetings in the 1980s and was subsequently taken up by the United Nations (UN) through negotiation of the UNFCCC. Australia ratified the UNFCCC and accepted its principle of 'common but differentiated responsibilities' for GHG emissions reductions and, as a developed nation, was listed as an Annex I party required to curb emissions. Although the UNFCCC expressed a goal for stabilising GHG concentrations in the atmosphere, this was subsequently quantified as national emissions targets for the Annex I nations in the UNFCCC's Kyoto Protocol (for the first commitment period).

Broadly, there have been three phases of Australia's international engagement with climate change corresponding with the changes in national government. Under the Labor Party governments headed by Bob Hawke and Paul Keating (1983–1996), Australia followed a path of middle international power diplomacy, promoting multilateral agreements and supporting international institutions, whilst pursuing its national economic and political interests. With the election of the Coalition government led by John Howard (1996–2007), Australian foreign policy emphasised stronger bilateral relationships (especially that with the United States), sought flexibility and pragmatism in its international relations and supported international institutions where these bolstered Australian interests. During this period, Australia and the United States held out from ratifying the Kyoto Protocol – the only Annex I parties to do so. Essentially, the government's rationale was that the Protocol was inequitable and ineffective because developing nations were not set quantified GHG reduction targets. During this time, Australia helped develop the Asia Pacific Partnership on Clean Development and Climate as a counter-measure to the Kyoto Protocol.

Climate change and the Kyoto Protocol featured in the national election of 2007. On this point, some commentators considered that the climate change issue was one of the major points of difference between the two major parties and a contributory factor to Labor's success (and the Coalition's failure). Newly elected Labor Party PM Kevin Rudd attended COP-13 at Bali and used the opportunity to ratify the Kyoto Protocol, thereby marking a third phase of Australia's explicit response to climate change negotiations and a return, of sorts, to a more multilateral approach to international relations. As part of its new cabinet, the Rudd government created a ministry for climate change and a separate federal department, thereby elevating the issue to Cabinet status for the first time. It appeared that the Rudd government was going to take climate change very seriously.

However, Australia's response to climate change is not quite as neat as this simple categorisation suggests. Australia's position has been consistently built on the Kyoto Protocol and Australia behaved through the period when it had not ratified the agreement (that is, 1996–2007) as if it had. All of the obligations for compiling the national emissions inventory have been met. Indeed, there was considerable investment in developing inventory methodologies suitable for measuring land use and ecosystem sources and sinks. Reporting of the national inventory and policy activity has been made to the UNFCCC Secretariat as required by the Kyoto Protocol, including reporting against the national emissions target that had not been officially accepted. This occurred right through the life of the Howard government, even though prominent Cabinet members were climate change 'sceptics'.

Contrary to the implications of the changes in national outlook on the issue, a case can be made that climate change policy has been remarkably consistent throughout its development. Prominent in this case is the primacy given to protecting national economic interests. In setting national emissions reduction targets for the Kyoto Protocol, Australia successfully achieved a target of 108 per cent of its 1990 levels, when nearly every other developed country accepted targets that required cutting emissions. Further, this target included emissions savings from land use activities, a decision that uniquely benefited Australia as it gained from policies reducing land clearing that were already in train. In effect, Australia's Kyoto Protocol target was a 'business as usual' target for the energy sector. During various UNFCCC conference negotiations, Australia was part of a shifting block of developed nations (frequently Japan, United States, Canada and New Zealand), which, amongst other things, argued for a weaker response for setting developed nations' quantitative targets, and endorsed emissions trading (Oberthür and Ott, 1999, pp. 17–18). Throughout its involvement in these diplomatic processes, Australia pursued arguments that have clearly favoured its interests over those seeking stronger protection of ecological values (Christoff, 1998, 2005; Hamilton, 2001). Australian delegations to the negotiations comprised many agencies, but it was the 'central' agencies (that is, Prime Minister, Treasury, and Trade departments) that determined the primary objectives focusing on political and economic goals.

National policy response

Domestic climate change policy has been the product of the same ideologies and values that have shaped the international response to climate change, both in terms of reflecting the shifting interests of the prevailing national governments and in expressing a fundamental consistency. As with the preceding observations on energy policy, climate change in Australia is probably best viewed as a policy field: besides the national formal policy, there is a wider array of policies formulated by the states, territories and local governments. For our purpose here, though, focusing on the national policy is sufficient.

To date, there have been several national climate change policies, notably the first in 1992 by the Council of Australia Governments (COAG, 1992) under the Hawke government, and then major policies in 1995, 1997, 1998 and the most recent in 2007 by the Howard government (DPMC, 2007). While the current Labor Party Gillard government (PM Julia Gillard replaced PM Rudd in June 2010) has not released an explicit climate change strategy, climate change has featured strongly in national politics since the election and a few key developments are of particular interest.

Giving primacy to established economic interests has been a feature of national climate change policy. Australian governments have long held the view – dating back at least to the federal government Cabinet decisions of the early 1990s – that Australia should not sign any international climate change agreement that could harm the Australian economy (Pearse, 2007). With the development of Australia's ecologically sustainable development strategy in 1992, climate change was recognised as an emerging issue, as was the need to cut GHG emissions. However, the strategy expressly stated that responses could only be framed while protecting national economic interests. Accordingly, the first *National Greenhouse Response Strategy* (COAG, 1992) re-iterated this requirement through two means, namely reliance on voluntary measures for emissions reduction and use of the 'no regrets' principle (meaning that any measures for climate change had to be worth taking in their own right). In retrospect, the first national policy was thin on content and was substantially a compilation of extant policy from related fields, more notably energy policy. Over time, more specific climate change initiatives were added, reflecting a growing institutional capacity and policy expertise within the federal public service. This succession of policies became more elaborate, committed greater funds and expressed some subtle shifts in emphasis and scope, such as the increasing recognition of the role of adaptation and further support for research. Nevertheless, a strong case can be made that, over this period, there was little progression in overall commitment to curbing national emissions.

On this last point, the promotion of carbon emissions trading as national policy is of particular interest. Since the first national policy there has been a consistent growth in developing emissions trading, to the extent that a proposed emissions trading scheme was the centrepiece of the Rudd government's climate change policy. This is neither novel nor unpredictable, but the result of the Kyoto Protocol's design that facilitates global emissions trading: Europe already has an emissions trading scheme, a regional scheme operates in north-eastern United States and the Australian state of New South Wales began its GHG Abatement System using emissions trading between electricity generators in 2003.

By virtue of both the expiry of the first commitment period of the Kyoto Protocol and because the emissions trading system selected is a 'cap and trade' model, Australia was going to have to set emissions targets regardless of which party held power federally – both sides of politics had promoted emissions trading and committed to remaining engaged in the UN response to climate change. Earlier work involved a National Emissions Trading Taskforce which undertook activity on a national scheme. This group established many of the intellectual and practical foundations for emissions trading in its 2006 discussion paper and then in its framework report. There was also a Prime Ministerial Task Group on Emissions Trading whose final report canvassed key issues for Australia. Part of the output of these groups was supported by federally funded consultancy studies and government agencies. Finally, the national climate change policy of the Howard government announced: '[T]he Government will introduce an emissions trading scheme, no later than 2012, as the primary mechanism for achieving the long term emissions reduction goal' (DPMC, 2007, p. vi). This has been interpreted as an electioneering announcement to counter growing public criticism of the government's performance on climate change, which was generally perceived as being very poor. Indeed, the Howard government sided with the fossil fuel industries, undermined climate change science and had many climate change sceptics in its ranks (Hamilton, 2001, 2007; Pearse, 2007). Doubtless there is considerable truth to the aforementioned claim, but it remains that the emissions trading proposal came at the end of a comprehensive technical investigation into emissions trading at the Howard government's instigation.

In late 2007, momentum was maintained by the incoming Rudd government that brought the emissions trading scheme debate into the public sphere via the agency of the Garnaut Climate Change Review, headed by economist Ross Garnaut. This review held extensive consultation and public meetings, and published several issues and working papers, before publishing its own *Final Report* (GCCR, 2008). Intellectually, the Garnaut review produced an antipodean version of the earlier British report – submitted by Sir Nicholas Stern to the Blair government – promoting emissions trading. Work on developing emissions trading continued and, soon in the term of the new government, the federal Minister for Climate Change, Penny Wong, announced the forthcoming national Carbon Pollution Reduction Scheme (CPRS). This was to follow the usual procedures of green and white papers (Australia, 2008), culminating then in a proposed raft of complex legislation.

For the CPRS, the Rudd government set 5–15 per cent reductions from the baseline year of 2000 (depending on the targets adopted by other nations) for 2020. In the lead-up to the Copenhagen climate conference, the government offered a 25 per cent cut by 2020 if a more ambitious global agreement occurred, but this did not eventuate. For its long-term target, the Rudd government sought a 60 per cent reduction against a baseline of year 2000 emissions by 2050 (all the states and territories have accepted this as their own targets). Many analyses, including the Garnaut review (GCCR, 2008), have argued that more stringent targets are necessary if global warming is to be kept below a 2°C increase.

This process went smoothly until the CPRS was stalled politically, firstly delayed by the Rudd government's concerns over the 2009 Global Financial Crisis and then stopped when the federal Senate rejected the enabling legislation, blocked by the Opposition and the Greens Party. Australia entered its 2010 federal election with the Gillard government offering to begin emissions trading (at the earliest) in 2013. The Liberal Party/National Party opposed the measure. Unexpectedly, the national vote of August 2010 produced a hung Parliament, with the Gillard government returning to office through the support of the Greens Party and three independent members.

It is now uncertain whether emissions trading will occur, as the Labor government can only pass lower house legislation with the assistance of its minority partners. It would not be surprising if the government changed course and adopted a national carbon tax in lieu of emissions trading.

Discussion and conclusions

Australian political interests opposing responses to climate change have generally worked in parallel with those in the United States, namely, the political alliance of major fossil fuel industries and their industrial clients, political interests from the right wing and conservative lobbyists and think tanks. Pearse (2007) provided a detailed account of the interaction of these political actors with the conservative Howard government, supporting the national position to align with the United States in refusing to sign the Kyoto Protocol. Christoff (1998, 2005), Hamilton (2007) and Stevenson (2009) drew on political economy and other approaches to explain the coincidence of these interests, including the relationship between national and foreign affairs policy. For while there may be doubts as to whether the federal government's position on climate change has served the national interests, there can be no doubt that it has provided comfort for the fossil fuel industries and their followers. At its most extreme form, the conservative position rejects the validity of climate change science, a position still openly held by many members of the Liberal and National Party national parliamentarians. Certainly, these conservative groups have invested considerably and effectively in maintaining a reasonable level of scepticism of climate change by a considerable section of the general public (Hamilton, 2007).

It may be instructive to close this chapter with some observations on Australian climate change and energy politics that tie together its key themes. Hamilton's (2001) account of climate change policy development in Australia describes three key beliefs that historically directed its international response. Similar arguments have appeared again in the most recent national report to the UNFCCC (DCC, 2010). Such outlooks provide a negotiating rationale for Australia to press its claims for having high GHG emissions and continue to underpin much of the nation's responses on these issues. The following section of the chapter will examine each response in detail.

Firstly, there is the view that Australia's high dependence on fossil fuels means that GHG emissions cuts will be more expensive for Australia than for its trading partners. Such a view was expressed in the first national climate change strategy (COAG, 1992) and remains a feature of Commonwealth government thinking. Empirically, there is not much to support this largely self-serving proposition; official economic modelling of these costs by the federal government has been derided for the political biases of its assumptions (e.g., Hamilton, 2001; Pearse, 2007). Unfortunately, there is a self-fulfilling aspect to these claims, in so far as the continued delays in cutting emissions surely increase the future costs and magnitude of future efforts to achieve such mitigation.

Secondly, there is a common belief that because of Australia's geographical size (it is the world's sixth-largest nation), its transport energy needs are especially high, given the need for trans-continental movement of passengers and freight. Again, empirically, this is largely invalid, as even cursory examination of transport GHG emissions data reveals that most emissions arise from fuel consumed by urban motorists (GCCR, 2008), of which the daily commute is the single largest category of trip type. There is comparatively little inter-city passenger and goods movement and, indeed, mode-switching much of road-based inter-state transport to rail offers the potential of considerable emissions savings (GCCR, 2008). Within the cities, there are considerable opportunities for cutting transport emissions, especially given that the Australian urban transport system – which incidentally features high levels of private car use – is emissions-inefficient, as much of the government's own research results demonstrate. Comparatively, there is nothing special about the scale of Australia's transport emissions, for, as a proportion of total GHG emissions, they are similar to Europe and North America.

Thirdly, in further reflection of the familiar rationale of protecting national economic (and associated vested) interests, there is concern regarding threats of the loss of export income should Australia be required to reduce its energy exports. What is so surprising about this argument is that it simply does not apply to the current Kyoto Protocol, as emissions accounting occurs at the point of release. Australia's exports of energy should impose no restraint on the national capacity for indigenous GHG emissions mitigation. Further, as Hamilton (2001) points out, a balanced view would determine the extent to which Australia 'imports' emissions as embodied emissions in imported products. Hamilton suggests that preliminary evidence has shown that national energy exports and embodied energy imports may, in fact, be similar. Finally, it is highly questionable to oppose GHG emissions reduction by other nations on the grounds that Australia's income from its energy exports will be harmed. Australia can make no call on how other nations chose to respond to climate change and, certainly, could not encourage them to continue to use high levels of fossil fuels in any international forum while retaining credibility as a nation that responds positively to global climate change.

Despite the contestability – not to mention downright weakness – of these three arguments, Australia's political leaders appear to remain in the thrall of these 'storylines', seemingly untroubled by suggestions that they lack basic veracity.

Ideologically, Australia's energy policy, energy security and climate change policies are in political accord, sharing a neo-liberal foundation. In these fields where there are many public goods and externalities, the neo-liberal response is not to rely on unrestrained markets, but to marshal governmental legitimacy and authority to create new markets and address market failures. National climate change policy has followed this general course since its inception, leading logically to proposals for emissions trading. One factor that makes the CPRS so attractive – as does the national investment in carbon capture and storage – is that Australia's legitimacy in international climate change negotiations is promoted.

Energy security is primarily directed towards securing the interests of the state and the large corporate entities linked to the energy sector by directing public investment for private corporate gain and for influencing international negotiations to align with the interests of these parties. Accordingly, energy security secures the *status quo*, which means further 'locking-in' fossil fuel energy systems and taking the wider Australian population further from the security of a predictable global climate. Two other implications arise. Firstly, through the ongoing neglect of renewable energy sources, there has been insufficient consideration concerning how to apply the concepts of energy security to these non-fossil fuel energy supplies. This is allied to the case that renewable energy needs to acquire the same legitimacy as an energy source as conventional energy forms by the central government agencies and given an equivalent institutional home. Secondly, access to energy varies greatly within the community, but energy security concerns 'national interests'. Opportunities for reducing the nation's need to secure the existing energy system could be directed towards increasing energy independence at the point of consumption. For example, furnishing the poor with independent energy sources would improve their energy security, and hence, at the collective level, enhance national energy security.

According to the Australian government, national energy security is to be achieved through continued domestic fossil fuel production, access to global markets for oil and the expectation of reasonably low future oil price increases. While Australians enjoy a globally high level of energy resources per capita, such a nation-centric and economy-centric perspective on energy security diverts attention from security of supply of energy services to households and the problems of fuel poverty. There are grounds for concern that national economic interests and social and economic values at the household scale are not in accord. For example, an examination of transport energy costs in major Australian cities – when combined with the effects of mortgage rates – found those places most distant from employment centres and, where the lack of public transport services made households car-dependent for transport, to be highly vulnerable to transport fuel price rises (Dodson and Sipe, 2008). Such high-vulnerability locations were also those of lower socio-economic standing; forecast rises in global fuel costs will greatly depress effective household income for these lower-income households. Official conceptualisations of energy security contain hitherto largely unexplored biases and assumptions that exclude the social dimensions of energy services and the associated implications of future changes in energy supply and costs, such as those caused by peak oil.

Ongoing faith in market forces to secure future oil supplies seems at odds with forecasts of increasing competition for oil and a return to greater reliance on OPEC suppliers (EIA, 2005; IEA, 2007). Given the transport sector's near-total reliance on petroleum products, the NESA seems to reject any notion of 'precaution' in protecting the nation from future price increase/supply disruptions from the volatile Middle East. It is also difficult to determine how the 'affordability' of energy fits with the conventional view of energy security, as transport energy is already a major cost for the economically disadvantaged in Australia. Under the 'peak oil' case, we have entered the end of the era of cheap oil, a proposition at odds with assumptions adopted by the NESA.

Not only is there optimism about the assured supply of imported and affordable oil under the conventional energy paradigm, but there is also technological optimism. There would seem to be much faith in technology-based systems, notably the experimental carbon storage projects and the development of new technologies for a low-carbon economy. Some commentators are sceptical about the prospects for such progress in the short term (for example, MacGill et al., 2006), particularly in the difficult transport sector (Moriarty and Honnery, 2004, 2008a, 2008b). For example, after nearly two decades of climate change policy, Australia's current motor car fleet has the same level of fuel economy achieved by the Model-T Ford.

Despite the ideological consistency of these policy developments over many years, the problem remains that making significant GHG emissions cuts that the nation has committed to achieving does not require abundant and low-cost fossil fuels to promote increased production. Cutting these emissions at this scale quickly requires a transition in the conventional energy system to one with reduced total energy demand and meeting energy service demands through low-emissions means – a task with both national and international dimensions. It is not going to be possible to capture the full economic value of the nation's energy resources (and its imported energy) while simultaneously maintaining the ecosystem values being degraded by the energy system. Certainly, such a task is well beyond the range of the proposed CPRS, a system whose beginning was marked by concessions to major polluting industries and other compromises.

International support for limiting future warming to 2°C continues to grow. Article 1 of the 2009 Accord arising from the UNFCCC Copenhagen Conference (2009), for example, interprets 'avoiding dangerous interference' in the global climate as requiring such a limit. A 75 per cent chance of limiting warming to 2°C requires that no more than 250,000 Mt of carbon be released (Meinshausen et al., 2009). Allen et al. (2009) estimate that, at current global emissions rates, the quantity of accumulated emissions in the atmosphere to cross the 2°C mark will be achieved in two decades. By implication, emissions reductions of this scale and rate require a transformation of the energy systems of the developed world, as this target can only be met by cutting GHG emissions by 25–40 per cent by the year 2020 and 80–95 per cent by 2050.

In closing, what is most urgently needed is not conventional energy supply 'security', but energy system 'resilience', namely a capacity not to resist change, but to respond dynamically and purposefully to such change. To talk of balancing conflicting goals between conventional energy systems and climate change is the language of equivocation. After nearly two decades of climate change policy and perhaps a decade's work on developing emissions trading, Australian leaders continue to seek an impossible balance, namely, to lower GHG emissions within an unconstrained fossil fuel energy system. By any reasonable deduction, Australia is simply not moving towards a low-carbon economy, unless rhetoric now counts as action.

References

Allen, M.R. D.J. Frame, C. Huntingford, C.D. Jones, J.A. Lowe, M. Meinshausen and N. Meinshausen (2009), 'Warming caused by cumulative carbon emissions toward the trillionth tonne', *Nature*, 458: 1163–1166.

Australia, Commonwealth of (2008), *Carbon Pollution Reduction Scheme: Australia's Low Pollution Future, White Paper, Vols. I and II* (Canberra).

Australia, Commonwealth of, Senate Standing Committee on Rural and Regional Affairs and Transport (2007), *Australia's Future Oil Supply and Alternative Transport Fuels: Final Report* (Canberra).

Australia, Commonwealth of (2004), *Securing Australia's Energy Future* (Canberra).

Australian Bureau of Agricultural and Resource Economics (ABARE) (2009), *End Use Energy Intensity in the Australian Economy* (Canberra).

ABARE (2010), *Energy in Australia 2010* (Canberra).

Christoff, P. (1998), 'From global citizen to renegade state: Australia at Kyoto', *Arena*, 10: 113–128.

Christoff, P. (2005), 'Policy autism or double-edged dismissiveness? Australia's climate policy under the Howard government', *Global Change, Peace and Security*, 17(1): 29–44.

Council of Australian Governments (COAG) (1992), *National Greenhouse Response Strategy* (Canberra: AGPS).

Department of Climate Change (DCC) (2010), *Australia's Fifth National Communication on Climate Change* (Canberra).

Department of Climate Change and Energy Efficiency (DCCEE) (2010), *National Inventory Report 2008, Volume 1* (Canberra).

Department of Prime Minister and Cabinet (DPMC) (2007), *Australia's Climate Change Policy: Our Economy, Our Environment, Our Future* (Canberra: Commonwealth of Australia).

Department of Resources, Energy and Tourism (DETR) (2009a), *National Energy Security Assessment* (Canberra).

DETR (2009b), *Energy White Paper: National Energy Policy Framework 2030: Strategic Directions Paper* (Canberra).

Diesendorf, M. (2007), *Greenhouse Solutions with Renewable Energy* (Sydney: University of New South Wales Press).

Dodson, J. and N. Sipe (2008), *Unsettling Suburbia: The New Landscape of Oil and Mortgage Vulnerability in Australian Cities*, Research Paper 17 (Brisbane: Urban Research Program, Griffith University).

Energy Information Administration (EIA) (2005), *International Energy Outlook 2005* (Washington, DC: EIA).

Garnaut Climate Change Review (GCCR) (2008), *Final Report* (Melbourne: Cambridge University Press).

Geoscience Australia and ABARE (2010), *Australian Energy Resource Assessment* (Canberra).

Hamilton, C. (2001), *Running from the Storm: The Development of Climate Change Policy in Australia* (Sydney: UNSW Press).

Hamilton, C. (2007), *Scorcher: The Dirty Politics of Climate Change* (Melbourne: Black Inc.).

International Energy Agency (IEA) (2007) *World Energy Outlook 2007* (Paris: OECD/IEA).

MacGill, I.F., T. Daly, and R. Passey (2006), 'The limited role for carbon capture and storage technologies in a sustainable Australian energy future', *International Journal of Environmental Studies*, 63(40): 751–763.

Meinshausen, M., N. Meinshausen, W. Hare, S.C.B. Raper, K. Frieler, R. Knutti, D.J. Frame and M.E. Allen (2009), 'Greenhouse gas emission targets for limiting global warming to 2°C', *Nature*, 458: 1158–1162.

Moriarty, P. and D. Honnery (2004), 'Forecasting world transport in the year 2050', *International Journal of Vehicle Design*, 35(1/2): 151–165.

Moriarty, P. and D. Honnery (2008a), 'Mitigating greenhouse: Limited time, limited options', *Energy Policy*, 36(4): 1251–1256.

Moriarty, P. and D. Honnery, (2008b), 'The prospects for global green car mobility', *Journal of Cleaner Production*, 16(16): 1717–1726.

Oberthür, S. and H.E. Ott (1999), *The Kyoto Protocol: International Climate Policy for the 21st Century* (Berlin and New York: Springer).

Pearse, G. (2007), *High and Dry: John Howard, Climate Change and the Selling of Australia's Future* (Melbourne: Penguin).

Randall, S.J. (2005), *United States Foreign Oil Policy since World War I* (Montreal and Kingston: McGill-Queens University Press).

Reidy, C. and M. Diesendorf (2003), 'Financial subsidies to the Australian fossil fuel industry', *Energy Policy*, 31(2): 125–137.

Saddler, H. (1981), *Energy in Australia: Politics and Economics* (Sydney: Allen and Unwin).

Schlapfer, A. (2009), 'Hidden biases in Australian energy policy', *Renewable Energy*, 34(2): 456–460.

Stevenson, H. (2009), 'Cheating on climate change? Australia's challenge to global warming norms', *Australian Journal of International Affairs*, 63(2): 165–186.

Syed, A., J. Melanie, S. Thorpe and K. Penny (2010), *Australian Energy Projections to 2029–30* (Canberra: ABARE Research Report 10.02).

UN FCCC (2009), *National Greenhouse Gas Inventory Data for the Period 1990—2007* (Geneva: United Nations Framework Convention on Climate Change Secretariat, Document: FCCC/SBI/2009/12).

Part III

Multilateral Energy Governance in the Era of Climate Change

12
Energy Security and Climate Change – Tensions and Synergies

Peter Christoff

Introduction

National energy and climate policies are becoming increasingly entwined. Energy security is an acknowledged and important factor in the domestic economic and energy policies of many states. The threat of global warming is forcing countries to consider rapid changes in their patterns of energy supply and consumption in order to reduce their contribution to global greenhouse emissions.

This chapter examines whether, and to what extent, energy security has played a significant role in shaping the climate negotiating positions of major energy-using and greenhouse gas emitting states. In particular, it seeks to identify the 'role' of energy security in the positioning of key state actors in climate negotiations. Confining attention to those states that are amongst the major national contributors to global emissions, it looks at energy security as one factor in states' climate negotiating behaviour amid shifting circumstances – shifts that relate to changing features affecting energy security, and changes affecting climate mitigation over the almost two decades since the United Nations Framework Convention on Climate Change (UNFCCC) was negotiated in 1992. Moreover, it considers which actors have been responsible for energy security becoming a determinant in national climate policy, and under what circumstances.

The chapter begins by examining the concept of energy security and its role in defining three different types of state. It then considers recent changes in global and regional energy circumstances and in the demands arising from the challenges of combating global warming. On this basis, it analyses how the energy profile of the world's 20 biggest national emitters may have influenced their negotiating performance, specifically in recent climate negotiations relating to the 'post-Kyoto' period, before concluding with observations about the 'role' of energy security in the positioning of states in climate negotiations.

Energy security

'Energy security' most often refers to the extent to which a state has 'access to secure, adequate, reliable and affordable energy supplies' (Bordoff et al., 2010, p. 214). There is therefore an understandable tendency, in assessing energy security, to concentrate on a state's independence in relation to critical energy supplies – often represented in terms of energy resource endowments and energy trade flows. Indeed, this chapter uses data on capacity, imports, exports and domestic use of specific energy resources, broadly to suggest states' levels of energy (in)security. However, such indicators may be contingent and unreliable in the final instance, as underlying aspects of energy security are shaped by national political and institutional capacities and by national choices relating to military, economic and – increasingly – environmental security.

For instance, a state may *appear* highly dependent on external energy sources, and therefore vulnerable, but also have the political, social, economic and other institutional capacities to respond rapidly to threats or challenges to its external energy supply. While such a state may appear to be narrowly dependent on one or two energy sources or resource types, it can in fact be flexible enough to quickly diversify supplies or politically robust enough to alter demand in ways that make its apparent insecurity only superficial or temporary. By contrast, another state may seem relatively diversified and 'secure' but because of its size, growth trajectory, and domestic political and other institutional rigidities, may be relatively inflexible in the face of challenge. The United States and China may fit this bill. These capacities to respond to energy threats are also, of course, critical issues for the climate narrative, which for some states demands major shifts from reliance on fossil fuels to renewables in a very short period of time.

Further, energy security and energy vulnerability are, in some senses, segmentable by sector and resource, into transport (oil); stationary power (coal/gas/uranium); and heating (gas/oil). For instance, although access to petroleum is a major concern for the transport sectors of oil-importing nations such as the United States, Australia and China – each is significantly dependent on external supplies – these states are independent when it comes to other energy resources, such as gas and coal.

Finally, energy security is a dynamic socially constructed phenomenon, changing according to shifts both in geopolitical circumstance and domestic political conditions. As an exploitable political resource, the energy security frame can be mobilised discursively to legitimise and preserve, advance, or retard and undermine, the commercial and political interests of specific groupings within and adjacent to government, depending on the configuration of the state. This occurs not merely in a rhetorical sense but also in a material one – where, for instance, manipulation of energy prices can be made to generate an 'energy security crisis', or where reliance upon a specific energy resource for national economic stability determines political legitimacy, power and success.

Similarly, the linked climate-energy security narrative will also transform over time, as individual national circumstances, capacities, aspirations and needs change. A state that aspires to be a regional or global power – including energy 'super power' – will have a different practical conception of its energy needs and energy security than one that is relatively restrained in its geopolitical ambitions. In all, it is possible that the shifting relationship between climate change and energy security will be one of tension for some states but synergetic for others.

Types of 'energy state'

The potential climate-negotiating imperatives of individual states may be clarified by considering three ideal types: energy independent, energy-import dependent, and energy-export oriented states. Depending on their underlying capacities, individual states have broadly sought to ensure energy security in one of three ways.

Energy independent states

States have traditionally sought energy independence by developing their domestic energy resources to meet national demand, by increasing the efficiency and reducing the intensity of domestic energy consumption and, less commonly, by tightening demand to diminish strains on limited supplies. Few developed or major developing states are energy independent – a situation largely reflecting the extent and diversity of their energy requirements, and the influence and economic impacts of globalised energy markets. Accordingly, a demand management path towards energy security has generally been set aside in favour of diversified energy trade.

Energy-import dependent states

More usually, energy-resource poor states have sought to enhance their economic development by importing energy. Energy security here depends on how the state goes about doing this – by using force or trade deals to secure relationships with a limited number of critical energy suppliers, or by developing resilience and diversity in its relations amongst a broad range of external suppliers and energy resources. Of course, the greater the level of energy-import dependence (including in relation to the range of energy resources imported, and the import ratio of the most critical resources) and the more volatile the energy trading partner, the greater the risk of energy insecurity.

For instance, some energy-dependent developed states – such as Japan and France – responded to the Organization of the Petroleum Exporting Countries (OPEC) oil crises of the 1970s by adopting energy security policies based on encouraging greater energy efficiency, and diversification of sources and suppliers (leading to the growth of the French and Japanese domestic nuclear power sector in the 1970s and 1980s, and dependency on uranium imports; see Chapter 7, p. 133–134). These states were consequently 'ahead of the game' and limited their 'easy' options for emissions mitigation (at least as far as stationary energy production was concerned) before climate change emerged as a policy concern.

The energy status of many developed states is nuanced by the interplay between capacity and need. Indeed states sometimes import and export the same type of energy resource according to changing market conditions: they may be resource-independent, or even exporters of certain energy commodities, but net importers of others. Australia is an example of such a complex energy profile: while it is the world's largest exporter of coal and fourth largest exporter of liquid natural gas, it is also a net importer of petroleum (Table 12.1).

Energy-exporting states

Finally, there are the energy-exporting states. Often, for such states, energy exports contribute significantly to national economic wealth and these states, victims of the 'Dutch disease', become increasingly reliant on the stability or growth of their energy resource markets for domestic political and economic security.

As Table 12.1 suggests, many states are an amalgam of these types – autonomous with regard to certain energy sources, while exporting or importing others. Canada and Russia are examples of fossil-fuel-based energy-independent states. Australia is energy-independent in coal and gas and a major exporter of these resources but also an oil importer. The situation for individual states – and for analysts – is further complicated by uneven dependencies across economic sectors: some states are dependent on coal or gas imported to sustain electricity production, others are dependent on importing petroleum to maintain their transport sector. As we will see, the complex individual energy characteristics of states, along with other important institutional features, makes it hard to find simple patterns linking energy policy, energy security status and climate-negotiating behaviour.

Changing circumstances

Changing energy circumstances

Over the past two decades the energy circumstances for many of the key state actors in climate negotiations have changed substantially, at the same time as the landscape of those negotiations has been transformed by shifting understandings of the pace of emissions mitigation required to address the problem of global warming. Increasing energy resource demand has coupled

Table 12.1 Major greenhouse gas emitting states and their energy characteristics

Country	Global emission status[a]	Global rank as crude oil producer[b]	Oil[c] and global rank[d]	Gas and global rank	Coal and global rank	Overall energy status[e]
China	1	5	3 Importer	Independent	**Independent** (1 producer; 2 importer)	Independent
United States	2	**3**	**1 Importer**	Independent (1 producer; 3 importer)	Independent (2 producer; 6 exporter)	**Importer**
Russia	3	**1**	**2 Exporter**	1 Exporter	3 Exporter	**Exporter**
Japan	4		**2 Importer**	1 Importer	1 Importer	**Importer**
India	5		4 Importer	Independent	**Independent** (3 producer; 4 importer)	Importer
Germany	6		**6 Importer**	2 Importer	6 Importer	**Importer**
Canada	7	**6**	**Exporter**	3 Exporter	9 Exporter	**Exporter**
Brazil	8		Independent	Importer	Importer	Independent
United Kingdom	9		**Exporter**	10 Importer	7 Importer	Independent
Australia	10		Importer	Exporter	**1 Exporter** (4 producer)	**Exporter**
Italy	11		**7 Importer**	4 Importer	9 Importer	**Importer**
France	12		**8 Importer**	Importer	Importer	**Importer**
Ukraine	13		Importer	**Importer**	Independent	Importer

Table 12.1 (Continued)

Country	Global emission status[a]	Global rank as crude oil producer[b]	Oil[c] and global rank[d]	Gas and global rank	Coal and global rank	Overall energy status[e]
Spain	14		**9 Importer**	Importer	10 Importer	Importer
Poland	15		Importer	Importer	**Independent** (9 producer)	Importer
Iran	16	**4**	**4 Exporter**	Independent	Importer	Exporter
Mexico	17	7	**Exporter**	Importer	Importer	<
South Africa	18		Importer	Importer	**5 Exporter**	Independent
Turkey	19		Importer	**Importer**	Importer	**Importer**
Indonesia	20		Independent	6 Exporter	**2 Exporter**	Exporter

[a]Ranked according to aggregate annual emissions, based on 2008 emissions data for the 20 highest emitting Annex 1 and non-Annex 1 countries, excluding Land Use Land-Use Change and Forestry (LULUCF). Including data from UNFCCC, 2005, 2010a.
[b]Status for columns 3–7 based on data from IEA (2010). The table also includes the top five OPEC oil producers: Saudi Arabia, Iran, Kuwait, United Arab Emirates and Venezuela.
[c]A country's status for a specific resource is designated along with its 2010 ranking by Mt (IEA, 2010). It is described as an energy *importer* when more than 30 per cent of net resource use (by energy balance) is imported; *independent* when over 90 per cent of net use (by energy balance) is domestically sourced and used; *exporter* when more than 50 per cent of net resource used (by energy balance) is exported. Countries that are exporters are, of course, also actually or potentially independent in the resource concerned. Overall status is assessed based on net energy flows [ktoe].
[d]A country's global ranking amongst the first ten nations (following IEA 2010), as an energy resource importer or exporter, is shown in brackets.
[e]A country's overall energy status is indicated in **bold** if this status is a defining characteristic of its resource economy.

with growing supply-side fragility produced by events such as massively fluctuating and intermittently soaring oil prices in 2008 and 2009, the growing political insecurity of supply from the Middle East, the threat of peak oil, and the consequences of natural and human-induced disasters like Hurricane Katrina in 2005 and the *Deepwater Horizon* oil spill in the Gulf of Mexico in 2010. This combination has reshaped the political landscape for climate negotiations and energy policy for both developed and developing states – especially for countries where political stability rests on low costs of energy supply. It has led to what at least one commentator (Muller-Kraenner, 2007, p. 29) has called the new 'Great Game', in which major powers with growing energy demands (such as China, India and the United States) and those with energy resources (Russia and Iran) compete for influence.

This competition has been shaped by the declining security of oil supply from the Middle East, the rise of Latin America, Africa and Russia as export sources, and the prospect of Canada entering this domain on the basis of its vast oil-shale reserves. The short-term inelasticity of demand for oil (especially in relation to transport) has made price and supply volatility a matter of policy concern in states dependent on oil imports. Although the price leap of 2008 has been ameliorated, ironically, by the recessionary economic downturn caused by the global financial crisis, the recession has also constrained private sector capacity to invest in new projects and therefore to ease supply concerns in the medium term. Natural gas has 'developed' as an accessible fuel source, its availability enhanced by new discoveries and also technological changes enabling its transportation as a liquid fuel, rather than constrained by piping it in gaseous form. The 'rise' of gas has also enhanced the international economic and political capacities of states such as Russia. On the other hand, the growth in the availability and economies of scale for energy-efficient consumer technologies, and renewable power technologies, has begun to offer 'escape routes' for energy-import dependent states.

Pascual and Zambetakis (2010, p. 11) comment that, given the relative inelasticity of demand in global energy markets, under volatile conditions (such as price fluctuations, and in short-term changes supply),

> [p]olitical power accrues in the hands of energy exporters, making it more difficult to gain consensus among net importers on international policies [...] Price volatility has also exacerbated the impact of bad economic policies in energy-exporting states when revenues have collapsed during economic downturns [...] Over the long term, reducing market volatility serves the self-interest of both energy importers and exporters.

Unfortunately this effect works against those interests pushing for rapid changes to the structure and content of energy markets. As a consequence, climate negotiations can be seen as a threat to the domestic political and economic stability of both energy exporters and inflexible energy importers, and tends to drive these states into a de facto alliance to reduce the pace of change. At best, they serve to buy time for diversification of capacity and/or supply, to reduce dependence on export revenue or predominant energy imports.

Changing climate circumstances

It is commonly recognised that global warming intensifies problems in most other policy domains. Perhaps nowhere is this clearer than in relation to national economic development, security and energy policies. If global average temperature is to be restrained to no more than 2 degrees above preindustrial levels, then global greenhouse emissions will have to peak by no later than 2015, emissions from developed countries will have to decline at minimum by between 80 and 95 per cent, and by at least 50 per cent for developing countries, by 2050, and dramatically thereafter – to approximately zero – within a decade or two thereafter (IPCC, 2007). These goals, although promoted by the Intergovernmental Panel on Climate Change (IPCC) in 2007, are already regarded as too high (too dangerous and too damaging) by parts of the climate scientific community (Allison et al., 2009). Such demands will place huge strains on the infrastructural, economic, social and therefore political capacities of developed and developing carbon-dependent economies, and stand in stark contrast to the relative inaction on this issue since the UNFCCC was signed some two decades ago, in 1992.

In recent times, climate negotiations have revolved around seven major themes. These include: the establishment of new targets for 2020 and 2050 for developed and developing countries; whether negotiations would lead to a new stage of the Kyoto Protocol or a new agreement altogether; whether or not that agreement would be legally binding; the nature of mechanisms associated with a global carbon market (including emissions trading, Clean Development Mechanism and Joint Implementation); adaptation funding; carbon offsets and Reducing Emissions from Deforestation and Degradation plus other measures (REDD+); and issues associated with the Measurable, Reportable and Verifiable (MRV) nature of commitments made by developing states.

On the issue of targets, there are four clear positions. The United States rejects the revision of the Kyoto Protocol and will only accept a new agreement involving binding targets for itself if major developing country emitters also agree to binding commitments. The European Union (EU) seeks revision of the Kyoto Protocol and new binding targets for itself, and is keen for, but not insistent on, targets for major developing states. Japan and Australia seek binding targets for developed and developing countries, and can accept this being negotiated as a revision of the Kyoto Protocol or under a new agreement. Finally, China, other major emerging developing country emitters, and most developing states insist on a revision of the Kyoto Protocol, and strong binding targets only for developed states.

Energy security and the logics of climate negotiation

What then might we expect from the intersection of energy security and climate concerns? It is important to note, at the outset, that even where energy security may play a role in shaping national (and bloc) climate negotiating strategies, it is only one amongst a number of influences and of varying importance over time. For instance, longstanding and entrenched disagreements between developed and developing countries continue to shape recent negotiations. Developing countries believe *en bloc* that it is the historical responsibility of the developed country bloc to lead in mitigation and to bear the burden of costs associated with adaptation and mitigation in the developing world – a view enshrined in the concept of 'Common But Differentiated Responsibility' or CBDR, embedded in Article 4 of the UNFCCC.

Nevertheless political economists and realists generally expect energy issues and energy security to play a powerful role amongst these influences. It might be said, for instance, that the energy/economic development imperative has been a significant factor in the near rupture between members of the G77-plus bloc, with the BASIC group – Brazil, South Africa, India, China – largely representing the interests of those major emergent emitters within that group at the expense of the claims and desires of weaker states, such as those in the Association of Small Island States (AOSIS) and African nations blocs.

Addressing the challenge of global warming depends on the international adoption of significant emissions reduction targets and a rapid transition away from fossil fuels and especially coal. But the faster the transition in the absence of cheap alternatives to coal, oil and gas, the greater the social and economic cost of transition. Clearly, the nature and timing of the transition away from fossil fuels will affect states unevenly – threatening some states (and major energy corporations) and benefitting others. Shifting from fossil fuel energy dependency imposes immediate economic, political and social costs on states, with the associated pain in turn dependent on the *rate* of transition and the national economy's level of reliance on fossil fuels. Under these circumstances, a rapid transition would – other things being equal – exacerbate the energy insecurity (marked by elevated energy prices and short-term economic and political stress) of heavily dependent fossil fuel economies, and would therefore lead such states to resist tough climate targets.

Given these considerations, domestic economic and institutional capacity and flexibility can be expected to be important underlying determinants of energy security. Large and inflexible economies are likely to be condemned to defend the carbon status quo from the scientific imperatives of rapid transformation to protect against global warming. Conversely, for more flexible economies, the demands for emissions reductions open up new possibilities for massive new global markets for renewable and low carbon technologies.

The different energy state 'types' suggest possible differences in climate-negotiating trends – which this chapter will investigate. For energy-independent states, greenhouse emissions mitigation 'merely' involves the challenge of adjusting domestic consumption patterns, technologies and energy resource streams to meet low emissions targets. Therefore one would expect little (or 'manageable') resistance to effective climate targets and support for a rapid transition to non-fossil fuel energies *if* the domestic capacity for such change is easily available or if the preparedness to accept greater reliance on more climate-benign imported energy sources is present (for instance, instead of using domestic coal, by importing gas, or deriving solar, wind or hydropower from a neighbouring state).

For energy-import dependent states, the logic of emissions minimisation and a shift away from fossil fuels can harmonise with and drive policies for improved energy security based on diversification of external energy sources or increased domestic energy autonomy – if domestic capacities for renewable energy (wind, solar, geothermal, etc.) exist. However, without alternative capacities and resources, these states are placed in a new 'energy security bind', where difficulties associated with present dependencies have to be assessed against the costs of transiting to alternative but potentially equally or more insecure relations with new producers – for instance, by shifting from a reliance on stable oil and coal importers to less stable suppliers' sources of gas or renewable energy.

For coal- and oil-exporting states, the logic of global emissions mitigation involves a direct challenge to national economic stability and, in the absence of alternatives, encourages resistance in negotiations and claims for compensation. Action to tackle climate change will favour gas exporting states if the transition is gradual, but may raise for them the same problems as faced by oil and coal exporters if the transition to renewable energy sources is rapid.

The logic of interests amongst exporting nations and the vulnerability of importing ones tends to a potentially nasty synergy, whereby threats to supply by the cartel of exporting nations (or energy multinationals) can lead to collusive or forced agreement by these states to opposition to – or at best only weak support for – emissions targets.

In each case, these imperatives cut across the definitional divide that dominates the UNFCCC, between developed and developing states. Climate negotiations and the prospect of mitigation challenge states differently, depending on which type of energy security best describes their situation and interests. This suggests that grouping states according to energy dependency status rather than development status should be a stronger predictor of – or at least a more illuminating basis for understanding – climate-negotiating postures.

Major state actors, energy and climate

With these points in mind, it is now possible to examine the energy security status and climate performance of the major greenhouse emitting states, which are actors critical to the resolution of the threat of global warming.

'Exceptional' states

As the planet's largest emitters, and the two states with claims to global hegemonic status, both the United States and China must be given priority in this discussion about state types, energy security and climate politics. For them, both energy security and climate change issues are explicitly bound up with and to a significant extent overwritten by other national political, security and economic agendas.

The United States, as the planet's largest economic and military power, occupies an exceptional place in this terrain. As the world's largest producer, importer and consumer of energy, it is presently highly dependent on fossil fuel energy for its economic capacity and growth: coal, oil and gas now provide about 80 per cent of energy consumed (EIA, 2010a). As a consequence, the United States is also the world's second largest emitter of greenhouse gases as well as the world's biggest cumulative historical emitter.

The United States is the world's second greatest producer, a major user, and sixth greatest exporter of coal. Coal is used to produce about half of US electricity and provides significant regional employment in 16 states (EIA, 2010b; EIA, no date). Changes to this profile would be expensive politically as well as economically. The United States has also become increasingly dependent on oil imports since the mid 1970s, given the decline in its domestic oil resource base. It currently imports more than 60 per cent of its oil – predominantly from the Middle East – and 16 per cent of its gas (EIA, 2010a). Competition with both China and India for petroleum has grown in recent times. These factors have increased US vulnerability to supply and price turbulence for oil.

Until the early 2000s, the Carter Doctrine's commitment to ensuring by any means 'the security of the Persian Gulf' as an oil source for the United States successfully provided Washington with an unchallenged form of energy security. In recent times, however, concerns about growing insecurity of supply – especially as a result of the cost of the two Iraq wars, and growing concerns about the security and long-term viability of other Middle Eastern oil sources – and the links between energy security, military security and climate change have gained high-level acceptance (see, for instance, CAN, 2007).

Recognition of these growing pressures on US foreign policy has initiated what appears to be a bi-partisan re-evaluation of the costs of such dependency. This has involved a recent rhetorical transition, reflected in statements by Presidents Bush Jnr and Obama that the United States must now adopt a doctrine of national energy security based on ensuring and expanding imported sources (Bush Jnr) and demand restraint, greater domestic energy efficiency, and discovering and exploiting additional and alternative domestic energy supply options, including Alaskan and Gulf oil (Bush and Obama). As Guri Bang (2010, p. 1645) notes

> as the dependence on imported oil and gas has become larger, the [US'] energy security concerns have increased due to rising prices, declining world reserves, and increasingly also fear of dependence on imports from the Middle East where instability and anti-Americanism is growing. Still, the changes in domestic policy directed at improving energy security and achieving energy independence over the past decades have been no more than incremental.

Several recent US energy bills have been framed by the energy security narrative and one observes the explicit convergence of energy security and climate narratives in the Waxman-Markey Bill, the *American Clean Energy and Security Act of 2009* (which was brought before the 111th Congress, approved in the House of Representatives but died in the Senate). Indeed, because the science of climate change remains politically contested in the United States, the narrative of dealing with 'energy security first' has been deployed to help legitimise actions to reduce greenhouse emissions. These bills intended to alter domestic patterns of energy efficiency, energy consumption and technological capacity in ways that would have additionally enabled the United States more confidently to pursue national emissions reductions commitments in international climate negotiations. But although one can argue that there has been a shift towards a narrative of energy security in US foreign policy and domestic energy/climate policy over the past five years, little progress is evident in real policy terms, even when energy dependency has been seen for over a decade as significant economic and military liability. Repeatedly, the passage of such bills has been slowed or thwarted politically, in part because there is no broad cross-party consensus about what energy security and energy independence might mean and how they should be achieved.

Bang (2010) recognises this as a puzzle and attributes the failure to convert domestic political concerns over energy security into policy action to two main factors: the design and structure of US political institutions, and the processes of agenda setting in the United States. The latter includes local political considerations related to employment in the fossil fuel-dominated energy sector and the self-protective lobbying and public influence of fossil fuel corporations (Lisowski, 2002; DeSombre, 2005). In all, one sees strong evidence of the importance of institutional and ideological factors other than those immediately relating to the issue of energy security, shaping US domestic and climate foreign policy.

The result of these influences has seen ongoing incoherence between the US domestic energy policy and climate policies, resulting in the United States playing an obstructive and destructive role in international climate negotiations.

Comparable political and economic (as opposed to institutional) factors have also slowed China's reaction to growing energy dependency and simultaneously framed its climate-negotiating strategy. Domestic political pressures and formal state commitment to Chinese domestic economic development largely guide China's energy strategies and also its climate-negotiating strategies. These domestic drivers are enhanced by China's longer-term strategic geopolitical ambition to become a global power able to compete with the United States. The stability of energy supply and energy prices is central to this ambition.

China is the global economy's manufacturing centre and, as a consequence, it is now the planet's second largest consumer of energy and its greatest producer of greenhouse emissions (EIA, 2010c). China is self-sufficient in coal, of which it is the world's largest producer and consumer and which largely fuels its electricity production. This dependency is economically and infrastructurally entrenched. However, since 1990, China has experienced a massive growth in demand and consumption of oil products (see Chapter 5, p. 92), leading to the depletion of its domestic oil reserves. As a result, it has moved from oil self-sufficiency in 1993 to become the world's third largest importer and second largest consumer of oil in 2009 (EIA, 2010c). This has placed it in direct competition with the United States for both geographically traditional (Middle Eastern) and alternative (African, Iranian, Central Asian, Canadian and Australian) energy supplies. To enhance its energy security, it has engaged through its energy corporations in a strategy of expansionist and diversifying investment in overseas energy resources – primarily oil but also gas. At the same time, it has used substantial state subsidies to keep energy prices low – a strategy that is unviable in the longer term, and will increase pressure for the pursuit of greater energy efficiency and alternative energy sources – elements prominent in the latest Chinese Five Year Plan.

While much has been written about the domestic influence of the energy and automobile sectors over US politicians and domestic and foreign energy and climate policy, little comparable attention has been paid to similar phenomena in China. Downs (2010) notes the importance of the three major Chinese national oil corporations (NOCs) which, since the liberalisation of China's energy sector in the 1980s, have grown in power, relative autonomy from central agency control and political influence. Largely because of their influence, China does not have a central energy ministry to coordinate their activities. Downs (2010, p. 77) comments,

> [T]he enormous profits earned by China's NOCs due to higher oil prices are also a source of clout with the party-state. In 2007, CNPC and Sinopec were the two largest state-owned enterprises by revenue, and the earnings of CNPC alone offset the losses of all loss-making state-owned enterprises... and of the [state-owned enterprises] under central government control, the [three major NOCs] accounted for... 40 per cent of taxes collected.

One can surmise that these corporations could and would exert pressure over climate and energy policy to advantage their prospects.

China's growing energy demand, growing oil dependency and increasing state-owned or controlled investments in foreign oil and gas ventures, together make its political alignments on climate issues increasingly complex and less easily consonant with the interests of other developing (G77) states. In recent climate negotiations, China's role has been largely negative – including trenchant refusal to accept global emissions targets under the international climate regime, binding and constraining emissions targets for developing countries, and persistent rejection of MRV national emissions accounting. These positions can be interpreted to primarily reflect a complex amalgam of domestic political and economic policy aims – promoting national development at a pace and in a form to be determined by China alone – and institutional requirements that extend beyond those relating to energy security. Nevertheless, domestically, China's programme of (weak) ecological modernisation of its energy sector shows considerable policy integration with, and leadership on, the climate issue – on China's own terms (Christoff, 2010), and has included massive investment in wind and solar power, the forced closure of older, dirtier coal-fired power stations, and a range of energy efficiency measures.

In summary, both the United States and China's climate-negotiating stratagems have been influenced by energy-related considerations, but factors other than energy security have been predominant in determining Chinese and US recalcitrant engagement with the climate regime, and China's proactive and climate-sensitive domestic development policies.

Energy exporters

Of the 20 major emitters, Russia, Canada and Australia are of particular interest in terms of their involvement in the evolution of the international climate regime.

Russia now controls over 20 per cent of global oil reserves and has the largest proven gas reserves in the world. It is the world's largest crude oil producer, the world's largest producer of natural gas and fifth largest producer of coal (EIA, 2010d; see Chapter 8, p. 143–144). It is more than self-sufficient in each of these resources and can be regarded as energy-independent as well as an energy exporter. The Russian energy sector, according to the International Monetary Fund and the World Bank, is responsible for about one-fifth of Russia's gross domestic product (GDP) and provides some 65 per cent of national tax revenues. Russia's political and economic stabilisation (with a significant growth in currency reserves) since the period of collapse that followed the demise of the Soviet Union has to a significant extent been built on its growth as an energy exporter. Specifically, Russia is the largest supplier of natural gas to Europe and currently supplies more than 30 per cent or more of all gas consumed to a large number of European states, including the Czech Republic, Greece, Austria, Hungary, Poland, Germany and Italy (Pascual & Zambetakis, 2010, p. 20). This places Russia in a very strong position to influence the economies of these states given the importance of this energy resource to their economies.

Russia aims to further consolidate its position as the major supplier of gas and oil to Europe in the future through development of the Nord Stream Gas pipeline. In recent times, under Vladimir Putin, it appeared that Russia's resurgent wealth and energy power have encouraged it to behave with increasing disregard for the concerns of its neighbours and other states. Its willingness to break continuity of gas supply in its confrontations with Ukraine in 2006 and 2008 has raised serious and enduring energy security concerns for these dependent European states, and transformed energy politics in Europe.

Energy security has not played a role in Russia's participation and positioning in recent climate negotiations, but its geopolitical strategic ambitions have. The UNFCCC established the 1990 baseline for recording developed country national emissions, reflecting the date at which climate change first was 'recognised' as a policy concern. This date, around which Kyoto Protocol emissions targets were later determined for developed countries, marked the start of the deep economic decline that occurred in former socialist states immediately following the collapse of the Soviet Union and which was accompanied by a steep drop in greenhouse emissions from these states. As a consequence, Russia and the Ukraine were awarded emissions reduction targets of 0 per cent below 1990 levels and they and other post-socialist states/economies in transition have not had to implement any climate-related strategies to date.

Russia was a late ratifier of the Kyoto Protocol, in 2004, an action undertaken to gain access to the newly formed EU/Kyoto emissions trading market into which it could sell its abundant carbon permits and reap very significant financial benefits. It also stands to be a major beneficiary of a global transition away from coal and oil to less carbon-polluting natural gas, of which it has major reserves and is the largest supplier into the European market. In this sense, Russia is not threatened by anything other than a rapid transition to renewable energy and a collapse of trade in fossil fuels. It has supported emissions trading, an emergent global carbon market and climate negotiations overall – but has been an erratic participant in recent climate negotiations. It appears that energy security has not played a significant part in its climate calculations.

By contrast, Australia and Canada have both played mainly negative roles in international climate negotiations in ways that can be largely attributed to their energy status. Both are major energy exporters: Australia is the world's largest coal exporter and fourth largest exporter of gas (but dependent on oil imports), while Canada is energy-independent and a net exporter of all fossil fuels and a major exporter of natural gas. Each state's climate policy seems largely to have been shaped by their economic dependency on energy exports – a point exemplified by Australia's performance over the past two decades.

Australia derives some 30 per cent of its export income from its trade in coal and natural gas, and is highly dependent on these industries, especially in key states and regions. In 1997, Australia, under the conservative Howard government, negotiated an exceptionally generous target under the Kyoto Protocol, which it signed before it joined the United States in 2001 in refusing ratification and working to undermine the Protocol (see Chapter 11, p. 204). Lobbying by key actors representing the fossil fuel sector has played a significant role in maintaining Australia's recalcitrance in international climate negotiations over the past 15 years while also minimising the intrusion of domestic climate policies on that sector's interests (Hamilton, 2007; Pearse, 2007).

Although other factors – such as Prime Minister Howard's climate scepticism, his strong adherence to Australia's alliance with the United States, and the narrowly realist approach to international politics adopted during his terms of office – also were important determinants of Australia's climate policy orientation (Christoff, 2005), it is clear that national energy policy drove climate outcomes domestically and in foreign policy. While Australia has now ratified the Kyoto Protocol – the first act of the incoming Rudd Labor government late in 2007 – its performance in climate negotiations has remained reticent: its proposed national emissions reduction targets for 2020 are amongst the weakest pledged by developed countries under the Copenhagen Accord.

Australia's current path for economic development – based on increasing its primary resource and energy exports – would be harmed by a global shift away from coal. Like Russia, Australia is a potential beneficiary of a transition to gas but is similarly threatened by any proposals for a rapid move away from fossil fuels overall. Consequently, Australia's understanding of its economic and energy security needs is in direct opposition to the requirements of effective climate policy.

Energy-dependent states

The EU is here first considered as a collective state actor, and then its key members are discussed separately. EU dependency on fossil fuel imports is set to grow from 50 per cent in 2009 to 70 per cent in 2030 under a business as usual scenario (CEC, 2006). This dependency, its high energy requirements, and its longstanding recognition of climate change as a policy problem, have – in combination – led to longer and stronger links being made between energy security and energy and climate policies, and between these policies and the EU climate-negotiating stance, than amongst other major state actors.

The EU's adoption of an emissions trading scheme in 2005 and its *Climate and Energy Package* in 2008 (which includes strong energy efficiency and renewable energy policies and targets for 2020) have together provided internal mechanisms for effecting a transition away from heavy dependency on fossil fuels. This confidence in momentum has been reflected in the EU's global championship of strong and binding targets for developed countries and, specifically, a strong EU emissions reduction target for 2020: at Copenhagen in 2009, the EU committed to a collective emissions reduction target of 20 per cent below 1990 levels by 2020, increasing to a 30 per cent cut in the context of a binding international agreement (UNFCCC, 2010b). However, as Patt (2010) reports, even within the EU, where delegation of national sovereignty has arguably progressed the furthest, energy policy stands out as an area where member states have retained almost complete national autonomy.

Consequently, while there are strong synergies between the Climate and Energy Package and climate policy, significant problems of integration exist between its members' energy policy, between its energy and climate policies and in the functioning of its Emission Trading Scheme, and these may yet undermine progress towards energy and climate targets (Adelle et al., 2009, section 2).

Like the United States, the EU increasingly faces energy insecurities – enhanced by instability in the Middle East, uncertainties associated with Russia and declining reserves in the North Sea. In particular, Russia's severance of gas supplies to the Ukraine in 2006 (with ancillary impacts on several other European states) led to a sharp re-evaluation of EU energy policy and the view that the EU had now entered a 'new energy era' of greater uncertainty and threat (CEC, 2006). The EU energy and climate initiatives are intended to go some way towards addressing what is acknowledged to be a problem of energy (in)security. Indeed the links between energy, climate and security are commonly made in all directions: the energy security narrative is also used to strengthen support for action about climate change even in states where climate policies are already well entrenched (see, for instance, Meah, 2010).

Germany, the United Kingdom and France are the EU's greatest energy consumers and produce the bulk of its emissions. While both Germany and the United Kingdom have domestic fossil fuel energy resources (coal, in the first instance, coal and gas for the United Kingdom – see Chapter 3, pp. 58–59), both are increasingly energy-dependent, as is France: Germany imports almost all its oil and gas, the United Kingdom almost all its oil. Germany and the United Kingdom have played leadership roles in proposing the EU's strong climate-negotiating targets and championing these in international climate negotiations. Moreover, each has adopted amongst the toughest emissions reduction targets accepted by developed countries. While the EU accepted a collective emissions reduction target of 8 per cent below 1990 levels for 2012, this could only be achieved with significant contributions by Germany (−21 per cent) and the United Kingdom (−12.5 per cent) under the EU's burden-sharing arrangement. Furthermore, their targets under the Copenhagen Accord are the most ambitious offered by developed countries: Germany has opted for a target of 40 per cent below 1990 levels, and the United Kingdom for −34 per cent. By contrast, Italy, and poorer EU states – Spain and Portugal, and new accession states such as Poland – have adopted weak Kyoto targets (adjusted for growth requirements under the EU's burden-sharing agreement), but appear likely to fail to meet even these goals through their domestic efforts.

In all, therefore, there appear to be significant links between the EU's climate and energy policies and its energy security dilemmas and objectives. Moreover, this link seems even clearer when one looks at the states' driving of EU climate policy, namely Germany and the United Kingdom. However there appears to be no clear pattern associated with the energy (security) status of energy import-dependent states (including Japan) and their dedication in pursuing strong climate objectives – suggesting the importance of other factors.

Conclusions

It is hard to find clear patterns of the influence of 'energy security' concerns in the climate-negotiating positions and performance of the major greenhouse gas emitting states (see Table 12.2).

For most of these states, other considerations, including normative ones, have predominated – especially in the initial stages of the development of the UNFCCC during the early 1990s. For instance, more fundamental concerns about climate adaptation capacity and basic survival have driven the negotiating stances of the poorest African states and of the members of the AOSIS.

When one looks at fossil fuel resource-rich states and at developed states highly dependent on imported energy resources, it seems possible to discern negotiating behaviours that are influenced or even defined by these

Table 12.2 Major greenhouse gas emitting states, their energy characteristics and emissions reduction efforts

Country[a]	Global emissions status[b]	Pledged emissions target (for 2020, at January 2011)[c]	Emissions reduction effort to date[d]	Overall energy status[e]
China	1	**–40% to –45% per unit GDP below BAU**	**Leader**	Independent
United States	2	**–17% below 2000 levels**	**Laggard**	**Importer**
Russia	3	**–15% to –25% below 1990 levels**	**Laggard**	**Exporter**
Japan	4	**–25% below 1990**	–	**Importer**
India	5	**–20% to –25% per unit of GDP below 2005 levels**	–	Importer
Germany	6	**–40% below 1990 levels**	**Leader**	**Importer**
Canada	7	**–17% below 2000 levels**	**Laggard**	**Exporter**
Brazil	8	**–36.1% to –38.9% below BAU**	**Leader**	Independent
United Kingdom	9	**–34% below 1990 levels**	**Leader**	Independent
Australia	10	**–5% below 2000 levels**	**Laggard**	**Exporter**
Italy	11	**[EU target –20% to –30% below 1990]**	**Laggard**	**Importer**
France	12	**[EU target –20% to –30% below 1990]**	–	**Importer**
Ukraine	13	**–20% below 1990**	–	Importer

Table 12.2 (Continued)

Country[a]	Global emissions status[b]	Pledged emissions target (for 2020, at January 2011)[c]	Emissions reduction effort to date[d]	Overall energy status[e]
Spain	14	**[EU target –20% to –30% below 1990]**	**Laggard**	Importer
Poland	15	**[EU target –20% to –30% below 1990]**	–	Importer
Iran	16	**No targets**	**Laggard**	Exporter
Mexico	17	**–30% below BAU**	–	
South Africa	18	**–34% below BAU**	–	Independent
Turkey	19	**No targets**	–	**Importer**
Indonesia	20	**–26% below BAU**	–	Exporter

[a]The table includes the 20 biggest national greenhouse emitters and the five biggest OPEC oil producers (Saudi Arabia, Iran, Kuwait, United Arab Emirates and Venezuela).

[b]Aggregate annual emissions, based on 2008 emissions data for the 20 highest emitting Annex 1 and non-Annex 1 countries, excluding LULUCF (UNFCCC, 2005, 2010) and other data (WRI, 2010).

[c]Targets pledged in the Copenhagen Accord (and therefore of uncertain legal status), enshrined in legislation or in implementable public policies. (At January 2011.)

[d]Assessment of developed countries' performance as leader or laggard includes performance against targets nominated under Kyoto Protocol, evaluation of Kyoto Protocol targets and actions against scientific estimates of required reductions, and a subjective assessment of the role played by the state in progressing or obstructing climate negotiations in the period 1992–2010; assessment for developing states includes, where possible, performance against BAU, and subjective assessment of the role played by the state in progressing or obstructing climate negotiations in the period 1992–2010.

[e]A country's overall energy status is indicated based on data drawn from IEA 2010. Overall status is assessed based on net energy flows [ktoe]. A country is shown in **bold** if this status is a defining characteristic of its resource economy. For more details, refer to Table 12.1.

states' energy status. However, it is apparent that energy security considerations are but one amongst a number of factors that intervene to determine climate-negotiating trajectory. Thee other factors include the configuration of domestic political institutions and stability, domestic economic capacity flexibility and aspirations, national 'identity', and regional and global normative, economic and military intentions.

Although domestic energy and economic growth concerns clearly influence the climate policy and negotiating positions of major states, energy (in)security does not appear to be a neat predictor of state behaviour during climate negotiations. States with energy security concerns (based on their dependency on energy imports) have not responded uniformly – as positive or negative influences – during climate change negotiations over the past two decades. More important seems to be the relationship between the state and private energy sector – in terms of the influence of the latter over the former, or regulatory control and authority of the former over the latter.

This is so even when one removes from consideration the two major energy-consuming states, the United States and China, both of which are dependent on their abundant domestic supplies of coal for electricity generation, but are also increasingly dependent on oil imports. A complex amalgam of economic size, global political ambitions and domestic political institutional factors have together proved more important determinants of their climate-negotiating strategies than energy security concerns alone.

An exception may be made in the case of countries whose economic security is dependent on a high level of energy (fossil fuel) exports. With their economic security apparently threatened by the prospect of rapid emissions reductions, major energy-exporting states have – with the notable exception of Norway – been uniformly recalcitrant actors during climate negotiations. Those major emitting states that are also major fossil fuel exporters (Russia, Australia and Canada) have proved the most obstructive and resistant on the issues of emissions reduction targets. This pattern extends to the other oil-exporting states. (The anomaly here is Norway, which has shifted in from being a laggardly member within the JUSCANNZ-plus group (which includes Japan, the United States, Canada, Norway, Australia and New Zealand) to becoming a leader in terms of its emissions reduction targets and in promoting the UN's collaborative programme on Reducing Emissions from Deforestation and Forest Degradation (REDD+.)).

While the UNFCCC continues to depend on consensus or near-consensus decision making for its development, these states will be able to influence outcomes disproportionately on the basis of their energy concerns.

However, the growing synergy of interests and material and institutional capacities amongst states pursuing policies to increase their energy security by reducing their dependency on imported fossil fuels has assisted some of these states to become leading advocates for strong emissions reduction targets.

In all, it seems that addressing domestic concerns about energy security might engender positive shifts in a state's climate-negotiating position, by incidentally generating the capacity for achieving related emissions targets. Conversely, the failure of major economies to address such concerns will condemn climate negotiations to stalemate – especially while the largest energy-dependent states (the United States and China) refuse to budge until their energy needs are met in ways that do not undermine their broader strategic domestic and foreign policy ambitions.

References

Adelle, C., M. Pallemaerts and J. Chiavari (2009), *Climate Change and Energy Security in Europe: Policy Integration and its Limits* (Stockholm: SIEPS).

Allison, I., N.L. Bindoff, R.A. Bindschadler, P.M. Cox, N. de Noblet, M.H. England, J.E. Francis, N. Gruber, A.M. Haywood, D.J. Karoly, G. Kaser, C. Le Quéré, T.M. Lenton, M.E. Mann, B.I. McNeil, A.J. Pitman, S. Rahmstorf, E. Rignot, H.J. Schellnhuber, S.H. Schneider, S.C. Sherwood, R.C.J. Somerville, K. Steffen, E.J. Steig, M. Visbeck and A.J. Weaver (2009), *The Copenhagen Diagnosis: Updating the World on the Latest Climate Science* (Sydney: The University of New South Wales Climate Change Research Centre).

Bang, G. (2010), 'Energy security and climate change concerns: Triggers for energy policy change in the United States?', *Energy Policy*, 38(4): 1645–1653.

Bordoff, J., P. Noel and M. Deshpande (2009), 'Understanding the interactions between energy security and climate change policy', in C. Pascual and J. Elkind (eds): *Energy Security: Economics, Politics, Strategies and Implications* (Washington, DC: The Brookings Institution Press).

CEC (2006), *Green Paper: A European Strategy for Sustainable Competitive and Secure Energy* (Brussels: CEC, COM[2006]105).

Christoff, P. (2005), 'Policy autism or double-edged dismissiveness? Australia's climate policy under the Howard government', *Global Change, Peace and Security*, 17(1): 29–44.

Christoff, P. (2010), 'Cold climate at Copenhagen: China and the United States at COP 15', *Environmental Politics*, 19(4): 637–56.

CNA Corporation (2007), National security and the threat of climate change [http://securityandclimate.cna.org/; accessed 05 January 2011].

DeSombre, E. (2005), 'Understanding United States unilateralism: Domestic sources of U.S. international environmental policy', in R. Axelrod, D.L. Downie and N. Vig (eds): *The Global Environment: Institutions, Law, and Policy* (Washington, DC: CQ Press).

Downs, E. (2010), 'Who's afraid of China's oil companies?', in C. Pascual and J. Elkind (eds): *Energy Security: Economics, Politics, Strategies and Implications* (Washington, DC: The Brookings Institution Press).

US Energy Information Administration (EIA) (undated), *[US] State Coal Profile* [http://www.eia.doe.gov/cneaf/coal/statepro/imagemap/usaimagemap.htm; accessed: 04 January 2011].

EIA (2010a), *Annual Energy Review 2010* [http://www.eia.gov/aer/pdf/pages/sec5_5.pdf; accessed 10 January 2011].

EIA (2010b), *Net generation by Energy Source* [http://www.eia.doe.gov/cneaf/electricity/epm/table1_1.html; accessed 10 January 2011].

EIA (2010c), *China Energy Profile* [http://www.eia.doe.gov/country/country_energy_data.cfm?fips= CH; accessed 10 January 2011].

EIA (2010d), *Russia Energy Profile* [http://www.eia.doe.gov/country/country_energy_data.cfm?fips= RS; accessed 10 January 2011].

Hamilton, C. (2007), *Scorcher: The Dirty Politics of Climate Change* (Sydney: Allen and Unwin).

International Energy Agency (IEA) (2010), *Key World Energy Statistics 2010* [http://www.iea.org/textbase/nppdf/free/2010/key_stats_2010.pdf; accessed: 10 January 2011].

IPCC (2007), *Climate Change 2007: Mitigation of Climate Change Summary for Policy Makers and Technical Summary* (Cambridge: Cambridge University Press).

Lisowski, M. (2002), 'Playing the two-level game: U.S. president Bush's decision to repudiate the Kyoto protocol', *Environmental Politics*, 11(4): 101–119.

Meah, N. (2010), 'Delivering GHG reductions and energy security: UK climate change and energy policies' [Achieving a Low Carbon Society 2nd Annual Meeting, Berlin 2010; http://lcs-rnet.org/meetings/2010/berlin/pdf/text_p1_2_Meah_prst.pdf; accessed: 10 January 2011].

Muller-Kraenner, S. (2007), *Energy Security* (London: Earthscan).

Pascual, C. and E. Zambetakis (2010), 'The geopolitics of energy: From security to survival', in C. Pascual and J. Elkind (eds): *Energy Security: Economics, Politics, Strategies and Implications* (Washington, DC: The Brookings Institution Press).

Patt, A. (2010), 'Effective regional energy governance – not global environmental governance – is what we need right now for climate change', *Global Environmental Change*, 20: 33–35.

Pearse, G. (2007), *High and Dry* (Melbourne: Penguin Books).

United Nations Framework Convention on Climate Change (UNFCCC) (2005), FCCC/SBI/2005/18/Add.2 [http://unfccc.int/resource/docs/2005/sbi/eng/18a02.pdf; accessed: 10 January 2011].

UNFCCC (2010a), FCCC/SBI/2010/18 [http://unfccc.int/resource/docs/2010/sbi/eng/18.pdf; accessed: 11 January 2011].

UNFCCC (2010b), Copenhagen Accord Appendix 1 [http://unfccc.int/home/items/5264.php; accessed: 12 January 2011].

WRI (World Resources Institute) (2010), Climate Analysis Indicator Tool [http://cait.wri.org/cait.php; accessed: 05 December 2010].

Yergin, D. (2008), 'Energy under stress', in K.M. Campbell and J. Price (eds): *The Global Politics of Energy* (Washington DC: The Aspen Institute).

13
Rethinking Energy Security in a Time of Transition

Jim Falk

Introduction

Energy security is widely invoked as a valued objective, notably in government reports. However, two contemporary challenges suggest that the idea of energy security might itself require re-examination or qualification: (a) the likelihood that we are approaching the peak of cheap oil production; and (b) the established relationship between the burning of fossil fuels, greenhouse gas (GHG) emissions and the increasingly pressing issue of climate change. In this sense, the concept of 'energy security' is now framed by a need to phase away from fossil fuels. But, as Joseph Camilleri and I argued in a recent book, there is a connected and bigger frame surrounding the challenge of climate change, characterised by the multiple ways in which the physical and social world of human beings is in a state of unprecedented physical and social transition (Camilleri and Falk, 2009).

Climate change is certainly a key factor in contemporary transitions. As a species, we face two key linked choices: how much more GHG do we propose to deliver to the atmosphere and at what rate? But associated with this is the question of what level of social transition we are prepared to undergo in order to avoid more extreme elements of the physical transition that will arise, both as a result of the gases already committed to the atmosphere, and from the gases which we propose to emit in the future.

Clearly the transition is not limited to the generation of energy and its impacts. Modern energy has enabled innovations in production and consumption that are not only reconstructing human societies but also instigating significant social changes and stresses. In this sense the transition is a complex process arising out of interwoven physical and social changes, covering different distances and also, as we will discuss, time spans. How we address these multiple components is pertinent to the conclusions that might be reached about how we conceive of energy security.

What is energy security?

In orthodox discourse 'security' is usually taken to include connotations of safety, freedom from anxiety, confidence and protection (Shorter Oxford English Dictionary, 1936, p. 1829). 'Energy security' tends to take meanings cast within the more restricted traditional conceptual domain of national security. However, as will be argued in more detail later, climate change forces us to think from an enlarged perspective, and to rethink from first principles what security itself is or should be about.

In the Australian context, energy security has been defined (DRET, 2009) within the usual orthodoxy of:

> [T]he adequate, reliable and affordable supply of energy to support the functioning of the economy and social development, where:
>
> - *Adequacy* is the provision of sufficient energy to support economic and social activity;
> - *Reliability* is the provision of energy with minimal disruptions to supply; and
> - *Affordability* is the provision of energy at a price which does not adversely impact on the competitiveness of the economy and which supports continued investment in the energy sector.

Here these dimensions of interest are understood to be

> [i]nterrelated and, to a large extent, mutually reinforcing. For example, if energy supplies are not adequate to meet the needs of the economy or community, the price of energy will need to rise or intervention in the market will be required to allocate scarce energy resources. However, as the price of energy rises to an extreme level, the affordability of energy will be reduced, thereby constraining economic and social activity. (DRET, 2009, p. 5)

Energy security, in this sense, remains a heavily constrained concept. Energy security is primarily seen as a matter of national concern, and thus focused along the dimension of economic strength.

Clearly energy security should not be understood simply as a goal in itself. It is a goal because of what energy brings, since it plays a central role in most human technologies, especially those of production. In this sense, energy security tends to be a leading consideration against other more lagging factors, including the different impacts of utilising the energy system to solve questions associated with water abundance and quality, transport, heating, food and commodity production, and much else. Stated in this way, within the frame of economics, a secure nation is seen as one with enough energy supply to keep the economy ticking over. Tying this to the discourse of national security requires only to add that economic strength is critically important to national well-being, and needs to be maintained, in particular in times of national stress – most notably in times of war.

Even if we do focus on the nation as the singular or most important domain of interest, consideration of the systems by which energy can be produced immediately raises areas of concern beyond that of economic strength. For example, if we consider the use of nuclear power, and the associated systems of the nuclear industry, many aspects of these systems can have dual purposes. The insecurity that comes with nuclear weapons proliferation accompanies the national security that may derive from a more certain supply of energy. The complex dance being carried out between the United Nations, United States and other states, vis-à-vis Iran, illustrates this ambiguity. But the same ambiguity applies in many other places (and indeed even arises around the pilot enrichment research, whose most recent manifestation is the Silex enrichment technology, which has taken place over many decades in Australia) (McMurtie, 2010).

Another example is provided by the relationship between energy and water security. In situations of water scarcity – like those experienced by South Eastern Australia or Israel – attempts to provide energy-using technologies that require large volumes of fresh water for the operation of cooling systems, are ultimately increasing water stress, not necessarily enhancing the overall security of the user community.

To reiterate: the central point here is that the orthodox concept of energy security tends to be developed in a way that is very restrictive, focusing primarily on the energy system and its capacity to provide energy for national economic growth. In that sense the discourse and conceptualisation of security is often set at a scale of national units, and is then focused on the energy system without much regard for its context. Beyond this orthodoxy, the meaning and shaping of energy security becomes much more elusive. One illustration of this is provided by energy security in the context of climate transition. This requires us to reconsider the concepts more subtly in terms of energy security within a number of overlapping contexts.

A time of transition

In our recent book, Camilleri and I have advanced evidence that, roughly beginning with the two world wars, human societies embarked on a major transition which is *physical, social and economic.* Various labels have been advanced for this unique and epochal transitional period. Crutzen (2000, p. 23) referred to it as the 'Anthropocene' – the epoch in which we are moving from the present interglacial 'Holocene' into an epoch whose physical characteristics are dominated by human behaviour. Camilleri and I refer to it as the Holocentric epoch – the epoch in which we, as a species, have the capacity and need to see what we are doing comprehensively across our societies if we are to have the best chance of securing a safe course through the transition (Camilleri and Falk, 2009). The transition is characterised in part by the four 'spikes' of population, consumption, extinction and GHGs, which are all following trajectories that, when viewed against the last two thousand years, are now thrusting upwards, ever more closely clinging to their vertical asymptotes (Ayres, 2000). But the transition is equally indicated by the rapid pace of technical and social innovation, as societies struggle to deal with an ever more complicated set of extensive socio-physical challenges.

The climate component is of course an important one. As Lester Brown (2008, p. 4) has put it:

> We are crossing natural thresholds that we cannot see and violating deadlines that we do not recognize. Nature is the time keeper, but we cannot see the clock. Among the other environmental trends undermining our future are shrinking forests, expanding deserts, falling water tables, collapsing fisheries, disappearing species, and rising temperatures

An important goal for the human species, and its constituent communities, is to pass through this composite transition as benignly (or from the evolutionary perspective, which Camilleri and I take) as adaptively as possible. Here we are thinking of adaptation in the evolutionary sense for our entire species, not the narrow and parochial sense – of local adaptation. Our species, given that it has developed a unique capacity to see consequences of its actions, has the capacity to change those actions in anticipation rather than just in response to their impacts. If we accept this framework, then it can be argued that the distinction between energy and climate security is spurious. The search for energy security becomes the task of finding the energy needed to navigate an adaptive path through the period of transition.

Security in the face of climate transition

Climate change undermines the orthodox view of energy security along a whole series of dimensions. The perturbation, and even chaos – which global warming adds to the global climate system – are caused by the global accretion of GHGs. As is well understood, mitigating climate change requires collaboration in reshaping patterns of energy usage and generation across the planet. Here, the distinction often made between adaptation and mitigation is also spurious, since a species that continues to destabilise its environment whilst seeking to adapt to the increasing impacts of that

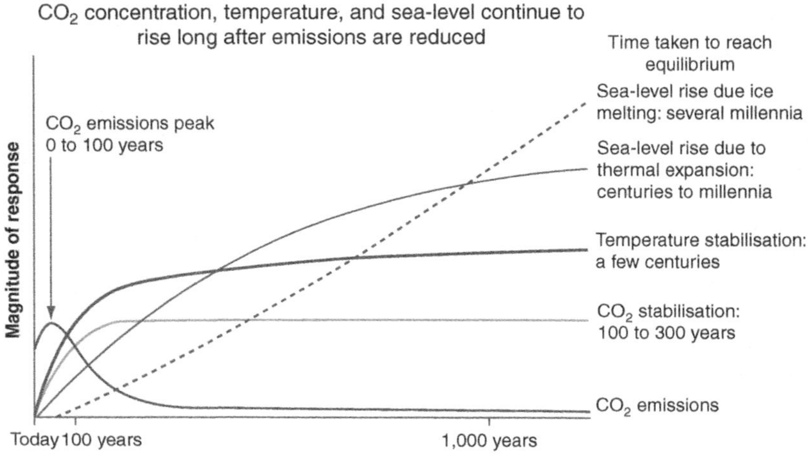

Figure 13.1 Intergovernmental Panel on Climate Change (IPCC) impacts of carbon dioxide emissions continue long after emissions cessation
Source: Camilleri and Falk (2009) adapted from IPCC (2007) Fig. SMP: 5.

destabilisation, is unlikely to be navigating a course that is likely to prove adaptive over the long term.

Figure 13.1 shows the long-range impacts of the GHGs accumulating now. Even if emissions were to be dramatically reduced immediately, the impacts of gases accumulated already will continue to rise and be felt well into the future. Climate change thus has the unfamiliar characteristic of requiring immediate action to offset long-term consequences.

In addition, the insecurity associated with GHG emissions is rapidly growing. As Parry, Lowe and Hanson (2009, p. 1102) have stressed, the world is not actually meeting the challenges of restraining emissions to a prudent level. Rather, the best realistic outcome of pledges made in the wake of the United Nations Framework Convention on Climate Change (UNFCCC) Copenhagen Conference points towards a rise of more than 2 degrees, perhaps of the order of 4 degrees which will run for several centuries. They note:

> [T]he window of opportunity for beginning effective long-term action on climate change is extraordinarily narrow. Urgent and major emissions reductions are essential to avoid the most severe effects. Yet even the most prompt and stringent action still risks overshooting a target of 2°C, and it will require centuries to achieve a roughly stable climate with tolerably low amounts of warming. The consequent demands on adaptation will be enormous, many times those currently envisaged. We should therefore give policies of adaptation much more urgent attention

Spatial scales

On account of the GHGs already accumulated in the atmosphere, the planet now faces a long period of climate transition. And the current likelihood is that this transition will be rendered much more challenging by anticipated future emissions. The transition will be both physical and social. Central to the generation of GHGs is the use and generation of energy, and in particular the use of carbon-based fuels.

What issues does climate change raise in relation to energy security? The first and most obvious is that climate transition is in one sense global. The overall cause is a global accumulation of GHGs, and in that sense, the global growth in use of carbon-based fuels. There are of course other causes, notably in agriculture, but also in such areas as mining and the release of methane, and other GHGs in processes of consumption and production, but energy production remains a centrally important driver. In particular, every nation, by securing its energy supply, may well be contributing to a worsening of the global GHG build-up, and to the destabilisation of climate worldwide, with many damaging economic consequences across the planet (Stern, 2006; Garnaut, 2008).

More broadly, global warming and the consequent changes to climate confront us with a requirement to think in unfamiliar ways across different spatial and accompanying social scales. Whilst in one sense the scale of both the problem, and its solution is global (because concentration of GHGs can only be brought down by collective changes across the entire planet), the scale on which governance is arranged remains primarily national, with collective agreement still being sought mainly through institutions based on the nation state. The UNFCCC and the Kyoto Protocol are both products of this process, and the disappointing outcomes of the UNFCCC meetings at Copenhagen and Cancún are forceful reminders of its limitations.

Further, the manifestations of climate change – its physical, biological, economic and social impacts – are frequently highly local and specific, varying enormously from region to region. An example is provided by the highly differentiated impacts of climate change on water, including the case of precipitation in Australia, along the North–South axis of the continent, with increasing likelihood of extreme flooding in the North, and extreme drought in the South.

A North–South axis, now across national borders, is well illustrated in relation to climate change and the water system of South Asia, where snow melt in the Himalayas from the Tibet-Qyinghai Plateau glaciers is a major source of water for the Yellow and Yangtze rivers. As snow melt accelerates, the extremes of water excess and reduction tend to grow both in scale and frequency. But these glaciers feed all the major rivers of Asia, including the Mekong, Ganges, Yellow and Yangtze rivers, so that changes to their flow have potentially major impacts on rice and wheat fields that service more than 1 billion people across many national borders.

Similar issues are also intensely local. For example, at the first workshop ever convened on the impacts of climate change in Srinagar, the 'Srinagar Statement' (November 2009) was collaboratively composed and read by the First Minister of the encompassing State of Jammu and Kashmir. The statement stressed the multiple ways in which climate change was likely to impact on the life of the region, proposed significant steps to meet that challenge and noted that: 'the 14th October 2009 will be marked in the history of Jammu and Kashmir as the day when Srinagar declared action on the impacts of climate change, for today, tomorrow and for future generations'.[1] Such a proposition illustrates the point, now widely understood, that both the impacts of climate change and potential proactive responses (whether in relation to mitigation or adaptation) are poorly understood when our attention is confined to the scale of single nation states. Related impacts and processes not only extend above the national scale all the way to the global level, but below, down to the fine but vitally important scale of the local level where everyday experience is constructed for most people.

Disruptions arising from climate change are ultimately based on integrated processes, which are not confined within national or cultural boundaries. This is true not only of the climate systems but also of many physical processes with which they interact. The result is that, in principle, there is no natural scale at which the climate challenge should be addressed: impacts and responses are simultaneously global, regional, national, provincial and local. It may be the case that there is considerable *de jure* decision-making power located at the level of the nation state. Nevertheless, increasingly effective and adaptive responses to highly integrated challenges – such as those associated with climate change – require collaboration of different entities across all the spatial scales mentioned above. Such collaboration often needs to encompass different social sites such as government, market, civil society and scientific research sectors. Camilleri and I have discussed this in considerable detail, in relation to a range of sectors of human activity, including those associated with climate change (Camilleri and Falk, 2009).

As already noted, human-generated (or collected) energy and the way it is used – for convenience let us refer to this as the 'energy system' – remains intimately connected to the anthropogenically driven changes to the climate system ('climate change'). This is in part because most GHG emissions derive from the use of energy, the majority of which in turn derives from the burning of fossil fuels.[2] But it is also because energy is needed to adapt to the impacts of climate change: for example, when it comes to changes to water availability, energy is needed for water treatment and recycling, desalination and pumping. This plays out at many points across the entire spectrum of adaptation choices.

Recent rounds of UNFCCC negotiations have illustrated a fundamental complication which confounds the political response to climate change: this is that the most intense climate impacts do not necessarily occur at the places that are responsible for the highest GHG emissions. The dominant role of energy generation and use in the creation of GHG emissions is at its most intense in the richest parts of the world, especially the cities, whilst the impacts are often most intense in the least resilient and poorest regions. The pattern is of course more nuanced than that – it is multidimensional and increasingly complex, mirroring the complex pattern of global production and trade, with absolute energy use and consequently GHG emissions now dominated by the United States and China (now the world's largest absolute emitter).

Given the close relationship between energy use and GHG emissions, it is useful to observe this pattern of emissions, in terms of energy use, in the distribution of countries plotted in terms of energy use per capita on one axis versus gross domestic product (GDP) per capita on the other (2007 data) – see Figure 13.2.

One key conclusion is that since reducing the rate of emissions of GHGs is ultimately a global problem – although one whose resolution requires dispersed responses – quite a lot will almost certainly need to be done by the richer countries and richer communities to gain the collaboration of other

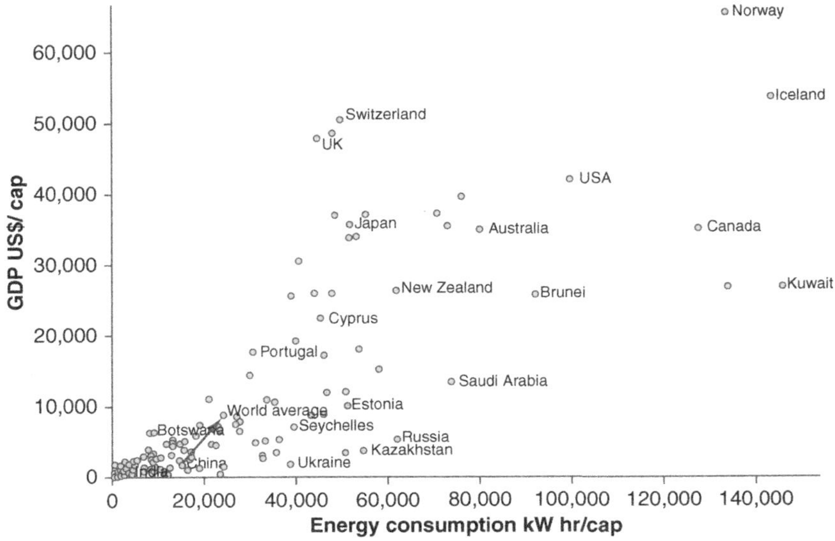

Figure 13.2 Selected countries: GDP per capita/annual per capita energy consumption

Source: Camilleri and Falk (2009, p. 302).

countries and communities in addressing that challenge. A second conclusion is that rich countries will need to give up more of actual use, whilst the poorer communities and countries will need to surrender more potential growth. The conclusion of the Garnaut Report, which examines the resulting dilemma in some detail, is that to gain such collaboration there must at least be an agreed ultimate objective of moving emissions per capita to a common target (the position proposed is referred to as 'contraction and convergence'). After canvassing a range of widely debated principles for allocation of emissions caps and reductions across the world, the Report (Garnaut, 2008, p. 202) concludes:

> While all of these approaches have strengths and weaknesses, the approach that seems to have the most potential to combine the desired levels of acceptability, perceived fairness and practicality is one based on gradual movement towards entitlements to equal per capita emissions. An approach that gives increasing weight over time to population in determining national allocations both acknowledges high emitters' positions in starting from the status quo and recognises developing countries' claims to equitable allocation of rights to the atmosphere.

Energy security bought at the cost of an increasingly chaotic climate may buy neither economic nor social stability. The two major studies of the costs of mitigation versus the costs of adaptation conclude that adaptation is much more expensive than the costs of averting the need to adapt through mitigation (Stern, 2006; Garnaut, 2008). From this point of view, energy security requires sufficient allocative justice to create the basis for a global consensus sufficient for the purpose of meeting the challenge of climate mitigation.

In summary, orthodox discussions of energy security have tended to focus on national energy security. But the security of people is no longer shaped solely on that basis, and, in the case of climate change, even primarily at that scale. Further, the actions that need to be taken in relation to energy to produce security are no longer capable of being determined simply at national scale. Consequently the concept of energy security needs to be extended to take account of its simultaneous interaction with society at different spatial scales. Similar considerations, however, can also be seen to apply across temporal scales.

Temporal scales

Energy security, in its orthodox sense, is usually constructed in relation to threats to supply emerging within comparatively close time horizons. The time scales used for thinking about security tend to be determined by the natural horizon of a human life, and then compacted further by much shorter horizons of social institutions such as governments (3–5-year election cycles) and corporations (1-year profit reporting cycle). The oil shocks of the 1970s created a strong sense of energy vulnerability, with a focus on the need to create a reliable form of supply.

The difficulty in taking into account longer-term horizons is shown by the reluctance most policy makers evidence in thinking through the likelihood that we are at, or approaching, the point of peak oil production. Historically, governments have shown similar reluctance to provide the necessary long-term support for the innovation process to develop renewable sources of energy to the point where they could become serious contenders to replace more problematic existing mainstream energy sources. The feasibility of moving to sustainable energy paths has been articulated over an extended period of time. For example, in 1973 the US Atomic Energy Commission concluded that solar energy could supply 15–30 per cent of US energy requirements by the year 2000, and 30–50 per cent of all heating and cooling (Office of Technology Assessment, 1978, pp. 18–24). But this would have required a significant shift in policy. As the World Commission on Environment and Development (Brundtland, 1987, p. 173) put the dilemma for policy makers in 1987:

> The crucial point about these lower, energy-efficient futures is not whether they are perfectly realizable in their proposed time frames. Fundamental political and institutional shifts are required to restructure investment potential in order to move along these lower, more energy efficient paths.

As discussed by both Stern (2006) and Garnaut (2008), amongst many others, the use of a discount rate to preference investment for immediate returns, as opposed to future benefit, creates an institutional pressure within market economies to avoid investments in renewable energy systems designed to create long-term climate-energy security.

The politics of climate transition, however, have the potential to force other factors into the security and energy security discourses. As already noted, many of the most severe impacts of climate change develop over long time spans, potentially affecting many future generations and, even if the anthropogenic emissions of GHGs were to completely cease now, the impacts of the increased concentrations already committed to the atmosphere would continue to change the behaviour of some of the earth's systems (notably sea level) for more than a millennium (see Figure 13.1).

If energy security is ultimately the task of finding an adaptive path through the current transition across communities at all spatial scales, then the climate component reminds us that the temporal scale of that path stretches also from the immediate to the millennial. Our institutions are poorly geared to enable future energy security to be considered in the pressure of current contexts. The design and actual transformation of our institutions to those that can take this into account in a manner likely to lead to an adaptive passage through the transition remains an unsolved challenge that will involve much institutional and even normative development if it is to be successfully addressed.

Scales of security, legitimacy, and trust

One further consideration, which might inform discussions of energy security, is the relationship between security and risk. The subtext of managing risk is, for example, invoked in the goal that present communities have adequate assurance that needed energy will be available in the future. Various proposals are advanced for achieving this end. Suggestions of what might be preferred to the current reliance on fossil fuels include, on the one hand, highly centralised systems such as nuclear reactors, massive desert-based collectors of solar energy feeding into either electricity grids or hydrogen transport, and on the other dispersed smaller systems, including photovoltaic panels on rooftops, windmills, small-scale hydro-electric systems, and many more. There is an important consideration to be introduced in the evaluation of the potential contribution of these different offerings to energy security. It is the question of trust.

Trust is an important component in a community, of whatever scale, feeling assured that necessary energy, with appropriate characteristics for overall adaptive success, can be made available. And that trust is vested potentially, not merely in the capacity of the technological systems but also in the institutions that will run them. There is a general question here of what sorts of institutions are most amenable to trust. This issue arose early in the course of the intended rapid deployment of commercial nuclear power generation in the 1970s.

In 1974, official predictions from the Australian Atomic Energy Commission, the Organization for Economic Co-operation and Development (OECD) and International Atomic Energy Agencies, predicted that some 3500 GWe of nuclear-generated electricity, representing some 3500 nuclear reactors, would be operating in 2000. By 1981 the estimates had dropped to less than 500 (Falk, 1983, p. 205). The actual number operating in 2000 was 438, producing 351 GWe of electricity (IAEA, 2001). A decade later, in 2010, this was largely unchanged with 437 operating with a generating capacity of 371 GWe – 1.5 GWe less than operated in 2009 (IAEA, 2010, p. 4).

I have argued elsewhere (much closer to the period in question) that this rapid decline in expectations was caused by the interaction of economic constraints and a global movement of social opposition, which spread rapidly and energetically during the 1970s (Falk, 1982). It built in part around the many dangers seen to be associated with nuclear power (for example, impacts of radiation, dangers of nuclear major accidents, unresolved problems associated with the permanent disposal of nuclear waste, issues associated with decommissioning nuclear reactors, and the dangers of proliferation of nuclear weapons associated with the spread of the nuclear fuel cycle). However, an additional factor was the striking correlation between the extent of opposition and those sites where nuclear reactors and other hazardous elements of the nuclear fuel cycle (together with their perceived risks) were imposed on regional communities to provide nuclear power for cities, often far away (Falk, 1982, pp. 172–199). Similar tendencies can be seen in contemporary opposition to wind farms deployed in rural areas, which are seen as imposing risk and aesthetic detriment in order to provide electricity elsewhere.

In short, energy generation, particularly if the technology is seen to carry significant risk, has the potential to carry a burden of mistrust and perceived illegitimacy, especially where generation facilities are highly centralised, and this leads also to a concentration of risk. A further observation is that the highly centralised institutions that are required to invest in and manage such energy systems themselves run an enhanced danger of being seen as remote and uncaring in relation to the risks perceived to be associated with their operations.

Whilst much more could be said on this complex social dimension of energy supply, it is sufficient here to note that it can be a significant dimension of energy security. This is first because this sort of distrust and lack of legitimacy reduces the security in the localities where the technologies are deployed. But, second, it reduces the reliability of plans heavily dependent on high levels of deployment of such technologies for producing future assurance of supply.

Writing in the specific context of comparing future plans based on nuclear power and renewable energy systems, I noted (Falk, 1982, p. 329):

> A more secure future might be provided by placing emphasis on resilience through the use of a variety of energy technologies. However, this is impossible if large, complex, capital intensive technologies, requiring the major share of the energy generation to pay for their development, are to be used. The requirement for resilience dictates the use of more diverse decentralized technology in energy programmes.

The events of the subsequent three decades seem, if anything, to have added additional support for this proposition.

Energy security in an era of transition

Enough has been said in this short chapter to suggest that some renovation is appropriate in the way in which energy security is conceived and discussed, notably in a world complicated and challenged by rapid transition. Against the old restricted focus on energy alone and on the nation state's access to assured energy, energy needs to be seen as only one dimension of security. At a time of unprecedented physical and social transition, the generation of energy, and its use, needs to be seen as part of the cause, as well as solution, to the challenges of that transition. In a world increasingly complicated by ever more significant and numerous interactions across the boundaries of nation states, energy needs to be understood as a factor that transcends boundaries, and affects communities, at all levels of scale from the local to the global. And, at a time when the effects of the manner in which energy is generated and the purposes to which it is applied, may affect many generations, the security supplied by different energy choices needs to be considered in sum along the long temporal history of its potential consequences.

In these circumstances it is reasonable to cast energy security as one component of a broader challenge to human communities of all scales: to follow an adaptive pathway, optimising human well-being, through a period of rapid and challenging transition. In the search for this, it is inappropriate to rely on a distinction between mitigation of the causes of transition (for example, GHGs) and adaptation. In the end, a species which continues to disrupt the stability and sustainability of its environment is not likely to navigate an adaptive course.

In considering what might comprise an adaptive pathway in energy development, it is necessary to think beyond the quanta of energy being generated, and even beyond the physical requirements and impacts of various technological options to take account of the:

- Requirements for adaptation at all scales, both spatial and temporal;
- Social capacity to produce and adopt the chosen technological innovations, including the capacity to develop necessary levels of trust and legitimacy in the institutions required to produce them, and this also at all scales;
- Extent to which dispersed or centralised mixes of energy technologies, and their associated sets of risks, benefits and costs will be conducive to enabling that capacity;
- Need to address barriers to collaboration across scales, including the need for intercultural dialogue, addressing major and growing disparities in access to resources including financial resources; such dialogue would facilitate engagement with the challenges which energy is needed to fulfil;
- Balance between distributed and centralised energy sources, which would support a long-term adaptive relationship across communities of different scales between distributed and centralised political power.

In this sense, energy security is emerging as a central consideration of the struggle by human societies in the task of adaptation in a time of rapid transition. It needs, however, to be understood as a more generalised form of energy security, shaped to respond to the increasing complexity of the physical and social world that humans are constructing, and responding to the most important challenge of all: to reconcile the needs and aspirations of humans as they live at small scales, with the needs and aspirations of the human race, who in the end must live and shape their future adaptively on a finite and stressed planet.

Notes

1. Transcribed by the author, 14 October 2009, Srinagar.
2. The IPCC (2007, p. 36) reported that 26 per cent directly in energy generation, 13 per cent in transport, 8 per cent in powering residential and commercial buildings, 19 per cent in industry and 57 per cent of emissions derive directly from fossil fuel use.

References

Ayres, E. (2000), 'The four spikes', *Futures*, 32: 539–554.

Brown, L. (2008), *Plan B 3.0: Mobilizing to Save Civilization* (New York-London: W.W. Norton & Company).

Brundtland, G.H. (1987), *Our Common Future* (Oxford: Oxford University Press).

Camilleri, J.A. and J. Falk (2009), *Worlds in Transition: Evolving Governance across a Stressed Planet* (Cheltenham: Edward Elgar).

Crutzen, P.J. (2000), 'Geology of mankind – the Anthropocene', *Nature*, 415(31 January): 23.

Department of Resources, Energy and Tourism (DRET) (2009), *National Energy Security Assessment, 2009* (Canberra: Australian Government).

Falk, J. (1982), *Global Fission: The Battle Over Nuclear Power* (Melbourne: Oxford University Press).

Falk, J. (1983), *Taking Australia off the Map* (Melbourne: Penguin Australia).

Garnaut, R. (2008), *The Garnaut Climate Change Review: Final Report* (Cambridge: Cambridge University Press, 2008).

Greenpeace (2004), *Secrets, Lies and Uranium Enrichment: The Classified Silex Project at Lucas Heights, Sydney* (Greenpeace Australia Pacific).

International Atomic Energy Agency (IAEA) (2001), 'IAEA releases nuclear power statistics for 2000' (Press Release, 3 May; http://www.iaea.org/NewsCenter/PressReleases/2001/prn0107.shtml; accessed: 23 November 2010).

IAEA (2010), *Nuclear Technology Review 2010* (Vienna: IAEA).

Intergovernmental Panel on Climate Change (IPCC) (2001), *Climate Change 2001: Synthesis Report Summary for Policy makers* (Cambridge: Cambridge University Press).

IPCC (2007), *Fourth Assessment Report Synthesis Report* (AR4 Synthesis report).

Little, W., H.W. Fowler, J. Coulson and C.T. Onions (1936), *The Shorter Oxford English Dictionary* (Oxford: Clarendon Press).

McMurtie, C. (2010), 'Australian laser "threatens nuclear security"' *ABC News* [http://www.abc.net.au/news/stories/2010/04/13/2870904.htm; accessed: 13 April 2010].

Office of Technology Assessment (Congress of the United States) (1978), *Application of Solar Energy to Today's Energy Needs* (Washington, DC: US Government Printing Office, Stock No. 052-003-22539-5).

Parry, M., J. Lowe and C. Hanson (2009), 'Overshoot, adapt and recover', *Nature*, 458(30 April): 1102.

Stern, N.H. (2006), *Stern Review on the Economics of Climate Change* (London: HM Treasury).

14
Energy Governance in the Era of Climate Change

Joseph A. Camilleri

Energy or the powering of human economies has been integral to the course of human evolution. It has played a decisive role in the changing forms of social interaction and levels of organisational complexity. Patterns of energy production and consumption closely correlate with the size of communities, their mode of economic activity, degree of technological sophistication and ensuing economic and social division of labour. They also reflect particular relationships to space, both physical space (land, water, air) and social space (the way social relationships are understood and practised). As a corollary of this, the sources and end uses of energy as well as the quantities and forms in which it is produced and consumed bear directly upon the society's authority structures, political institutions and decision-making processes. It should therefore come as no surprise that anthropogenic climate change should have generated in a relatively short time frame a far-reaching response in human governance.

Over millennia, humans have extended and expanded their access to energy, first by the use of fire, followed by the exploitation of animal power and later by harnessing the power of wind and water – these would prove critical factors in the development of agriculture some 10,000 years ago. However, it is only with industrialisation and the intensive use of fossil fuels that human societies managed to free themselves from the limitations of natural energy flows. By unlocking the Earth's stores of coal, oil and natural gas, they were able to accelerate with unprecedented speed the rate at which energy could be channelled into the human economy. The net effect has been the most radical social transformation in human evolution, the full ramifications of which are still only dimly perceived (Price, 1995).

The history of energy production and consumption in the United States represents the single most dramatic expression of this trend (see Figure 14.1). Wood remained the dominant energy fuel from the founding of the first American colonies in the early seventeenth century until the late nineteenth century. Coal did not surpass wood until about 1885. By the end of the First

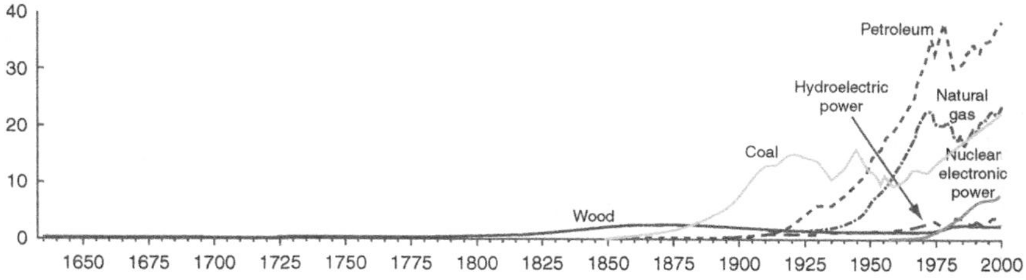

Figure 14.1 Energy consumption by source (1635–2000, quadrillion Btu)
Source: US Energy Information Administration (2001), Annual Energy Review 2001, Appendix F, Tables F1a and F1b.

World War, it accounted for 75 per cent of US total energy use, only itself to be surpassed in 1951 by petroleum and then by natural gas a few years later. The annual consumption of both petroleum and natural gas would exceed that of coal in 1947 and quadruple in the space of just three decades (US Energy Information Administration, 2009). Neither before nor since has any source of energy achieved such rapid dominance.

Cars and trucks soon replaced the railway as the primary form of transport and natural gas acquired extensive heating applications in both industry and the home. The coal industry survived, however, as electricity utilities competed to fill the nationwide demand for electricity. In 2000 fossil fuels accounted for 80 per cent of total energy production and were valued at an estimated $148 billion (nominal dollars).

Though the United States remained by far the largest single user of energy per capita in the world, the same general trend applied to the industrialised world as a whole, and to most of the emerging economies.

The scale, structure and impact of global energy usage (see Figure 14.2) have in recent decades become the subject of mounting concern on the part of scientists, policy makers and the wider public. In question are policy imperatives that are integral to the climate change debate The emerging scientific consensus, to which the Assessment Reports of the Intergovernmental Panel on Climate Change (IPCC) have significantly contributed,[1] points to a number of relatively well-known propositions: that atmospheric concentrations of greenhouse gases have increased due to human activities, and that as a consequence global mean surface temperatures have increased, precipitation patterns have changed, sea levels have risen, the El Niño weather phenomenon has become more intense, frequent and persistent, biophysical systems have changed and economic damages arising from extreme weather conditions have markedly increased (see Figure 14.3). These effects were expected to become progressively more pronounced, and if current patterns of energy use remained unchanged, were likely to have far-reaching and negative impacts on environmental and economic conditions in almost every region of the world.

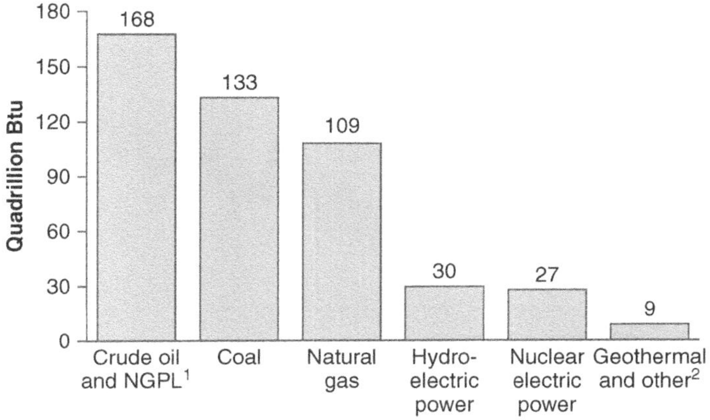

Figure 14.2 World primary energy production by source (2007)
N.B.: Data for United States also include other renewable energy
Source: US Energy Information Administration (2009), *Annual Energy Review 2009*, Chapter 11, Figure 11.1, p. 306.

Contrary to a widely shared view, this chapter argues that the challenge posed by climate change has already elicited substantial policy responses on the part of governments, international organisations, the corporate sector and a wide range of civil society actors (Camilleri and Falk, 2009, pp. 260–267, 304–313). Fifty, let alone a hundred, years ago the scale of these responses, the range of actors involved in both consultative and decision-making processes, and the scope of institutional innovation would have been scarcely imaginable. This is not to say that the normative, legal and political steps taken thus far are equal to the task; far from it. Yet, a significant policy shift is under way, one that is paralleled by an even more pronounced shift in governance arrangements. The scale of the institutional shift has yet to be fully appreciated, in part because so much scholarly attention, has focused on policy formulation rather than institutional innovation, on outcomes rather than process. Moreover, the assessment of change has tended to focus on the failure to achieve desirable or even declared objectives rather than on the herculean organisational task which climate change poses to a Westphalian, or even early post-Westphalian, system of governance.

Compounding the problem of analysis is that, so far as policy is concerned, a clearly discernible gap has emerged between declaratory and operational policy – a gap which much of the literature has somewhat simplistically sought to explain by reference to the competing interests of states, hence their failure to arrive at a universal and legally binding climate change regime. However, this reading tells us but one part of the story. Three other defining features of the governance response to date must also inform our

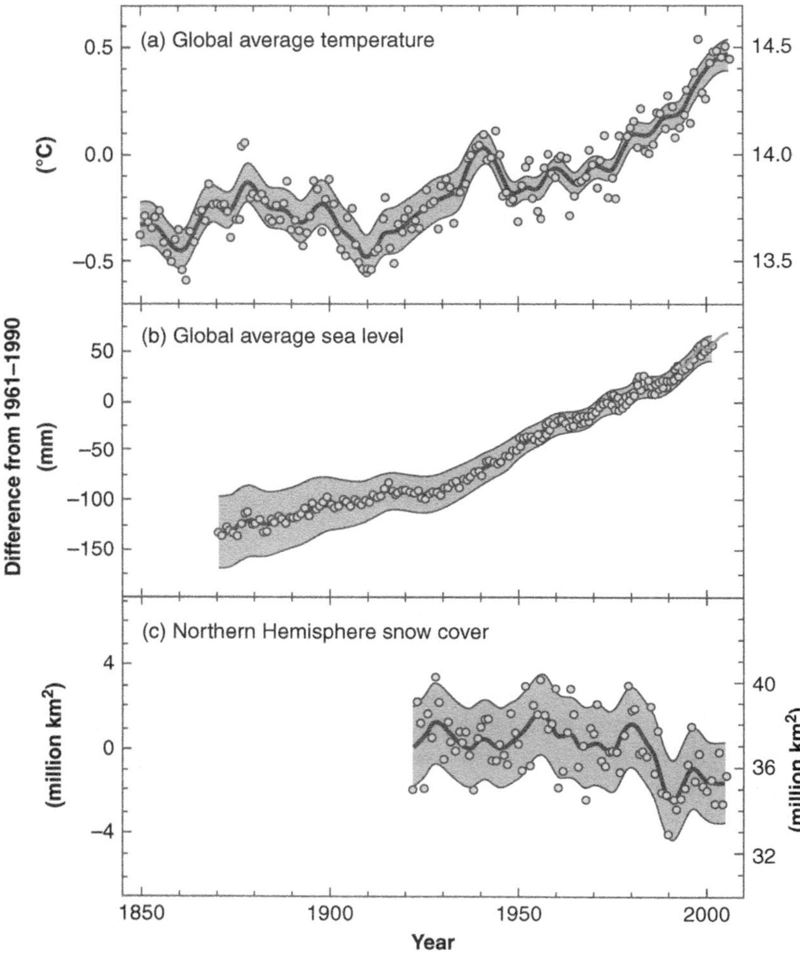

Figure 14.3 Changing temperatures, sea levels and ice and Northern Hemisphere snow cover

Note: Observed changes in (a) global average surface temperatures; (b) global average seas level from tide gauge and satellite data; and (c) Northern Hemisphere snow cover for March–April. All differences are relative to corresponding averages for the period 1961–1990. Smoothed curves represent decadal averaged values while circles show yearly values. The shaded areas are the uncertainty intervals estimated from a comprehensive analysis of known uncertainties (a and b) and from the time series (c). {WG1 FAQ 3.1 Figure 1, Figure 4.2, Figure 5.13, Figure SPM.3}

Source: IPCC (2007), *Climate Change 2007: Synthesis Report*, Chapter 1, Figure 1.1, p. 31.

analysis: the uncoordinated and at times contradictory ways in which the multiple tiers of governance interact, the intricate and often elusive web of linkages that connect state, market and civil society, and the propensity to reduce climate change policy to a set of technical fixes that glosses over the deeper societal and cultural underpinnings of energy policy. To illuminate these critical aspects of the challenge–response dynamic, we must first review, however briefly, the policy and institutional trajectory since the 1988 Toronto Conference on the Changing Atmosphere.

From Rio to Copenhagen

The multilateral response to climate change is best characterised by reference to a number of thresholds (Camilleri and Falk, 2009, pp. 49–50), each of which was followed by a period of intense and often acrimonious negotiation (see Figure 14.4). These thresholds and the intervening phases are reviewed here because of the light they shed on the scope, modalities and trajectory of institutional innovation. Specifically, they are revealing of the tensions and incongruities that have emerged between different decision-making arenas (notably states, markets and civil society), between different policy domains (notably energy, economy, security and environment) and between different tiers of governance (notably local, provincial, national, regional and global).

The first threshold came with the 1988 Toronto Conference on the Changing Atmosphere, which was the first major international meeting bringing together governments and scientists to consider the international policy challenge posed by climate change. The conference produced two notable achievements: industrialised countries reached a consensus on the need to reduce greenhouse gas emissions by 20 per cent by 2005 (the so-called 'Toronto target'); and a decision was taken to establish the IPCC, an international grouping of over 300 leading climate scientists charged with articulating in authoritative fashion the developing scientific understanding of the magnitude and implications of climate change. In August 1990 the first IPCC report was sufficiently alarming for the United Nations (UN) General Assembly to launch negotiations for a new treaty. In December 1990, it established the Intergovernmental Negotiating Committee (INC) (United Nations General Assembly, 1990). Following five formal meetings, the INC developed a proposal for a *UN Framework Convention on Climate Change* (UNFCCC) (United Nations, 1992).

The second threshold came with the UN Conference on Environment and Development (UNCED) which convened in Rio de Janeiro on 3–14 June 1992, and at which the UNFCCC was opened for signature. The Convention, which entered into force after the fiftieth ratification on 21 March 1994 (as of October 2010 194 ratifications had been secured), had as its ultimate objective to stabilise greenhouse gas concentrations in the atmosphere at

Year	Event	Threshold		COP	MOP	Outcomes
1988	Toronto Conference on the Changing Atmosphere	**1. Creation of IPCC**				
1989						
1990						
1991						
1992	Rio de Janeiro United Nations Conference on Environment and Development	**2. UNFCCC adopted and open for signature**				
1993						
1994	Entry into force of UNFCCC					
1995				COP1		Berlin Mandate
1996				COP2		
1997	Kyoto Conference	**3. Approval of Kyoto Protocol**		COP3		Kyoto Protocol
1998	Kyoto Protocol open for signature			COP4		Buenos Aires Action Plan
1999				COP5		
2000	Kyoto Protocol open for ratification			COP6		Bonn Agreements
2001				COP7		Marrakesh Accord
2002				COP8		
2003				COP9		
2004	Kyoto Protocol ratified by Russian Federation			COP10		
2005		**4. Entry into force of Kyoto Protocol**		COP11	MOP1	Montreal Action Plan
2006			Period of validity of the Kyoto Protocol	COP12	MOP2	
2007				COP13	MOP3	Bali Road Map
2008	First Commitment Period of Kyoto Protocol			COP14	MOP4	
2009		5. ???		COP15	MOP5	Copenhagen Accord
2010				COP16	MOP6	Cancun Agreements
2011				COP17	MOP7	
2012						

Figure 14.4 Chronology of the negotiating process
Source: Spanish Ministry of Environment (2008), *Guía para periodistas sobre cambio climatico y negociación internacional*, Chapter 2, *Cronologia Del Proceso Negociador*, p. 12.

a level that would prevent dangerous human interference with the climate system. To this end the Convention instituted the Conference of the Parties (COP), an association of all the countries that were Parties to the Convention, with a view to keeping international efforts to address climate change on track. Its task was to review the implementation of the Convention and examine the commitments of Parties in light of the Convention's objective, new scientific findings and experience gained in implementing climate change policies. A profound normative, legal and even institutional shift was underway, though the process was at times contradictory, often highly acrimonious and generally improvised and uncoordinated.

A period of protracted and contentious negotiation ensued on ways of implementing the Convention. The first of a series of COP meetings, held in Berlin in March–April 1995, produced the *Berlin Mandate*. Two key problems had to be surmounted. The first had to do with the question of unequal responsibility. Although the Mandate acknowledged the general principle that reducing greenhouse gas emissions would impose considerable costs to national economies, how these costs would be distributed was left unresolved. On the other hand, it was agreed that the least developed countries (Annex 2 countries) should not have to make any new commitments. The other difficult question, how to institute legally binding emissions targets, was left for consideration by a future COP-3 meeting.

Competing interests, perceptions and attitudes would play out against the backdrop of a rapidly solidifying scientific consensus. In December 1995 the IPCC released its *Second Assessment Report* elaborating and sharpening its evaluation of core concerns. The hardening scientific conclusions were, however, at odds with increasing doubts as to the capacity of international decision-making processes to devise appropriate remedial action. The widespread view was that the industrialised world (Annex 1 countries) would not be able to cut its emissions to 1990 levels by 2000. Reflecting the heightened sense of urgency emanating from the IPCC's *Second Assessment Report*, the Geneva Declaration issued by COP-2 (7–19 July 1996) nevertheless reaffirmed the commitment that COP-3 should set binding emissions reduction targets. For its part, the US Administration called for further negotiations and more realistic targets. In the eyes of many, especially the environmental lobby, the US response reflected the powerful pressure exerted by energy companies and their unrelenting lobbying and media campaigns as they attempted to delegitimise the emerging scientific consensus (Beder, Brown and Vidal, 1997, p. 4; Beder, 1999).

Held in the midst of this highly charged atmosphere, the COP-3 meeting, which convened in Kyoto in December 1997 with some 10,000 participants, constituted the third threshold. Significantly, national government delegates were outnumbered by civil society and corporate representatives. COP-3 did not put an end to heated disagreement amongst state actors or between them and a range of non-state actors, but it did pave the way for the signing of the *Kyoto Protocol to the UN Framework Convention on Climate Change*.

The agreement endorsed more sharply than ever before the scientifically legitimised proposition that the burning of fossil fuels released greenhouse gases (in particular carbon dioxide, methane, nitrous oxide, hydrofluorocarbons, perfluorocarbons and sulphur dioxide), which led to global warming and climate change. It provided for an overall reduction of greenhouse gas emissions by Annex 1 countries over 2008–12 by an average of 5.2 per cent from 1990 levels. Each Annex 1 country was given a specific target as its contribution to this overall outcome. Developing and least developed countries were exempted from making cuts for the foreseeable future. The protocol would come into force when 55 countries – including Annex 1 countries that emitted 55 per cent of greenhouse gas emissions in 1990 – ratified the protocol.

Notwithstanding the agreement reached, the Kyoto Conference was followed by a period of even sharper contestation. Estimates varied widely as to how onerous these targets would be, since the burden depended on the extent to which emissions would have grown in the absence of intervention (Oil and Gas Journal, 2000). Conflicting assessments of the projected impact of national emissions targets on economic growth mirrored and reinforced the divergent positions of the United States and the European Union (positions in each case shared by powerful voices in their respective corporate sectors) on the feasibility and desirability of implementing the treaty. The incoming Bush Administration soon made it known that it would not ratify the Kyoto Protocol, with Australia immediately following suit, even though its target allowed for an 8 per cent increase in emissions. US recalcitrance represented a severe blow to the prospects for ratification, since the United States accounted for about one-quarter of the world's emissions. It was only with Russia's belated decision in September 2004 in favour of accession (in part the result of immense pressure exerted by the European Union) that the Kyoto Protocol entered into force on 16 February 2005 (BBC News, 2005).

Ratification was a significant political milestone, and may be considered the fourth threshold. It was the strongest multilateral affirmation yet that states responsible for the bulk of greenhouse gas emissions were prepared to take mitigative action. Especially significant was the fact that fierce US opposition had failed to derail ratification. However, the Protocol's strength was also its weakness.[2] The United States and Australia, two of the world's highest per capita emitters, both initially remained outside the treaty. Meanwhile, rapidly industrialising economies, notably China, India and South Africa, whose economic growth trajectories were predicated on high and rising levels of coal burning did not commit to any emissions reductions (US Energy Administration, 2010).

The Kyoto agreement would encounter a number of other difficulties (Victor, 2001). The adequacy of the Protocol's monitoring and enforcement mechanisms, and more importantly the adequacy of the targets themselves now came under sharper scrutiny. Even if Kyoto did reach its goal – a 5 per cent fall in 1990 emissions by 'Annex I' countries over 2008–2012, this would still be well short of the IPCC's call for a 60–80 per cent cut in global emissions. The exemption of Annex II countries from legally binding targets, ethically defensible though it was, would soon become a persistent source of tension. The fact that these countries were required to report their emissions, improve their emissions accounting practices and participate in clean development mechanisms, did little to placate those arguing for universal burden sharing. Finally, ratification of the Protocol highlighted a number of unanswered questions relevant to the process of implementation: how would commitments under the Protocol relate to the Global Environment Facility (GEF) which was established in 1991 to help developing countries fund environmental projects and programmes? Similarly, what role might other international organisations both outside and within the UN system, in particular the United Nations Development Programme (UNDP), the United Nations Environment Programme (UNEP, UN Population Fund and the World Bank, whose mission straddled the energy, development and environment policy domains, play in promoting the objectives of the Kyoto Protocol?

Well before the Kyoto Protocol had come into force, international negotiations for a post-Kyoto climate change regime were already under way. The negotiating process had to contend with sharply competing political and economic priorities on the one hand and an increasingly confident scientific assessment of the dangerous implications of rising levels of fossil fuel consumption on the other. In this context, the scenarios constructed by various international agencies merit attention not so much for their predictive accuracy as for the light they shed on the implications for governance. Here, we confine our attention to the *World Energy Outlook 2008* prepared by the International Energy Agency (IEA) – an assessment echoed by a number of other reports (e.g. Stern, 2007; Garnaut, 2008) but one which carried particular weight given the IEA's coordinating function amongst Organization for Economic Co-operation and Development (OECD) countries.

The IEA Report contrasted three climate change policy scenarios: the reference scenario (or business as usual with world energy demand expanding by 45 per cent by 2030) and two scenarios predicated on greenhouse gas emissions reductions to 550 and 450 ppm CO_2e, respectively (see Figure 14.5). It is worth stressing that both reduction scenarios envisaged that, while technological innovation would play a part, most energy savings would derive from efficiency gains and the deployment of existing low carbon energy technologies. The 450 policy scenario, which corresponded to a 2°C global temperature rise, envisaged energy demand growing half as fast as in the Reference Scenario. This outcome would be secured through the rapid deployment of low carbon technologies, in particular carbon capture and storage (CCS), a substantial reorganisation of energy consumption patterns in non-OECD countries, the introduction of carbon pricing (the CO_2 price in 2030 would reach US$180 per tonne) and additional investment equal to 0.6 per cent of gross domestic product (GDP).

Though these policy assessments were fiercely resisted by industries most likely to be adversely affected by their implementation, they were nevertheless influential in setting the tone for policy discourse, especially in Europe. In December 2005, the first Meeting of the Parties to the Kyoto Protocol (MOP1) established the Ad Hoc Working Group on Further Commitments by Annex 1 Parties under the Kyoto Protocol (AWG-KP). Two years later COP13, meeting in Bali in December 2007, adopted the Bali Action Plan which established the Ad Hoc Working Group on Long-Term Cooperative Action

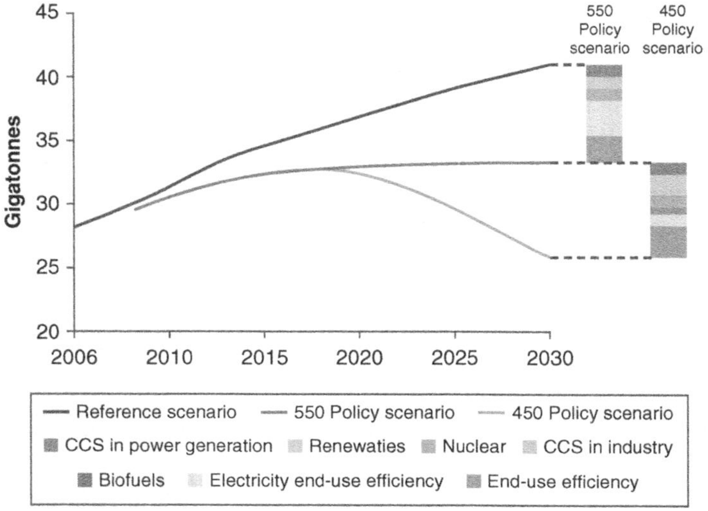

Figure 14.5 Energy-related CO_2 emissions by source in the 550 and 450 Policy Scenarios relative to the Reference Scenario
Source: OECD/IEA (2008), *World Energy Outlook 2008*, Chapter 18, Figure 18.4, p. 446.

under the UNFCCC (AWG-LCA) with a mandate to focus on mitigation, adaptation, finance, as well as technology- and capacity-building. The Bali conference also agreed on a two-year process, the Bali Roadmap, which envisaged parallel and interlinked negotiations under UNFCCC and the Kyoto Protocol leading to a legally binding agreement to be concluded at COP15/MOP5 in Copenhagen in December 2009. As the UNFCCC Copenhagen Conference approached, the prevailing sentiment was that the two working groups had made moderate progress on the issues of adaptation, technology- and capacity-building, but that deep divisions remained on mitigation and key aspects of finance.

Copenhagen and its aftermath

The UN Climate Change Conference held in Copenhagen on 7–19 December 2009 attracted unprecedented international attention and the attendance of 120 heads of state and government. Participants included 10,500 delegates, 13,500 observers and more than 3000 media representatives. Delegates engaged in some 1000 official, informal and group meetings, while observers took part in more than 400 meetings and media attended over 300 press conferences. Some 220 exhibits had been prepared by governments, the UN, other multilateral agencies and civil society organisations. The negotiations, which took place in the context of COP15 and MOP5 and in conjunction with meetings of the AWG-KP and AWG-LCA, had two clear goals: a legally binding treaty to cover the period 2013–20, and a well-defined vision for long-term collaborative action beyond 2020. Might this be the occasion for the elusive fifth threshold?

As many had feared, the Conference produced a cacophony of voices, most of them rehearsing well-known arguments, with both weak and powerful states seemingly unable to deviate far from their prepared scripts. The only substantial document to emerge was the Copenhagen Accord, brokered by the United States in discussions with four of the leading industrialising economies (China, India, Brazil and South Africa). Key elements included: a general commitment to limit the rise in global temperatures to 2°C, a process whereby countries would indicate mitigation pledges by 31 January 2010, broad principles for reporting and verification of undertakings by national governments, a collective pledge by developed countries to provide developing countries with additional funds 'approaching $30 billion' for the period 2010–12 to assist with mitigation and adaptation efforts and a promise to mobilise US$100 billion dollars a year by 2020 to address their needs through a mix of bilateral and multilateral, public and private resources. The Accord also envisaged the creation of the Copenhagen Green Climate Fund, a High Level Panel to explore ways of meeting the 2020 finance objective, and a new Technology Mechanism (Pew Centre on Global Climate Change, 2010).

For many the outcome was deeply disappointing. The hoped for new (fifth) threshold had not materialised. The Conference failed to produce a binding agreement or a feasible pathway for achieving that objective and merely 'took note' of the Accord, although more than 120 states, responsible for more than four-fifths of global greenhouse gas emissions, opted to engage with the provisions of the Accord. No agreement was reached on a timetable for achieving emissions reduction targets. A global coordination mechanism, a viable verification system and ways of enforcing compliance even with self-imposed targets remained similarly out of reach.

The undertakings given by states in response to the Copenhagen Accord were at best uneven. As of December 2010, 140 parties (counting the 27 member states of the European Union as a single party) had expressed their intention to be listed as agreeing to the Accord. In line with the Accord, the UNFCCC received quantified economy-wide emissions targets for 2020 from 42 industrialised countries, and 43 developing countries submitted nationally appropriate mitigation actions (UNEP, 2010, p. 20). However, the total emissions reductions proposed fell far short of what was needed to achieve the 450 ppm pathway by 2020. According to one authoritative assessment, global emissions in 2020 would depend on the pledges implemented and the rules surrounding them. On one hand, emissions in 2020 could be as low as 49 Gt CO_2e (range: 47–51 Gt CO_2e) when countries implemented their conditional pledges with 'strict' accounting rules. On the other hand, they could be as high as 53 Gt CO_2e (range: 52–57 Gt CO_2e) when countries implemented unconditional pledges with 'lenient' accounting rules. In the latter case, the gap for reaching the 450 ppm pathway by 2020 could be as high as 9 Gt CO_2e (UNEP, 2010, p 16). Most assessments pointed to rising global temperatures of between 3.0 and 3.9 degrees Celsius (Pew Centre on Global Climate Change, 2010). As for the financing arrangements, the amounts envisaged were not pegged to inflationary pressures, were generally less than UN agencies considered necessary and riddled with ambiguities as to the source of funding. Nor was it entirely clear how much new money was involved and how much was simply the repackaging of existing aid programmes (Ballesteros et al., 2010).

This cursory review of the Copenhagen Accord is instructive not so much for what it tells us about the complexities of climate change policy but for the light it sheds on the dynamics of energy governance in a period of profound transition. Why did the decision-making framework painstakingly developed over two decades of sustained international negotiations not yield the desired outcomes? In the wake of Copenhagen the scepticism with which multilateral processes and institutions had been viewed for some time quickly gathered pace.

Some now advocated the imposition of sanctions to discourage non-compliance, others canvassed mechanisms designed to dissuade 'free-riders' and agreements to limit in modest but explicit ways traditional notions of state sovereignty. Others still made the case for numerically more manageable negotiating forums paving the way for bilateral or 'minilateral' accords. Negotiations, it was argued, would make more headway if they centred on

> [...] the small number of actors responsible for the lion's share of the world's carbon dioxide emissions, including China (21.5 per cent), the United States (20.2 per cent), the European Union (13.8 per cent), and a handful of other developed and emerging economies. (Council on Foreign Relations, 2010)

Smaller, less formal frameworks, including the G20, the G8+5,[3] and the Major Economies Forum on Energy and Climate (MEF)[4] already existed, but they did not as yet occupy centre stage. Selective state-based forums on climate change were proposed as preferable sites of negotiation precisely because they operated outside the universal structure of the UNFCCC regime. For Steve Rayner and Gwyn Prins (2007) the politics of inclusion risked becoming a recipe for gridlock:

> Relying on an international agreement that requires the consent of all national governments inevitably results in the very lowest of common denominators. Since fewer than twenty countries account for 80% of the world's emissions [...] it would be better for diplomacy to focus upon them. In these early stages, the other 150 countries only get in the way.

In the interests of more effective decision making, some argued that the UNFCCC negotiations should replace the consensus principle, which gave each state a virtual power of veto, with a majority-based system of decision making, while others were attracted to the notion of 'complementary processes'. 'Coalitions of the willing', precisely because they brought together the like-minded, were thought more likely to reach agreement and take initiatives and so demonstrate the kind of progress that others might wish to emulate at a later date. Others still questioned the wisdom of those who saw verifiable, legally binding commitments as the only way to guarantee that countries would cut their emissions (Pew Centre on Global Climate Change, 2009). They argued instead that such commitments would be difficult or impossible to secure, and in the unlikely event that they could be secured, the risk of non-compliance would remain high (Aldy and Stavins, 2007). A more promising strategy might be to seek an international agreement based on political pledges supported by legal domestic targets. In short, a multifaceted intellectual effort was underway to reassess the institutional and legal foundations of climate change policy in the light of the disappointing outcome at Copenhagen and the tortuous process that had led to it.

Rethinking the governance agenda

Commendable though it was, much of the emerging academic and policy discourse seemed strangely unable to grasp the import of two inescapable realities: the multidimensional character of the policy challenge posed by climate change and the magnitude of what had already been attempted by way of institutional innovation over the preceding decades.

Normative, legal and institutional responses to any policy challenge are unlikely to prove equal to the task unless they rest on a lucid assessment of that challenge. When it comes to climate change, both the scientific evidence and the responses of both experts and policy makers have rightly focused on the magnitude of societal risks associated with rising temperatures, rising sea levels and other shifts in weather patterns. To keep these risks to manageable proportions, the conclusion has been reached that an appropriate policy goal is to limit the rise of global average temperatures to 2°C, which then translates to a carbon emissions target of 450 ppm. The problem with this technical formulation of the risks involved and of the measures needed to mitigate or adapt to those risks is that it loses sight of the many other foreseen and unforeseeable consequences associated with high and rapidly rising levels of energy consumption, of which climate change is but one, albeit the most dramatic, manifestation. In other words, in both academic and policy discourse a clearly discernible trend has emerged, which treats climate change policy – and the governance processes needed to give effect to it – in relative isolation from the many other areas of policy formulation and implementation with which it is integrally connected.

In both theory and practice climate change governance is inseparable from energy governance. The rise of new and high-energy consuming economies (notably China and India), the uncertainties generated by the global financial crisis and economic slowdown, the accelerating shift in the global geopolitical and geoeconomic balance, the shifting geography of fossil fuel supplies and the complex geopolitical and strategic considerations associated with long-distance transport of oil and gas, the fast approaching peak of oil production and the inevitable rise in the price of oil, the risks surrounding the foreshadowed expansion of the nuclear industry and the vagaries of renewable energy markets are as integral to climate change policy as they are to 'energy security' calculations (Westphal, 2006).

There is in any case much more to energy security, and by extension to energy policy, than a simplistic geopolitical calculus would suggest. Conventionally defined in geopolitical terms to mean the scramble by states for energy supplies (at acceptable cost), energy security as a concept and the complex mix of stated and unstated values and objectives on which it rests have become the subject of increasing contestation. On the one hand energy security can be understood with reference to such state-centric norms as national economic growth and national security, but other critical considerations now include: profitability of key industries, employment, financial flows, levels of consumption and delivery of pubic goods (all of which to a greater or lesser extent involve the complex interaction of states, markets and civil society). More recently, ecological values and notions of equity have gained greater prominence (both of which are by definition international and transnational in scope and impact). The vicissitudes of climate change policy cannot but reflect the multidimensional character of energy security and energy policy generally. The governance challenges posed by climate change and the responses to them make sense only if they are placed in the larger energy policy context and the complex interdependence of actors and policy priorities on which it rests.

What all this tells us is that climate change governance requires a normative, legal and institutional framework equipped to handle the multiplicity of policy challenges which lie at the interface of economy, security and environment. Climate-friendly 'national development' and 'decarbonisation' of the national economy may at first sight seem commonsensical objectives amenable to relatively straightforward technical measures. But even the most cursory examination soon reveals a highly fractured terrain, in which competing values, interests and perceptions in widely different domains are vying for influence and attention. Is an effective climate change policy compatible with higher levels of economic prosperity for everyone? Or is it predicated on diminished economic prospects, whether in absolute or relative terms, at least for some? Once the question is framed in such stark terms, whether in a local, national or international setting, the intensity of the contestation becomes readily apparent. The technical formulation of mitigation and adaptation measures and financing and technology transfer mechanisms might serve to obscure but cannot eliminate fundamental and disturbing questions about the future organisation of human affairs. These questions relate to notions of distributive justice (how the costs and benefits of energy policy in the era of climate change will be distributed within and between countries), to the inclusiveness of decision making (who will have an effective say over the vital decisions to be made) and to the efficacy of policy making (will the policies adopted and implemented effectively cope with the mounting threats to economy, security and environment).[5] The principle of 'common and differentiated responsibilities' (adopted within the UNFCCC framework) and notions of trust-building (in relation to the monitoring and verification of national commitments) are but small steps in this direction.

Enough has been said to indicate that the effectiveness of climate change governance will in large measure depend on the extent to which it recognises the complex interconnectedness that lies at the core of the energy (and climate change) policy domain and the contentiousness of the issues to be addressed. It is difficult to see how any emerging normative, legal and institutional framework can effectively manage these two realities unless inclusiveness and cooperation are made a defining feature of that framework. Inclusiveness, it should be noted, operates along two axes. One axis denotes the tiers of governance (municipal, provincial, national, regional and global), and the other the sites (states, markets and civil society) within which authoritative and influential actors (or stakeholders) operate (Camilleri and Falk, 2009, pp. 162–167). The emerging framework of energy governance may be said to be inclusive to the extent that it incorporates in different yet complementary ways all tiers of governance and all three sites of decision making. The question arises: how are inclusiveness and cooperation to be institutionalised? The large and diverse gatherings, exemplified by the Rio (1992), Kyoto (1997), Bali (2007) and Copenhagen (2009) Conferences represent one possible model – a model that has been applied, at least intermittently, to other policy domains, including development, human rights population, food, and disarmament and arms control. Participants at these world summits were drawn not just from national governments but from all other tiers of governance, and at the same time encompassed a wide cross-section of influential actors operating in civil society and the marketplace. The sheer number and range of voices to be heard and the sheer scale of the attempted dialogue have prompted theorists and practitioners alike to question the utility of a single global multilateral framework, and to advocate instead 'polycentric' approaches of one kind or another (e.g. Ostrom, 2009; World Bank, 2010).

As already noted, a common reaction to the apparent failings of the inclusive multilateralist design of the UN climate regime has been to propose increasing reliance on 'minilateral' approaches and innovations. Smaller clusters of states, it is argued, formed by virtue of economic weight (e.g. G8, G20), common interests (e.g. the Brazil, Russia, India and China grouping) or regional integration (e.g. the European Union, the Asia Pacific Economic Cooperation group), are more likely to make for coherent decision making and to spawn energy-specific organisational forms (e.g. Asia Pacific Partnership on Clean Development and Climate) tailored to particular needs or interests (Victor, 2006; Naím, 2009, pp. 136–137). This approach, also labelled 'exclusive minilateralism', has the advantage that it acknowledges the profound divisions that continue to obstruct the emergence of a global policy consensus. They seek to take advantage of the benefits said to derive from smaller hence more manageable forums and from likeminded groupings or 'coalitions of the willing'. Perhaps the most incisive contribution to this discourse has been the proposition that, in the absence of an integrated, comprehensive climate change regime, we are seeing the emergence of a 'regime complex', that is, a cluster of arrangements of the loosely coupled variety, 'with no clear hierarchy or core yet many of its elements linked in complementary ways' (Keohane and Victor, 2010). Significantly, the proponents of this formulation see it not only as a faithful representation of emerging trends but as a more promising approach to the imperatives of climate change than the globalist ambition of the UNFCCC regime.

At one level the notion of a loosely structured regime complex appears to have a surface plausibility to it. There is no denying that the last 20 years have witnessed the growth of a great many unilateral, bilateral and multilateral initiatives to which individual states and diverse inter-governmental bodies (e.g. IPCC, G8, G20, MEF, specialised UN agencies, multilateral development banks) have contributed at different times and in different ways. This conceptualisation is nevertheless deeply flawed on three counts: it reveals only one facet of the complex multilateral patchwork that has unfolded; its conceptual orientation remains unconvincingly state-centric; and it fails to provide a satisfactory explanation of the way these diverse initiatives, forums and mechanisms can or are likely to be integrated into anything approaching a coherent policy framework.

The first deficiency – the tendency to concentrate on certain types of initiatives and ignore others – derives from the failure to connect climate change with the larger energy policy domain. The reality is that a great many institutions now exist – the IEA and Organization of the Petroleum Exporting Countries (OPEC) are two obvious examples, which have a global impact on energy policy and governance mechanisms. The World Trade Organization and various regional trade bodies bear considerably upon both national energy policy and international negotiations. The issue here is not so much that the multilateral patchwork is more extensive or diffuse than even Keohane or Victor appear to realise, but that, as we have already noted, climate change responses are inseparable from the larger energy policy nexus, in which economic, environmental and security concerns all play a decisive role. It follows that the framework for climate change policy, if it is to be at all coherent or viable, must somehow take account of highly interconnected policy domains that are now central to the task of international coordination and regulation. It is not at all clear how the loosely coupled 'climate change regime complex' described by Keohane and Victor does, or could in the future, manage this complex interconnectedness.

The second difficulty, closely related to the first, is the state-centric rendition of the governance problématique. Crucial here are the significant functions now performed by markets and civil society. Energy policy is increasingly a product of decisions made in global energy markets. As Goldthau and Witte have succinctly observed, markets are structured by a broad variety of different actors, private as well as public: 'In addition to governments, private companies, i.e. international energy firms, financial institutions and others interact through market-based transactions, and thus determine outcomes in global energy' (Goldthau and Witte, 2010, p. 1). Put simply, the production, distribution and consumption of fossil fuels, nuclear energy and their renewable counterparts are organised largely by private actors that engage with one another primarily through market-based interactions, though these are increasingly embedded by international rules and institutions.

Civil society relates to international multilateralism in strikingly different ways, yet its impact on the policy-making process is no less significant. Expressed simply, any society's 'intent to decarbonise' is inextricably linked to the community's understanding of energy options and level of support for ambitious climate policy. What any one state is able or willing to do, regardless of the complexion of its political system, cannot but take account of societal capacities and dispositions. The positions adopted by political elites, whether in the United States, Europe, India or China, cannot deviate far from prevailing public attitudes and perceptions – given that energy consumption patterns are such an integral part of quality of life expectations. The societal and cultural underpinnings of the political process are evident in the rise to prominence of significant initiatives in energy policy at the municipal, provincial, regional and global tiers of governance. A growing number of highly skilled and well-organised civil society actors have found in these different arenas new and expanding opportunities to shape the policy agenda across a range of time frames. The immense impact of the scientific community, through the IPCC and just as importantly through prestigious national and international peak bodies, has been widely observed (Camilleri and Falk, 2009, pp. 308–313). The development of local, national and international environmental networks, which operate in increasingly flexible spatial and temporal domains points to a markedly enhanced capacity to influence the context and even the outcome of political negotiation.

Finally, the regime complex hypothesis, while it correctly highlights the diffuseness and fluidity of the emerging policy-making process in relation to climate change, seems unable to account for the persistent and not altogether negligible steps already taken in the development of a global regulatory framework, not to mention those contemplated for the coming decade and beyond. That these steps have often been hesitant and subject to acute contestation is hardly surprising. How could it be otherwise? What is especially striking, however, is that despite the roadblocks and disappointments, key actors have continued to engage in global negotiations, partly because the pressure to do so remains intense – pressure that emanates largely from civil society but also with increasing vigour from the marketplace, and is graphically and continuously relayed through a vast array of interconnected media and educational channels. There is, however, another contributing influence, namely the exigencies of the present conjuncture. Though unilateral, bilateral and minilateral initiatives will remain an important feature of the policy response to climate change and energy security, these arrangements require an overarching framework which alone can give them guidance and potency.

It should come therefore as no surprise that the COP16 negotiations which concluded in Cancún on 10 December 2010 should have given renewed momentum to the process that had seriously faltered the year before at Copenhagen. It is worth noting in parenthesis that, as at previous COP meetings but with greater vigour and sharpness on this occasion, business representatives meeting outside the official negotiations focused on the emerging opportunities for cooperative climate change initiatives which they now saw as critical to any long-term strategy designed to achieve greater energy cost savings, reduce risks and increase profit margins (Starkbuck, 2010). In the official negotiations, Cancún registered several modest but significant outcomes. First, the negotiations (under the UNFCCC or AWG-LCA track) formally approved the UN REDD+ (Reducing Emissions from Deforestation and Degradation plus other measures such as conservation and land management) mechanisms to help developing countries prevent deforestation. Second, COP16 codified a Green Climate Fund as part of the UN process to help poor and developing countries adapt to the impacts of climate change and support low-carbon development. Third, a more advanced discussion on climate adaptation led to the adoption of the Cancún Adaptation Framework and the establishment of an Adaptation Committee to support state-level measures. Fourth, agreements were reached to facilitate the flow of low-carbon technologies between developed and developing countries. Finally, COP16 made progress with regard to monitoring, reporting and verifying national emissions cuts through standardised self-reporting mechanisms and international verification mechanisms (Ewing and Kuntjoro, 2010).

Cancún, it is true, did not adequately address the elephant in the room: no agreement was reached on a framework to replace the Kyoto Protocol, which had served as the foundation of contemporary international emissions regulation and was set to expire in 2012. Yet, even here important steps were taken. The preamble of the Cancun statement under the Kyoto track included important language that recognised the need for Annex I Parties as a group to reduce their emissions in the range of 25–40 per cent below 1990 levels by 2020. The decision also took note of the undertakings given by Annex I countries, thereby formalising targets which were put forward in the context of Copenhagen and placing them under the UNFCCC and the Kyoto Protocol. Finally, it was agreed that further work was needed to convert these targets into actual binding commitments under the Kyoto Protocol (Morgan, 2010).

Cancún had not delivered the elusive fifth threshold, and the timeframe for the introduction of a new legal framework was rapidly closing. On the other hand, it had brought this threshold closer to the realm of the feasible. Simply put, it had reaffirmed the principle that an integrated international normative and political accord remained the necessary destination, however faltering and painful the intervening steps might be. In the coming years the scaffolding would continue to rise, at times slowly, often messily and unevenly, yet an 'umbrella' framework was gradually emerging. The construction of this normative, legal and institutional edifice remained the necessary though not sufficient condition for the global transition to sustainable development, and for animating the old and new coalitions capable of yielding this outcome.

Notes

1. The four Assessment Reports published thus far (1990, 1995, 2001, 2007) have painted an increasingly bleak picture of the severity of the problem, and argued with increasing confidence that the problem is attributable largely to human economic activity.
2. Though the European Union had largely spearheaded the Kyoto process, it nevertheless acknowledged that a number of weaknesses would have to be addressed (European Commission, 2010, pp. 5–6).
3. The G8+5 includes the heads of government from the G8 nations as well as those from the five leading emerging economies (Brazil, China, India, Mexico and South Africa).
4. The MEF, which consists of the major economies, was launched in March 2009 to facilitate a candid dialogue on climate change among major developed and developing economies.
5. This is in some respects a simpler yet more revealing statement of the hurdles which an effective climate change governance regime must overcome than the six dimensions (coherence, accountability, effectiveness, determinacy, sustainability and epistemic quality) proposed by Keohane and Victor (2010, pp. 19–20).

References

Aldy J. and R.N. Stavins (eds) (2007), *Architectures for Agreement: Addressing Global Climate Change in the Post-Kyoto World* (Cambridge: Cambridge University Press).

Ballesteros, A., C. Polycarp, K. Stasio, E. Chessin, Xing Fu-Bertaux and K. Hurlburt (2010), 'Summary of Developed Country "Fast-Start" Climate Finance Pledges' [World Resources Institute, 6 October http://www.wri.org/publication/summary-of-developed-country-fast-start-climate-finance-pledges; accessed: 15 October 2010].

BBC (2005), Kyoto Protocol comes into force, *BBC News* [http://news.bbc.co.uk/2/hi/science/nature/4267245.stm#_jmp0; accessed: 05 March 2008].

Beder, S. (1999), 'Corporate Hijacking of the Greenhouse Debate', *The Ecologist*, 29(2): 119–122.

Beder, S., P. Brown and J. Vidal (1997), 'Who Killed Kyoto?', *The Guardian*, 29 October, p. 4.

Camilleri, J.A. and J. Falk (2009), *Worlds in Transition: Evolving Governance across a Stressed Planet* (Cheltenham: Edward Elgar).

Council on Foreign Relations (2010), 'The Global Climate Change Regime', *Backgrounder*, 20 April [http://www.cfr.org/publication/21831/global_climate_change_regime.html#p2; accessed: 03 November 2010].

European Commission (2010), 'International Climate Policy Post-Copenhagen: Action now to Reinvigorate Global Action on Climate Change' [www.ec.europa.eu/environment/climat/pdf/com_2010_86.pdf; accessed: 29 November 2010].

International Energy Agency (IEA) (2008), *World Energy Outlook* (Paris: OECD/IEA).

Stern, N. (2007), *The Economics of Climate Change: The Stern Review* (Cambridge: Cambridge University Press).

Garnaut, R. (2008), *The Garnaut Climate Change Review: Final Report* (Cambridge: Cambridge University Press).

Goldthau A. and J.M. Witte (2010), 'From Energy Security to Global Energy Governance', *Journal of Energy Security*, 23 March (accessed on-line at http://tinyurl.com/y52mljp on 9 September 2010).

Keohane R. and D. Victor (2010), 'The Regime Complex for Climate Change', *The Harvard Project on International Climate Agreements*, Discussion Paper 10–33.

Oil and Gas Journal (2000), 'The Collapse of Kyoto' (editorial), 4 December, 49: 25.

Ostrom, E. (2009), 'A Polycentric Approach for Coping with Climate Change', World Bank Policy Research working paper no. WPS 5095, October.

Pew Centre on Global climate Change (undated), *Summary: Copenhagen Climate Summit* [http://www.pewclimate.org/international/copenhagen-climate-summit-summary; accessed: 02 November 2010].

Pew Centre on Global Climate Change (2009), 'A Copenhagen Climate Agreement' [http://www.pewclimate.org/international/copenhagen-climate-agreement; accessed: 21 November 2010].

Pew Centre on Global Climate Change (2010), 'Adding up the Numbers: Mitigation Pledges under the Copenhagen Accord' [http://www.pewclimate.org/copenhagen-accord/adding-up-mitigation-pledges; accessed: 04 November 2010].

Price, D. (1995), 'Energy and Human Evolution', *Population and Environment: A Journal of Interdisciplinary Studies*, 16(4): 301–319.

Prins, G. and S. Rayner (2007), 'The Wrong Trousers: Radically Rethinking Climate Policy' [http://www.lse.ac.uk/collections/mackinderProgramme/pdf/mackinder_Wrong%20Trousers.pdf; accessed: 02 November 2010].

US Energy Information Administration (2009), *Annual Energy Review*.

US Energy Administration (2010), *Country Analysis Briefs* [http://www.eia.doe.gov/cabs/index.html; accessed: 04 November 2010].

United Nations (1992), *Annex 1 to the report of the Intergovernmental Negotiating Committee for the framework convention on climate change on the work of its fifth session*, 9A/AC.237/18(Part II)/Add.1.

United Nations General Assembly (UNGA) (1990), *Protection of Global Climate for Present and Future Generations of Mankind*, A/RES/45/212.

Victor, D. (2006), 'Toward Effective International Cooperation on Climate Change: Numbers, Interests and Institutions', *Global Environmental Politics*, 6(3): 90–103.

Naím, M. (2009), 'Minilateralism', *Foreign Policy*, 163: 136–137.

Westphal, K. (2006), 'Energy Policy between Multilateral Governance and Geopolitics: Whither Europe?', *IPG*, 4(44): 44–62.

15
Interconnections between Climate and Energy Governance

Jonathan Symons

Introduction

'Energy security' is usually understood as the achievement of low-cost, diverse, stable energy supplies (Yergin, 2006, p. 70); importantly, the agent who 'secures' energy is usually a state or sub-state government. A cursory analysis of this definition suggests that reducing greenhouse gas (GHG) emissions and attaining energy security will, after cost-neutral energy efficiency gains are exhausted, be contradictory goals (see Chapter 2). This is because the higher price of low-emissions energy sources (OECD, 2010) runs counter to the 'low-cost' goal of traditional energy security policy. Yet, a paradoxical flipside emerges: while GHG emissions reductions and energy security are largely contradictory objectives within the domestic policy making of any individual state (Brown and Huntington, 2008), an effective global agreement mitigating climate change would bring considerable side-benefits for aggregate global energy security. This chapter outlines why an effective global climate agreement would stimulate investment in both energy research and developing world infrastructure and argues that these developments would unlock benefits via improved cooperation in energy distribution. Nevertheless, it is unclear whether these side-benefits are sufficient to fully compensate for the higher cost of low-emissions energy sources.

The links between mitigation of climate change and pursuit of energy security are dense. Most importantly, averting dangerous climate change would require massive investment in developing world low-emissions energy infrastructure and a transformation of global energy governance. These interconnections become apparent when we consider that:

(1) Combustion of fossil fuels is responsible for approximately 57 per cent of global GHG emissions (IPCC, 2007, Figure SPM.3.(b));
(2) It is projected that non-Organization for Economic Co-operation and Development (OECD) countries will account for around 97 per cent of

increases in energy-related carbon dioxide (CO_2) emissions before 2030 under a business as usual scenario (IEA, 2008, p. 46);

(3) In the coming century at least two-thirds of least-cost mitigation opportunities and associated investment needs will be located in the developing world (Edmonds et al., 2008; Hope, 2009).

I argue that this distribution of investment needs means that any successful response to climate change must apply western scientific and financial resources to the task of providing low-emissions energy infrastructure in the developing world.

Necessary investment in low-emissions energy infrastructure in the developing world could theoretically be achieved through a variety of different political structures. For example, current negotiations under the United Nations Framework Convention on Climate Change (UNFCCC) centre on adoption of national emissions reduction targets. States are each individually responsible for meeting their emissions targets, even though negotiations encompass specific promises of international assistance. Alternatively, many developing states and advocates of climate justice call for the West to repay its accrued 'climate debt' by providing unconditional financial and technological assistance (Wen, 2009). Where the impracticality of the current UNFCCC approach is demonstrated by the failure of existing negotiations to achieve a global agreement with sufficient ambition to avert dangerous climate change (discussed in detail below), the altruism of the debt–repayment approach has no historical precedent. Neither approach appears likely to achieve the necessary speed or quantum of investment in emissions abatement.

Admittedly, the prospects for an effective global climate agreement are poor. However, were one to be achieved, it would likely involve a much more substantial compromise between developed and developing countries than has been offered at UNFCCC negotiations in Copenhagen or Cancún. The developed world's contribution to developing world emissions constraint would need to increase in exchange for binding developing world emissions limits. Western governments would need to direct financial assistance in excess of that envisaged under the 'Copenhagen Green Climate Fund' in exchange for binding developing world emissions limits and governance concessions. What shape might such a deal take? The approach that is most consistent with both the competitive logic of the international system and with prevailing international norms would use market mechanisms to make investment in emissions abatement in the developing world commercially attractive. Achieving the necessary levels of international investment in the developing world's energy sector through market mechanisms would also require harmonisation of emissions trading, taxation and investment rules (Blyth, 2010, pp. 138–139). Such changes would deepen international cooperation in the energy sector and involve a significant intensification of economic globalisation. Many people would reflexively oppose these developments because of their obvious, negative consequences for national democratic autonomy. One purpose of this chapter is to reflect on the wider ramifications of enhancing global governance within the energy sector.

To date there has been only limited progress towards realising synergies between climate change and energy security policy. As some chapters included in the second section of this book have argued national climate policies often do little more than tweak and re-brand energy security initiatives (see Chapter 6, pp. 114–116). Even though the Kyoto Protocol's 'Clean Development Mechanism' (CDM) has financed some projects in some developing countries, measures promoting first world investment in emissions abatement in the developing world have been poorly designed and have achieved only a tiny fraction of the required investment (Victor and Cullenward, 2007). Looking forward, it is most likely that the UNFCCC negotiation process will continue to fail to reach an agreement that might avert dangerous climate change, and that increased national control of energy production will continue to limit the liberalisation of energy distribution. For these reasons, the arguments developed in this chapter describe a hypothetical scenario – for the foreseeable future it appears unlikely that climate concerns will be the dominant force shaping energy governance at a global level, even if particular regions (such as the European Union (EU)) partially diverge from this trend. As a result, it is extremely unlikely that synergies between climate and energy policy will be fully realised (see Chapter 12); however, capitalising on these opportunities remains an important goal.

This chapter begins by outlining the structure of the international challenge in energy and climate governance, respectively. After detailing why an effective response to climate change would deepen multilateral cooperation and economic globalisation, it goes on to explore the global implications for energy security of the consequent entrenchment of markets within the energy sector. Such an intensification of global energy governance through the creation of global emissions markets would, other things being equal, carry benefits for aggregate global energy security. This is because a comprehensive international climate change mitigation agreement would lock states into rule-based energy distribution and emissions-abatement markets. This, in turn, would encourage investment in new energy sources and minimise the risk of descent into a zero-sum game of competitive national appropriation of existing energy reserves. The chapter outlines both the potential for complementarity in global climate and energy security efforts and the factors that will likely prevent the realisation of such synergies. In both domains policy must grapple with allocation and conservation of a limited global resource – of safe GHG emissions and accessible fossil fuel reserves, respectively. However, the structures of the two cooperation problems are quite different. The chapter concludes by reflecting on some of the normative implications for international society of the energy security challenge.

Global energy security

The global politics of energy are often discussed in geopolitical terms that presume competition for energy must be a 'zero-sum game' (Goldthau and Witte, 2010, p. 2). This perspective emphasises reasons to be fearful of a looming energy supply crunch: the rise of developing energy consumers such as China and India; declining availability of low-cost energy reserves; declining levels of investment in energy production (other than refining capacity); and the exhaustion of non-Organization of the Petroleum Exporting Countries (OPEC) oil reserves which is leading to a concentration of oil and gas production within a limited number of often-unstable areas (Correljéa and van der Linden, 2006; IEA, 2008). These fears often dovetail with wider security concerns about the rise of China – China's unprecedented demand for resources has become a major factor shaping its foreign policy, transforming political relationships and creating opportunities for energy-exporting developing states (Zweig and Jianhai, 2005). Moreover, other states are also increasingly asserting national control over energy production and using diplomatic measures to leverage stable, favourable long-term energy supply agreements. These measures also undermine the liberalisation of global energy markets.

Yet, there is a clear alternative to the competitive zero-sum approach to energy. The factors described above have not yet reversed the long-term trend towards liberalisation of energy distribution instigated by institutional reforms made in the wake of the 1970s oil crises (Goldthau and Witte, 2010, pp. 10–11). Today the bulk of oil is traded on international exchanges via relatively short-term contracts, rather than tied up through bilateral arrangements. A global market for gas is also emerging thanks to the growing trade in highly transportable liquid petroleum gas (Goldthau and Witte, 2010, pp. 4–6). While threats to energy supply and bilateral agreements over energy resources were once widely used as instruments of statecraft, distribution of energy resources is now significantly shaped by market forces. This development has boosted aggregate global energy security by creating various economic efficiencies and providing a more reliable climate for investment. Whereas national competition over energy resources is a zero-sum game in which political instability commonly undermines net energy production, market-based international distribution allocates energy according to the logic of economic efficiency rather than the logic of power and so should theoretically maximise the incentives for energy investment.

This analysis suggests two narratives that might describe potential scenarios in energy politics. The first, which has been termed a narrative of 'markets and institutions' (Correljéa and van der Linden, 2006), denotes a world of intensifying economic globalisation where markets and cooperative economic institutions – primarily the World Trade Organization (WTO), the International Energy Agency (IEA), OPEC, the International Monetary

Fund and regional free trade organisations coordinate the free flow of energy resources. A second narrative, of 'regions and empires' (Correljéa and van der Linden, 2006), sees the globe divided into competing spheres of influence (US, EU, Russian, Japanese and Chinese) such that national security concerns limit the development of global energy markets and impede movement of strategic goods and capital. In this scenario the importance of bilateral trade relationships and treaties to energy supply security promotes formation of 'integrated blocks with satellite regions that compete for markets and energy resources' (Correljéa and van der Linden, 2006). While the last decade has seen strong forces pushing towards the regional energy distribution model the future of energy politics remains unclear.

Importantly, there is a significant commonality amongst the interests of all parties in global energy politics. First, despite competition for resources, energy consumer states share a common interest in preserving reliability of energy supply and nurturing market institutions that prevent cartel-like behaviour amongst energy suppliers. It was these factors that led OECD members to form the IEA in response to the energy crisis of 1973–1974. Although the IEA remains the major institutional actor promoting stability of energy supply (and the efficient operation of global energy markets), its work is hampered by its limited membership (OECD members only) and the tendency for member states' foreign policies to work against organisational goals. Recent developments – such as China's deepening bilateral agreements with energy exporters, the lack of progress in WTO and UNFCCC negotiations, the slow progress of EU power and gas market liberalisation and unilateral US foreign policy over Iraq – point to a move away from the markets and institutions story line (Correljéa and van der Linden, 2006). However, the capacity for the IEA to work cooperatively with the new energy consumer states, and the shared national interest in cooperation, give grounds for optimism. There is also a fundamental symmetry connecting the interests of consumer states and producer states. Where the former wish to preserve stability of energy supply, the latter seek stability of energy demand and revenue. Obviously the interests of the two groups diverge around price; however, each side has reasons to assist in maintenance of international institutions governing energy distribution.

This chapter began by observing the paradox that there are significant synergies between climate and energy agendas at a global level despite the conflict between pursuit of climate change mitigation and energy security domestically. The primary explanation for this paradox is that such a global agreement will lock the politics of energy into a cooperative, market-based pattern that is conducive to technological innovation and development of new energy sources. Consider the two narratives described above – of regulated, global energy *markets* versus *regional* supply models structured by the bilateral relationships of great powers. Whereas the former *market*-based model involves cooperation and the potential for positive sum gains, the latter involves zero-sum contests for control of existing resources. For this reason, exclusive focus on national energy security might result in sub-optimal levels of international cooperation and a consequent reduction in aggregate global energy security. By contrast, an effective climate regime would require such a significant intensification of economic globalisation (and global regulation) in the energy sector, that it would also facilitate a cooperative international response to energy security. An effective global climate agreement would ensure that the narrative of markets and institutions prevails in energy distribution even if the trend towards national control of production continues.

Scale of the global climate challenge

Substantiating my argument that a successful outcome would both stimulate significant research into new energy technologies and intensify economic globalisation and energy sector governance requires analysis of the scale and structure of the global challenge posed by climate change. The first point to observe is that the challenge of averting dangerous climate change is daunting.

While the scientific reality of climate change is now very widely accepted and the processes causing warming are well understood, considerable uncertainty remains about the sensitivity of the global climate system and therefore about what would constitute a safe atmospheric concentration of GHG. Although 450 ppm CO_2e[1] is widely accepted as the point beyond which warming in excess of 2°C becomes likely (Hassol, 2007), it seems increasingly improbable that emissions can be limited to this level. Partly for this reason major policy analyses, such as those provided by the *Stern Review* (2006) and *Garnaut Climate Change Review* (2008), have advocated targets between 450 and 550 ppm of atmospheric CO_2 equivalent. Although scientific analysis of the impact of emissions is complex and subject to a high level of uncertainty, the arithmetic justifying pessimism about our capacity to limit emissions to 450 ppm CO_2e is straightforward (Blyth, 2010, p. 136). At present, human activity results in emissions of around 50 gigatonnes of CO_2e each year, which produces an annual increase of about 2 parts per million in the atmospheric concentration of CO_2. In 2010, the atmospheric concentration of CO_2 stood at around 389 ppm. While the relationship between CO_2 and CO_2 equivalent is disputed, some analyses suggest this figure may equate to about 430 ppm of CO_2e (Stern, 2006; Hassol, 2007, p. 3). Since annual emissions of GHG are currently rising rather than falling, present trends suggest that atmospheric concentrations of GHG will enter an unsafe danger zone at some point in the next two decades.

Two important caveats qualify this prediction. First, is the view held by some leading scientists that 450 ppm CO_2e – which represents a doubling of pre-industrial levels – is itself unsafe. According to this view, analysis of paleoclimate data reveals various slow feedback mechanisms not included in the Intergovernmental Panel on Climate Change (IPCC) climate assessments on which the 450 ppm figure is based. For this reason, James Hansen and others (2008, p. 217) have argued that

> if humanity wishes to preserve a planet similar to that on which civilisation developed and to which life on Earth is adapted [...] CO_2 will need to be reduced from its current 385 ppm to at most 350 ppm.

A second caveat concerns possible technological fixes to global warming. It is conceivable that geo-engineering measures may ultimately offer a low-cost substitute for some emissions reduction (Barrett, 2007; Victor et al., 2009). These are technologies that alter the planet's temperature by reducing the amount of solar energy that is absorbed (e.g. through aerosol particles that reflect light into space) or increasing sequestration of atmospheric carbon (e.g. by encouraging algal growth in the ocean). While there are many unanswered questions about the effectiveness of geo-engineering technologies, it seems almost inevitable that they will be utilised to some degree. Since atmospheric concentrations of GHGs will almost certainly exceed 'safe' levels in the coming decades, geo-engineering techniques, if they prove viable, will probably be used to manage the period of 'overshoot' prior to emissions being reduced to below the rate of their natural removal from the atmosphere. However, since geo-engineering measures cannot address all the issues linked to GHG emissions (e.g. ocean acidification) and will have various unintended impacts, emissions reduction will remain an urgent priority.

A picture of the scale of the challenge involved in limiting emissions to a safe level and the likely consequences of failure can be gained by comparing IPCC climate projections against emissions trends predicted in the International Energy Agency's annual *World Energy Outlook* reports. The IEA's reference scenario, which predicts future carbon emissions factoring in conservation measures that have already been committed to, sees global energy-related CO_2 emissions rising from 28 Gt in 2006 to 42 Gt in 2030 (IEA, 2008, p. 11). This suggests a doubling of the concentration of GHGs in the atmosphere by 2100 and entails 'eventual global average temperature increase of up to 6°C' (IEA, 2008, p. 11). Such warming risks taking the planet past tipping points that would trigger catastrophic changes (Hansen et al., 2008). Alarmingly, China's annual growth in CO_2 emissions between 2005 and 2009 (8.4 per cent) significantly exceeds figures used in the IEA scenarios (World Bank, 2010, p. 15).

The scale of action required to achieve the IEA's alternative emissions trajectories is also sobering. Two alternative emissions scenarios are considered. The more plausible – which nevertheless requires much more stringent emissions limitations than we have seen to date – results in atmospheric concentrations of 550 ppm CO_2e (2008, p. 48). The mid-point of estimates for additional warming in this case is about 3°C. As we have seen, if the global community wishes to have a strong chance of limiting warming to the 2°C 'safe' level, atmospheric concentrations must be stabilised at no more than 450 ppm CO_2e. However, the IEA's 450 ppm emissions trajectory demonstrates that achieving this target would require unprecedented financial, scientific and political commitment. The IEA report (2008, p. 48) notes:

> The scale of the challenge in the 450 Policy Scenario is immense: the 2030 emission level for the world as a whole in this scenario is less than the level of projected emissions for non-OECD countries alone in the Reference Scenario. In other words, the OECD countries alone cannot put the world onto the path to 450-ppm trajectory, even if they were to reduce their emissions to zero [...] [I]t is uncertain whether the scale of the transformation envisaged is even technically achievable, as the scenario assumes broad deployment of technologies that have not yet been proven.

This analysis exposes the inadequacy of the Kyoto Protocol, which imposed no constraints on developing countries and only sought to clip developed world emissions by an average 5.2 per cent. Importantly, the IEA emissions trajectories demonstrate the need for any global climate agreement to limit developing world emissions. In the reference scenario a full three-quarters of the projected increase in energy-related CO_2 emissions arise in China, India and the Middle East, while 97 per cent of increases are sourced from non-OECD countries. The developing world's growing energy demand only adds to the urgency of cuts in industrialised states. For example, the IEA's 450 ppm emissions trajectory 'requires emissions in OECD countries to be reduced by almost 40 per cent in 2030, compared with 2006 levels', while major developing economies must limit their emissions growth to 20 per cent (IEA, 2008). The IEA also points out that the long life of electricity infrastructure means that most emissions for the next 20 years are effectively 'locked in'. The cost of past policy failures is high.

The enormity of developing world financing needs is further illustrated by two recent World Bank reports which found that (1) achieving emissions restraint consistent with limiting global warming to 2°C will impose annual mitigation costs on developing countries of approximately US$140 to US$175 billion a year over the next 20 years (World Bank, 2010, p. 257); and (2) adapting to the consequences of climate change alone will cost the developing world US$75–100 billion annually between 2010 and 2050 (Margulis et al., 2009). These figures dwarf previous international assistance provided by developing countries by orders of magnitude (Müller, 2008, p. 7; Harris and Symons, 2009). The December 2009 Copenhagen Accord (UNFCCC, 2009) does contain a vague pledge of additional funding which rises towards a 'goal' of US$100 billion dollars per annum by 2020. However, despite some progress in negotiations at Cancún, this funding remains an unfulfilled promise – even in the unlikely event that commitments are honoured in full, the fund will finance only a modest fraction of adaptation and mitigation expenses.

Structure of the climate challenge

The global community's failure to avert dangerous climate change is unsurprising. Both the vast scale and specific features of the climate challenge make global cooperation difficult to achieve. Preservation of a habitable climate is a classic example of a 'public good' – this being a good that is both non-excludable, in the sense that no state can be prevented from enjoying the benefits of averting dangerous climate change, and non-rival, in the sense that any state's enjoyment of a safe climate does not detract from others'. In the absence of government, public goods are notoriously difficult to supply: since the benefits are equally available to all it is in the interests of each actor to free-ride on others' contributions to their attainment. Despite these difficulties, the global community has worked together cooperatively to supply some public goods. Elimination of the small-pox virus and phasing out of ozone-destroying substances are two prominent examples. Analysis of these successful cases suggests that such cooperation is most likely where the ratio between the costs of providing the good and the anticipated benefits is very high, or where one (or a few) parties have the capacity and motive to supply the good unilaterally (Barrett, 2007). Judged from this perspective the ratio of costs to benefits derived from climate change mitigation is not highly favourable. First, the costs of fully mitigating climate change are orders of magnitude higher than those associated with any previous instance of global cooperation. Second, the greatest benefits from climate change mitigation arise many decades into the future – if a standard 'discount rate' is applied, even very large benefits in the distant future have limited present day value and so the relative return on investment is assessed as low (Barrett, 2007, p. 95).[2]

The consequent challenge for global climate governance might also be characterised as a classic 'collective action problem'; since the benefits from investment in emissions reduction accrue globally while costs are borne locally, rational states acting independently in pursuit of self-interest will select a level of investment in climate change mitigation that is far below that necessary to achieve an optimal collective outcome. For example, while investment in renewable electricity generation (which is comparatively expensive) contributes to lowering global emissions, it generally does not bring immediate benefits to the state that undertakes the investment. By contrast, the entire value of adaptation measures, such as construction of storm-resistant infrastructure, sea walls and improvements in agricultural practices, accrues locally. Because these benefits are more immediate and obvious they are also likely to be more politically attractive. It follows that a rational state, if concerned with local welfare rather than aggregate global welfare, will invest in adaptation measures rather than mitigation, unless there is some kind of agreement through which other states' mitigation expenditure is guaranteed as a *quid pro quo* for local expenditure.

Of course, this stylised story of rational states failing to achieve a cooperative outcome does not accurately describe the complex forces at work in climate negotiations. Domestic climate policies are generally shaped by internal political forces that have little connection to global negotiations or the logic of the international system. For example, since China and the United States are the two largest emitters of GHGs their participation will be crucial to any successful international agreement mitigating climate change. Yet, the limited capacity of either the People's Republic of China to secure full compliance with central government policies, or of the US Administration to gain congressional support for emissions constraint explains these states' reluctance to accept binding (China) or significant (United States) emissions constraints. Additional features of global warming create extreme and unusual forms of 'moral hazard' and temptations to under-invest in mitigation. First, the international collective action problem described above is amplified by a series of domestic collective action problems, wherein those actors who would face major near-term losses from emissions limitations are the most motivated to influence political outcomes (Olson, 1971). For this reason, the interests of mining and energy sectors have been able to shape climate policy in defiance of public opinion in several states – such as Australia (Hamilton, 2007; see Chapter 11, p. 208). Likewise, in the United States, the Obama Administration advocates for more aggressive action than is supported by Congress, as is reflected by US Special Climate Envoy Todd Stern's colourful assertion that the administration is 'jumping as high as the political system will tolerate' (Telegraph, 2009). In addition, the multi-decade delay between emissions of GHGs and their environmental impact creates a powerful temptation for present-day welfare to be prioritised over aggregate long-term welfare.

In summary, mitigating dangerous climate change through emissions reductions can be seen as a global public good whose scale and pay-off structure means that climate security cannot be achieved unilaterally by any single state, but will instead require simultaneous intense efforts within every major economy. This picture could potentially change if geo-engineering technologies prove effective. However, it seems safe to assume that preserving a safe climate will require both development of new low-emission energy technologies and deployment of these new technologies on a global scale. This transition to a low-carbon economy will require multilateral cooperation to ensure that both price signals and technology policy are actively used to pursue these goals.

The failure of the Kyoto Protocol and the path beyond Cancún

My scepticism concerning the likelihood of an effective global climate agreement runs counter to the argument advanced by Joseph Camilleri in the previous chapter. While Camilleri is correct to point to the many forms of cooperation achieved, the inadequacy of existing international responses to climate change over the last 20 years is also unambiguous. The first IPCC report of 1990 confirmed the scientific evidence for anthropogenic climate change and prompted negotiation of the UNFCCC in 1992. Despite these clear warnings and promising early responses, subsequent negotiations have done almost nothing to slow the pace of emissions growth, as is illustrated by Figure 15.1. The Kyoto Protocol was always intended as only a first step and a foundation upon which future negotiations would build. Nevertheless, in the period 2000–2006, global CO_2 emissions increased at an annual rate of 3.1 per cent – a rate of increase which is more than double that of the 1990s (van Vuuren and Riahi, 2008, p. 241). The two decades since the first IPCC report have been a period of seemingly unconstrained emissions growth in which atmospheric GHG concentrations have overshot a level of relative 'safety'.

The current deadlock in climate negotiations must be overcome if an agreement leading to swift emissions reductions is to emerge. On the one

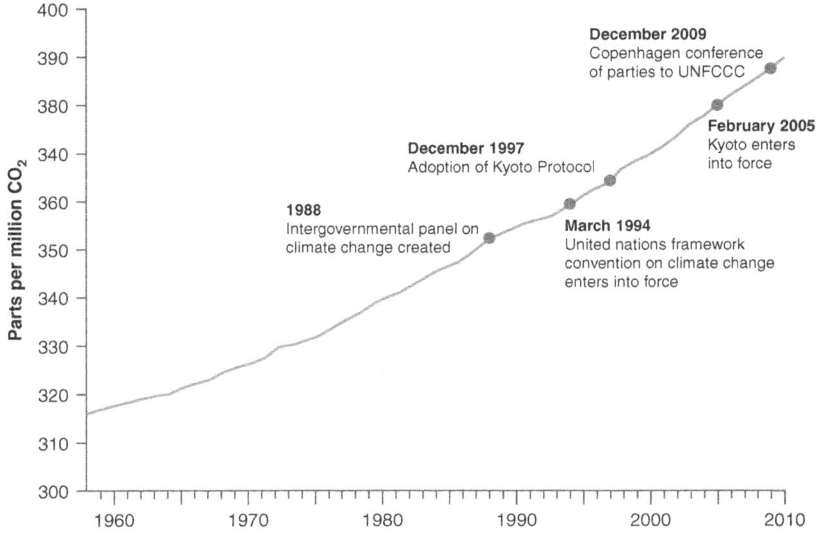

Figure 15.1 Rises in atmospheric concentrations of CO_2 – measurements from Manua Loa Observatory

Source: Elaborated by the author with data from Earth System Research Laboratory [http://www.esrl.noaa.gov/gmd/ccgg/trends/].

hand developed states, such as the United States, insist that any agreement must include binding emissions targets for the developing world, which is the major source of emissions growth. They argue that any new agreement that imposes binding and verifiable constraints on developed state emissions but not developing world emissions would be unfair and ineffective. By contrast, the developing world asserts that the West, which is responsible for the vast majority of historical emissions, has an 'unshirkable moral duty' to provide technological and financial assistance to aid developing world mitigation and adaptation efforts (Wen, 2009). Although couched in the language of justice, this deadlock amounts to brinkmanship in pursuit of comparative economic advantage. It provides some clues as to the nature of a possible future compromise: it might provide the financial and technological assistance the developing world demands, but do so in exchange for governance compromises and acceptance of binding and verifiable emissions limits by all parties. In order to build support within developed states for the necessary flows of international assistance, an effective climate agreement would probably need to win advocates amongst first world corporations by guaranteeing equal access to projects funded by international assistance.

The outcomes that any effective climate agreement must achieve on the ground are clear. Ultimately efforts to reduce GHG emissions must either create an effective price on GHG emissions (through taxes, emissions caps or other regulatory measures that create a 'shadow' price) or else utilise technology-based policies to make low-emissions energy sources more competitive (World Bank, 2010, p. V). The scale of the global climate challenge suggests that both approaches must be implemented; any effective agreement must both achieve rapid global deployment of existing low-GHG technologies by placing a shadow-price on emissions, and also generate (through incentives or direct funding) significant new investment in research and development.

To achieve these goals and win political acceptance amongst a preponderance of states (which requires winning support amongst corporate actors and public opinion in leading states), I argue that a global agreement will likely involve measures that intensify economic globalisation by:

1) Creating mechanisms to finance investment in low-emissions technology in the developing world;
2) Strengthening international investment rules and intellectual property protection to promote continued research and development;
3) Utilising market mechanisms on a global scale to minimise the total cost of mitigation efforts by identifying the lowest-cost GHG emissions abatement opportunities.

The first two of these points have particular relevance for energy security. The need for financing of developing world energy infrastructure is relatively uncontroversial, even if progress towards this goal is slow. The Kyoto Protocol's CDM was a small but significant early step towards achieving this goal. CDM aimed to allow developed state parties (Annex I) to the Kyoto Protocol to offset domestic emissions through investment in developing world abatement projects. Between 2001 and 2012 – the full commitment period in which CDM projects could be registered – it is estimated that CDM projects will create 1.5 billion tons of CO_2 equivalent in emissions reductions in the developing world (World Bank, 2010, p. 262). The primary purpose of these measures is to enable developed states to lower the cost of meeting their emissions targets through access to low-cost developing world abatement opportunities (CDM reductions are not additional to Kyoto targets). However, CDM also raises finance for infrastructure in the developing world and has enhanced local capacity (particularly Chinese) in low emissions industries. It is estimated that the revenues raised by CDM projects will be between US$15billion and US$24 billion (World Bank, 2010, p. 262). This figure represents only a tiny fraction of estimated needs, and CDM has involved only about 1 per cent of global emissions (Blyth, 2010, p. 145). Nevertheless, it is hard to imagine a successful global climate agreement that does not include a better designed and more extensive scheme to distribute the costs of low-emissions developing world energy infrastructure on a global basis.

The second point, concerning the harmonisation of investment and intellectual property laws, is more controversial. The World Bank's estimate of the mitigation costs facing the developing world (US$140–US$175 billion annually) far exceeds the capacity of the developing world's public or private sectors (World Bank, 2010, p. 257). Attracting the necessary private capital for long-term investments such as low-emissions energy infrastructure in the developing world requires credible guarantees concerning long-term carbon pricing and investment security (protection against nationalisation, changes in emissions pricing, etc.). A binding international agreement establishing investor rights and emissions constraints under international law would provide additional security, which can be especially valuable in those states where political polarisation or instability might otherwise make it difficult for governments to make credible, binding commitments.

Governance reform is also necessary within national economies – particularly around energy subsidies. While energy subsidies are fundamental to regime stability in many developing countries, the levers of emissions reduction policy (price signals or technology policies) are ineffective where particular forms of emissions-intensive energy are heavily subsidised. Eliminating energy subsidies is thus an essential aspect of mitigation policy – especially in the developing world. Importantly, energy subsidies in the developing world are overwhelmingly regressive (see Chapter 9, p. 164, p. 170). Because modern energy sources are accessed only by the more affluent households energy subsidies are typically a form of middle class welfare (World Bank, 2010, p. 42). For example, in the case of Indonesia, it is estimated that about half of energy subsidies go to the richest 10 per cent of households (World Bank, 2010, p. 42).

The challenge of lifting investment in research to the required level is similarly daunting. Recent analysis suggests that US$51–100 billion must be spent on energy research and development annually if global emissions are to be halved by 2050 (Levi et al., 2010). In contrast, current public spending on research and development of clean energy technologies is around US$10 billion annually and even this inadequate expenditure will reduce as global stimulus spending is exhausted (Levi et al., 2010). Private financing of clean energy is estimated to contribute only around another US$10 billion annually (Levi et al., 2010). Underinvestment in energy sector innovation is itself a form of market failure, which results from the huge capital requirements, long investment horizon and difficulty of capturing the full value of research and development. These considerations underscore the enormity of the investment challenge and suggest that direct government funding of research will be needed in addition to governance measures that assist companies to profit from low-emissions technologies. The research challenge is also of a scale that means it is unlikely to be met by a single state. Cooperation might occur through inter-state agreements stipulating specific forms of cooperation and investment, or through market-based measures that improve the likely returns on investment in energy innovation. Such market-based measures would place a *de facto* price on carbon. In addition to prompting innovation in low-emissions technologies they should also prompt efficiency measures, and achieve GHG emissions reductions at a much lower cost than would be possible through unilateral action by any single state (Garnaut, 2008).

Although many advocates of climate justice would propose that the affluent developed-world beneficiaries of past pollution should provide unconditional assistance to the developing world, such a path is politically improbable. Instead, an effective response to climate change will likely involve a dramatic intensification of the processes of economic globalisation as it would entail the imposition of a price on carbon in all major economies, elimination of energy subsidies and significant integration of global energy markets. Such an agreement would be a powerful force moving dynamics of energy distribution towards the global *markets and institutions* narrative described above – a scenario under which the incentives for energy research and development of new energy infrastructure are optimised.

Conclusions

States have traditionally adopted 'energy security' policies because unregulated markets tend to produce socially and economically sub-optimal outcomes due to underinvestment in energy infrastructure. Traditional 'energy security' policy can therefore be understood as a nation-level market intervention aimed at securing public goods. As hundreds of millions of people in the developing world seek access to modern energy, rising global emissions pose a threat to the global public good of a habitable atmosphere. This challenge to the fundamental interests of people everywhere demands that provision of public goods be pursued globally as well as nationally, and that the externalised costs associated with energy production be internalised through some form of emissions pricing. Although estimates of these externalities vary considerably, in 2006 the Stern report calculated the 'social cost of carbon' resulting from each ton of CO_2 at approximately US$85 (social cost of carbon is a measure of the current day economic value of the future impacts of emissions) (Stern, 2006, p. 322). Building such significant externalities into the price of energy would involve massive social, political and economic changes. Attempting to transform energy systems on a global scale will also create pressing questions of justice.

Globally, around 1.5 billion people lack access to electricity. Amongst state members of the Asia-Pacific Economic Cooperation forum, 120 million people lack access (World Bank, 2010, pp. 39–40). Many hundreds of millions more are eager to gain access to modern energy that people in the West take for granted. For example, 730 million people in China, 120 million in Indonesia and 55 million in Vietnam still rely on biomass and coal for their cooking (World Bank, 2010, pp. 39–40). In Indonesia alone, 81 million people (35.5 per cent of the population) still lack access to electricity (World Bank, 2010, pp. 39–40). As we have seen, the developing world's demand is a key driver of global emissions growth, and satisfying this demand with low emissions energy sources presents a key challenge for national and global governance. Asking developing world populations to finance low-emissions energy infrastructure unassisted would be both politically impossible and unethical, since doing so would likely deprive vulnerable populations of access to modern energy.

Implementation of effective global climate policy will require a degree of cooperation and economic integration that will undermine widely accepted principles of national autonomy and democratic self-determination. Fortunately energy policies that more fully reflect the social cost of energy use should benefit the global poor over the long term. If this internationalisation of social and environmental costs can only be achieved by shifting the locus of energy policy formation from the national to the global level, there will be significant negative impacts on national autonomy. However, the challenge posed by climate change is daunting, global and immediate and an effective response will require that energy prices come to reflect the social costs of energy production in all significant economies. Obviously such a transition will be difficult – some patterns of life that have evolved in the era of cheap energy, together with the associated economic and political structures, may be destabilised. However, no matter what choices are made the coming century will be a period in which human environmental impacts have planetary dimensions. Our capacity to maintain both energy security and environmental security will turn on our ability to find forms of governance that regulate our behaviour on a global scale.

Notes

1. CO_2 equivalent is a measure used to assess the warming impact of all GHGs, such that 450 CO_2e refers to an atmospheric concentration of all GHGs that would create the equivalent level of warming as 450 parts per million of CO_2 in the atmosphere.
2. Barrett suggests that while the cost:benefit ratio for addressing ozone depletion was 11:1, using standard discount rates the ratio for climate mitigation action is only 0.5:1 (Barrett, 2007, p. 95).

References

Barrett, S. (2007), *Why Cooperate? The Incentive to Supply Global Public Goods* (Oxford: Oxford University Press).

Blyth, W. (2010), 'Carbon Markets and Energy Sector Investment', in A. Goldthau and J.M. Witte (eds): *Global Energy Governance: The New Rules of the Game* (Washington, DC: Brookings Institution).

Brown, S.P.A. and H.G. Huntington (2008), 'Energy Security and Climate Change Protection: Complementarity or Tradeoff?' *Energy Policy*, 36(9): 3510–3513.

Correljéa, A.B. and P.J. van der Linden (2006), 'Energy Supply Security and Geopolitics: A European Perspective', *Energy Policy*, 34(5): 532–543.

Edmonds, J., L. Clarke, J. Lurz and M. Wise (2008), 'Stabilizing CO_2 Concentrations with Incomplete International Cooperation', *Climate Policy*, 8(4): 355–376.

Garnaut, R. (2008), *The Garnaut Climate Change Review* (Melbourne: Cambridge University Press Australia).

Goldthau, A. and J.M. Witte (2010), 'The Role of Rules and Institutions in Global Energy: An Introduction', in A. Goldthau and J.M. Witte (eds): *Global Energy Governance: The New Rules of the Game* (Washington: Brookings Institution).

Hamilton, C. (2007), *Scorcher: The Dirty Politics of Climate Change* (Melbourne: Black Inc.).

Hansen, J. Mki. Sato, P. Kharecha, D. Beerling, R. Berner, V. Masson-Delmotte, M. Pagani, M. Raymo, D.L. Royer, and J.C. Zachos (2008), 'Target Atmospheric CO2: Where Should Humanity Aim?', *Open Atmospheric Science Journal*, 2: 217–231.

Harris, P. and J. Symons (2009), 'Justice in Adaptation to Climate Change: Cosmopolitan Implications for International Institutions', *Environmental Politics*, 19(4): 617–36.

Hassol, S. (2007), 'Questions and Answers Emissions Reductions Needed to Stabilize Climate', for the Presidential Climate Action Project [www.climatecommunication.org/PDFs/HassolPCAP.pdf; accessed: 12 January 2011].

Hope, C. (2009), 'How Deep Should the Deep Cuts Be? Optimal CO2 Emissions over Time under Uncertainty', *Climate Policy*, 9(1): 3–8.

International Energy Agency (IEA) (2008), *World Energy Outlook 2008: Executive Summary* (Paris: International Energy Agency).

Intergovernmental Panel on Climate Change (IPCC) (2007), 'Summary for Policymakers', in B. Metz, O.R. Davidson, P.R. Bosch, R. Dave and L.A. Meyer (eds.):

Climate Change 2007: Mitigation. Contribution of Working Group III to the Fourth Assessment Report of the Intergovernmental Panel on Climate Change (Cambridge-New York: Cambridge University Press).

Levi, M., E.C. Economy, S. O'Neil and A. Segal (2010), 'Globalizing the Energy Revolution', *Foreign Affairs*, 89(6): 111–123.

Margulis, S. et al (2009), *The Costs to Developing Countries of Adapting to Climate Change, New Methods and Estimates: the Global Report of the Economics of Adaptation to Climate Change Study (Consultation Draft)* (Washington DC: World Bank) [http://siteresources.worldbank.org/INTCC/Resources/EACCReport0928Final.pdf; accessed: 12 January 2011].

Müller, B. (2008), *International Adaptation Finance: The Need for an Innovative and Strategic Approach, EV 42* (Oxford: Oxford Institute for Energy Studies) [www.oxfordenergy.org/pdfs/EV42.pdf; accessed: 12 January 2011].

OECD and International Energy Agency (2010), *Projected Costs of Generating Electricity – 2010 Edition* (Paris: OECD Publishing).

Olson, M. (1971), *The Logic of Collective Action: Public Goods and the Theory of Groups* (Harvard: Harvard University Press).

Stern, N. (2006), *Stern Review on the Economics of Climate Change* (London: HM Treasury).

The Telegraph (2009), *US 'will not speed up emissions cuts'*, 24 May [www.telegraph.co.uk/news/worldnews/northamerica/usa/barackobama/5380137/US-will-not-speed-up-emissions-cuts.html; accessed: 16 December 2010].

United Nations Framework Convention on Climate Change (UNFCCC) (2009). Copenhagen accord (New York: United Nations; http://unfccc.int/home/items/5262.php; accessed: 16 December 2010).

World Bank (2010), *Climate Change and Fiscal Policy: A Report for APEC* (Report no. 56563-EAP, Washington DC: World Bank).

Victor, D.G., M.G. Morgan, J. Apt, J. Steinbruner and K. Ricke (2009), 'The Geoengineering Option', *Foreign Affairs*, 88(2): 322–336.

Victor, D. and D. Cullenward (2007), 'Making Carbon Markets Work', *Scientific American* 297(6): 70–77.

van Vuuren, D.P. and K. Riahi (2008), 'Do Recent Emission Trends Imply Higher Emissions Forever?', *Climatic Change*, 91: 237–248.

Wen, J. (2009), 'Build Consensus and Strengthen Cooperation to Advance the Historical Process of Combating Climate Change', *Address at the Copenhagen Climate Change Summit by Wen Jiabao*, Copenhagen, 18 December [http://sy.chineseembassy.org/eng/xwfb/t647462.htm; accessed: 12 January 2011].

World Bank (2010), *World Development Report 2010: Development and Climate Change* (Washington DC: World Bank).

Yergin, D. (2006), 'Ensuring Energy Security?', *Foreign Affairs*, 85(2): 69–82.

Zweig, D. and B. Jianhai (2005), 'China's Global Hunt for Energy', *Foreign Affairs*, 84(5): 25–38.

Index

The manufacturer's authorised representative in the EU is Springer Nature Customer Service Centre GmbH, Europaplatz 3, 69115 Heidelberg, Germany. If you have any concerns regarding our products, please contact ProductSafety@springernature.com

Printed and bound by CPI Group (UK) Ltd, Croydon, CR0 4YY
10/10/2026
02231232-0003